pwc

普华永道

普华永道国际财务报告准则实务指引——金融工具系列（第三册）
PricewaterhouseCoopers IFRS Manual of Accounting — Financial Instruments Series (Volume Three)

IFRS Manual of Accounting — Financial Instruments

Chapter 5 – Embedded derivatives in host contracts
Chapter 9 – Measurement of financial assets and liabilities

国际财务报告准则实务指引——金融工具

第五章—主合同中的嵌入式衍生工具
第九章—金融资产和金融负债的计量

中英文对照

主译　陈燕华
翻译组主要成员　李家胜　程江　王洁

中国财政经济出版社

This book has been prepared for general guidance on matters of interest only, and does not constitute professional advice. You should not act upon the information contained in this book without obtaining specific professional advice. No representation or warranty (express or implied) is given as to the accuracy or completeness of the information contained in this book, and, to the extent permitted by law, PricewaterhouseCoopers does not accept or assume any liability, responsibility or duty of care for any consequences of you or anyone else acting, or refraining to act, in reliance on the information contained in this book or for any decision based on it.

This book covers one of the chapters of the English version and its Chinese translation, which the English version remains the definitive source of guidance. The publishers and the authors cannot accept any responsibility for any errors or misunderstandings arising from the English version and its Chinese translation. Neither can the publishers and the authors accept any responsibility for loss occasioned to any person acting or refraining from action as a result of the material in this book.

编写本书之目的是对感兴趣的事项给予一般性的指导，而非提供专业建议。未征得具体专业意见之前，不应依据本书所述内容采取任何行动。我们不对书中所述信息是否准确或完整作出任何明示或暗示的承诺或保证。除非法律另有明文规定，普华永道不对任何个人或单位因为阅读了本书而采取或未采取某项行动的后果、或基于本书所作出的任何决定承担任何责任。

本书内容为英文本中的一个章节及其中文译文，指导概以英文为准。出版社和编译者不对英文原文及中文译文的偏差或误解承担任何责任，也不对任何个人或单位因为阅读了本书而采取或未采取某项行动所发生损失承担任何责任。

Preface

Recent years have seen major changes in financial reporting worldwide with the single most important change being convergence around IFRS. There has also been a keen focus to improve the long term development of the CPA profession within China. As the Ministry of Finance and other regulatory bodies continue to promulgate legislation to promote the development of the Chinese CPA profession, we hope the release of our IFRS Manual of Accounting with Chinese Translation will also contribute to this effort.

The Ministry of Finance issued the Accounting Standards for Business Enterprises (hereafter referred to as "China Accounting Standards" or "CAS") in 2006. CAS incorporates all of the principles of IFRS and there has been a continued focus on convergence over the last few years. Additionally, IFRS is becoming increasingly important for many companies in China, including domestic companies seeking to raise capital overseas, as well as for foreign companies that have operations in China. With the continued convergence of CAS and IFRS, the release of our IFRS Manual of Accounting with Chinese Translation brings to China the extensive collective experience of the PwC's global network of firms in applying IFRS.

We hope this Manual will play a part in promoting consistent, comparable, relevant and reliable IFRS financial information and will serve as a reference tool for accounting students, academics, practitioners and users of financial statements in better understanding and implementing IFRS. More importantly, we hope the advice given in this text will assist those dealing with the many issues faced in preparing IFRS financial statements and provide helpful insight to users of such statements.

Raymund Chao
Asia Pacific Assurance Leader
PwC

前言

近年来，全球财务报告领域发生了重大变化，其中最为重要的一项变化是与国际财务报告准则的趋同。同时人们也热切地关注着中国境内注册会计师行业的长期发展。财政部及其他监管机构不断完善法规，推动中国注册会计师行业的发展，我们希望这本中英文对照的国际财务报告准则实务指引能够对此作出贡献。

财政部于2006 年颁布了《企业会计准则》（以下称为中国会计准则，或CAS）。CAS 包含了 IFRS 中的所有原则，且在过去的几年里持续趋同。此外，IFRS 对于中国的许多公司来说越来越重要，包括寻求筹集海外资本的国内公司，以及在中国境内运营的外国公司。随着 CAS 与 IFRS 的持续趋同，本书的发行将给中国读者带来普华永道全球成员机构网络在应用 IFRS 方面积累的丰富的经验。

我们希望本书能够在推广一致的、可比的、相关的以及可靠的 IFRS 财务信息方面起到作用，并且可以作为会计领域的学生、学者、从业人员及财务报表使用者更好地理解及运用 IFRS 的参考工具。更为重要的是，我们希望本指引中提出的建议能够帮助其处理在编制 IFRS 财务报表时遇到的问题，并向此类财务报表使用者提供有用的观点。

赵柏基
普华永道亚太区审计部主管合伙人

Overview/Introduction

The IFRS Manual of Accounting is a practical guide to International Financial Reporting Standards. With close to 70 countries that have converged their local accounting standards with IFRS as at the time of writing, the application of IFRS has attracted significant attention in the world stage. At the same time, as more and more countries adopt IFRS (or its equivalent local standard), views continue to develop or evolve as to how particular aspects of a standard should be interpreted and applied. The views expressed in this Manual are based on years of experience from PricewaterhouseCoopers' Global Accounting Consulting Services team. The views expressed are a guide to applying IFRS rather than a set of definitive interpretations. The application of IFRS to a specific company is a matter of judgement given its particular facts and circumstances. Moreover, the application of IFRS might be influenced by the views of regulators.

The Manual covers diverse areas of accounting from the recognition and measurement of financial instruments to accounting for deferred taxation, business combinations and share-based payments. It explains in detail the rules that apply to preparing consolidated financial statements and considers the other statements that appear in annual reports such as cash flow statements as well as disclosures required by each specific standard.

Due to the continued convergence of China Accounting Standards and IFRS, PwC China has undertaken a significant project to translate our Global IFRS Manual of Accounting into Chinese. We sincerely hope that our IFRS Manual of Accounting with Chinese Translation provides practical insights to transactions commonly-seen in China and can help preparers, auditors, analysts and other users of financial statements to bridge the gap between accounting principles and their applications.

Yvonne Kam
Accounting Consulting Service Lead Partner
PwC China and Hong Kong

概述/引言

《国际财务报告准则实务指引》是应用国际财务报告准则的实务指南。于撰稿之时，已有近70个国家将其本国的会计准则与国际财务报告准则趋同，在世界范围内，国际财务报告准则的应用已广受重视。与此同时，随着越来越多的国家采用国际财务报告准则（或其等同的本地准则），关于某条准则特定方面应如何解释及应用的各种观点在持续发展或演变。本实务指引中所表达的观点是基于普华永道全球会计专业咨询服务团队以往多年的经验得出。我们所传达的观点是应用国际财务报告准则的指南，而非一系列确定的解释。一家特定的企业在应用国际财务报告准则时需根据特定的事实和环境作出判断。此外，国际财务报告准则的应用也可能受到监管机构观点的影响。

本实务指引涵盖从金融工具的确认和计量到递延税项、业务合并和以股份为基础的支付的核算等不同的会计领域。它详细解释了编制合并财务报表所应用的原则，并考虑了年报中出现的其他报表，如现金流量表以及每条特定准则所要求的披露。

鉴于中国会计准则与国际财务报告准则的持续趋同，普华永道中国启动了一项具有重大意义的项目，即将《国际财务报告准则实务指引》译成中文。我们诚挚地希望这套中英文对照的《国际财务报告准则实务指引》能够为中国常见的交易提供实用的见解，为编制者、审计人员、分析人员以及其他财务报表使用者们在会计原则与其具体应用之间架起一座桥梁。

金以文
会计专业咨询服务首席合伙人
普华永道中国及香港

How to use this publication

Given the increasing importance of IFRS in China and the continued convergence of CAS and IFRS, the Accounting Consulting Services team of PwC China and Hong Kong have undertaken a significant project to translate the IFRS Manual of Accounting into Chinese.

The Manual is a practical guide in applying IFRS and the views are based on the extensive experience of the PwC's global network of firms. However, IFRS is not static and is continuously developing. The views on its interpretation and application will adapt and evolve. The views expressed in this Manual are a guide to applying IFRS rather than a set of definitive interpretations. The application of IFRS requires significant judgement and specific facts and circumstances should be carefully considered.

IFRS Manual of Accounting with Chinese Translation will be released in different volumes. Depending on the topic, each release may be a chapter or a combination of a number of chapters from the Manual.

Because of the interdependencies between individual IFRS, there are many cross references between different chapters of the Manual. Although the IFRS Manual of Accounting with Chinese Translation will be released in different volumes, the cross references have been maintained. Users are encouraged to refer to those cross references in other translated chapters or to the English version of the Manual if it helps in their understanding.

This book is the third volume of IFRS Manual of Accounting – Financial Instruments 2011 Series with Chinese Translation. The content covers Chapter 5 – Embedded derivatives in host contracts, Chapter 9 – Measurement of financial assets and liabilities of the English version and its translation. While every effort has been made to ensure an accurate translation, reference should be made to the English version in the event there are any differences between the Chinese and English versions.

使用说明

鉴于 IFRS 在中国愈发重要以及 CAS 和 IFRS 的持续趋同，普华永道中国及香港的会计专业咨询服务小组已着手开始了一项具有重大意义的项目，即将《国际财务报告准则实务指引》译成中文。

《国际财务报告准则实务指引》是对应用 IFRS 的实务指引，其中的观点是基于普华永道全球成员机构网络丰富的经验。然而，IFRS 不是静止的，而是持续发展的；因此，对 IFRS 的解释和适用会有所改变和发展。本指引表达的观点是对应用 IFRS 的一种指引，而非一套具有决定性的解释。IFRS 的应用需要大量的判断，还应当谨慎考虑特定的事实及所处的环境。

IFRS 实务指引及其中文翻译版将分成多册发行。根据主题，每一册可能是本指引的某一章节或是包含某几个章节。

由于各个 IFRS 准则之间的相互依存，因此本指引中不同的章节会相互参照索引。尽管 IFRS 实务指引及其中文翻译版将分成多册发行，但仍保留此类相互参照索引。如果有助于理解，我们鼓励读者阅读此类相互参照索引时参考其他已翻译的章节或指引的英文版。

本书为普华永道国际财务报告准则实务指引——金融工具系列（中英文对照）的第三册。内容为英文原版的《国际财务报告准则实务指引——金融工具》中的《第五章——主合同中的嵌入式衍生工具》和《第九章——金融资产和金融负债的计量》及其中文翻译。我们已尽最大的努力来确保翻译的准确，但中文翻译版与英文版出现不一致时，应参考英文版。

The chapters of our IFRS Manual of Accounting have been restructured in 2013 and changes have been marked as follow:

IFRS Manual of Accounting (MoA)

Accounting rules and principles

01 – Introduction

02 – Accounting principles and applicability of IFRS (combined with chapter 1 in MoA 2013)

03 – First-time adoption of IFRS

04 – Presentation of financial statements

05 – Accounting policies, accounting estimates and errors (chapter 3 in MoA 2013)

06 – Hyper-inflation (chapter 31 in MoA 2013)

07 – Foreign currencies

08 – Insurance contracts

Income statement and related notes

09 – Revenue and construction contracts

10 – Segment reporting

11 – Employee benefits

11A – Employee benefits (IAS 19 revised)

12 – Share-based payment

13 – Taxation

14 – Earnings per share

Balance sheet and related notes

15 – Intangible assets

16 – Property, plant and equipment

17 – Investment property

18 – Impairment of assets

19 – Lease accounting

20 – Inventories

英文原版《国际财务报告准则实务指引》的章节已在2013年再版时重新排列，变动已列示如下：

国际财务报告准则实务指引

会计规则和原则

01 – 引言
02 – 会计原则和国际财务报告准则的适用性（在2013版中与第一章合并）

03 – 首次采用国际财务报告准则
04 – 财务报表的列报
05 – 会计政策、会计估计和差错（在2013版中为第三章）
06 – 恶性通货膨胀（在2013版中为第三十一章）
07 – 外币
08 – 保险合同

利润表及相关附注

09 – 收入与建造合同
10 – 分部报告
11 – 职工福利
11A – 职工福利（IAS 19修订版）
12 – 以股份为基础的支付（“股份支付”）
13 – 所得税会计
14 – 每股收益

资产负债表及相关附注

15 – 无形资产
16 – 不动产、工厂和设备
17 – 投资性房地产
18 – 资产减值
19 – 租赁会计
20 – 存货

21 – Provisions and contingencies
22 – Events after the reporting period and financial commitments
23 – Share capital and reserves

Consolidated financial statements
24 – Consolidated and separate financial statements
24A – Consolidated financial statements
25 – Business combinations
26 – Disposal of subsidiaries, businesses and non-current assets
27 – Equity accounting
28 – Joint ventures
28A – Joint arrangements

Other subjects
29 – Related party disclosures
30 – Cash flow statements
31 – Interim reports and preliminary announcements (seperate book in 2013)
32 – Agriculture
33 – Service concession arrangements
34 – Fair Value (chapter 5 in MoA 2013)
35 – Management commentery

IFRS Manual of Accounting—Financial Instruments (chapter 6 in MoA 2013)

01 – Overview (chapter 6.1 in MoA 2013)
02 – Introduction (combined with chapter 6.1 in MoA 2013)
03 – Objectives and scope of IAS 32, IAS 39 and IFRS 7 (combined with chapter 6.1 in MoA 2013)
04 – Nature and characteristics of financial instruments (chapter 6.2 in MoA 2013)
05 – Embedded derivatives in host contracts (chapter 6.3 in MoA 2013)

06 – Classification of financial instruments (chapter 6. 4 in MoA 2013)
07 – Financial liabilities and equity (chapter 6. 5 in MoA 2013)
08 – Rccognition and dcrccognition (chapter 6. 6 in MoA 2013)
09 – Measurement of financial assets and liabilities (chapter 6. 7 in MoA 2013)
10 – Hedge accounting (chapter 6. 8 in MoA 2013)
11 – Presentation and disclosure (chapter 6. 9 in MoA 2013)
12 – IFRS 9, "Financial Instruments" (chapter 6. 10 in MoA 2013)

International standards and interpretations

International standards

IFRS 1	First-time adoption of International Financial Reporting Standards
IFRS 2	Share-based payment
IFRS 3	Business combinations
IFRS 4	Insurance contracts
IFRS 5	Non-current assets held for sale and discontinued operations
IFRS 6	Exploration for and evaluation of mineral resources
IFRS 7	Financial instruments: Disclosures
IFRS 8	Operating segments
IFRS 9	Financial instruments
IFRS 10	Consolidated financial statements
IFRS 11	Joint arrangements
IFRS 12	Disclosure of interests in other entities
IFRS 13	Fair value measurement
IAS 1	Presentation of financial statements
IAS 2	Inventories
IAS 7	Cash flow statements
IAS 8	Accounting policies, changes in accounting estimates and errors
IAS 10	Events after the balance sheet date
IAS 11	Construction contracts
IAS 12	Income taxes
IAS 16	Property, plant and equipment
IAS 17	Leases
IAS 18	Revenue
IAS 19	Employee benefits
IAS 20	Accounting for government grants and disclosure of government assistance
IAS 21	The effects of changes in foreign exchange rates
IAS 23	Borrowing costs

国际财务报告准则及解释公告

国际财务报告准则

国际财务报告准则第 1 号	首次采用国际财务报告准则
国际财务报告准则第 2 号	以股份为基础的支付
国际财务报告准则第 3 号	企业合并
国际财务报告准则第 4 号	保险合同
国际财务报告准则第 5 号	持有待售的非流动资产和终止经营
国际财务报告准则第 6 号	矿产资源的勘探和评价
国际财务报告准则第 7 号	金融工具：披露
国际财务报告准则第 8 号	经营分部
国际财务报告准则第 9 号	金融工具
国际财务报告准则第 10 号	合并财务报表
国际财务报告准则第 11 号	合营安排
国际财务报告准则第 12 号	对其他主体中权益的披露
国际财务报告准则第 13 号	公允价值计量
国际会计准则第 1 号	财务报表的列报
国际会计准则第 2 号	存货
国际会计准则第 7 号	现金流量表
国际会计准则第 8 号	会计政策、会计估计变更和差错
国际会计准则第 10 号	报告期后事项
国际会计准则第 11 号	建造合同
国际会计准则第 12 号	所得税
国际会计准则第 16 号	不动产、工厂和设备
国际会计准则第 17 号	租赁
国际会计准则第 18 号	收入
国际会计准则第 19 号	职工福利
国际会计准则第 20 号	政府补助的会计和政府援助的披露
国际会计准则第 21 号	汇率变动的影响
国际会计准则第 23 号	借款费用

IAS 24	Related-party disclosures
IAS 26	Accounting and reporting by retirement benefit plans
IAS 27	Consolidated and separate financial statements
IAS 28	Investments in associates
IAS 29	Financial reporting in hyper-inflationary economies
IAS 31	Interests in joint ventures
IAS 32	Financial instruments: Presentation
IAS 33	Earnings per share
IAS 34	Interim financial reporting
IAS 36	Impairment of assets
IAS 37	Provisions, contingent liabilities and contingent assets
IAS 38	Intangible assets
IAS 39	Financial instruments: Recognition and measurement
IAS 40	Investment property
IAS 41	Agriculture

Interpretations

IFRIC 1	Changes in existing decommissioning, restoration and similar liabilities
IFRIC 2	Members' shares in co-operative entities and similar Instruments
IFRIC 4	Determining whether an arrangement contains a lease
IFRIC 5	Rights to interests arising from decommissioning, restoration and environmental rehabilitation funds
IFRIC 6	Liabilities arising from participating in a specific market – Waste electrical and electronic equipment
IFRIC 7	Applying the restatement approach under IAS 29 Financial reporting in hyper-inflationary economies
IFRIC 8	Scope of IFRS 2
IFRIC 9	Re-assessment of embedded derivatives
IFRIC 10	Interim financial reporting and impairment
IFRIC 11	IFRS 2 – Group and treasury share transactions
IFRIC 12	Service concession arrangements

国际会计准则第 24 号	关联方披露
国际会计准则第 26 号	退休福利计划的会计和报告
国际会计准则第 27 号	合并财务报表和单独财务报表
国际会计准则第 28 号	联营中的投资
国际会计准则第 29 号	恶性通货膨胀经济中的财务报告
国际会计准则第 31 号	合营中的权益
国际会计准则第 32 号	金融工具：列报
国际会计准则第 33 号	每股收益
国际会计准则第 34 号	中期财务报告
国际会计准则第 36 号	资产减值
国际会计准则第 37 号	准备、或有负债和或有资产
国际会计准则第 38 号	无形资产
国际会计准则第 39 号	金融工具：确认和计量
国际会计准则第 40 号	投资性房地产
国际会计准则第 41 号	农业

解释公告

国际财务报告解释公告第 1 号	现有退役、复原和类似负债的变动
国际财务报告解释公告第 2 号	成员在合作主体中的股份和类似工具
国际财务报告解释公告第 4 号	确定一项协议是否包含租赁
国际财务报告解释公告第 5 号	退役、复原和环境恢复基金产生的权益
国际财务报告解释公告第 6 号	参与废弃电器和电子设备特定市场产生的负债
国际财务报告解释公告第 7 号	应用《国际会计准则第 29 号——恶性通货膨胀经济中的财务报告》中的重述法
国际财务报告解释公告第 8 号	《国际财务报告准则第 2 号》的范围
国际财务报告解释公告第 9 号	嵌入衍生工具的重估
国际财务报告解释公告第 10 号	中期财务报告和减值
国际财务报告解释公告第 11 号	《国际财务报告准则第 2 号》：集团和库藏股交易
国际财务报告解释公告第 12 号	特许服务权安排

IFRIC 13	Customer loyalty programmes
IFRIC 14	IAS 19 – The limit on a defined benefit asset, minimum funding requirements and their interaction
IFRIC 15	Agreements for the construction of real estate
IFRIC 16	Hedges of a net investment in a foreign operation
IFRIC 17	Distributions of non-cash assets to owners
IFRIC 18	Transfers of assets from customers
IFRIC 19	Extinguishing financial liabilities with equity instruments
IFRIC 20	Stripping costs in the production phase of a surface mine
SIC 7	Introduction of the euro
SIC 10	Government Assistance – No specific relation to operating activities
SIC 12	Consolidation – Special purpose entities
SIC 13	Jointly controlled entities – Non-Monetary contributions by venturers
SIC 15	Operating leases – Incentives
SIC 21	Income taxes – Recovery of revalued non-depreciable assets
SIC 25	Income taxes – Changes in the tax status of an entity or its shareholders
SIC 27	Evaluating the substance of transactions in the legal form of a lease
SIC 29	Service Concession Arrangements: Disclosures
SIC 31	Revenue – Barter transactions involving advertising services
SIC 32	Intangible assets – Web site costs

国际财务报告解释公告第 13 号	客户忠诚度计划
国际财务报告解释公告第 14 号	《国际会计准则第 19 号》：对设定受益资产的限制、最低资金要求及其相互作用
国际财务报告解释公告第 15 号	房地产建造合同
国际财务报告解释公告第 16 号	对境外经营净投资的套期
国际财务报告解释公告第 17 号	以非现金资产对所有者进行分配
国际财务报告解释公告第 18 号	从客户处转移资产
国际财务报告解释公告第 19 号	以权益工具解除金融负债
国际财务报告解释公告第 20 号	露天矿生产阶段的剥离成本
国际会计准则解释公告第 7 号	引入欧元
国际会计准则解释公告第 10 号	政府援助：与经营活动没有特定联系的政府援助
国际会计准则解释公告第 12 号	合并：特殊目的主体
国际会计准则解释公告第 13 号	共同控制主体：合营者的非货币性投入
国际会计准则解释公告第 15 号	经营租赁：激励措施
国际会计准则解释公告第 21 号	所得税：已重估非折旧资产的收回
国际会计准则解释公告第 25 号	所得税：主体或其股东纳税状况的改变
国际会计准则解释公告第 27 号	评价涉及租赁法律形式的交易实质
国际会计准则解释公告第 29 号	特许服务权安排：披露
国际会计准则解释公告第 31 号	收入：涉及广告服务的易货交易
国际会计准则解释公告第 32 号	无形资产：网站成本

Abbreviations and terms used

Accounts	financial statements
AG	Application Guidance
App	Appendix
ARC	Accounting Regulatory Committee
BC	Basis for Conclusions (to an accounting standard)
C	currency unit
Chp	Chapter
chapter (1)	'PricewaterhouseCoopers' Manual of accounting' – chapter (1)
CESR	Committee of European Securities Regulators
CPP	current purchasing power
DP	discussion paper
EBIT	earnings before interest and tax
EBITDA	earnings before interest, tax, depreciation and amortisation
ED	exposure draft
EFRAG	European Financial Reporting Advisory Group
EPS	earnings per share
EU	European Union
FASB	Financial Accounting Standards Board (US)
Framework	Framework for the preparation and presentation of financial statements
GAAP	generally accepted accounting principles (and practices)
IAS	International Accounting Standard (see also IFRS)
IASB	International Accounting Standards Board
IFRIC	International Financial Reporting Interpretations Committee
IFRS	International Financial Reporting Standard (see also IAS)
IG	Implementation Guidance (to an accounting standard)

缩写及词汇对照

财务报表
实施指南
附录
会计监管委员会
（某一准则的）结论基础
货币单位
章
第一章　普华永道《国际财务报告准则实务指引》——第（一）章

欧洲证券监管委员会
现行购买力
讨论稿
息税前收益
扣除利息、所得税、折旧和摊销之前的收益
征求意见稿
欧洲财务报告咨询组
每股收益
欧盟
（美国）财务会计准则委员会
编报财务报表的框架

公认会计原则
国际会计准则（亦请参见 IFRS）
国际会计准则理事会
国际财务报告解释委员会
国际财务报告准则（亦请参见 IAS）
（某一准则的）应用指南

para(s)	paragraph(s) of Schedules to the Companies Acts, or IFRSs or IASs or FRSs, or SSAPs, or FREDs, or EDs, or DPs, or text
PPE	property, plant and equipment
US SEC	US Securities and Exchange Commission
SIC	Standing Interpretation Committee of the IASC (see IFRIC)
SPE	special purpose entity
UK	United Kingdom
US	United States of America

段落（公司法、国际财务报告准则、国际会计准则、财务报告准则、会计实务准则、财务报告征求意见稿、征求意见稿、讨论稿或文章中的段落）

不动产、工厂和设备

美国证券交易委员会

国际会计准则委员会的常设解释委员会（参见 IFRIC）

特殊目的主体

英国

美国

Content

IFRS Manual of Accounting—Financial Instruments Series (Volume Three)

目　录

国际财务报告准则实务指引——金融工具系列（第三册）

Chapter 5 Embedded derivatives in host contracts

Content

第五章　主合同中的嵌入式衍生工具

目　录

Introduction

5. 1 A derivative instrument that falls within IAS 39's scope need not be free-standing. Terms and conditions may be embedded in a financial instrument or non-financial contract (as the ' host ' contract) that behave like a free-standing derivative. These are referred to as embedded derivatives. The combination of the host contract and the embedded derivative is a ' hybrid instrument'.

5. 2 An embedded derivative can arise from deliberate financial engineering, for example to make low interest-rate debt more attractive by including an equity-linked return. In other cases, they arise inadvertently through market practices and common contractual arrangements, such as leases and insurance contracts. Even purchase and sale contracts that qualify as executory contracts may contain embedded derivatives. In fact, they may occur in all sorts of contracts and instruments – the objective being to change the nature of cash flows that otherwise would be required by the host contract and effectively shift financial risks between the parties.

5. 3 Analysing non-derivative financial instruments and executory contracts for potential embedded derivatives is one of the more challenging aspects of IAS 39. However, the challenge does not end there. As will be apparent later, a derivative identified in a host contract needs further evaluation to determine whether it should be accounted for separately as a stand alone derivative at fair value. Not all embedded derivatives need to be accounted for separately from the host contract.

Definition and key characteristics

5. 4 An embedded derivative is a component of a hybrid instrument that also includes a non-derivative host contract – with the effect that some of the cash flows of the hybrid instrument vary in a way similar to a stand-alone derivative. An embedded derivative causes some or all of the cash flows that otherwise would be required by the contract to be modified according to a specified interest rate,

引言

5.1　符合 IAS 39 适用范围的衍生工具不一定是独立存在的。嵌入到金融工具或非金融合同（以下称为“主”合同）中的条款和条件，也可以和独立存在的衍生工具一样起到相同的作用。这些条款和条件被称为嵌入式衍生工具。主合同及嵌入式衍生工具的组合被称为“混合工具”。

5.2　嵌入式衍生工具可能产生于有意的金融设计，例如通过纳入与权益挂钩的回报，使低利率债务更具有吸引力。有时，嵌入式衍生工具是无意间产生于市场惯例和常规合同安排，比如租赁合同和保险合同。甚至作为待执行合同的购销合同，也可能包含嵌入式衍生工具。事实上，嵌入式衍生工具可能出现于各种类型的合同和工具中——其目的就是改变主合同所要求的现金流特性，并在合同各方之间有效地转移金融风险。

5.3　分析非衍生金融工具和待执行合同中潜在的嵌入式衍生工具是 IAS 39 中更具挑战性的领域之一。但是，挑战并未到此结束。之后愈发明显，主合同中识别的衍生工具需要进一步评估，以确定是否应将其作为独立的衍生工具按公允价值单独进行会计处理。并非所有的嵌入式衍生工具都需要与其主合同分开进行会计处理。

定义和关键特征

5.4　嵌入式衍生工具是混合工具（该混合工具还包括一个非衍生主合同）的组成部分——从而使得混合工具的部分现金流量以一种类似于独立衍生工具的方式进行变化。嵌入式衍生工具使合同所要求的部分或全部现金流量随特定利率、金融工具价格、商品价格、汇率、价格指数或费率指数、信用等级或信用指数，或其他变量的变动而变动；变量为非金融变量的，其与合同的

financial instrument price, commodity price, foreign exchange rate, index of prices or rates, credit rating or credit index, or other variable, provided in the case of a non-financial variable that the variable is not specific to a party to the contract. [IAS 39 para 10]. Variation of the cash flows over the contract's term is a critical indicator of the presence of one or more embedded derivatives. An example of a hybrid instrument is a loan that pays interest based on changes in the FTSE 100 index. The component of the contract that is to repay the principal amount is the host contract – this is the 'base state' with a pre-determined term and pre-determined cash flows. The component of the contract that is to pay interest based on changes in the FTSE 100 index is the embedded derivative – this component causes some or all of the cash flows of the host contract to change. The following diagram demonstrates this:

Hybrid (combined) instrument

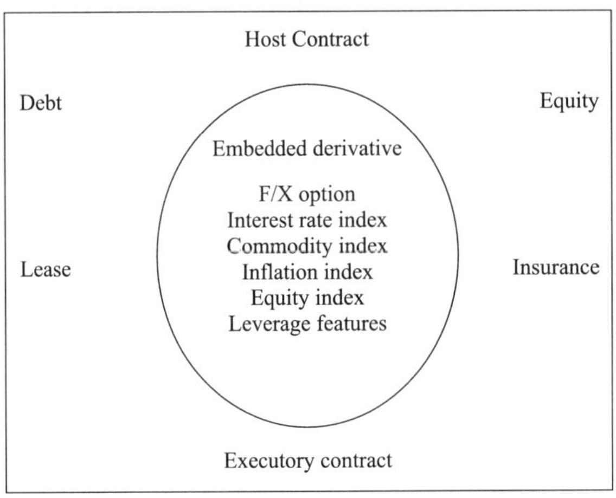

5.5 A derivative that is attached to a financial instrument but is contractually transferable independently of that instrument, or has a different counterparty from that instrument, is not an embedded derivative, but a separate financial instrument [IAS 39 para 10]. An example is a bond with a detachable warrant. The owner of the bond-warrant package can exercise the warrant and buy shares for cash but keep the bond. This is unlike an owner of a convertible bond where the owner has to give up the bond in order to exercise the option.

任一方不存在特定关系［IAS 39 第 10 段］。合同期内现金流量的变化是存在一个或多个嵌入式衍生工具的重要迹象。比如：基于 FTSE 100 指数的变化来支付利息的贷款便是一个混合工具。其中，偿还本金的合同部分是主合同，即预定期限和预定现金流量的“基本状态”。基于 FTSE100 指数变化来支付利息的合同部分是嵌入式衍生工具——该部分使主合同的全部或部分现金流量产生变化。以下是对上述说明的图解：

混合（组合）工具

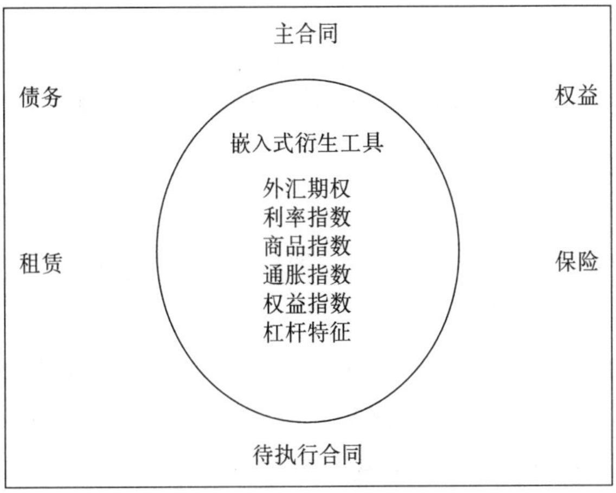

5.5　附属于一项金融工具，但依合同约定可以独立于该工具进行转让，或具有不同于该工具交易对方的衍生工具，不是嵌入式衍生工具，而是单独的金融工具［IAS 39 第 10 段］。比如：附有可分离认股权证的债券。这种债券认股权证组合的持有人可以行使认股权证以现金购买股票，但保留债券。这就与可转换债券的持有人不同，为了行使转换权可转换债券持有人必须放弃债券。

Conditions for separation

5.6 Paragraph 11 of IAS 39 states that an embedded derivative should be separated from the host contract and accounted for as a derivative if all of the following three conditions are met:

- the economic characteristics and risks of the embedded derivative are not closely related to the economic characteristics and risks of the host contract;
- a separate instrument with the same terms as the embedded derivative would meet the definition of a derivative; and
- the hybrid instrument is not measured at fair value with changes in fair value recognised in profit or loss.

5.7 In relation to the third bullet point above, paragraph 11A of IAS 39 states that if a contract contains one or more embedded derivatives, an entity may designate the entire hybrid contract as a financial asset or financial liability at fair value through profit or loss unless:

- the embedded derivative(s) does not significantly modify the cash flows that otherwise would be required by the contract; or
- it is clear with little or no analysis when a similar hybrid instrument is first considered that separation of the embedded derivative(s) is prohibited, such as a pre-payment option embedded in a loan that permits the holder to pre-pay the loan for approximately its amortised cost.

5.8 The above requirements are summarised in the diagram below.

Questions that need to be asked

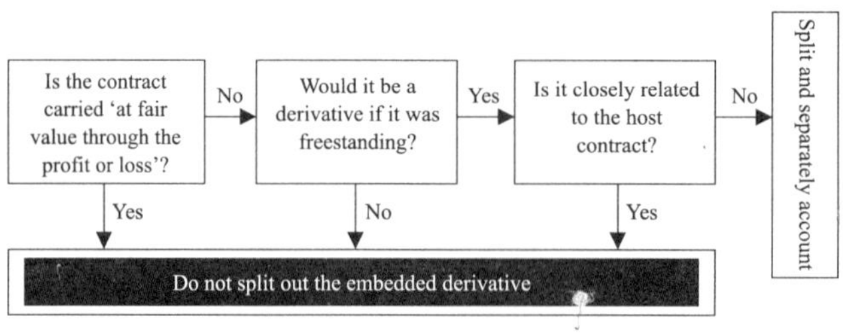

分拆条件

5.6　IAS 39 第 11 段规定，如果同时满足下列三个条件，嵌入式衍生工具应与主合同分开并作为衍生工具进行会计处理：

- 嵌入式衍生工具的经济特征和风险不与主合同的经济特征和风险紧密相关；
- 与嵌入式衍生工具有相同条款的独立工具符合衍生工具的定义；及
- 混合工具并未按照公允价值进行计量且其变动计入损益。

5.7　IAS 39 第 11A 段在阐述上述第三点内容的相关问题时指出，如果一项合同包括一项或多项嵌入式衍生工具，则主体可以将整个混合合同指定为以公允价值计量且其变动计入损益的金融资产或金融负债，除非：

- 嵌入式衍生工具对合同所要求的现金流量没有重大改变；或者
- 当首次考虑类似的混合工具时，仅进行少量分析或者不用分析就可以确定，不应分拆该嵌入式衍生工具，如一项贷款中嵌入的提前还款选择权，该选择权允许持有人以大致等于摊余成本的金额提前还款。

5.8　以上要求总结如下图。

需问的问题

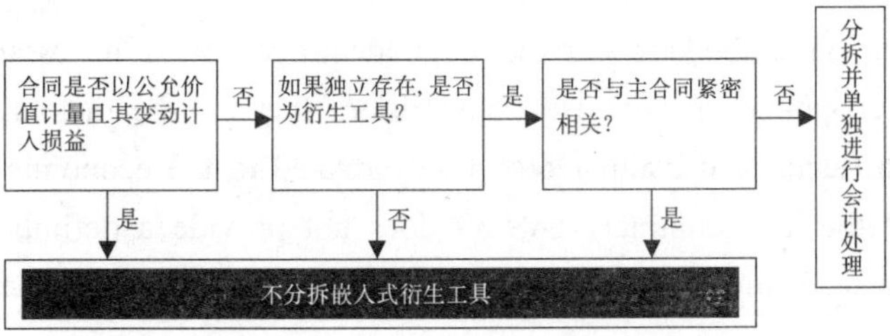

5. 9 The rationale for the above requirements is to ensure that all the underlying risks in an instrument are properly reflected in the accounting. For instance, a debt host contract may contain an embedded derivative that exposes the contract to risks that are non-interest related. If there were no requirement to separate the non-interest related exposure from the host debt instrument, entities would be able to achieve an accounting result different from the accounting result achieved if it had issued two separate contracts with the same combined economic effect. Therefore, separation of the embedded derivative not only ensures that the accounting faithfully represents the contract's underlying nature and its exposure to various risks, but also achieves consistency in accounting compared with freestanding derivatives. However, measuring an embedded derivative separately from its host contract requires judgement, and sometimes such measurements may be difficult. Therefore, as a practical expedient IAS 39 provides that an embedded derivative need not be separated if it is regarded as closely related to its host contract.

5. 10 Although the requirement to separate an embedded derivative from a host contract applies to both parties to a contract (that is, both the issuer and the holder of a hybrid instrument), the two parties to the contract might reach different accounting treatments when applying the decision tree in paragraph 5. 8 above. For example, an equity conversion feature embedded in a convertible debt instrument denominated in the functional currency of the issuer is not closely related to the host debt instrument from the perspective of the holder of the instrument. However, from the issuer's perspective, the equity conversion option is an equity instrument and excluded from IAS 39's scope, provided it meets the conditions for classification as equity under IAS 32. [IAS 39 para AG 30(f)].

Interpretation of 'closely related'

5. 11 Once an embedded derivative is identified, it is necessary to consider whether its economic characteristics and risks (that is, the factors that cause the derivative to fluctuate in value) are closely related to the economic characteristics and risks of the host contract. IAS 39 does not provide a definition of 'closely related'. Instead, the application guidance to the standard provides examples of

5.9 上述要求的原理是为了确保工具中的所有基础风险都在会计上得以正确反映。例如，债务主合同中包含的嵌入式衍生工具使得合同面临并非与利率相关的风险。如果没有将非利率相关风险敞口从主债务工具分拆出来的要求，主体达成的会计处理结果将不同于对假定签发两份单独的、但组合起来具有相同经济影响的合同所做出的会计处理结果。因此，嵌入式衍生工具的分拆不仅确保了会计处理如实体现合同的基础特性及其面临的各种风险，同时也与独立衍生工具的会计处理保持一致。然而，把嵌入式衍生工具与其主合同分开进行计量需要进行判断，有时该等计量可能会比较困难。因此，为方便实务核算，IAS 39 规定，嵌入式衍生工具如果与主合同紧密相关，可以不必进行分拆。

5.10 尽管把嵌入式衍生工具从主合同分拆的规定适用于合同双方（即混合工具的发行人及持有人），但合同双方在运用上述第 5.8 段中的决策树时，可能会得出不同的会计处理结果。例如，嵌入到可转换债务工具中的以发行人功能货币计价的转股特征，从工具持有人的角度来看与主债务工具并不紧密相关。但从发行人的角度来看，如果符合 IAS 32 下的分类条件，该转股权是一项权益工具，不在 IAS 39 的适用范围内。[IAS 39 AG 第 30（f）段]。

“紧密相关”的释义

5.11 嵌入式衍生工具一旦被识别，就需要考虑其经济特征和风险（即影响衍生工具价值波动的因素）是否与主合同的经济特征和风险紧密相关。IAS 39 并未对“紧密相关”进行定义，而是在准则应用指南中给出了嵌入式衍生工具是否与主合同紧密相关的示例。这些示例旨在关注嵌入式衍生工具的基础经济特征和风险与主合同的经济特征和风险表现方式是否一致的问题。

situations where the embedded derivative is, or is not, closely related to the host contract. Those examples have an underlying theme. They tend to focus attention on the question of whether the underlying economic characteristics and risks of the embedded derivative behave in a manner similar to the host contract's economic characteristics and risks.

5. 12 A key determinant in the closely related assessment process is likely to be risk. Risk in a derivative is determined by the underlying such as interest rate, foreign exchange, prices etc, and by any leverage in the formula for determining settlement. An embedded derivative such as a cap or floor on the interest rate (interest rate risk) that bears a close economic relationship to its host debt contract would be considered closely related. Conversely, when a derivative that is embedded in a debt instrument embodies an equity instrument's economic characteristics (for example, the derivative has a rate of return that is tied to the DAX 30 index), the economic characteristics of the derivative (equity-price risk) and host contract (interest rate risk) are different. In this situation, the embedded derivative would not be considered closely related to the host contract.

5. 13 The following example illustrates how quantitative as well as qualitative factors should be taken into account in determining whether the economic characteristics and risks of an embedded derivative are closely related to thosc of the host contract.

Example – Electricity contract linked to coal prices

Entity A, an electricity provider, operates in a country where electricity is not traded on a market, and has a number of electricity contracts that have prices linked to coal prices. Management believes that, from a qualitative perspective, the electricity price is linked to the price of coal, as coal is a major input to the electricity generation process. A quantitative analysis reveals that electricity prices are not directly correlated with coal prices.

A qualitative approach should be supported by quantitative analysis.

Whilst coal is an important input in the production of electricity, the price of electricity is driven by many other factors and, therefore, it is important to assess the extent to which the economic characteristics and risks of coal are in

5.12　在关于紧密相关的评估过程中，一个关键的决定因素很可能是风险。衍生工具的风险取决于利率、外汇、价格等，以及确定结算金额的公式中的任何杠杆作用。诸如利率的上限或下限（利率风险）等与主债务合同有着紧密经济关系的嵌入式衍生工具，将被认为是与主合同紧密相关的。相反，当嵌入债务工具中的衍生工具体现出权益工具的经济特征时（例如，衍生工具的回报率与 DAX 30 指数关联），该衍生工具的经济特征（权益价格风险）和主合同的经济特征（利率风险）是不同的。在这种情况下，嵌入式衍生工具不会被认为是与主合同紧密相关的。

5.13　下面示例说明，在确定嵌入式衍生工具的经济特征和风险是否与主合同的经济特征和风险紧密相关时，应如何考虑定量以及定性因素。

示例——与煤炭价格挂钩的电力合同

主体 A 是一家电力供应商，在其经营所在的国家，电力并不在市场上交易，该主体有很多电价与煤炭价格挂钩的电力合同。管理层认为，从定性的角度来看，电价与煤炭价格是相关联的，因为煤炭是发电过程中的主要投入。但定量分析却表明，电价与煤炭价格并不直接关联。

定性分析的方法应当由定量分析予以支持。

煤炭是电力生产的重要投入，但同时电价也会受到许多其他因素的影响，因此，对煤炭的经济特征和风险与电力的经济特征和风险实际上的紧密相关程度进行评估是非常重要的。而对相关性进行定量评估，可以有助

practice closely related to those of electricity. A quantitative assessment of correlation may be relevant to this determination and in this example may lead to the conclusion that the coal price is not closely related to the electricity price. The embedded derivative would, therefore, need to be separated.

Leverage embedded features in host contracts

5. 14 Leverage embedded features can significantly modify some or all of the cash flows that otherwise would be required by the host contract. IAS 39 does not define the term ' leverage', although the term appears in several examples in paragraph AG33. In general, a hybrid instrument is said to contain embedded leverage features if some or all of its contractually required cash flows, determined by reference to changes in one or more underlyings, are modified in a manner that multiply or otherwise exacerbate the effect of those changes. An example of this would be a lease with payments linked to an inflation index multiplied by a factor of 2. 5. The effect of leverage is only relevant for those embedded derivatives that would otherwise be ' closely-related' to the non-derivative host contract. This is because embedded derivatives that are not ' closely-related' would have to be separated out from the host contract in any event, irrespective of whether they are considered to be leveraged.

5. 15 Although, in general, leverage has a multiplying effect, the standard does not quantify a numerical measure of leverage for closely related embedded derivatives although it does include the notion of at least doubling the holders interest rate of return in relation to embedded derivatives in which the underlying is an interest rate or an interest rate index (see para 5. 31 below). In other words, although it may be clear that any embedded feature that leverages the exposure of the host contract to more than an insignificant amount would require separation, no guidance is given as to what would constitute an acceptable threshold. An example of this would be a contract for delivery of paper where the price is linked to a pulp index, transportation index and relevant inflation index where the indices are multiplied by percentages that reflect relative weighting of the cost factor in the production of paper. Such percentages would normally add up to 100 per cent. To support the closely related assertion it has to be demonstrated that it was the normal

于确定此种相关程度。在本示例中，可能因此得出煤价与电价并不紧密相关的结论。衍生工具可能因此需要分拆。

主合同中具有杠杆作用的嵌入特征

5.14　具有杠杆作用的嵌入特征可以显著地更改部分或全部主合同所要求的现金流量。IAS 39 没有对“杠杆作用”一词进行定义，虽然该词在 AG 第 33 段的几个示例中多次出现。一般情况下，如果混合工具中的部分或全部合同所要求的现金流量是根据一项或多项标的变化所确定的，且该现金流量以一种倍增或加剧这些标的变化的影响的方式进行变更，那么我们就说该混合工具包含嵌入的杠杆作用特征。比如，一项租赁中，其付款与通胀指数乘以 2.5 的系数进行挂钩。杠杆作用的影响仅仅和（在不考虑该影响时）与非衍生工具主合同“紧密相关”的嵌入式衍生工具相关。这是因为不论在何种情况下，不论嵌入式衍生工具是否具有杠杆作用，非“紧密相关”的嵌入式衍生工具一定会从主合同中分离出来。

5.15　虽然杠杆作用通常具有倍增效应，但准则并未对紧密相关的嵌入式衍生工具的杠杆作用确定一个量化指标，尽管准则确实在讨论标的是利率或利率指数的嵌入式衍生工具时，提出持有人的回报率至少应该翻倍的概念（见下述第 5.31 段）。换句话说，尽管很显然如果任何嵌入的杠杆作用特征使得主合同的风险敞口超过重大金额，应将其分拆，但是准则中并没有给出如何设定一个可接受阈值的指引。比如，一份纸张供应合同，合同中纸张的价格与纸浆指数、运输指数和相关通货膨胀指数挂钩，即这些指数与反映纸张生产中各成本因素相对权重的百分比相乘。权重的百分比通常加总为 100%。为了支持紧密相关的认定，必须证明这是纸张市场上在合同订立时，商业合同定价的一种常规方式。比如可以通过以下方式予以证明：参考相关行业协会、商品或货物交易所网站等。因此，应在考虑了特定情况下的所有相关事实和情形后再作出判断。

way to price commercial contract in the market for paper at the time when the contract entered into. That could be done, for example, by reference to web sites of relevant industry associations, commodity or goods exchanges, etc. Therefore, judgement should be exercised after considering all relevant facts and circumstances that are specific to the situation.

Identifying the terms of embedded derivative and host contracts

5.16 Because an assessment of whether an embedded derivative is 'closely related' to the host contract requires an understanding of the economic characteristics and risks of both the host contract and the derivative, it is necessary to consider the general principles that may be helpful in identifying the hosts and any derivatives that may be embedded in them.

5.17 Determining the type of host should not cause undue difficulty in practice as its economic characteristics and risks are readily transparent. Common host contracts that have derivatives embedded in them are given below:

- Debt instruments.
- Equity instruments.
- Leases.
- Executory contracts such as purchase and sales contracts.
- Insurance contracts.

The economic characteristics and risks of each of these contracts are considered in the application section below. Other hosts may exist, but as these are likely to be rare they are not considered in this chapter.

5.18 Searching for derivatives that may be embedded in the above hosts may be more challenging. Because few hybrid contracts actually use the term 'derivative', a thorough evaluation of a contract's terms must be performed to determine whether the contract contains an embedded derivative. Certain terms and

识别嵌入式衍生工具和主合同的条款

5.16　由于评估嵌入式衍生工具是否与主合同“紧密相关”要求对主合同和衍生工具的经济特征和风险进行了解，所以有必要考虑可能有助于识别主合同及任何可能嵌入的衍生工具的一般原则。

5.17　由于主合同具有明显的经济特征和风险，所以实务中确定主合同的类型应该不难。事实上，通常包含嵌入式衍生工具的主合同会有以下几种：

- 债务工具。
- 权益工具。
- 租赁合同。
- 待执行合同，如购销合同等。
- 保险合同。

上述每类合同的经济特征和风险将在下面的应用部分中考虑。可能还存在其他的主合同，但因为较为少见，所以未在本章中考虑。

5.18　在上述主合同中寻找可能嵌入的衍生工具，或许更具有挑战性。因为很少有混合合同中会实际使用“衍生工具”一词，所以必须对合同的条款进行全面评估，以确定合同是否包含嵌入式衍生工具。然而，某些条款和措辞可能会显示嵌入式衍生工具的存在。这些条款和措辞可能包括：

phrases, however, may indicate the presence of an embedded derivative. Such terms and phrases may include:

- Pricing based on a formula.
- The right to purchase/sell additional units.
- Exchange/exchangeable into.
- Indexed to/adjusted by/referenced to.
- Premium/strike/limits.
- The right to cancel/extend/repurchase/return.

5.19 Another method of determining whether a contract has an embedded derivative is to compare the terms of a contract (such as interest rate, maturity date(s), cancellation provisions, etc) with the corresponding terms of a similar, non-complex contract. In other words, an entity should ascertain whether there are differences between typical market terms and the terms of the contract that is being evaluated. An investigation of differences may uncover an embedded derivative.

5.20 The following list illustrates how the nature of a host contract and embedded derivative may be determined:

Instrument	**Host contract**	**Embedded derivative**
Convertible bond	Debt instrument	Purchased call option on equity securities
Debt paying interest quarterly based on an equity index	Debt instrument	Four forward contracts p. a. on equity index
A two-year fixed-quantity sales contract including maximum and minimum pricing limits	Purchase contract	Commodity price collar
A two-year fixed-quantity sale contract of mobile phones denominated in GBP between a French seller and German buyer both with euro functional currencies	Purchase contract	Foreign currency forward contract

- 基于公式的定价。
- 购买/出售额外单位的权利。
- 兑换成/可兑换成。
- 以……为指数/按……调整/……参考……。
- 溢价/执行价/限价。
- 取消/延期/回购/返还的权利。

5.19　另一种确定合同是否包含嵌入式衍生工具的方法是把合同条款（如利率、到期日、取消条款等）与另一个类似的非复杂合同的相应条款进行比较。换言之，主体应确定典型的市场条款与所要评估的合同条款之间是否存在差异。通过对差异的调查分析，就可能发现嵌入式衍生工具。

5.20　下表说明了如何确定主合同及嵌入式衍生工具的性质：

工具	主合同	嵌入式衍生工具
可转换债券	债务工具	买入的权益性证券看涨期权
基于权益指数每季度支付利息的债务	债务工具	每年四个基于权益指数的远期合同
包括最高和最低价格的两年期定量销售合同	采购合同	商品价格上下限
法国卖方和德国买方之间以英镑计价的两年期定量手机销售合同，双方均以欧元作为功能货币	采购合同	外币远期合同

Assessment of closely related criterion

5.21 It is clear that the assessment of the closely related criterion should be made when the contract is initially recognised, which is usually at inception of the contract. The question arises as to whether this initial assessment should be revisited during the contract's life. For example, an entity may determine, based on market conditions existing at the date of inception, that an embedded derivative in a host contract is closely related. Subsequently, market conditions change and the entity concludes that the embedded derivative is no longer closely related. The converse situation can also arise. The issue is in which circumstances the entity should make this re-assessment.

5.22 The above issue is addressed in IFRIC 9. IFRIC 9 re-confirms the treatment in IAS 39 that an entity should assess whether an embedded derivative is required to be separated from the host contract and accounted for as a derivative when the entity first becomes a party to the contract. This initial assessment is not revised, unless the contractual terms change and the change significantly modifies the expected future cash flows associated with the embedded derivative, the host contract or both relative to the previously expected cash flows on the contract. [IFRIC 9 para 7]. It follows that if the market conditions change and the market was the principal factor in determining whether the host contract and the embedded derivative are closely related, no re-assessment is required, unless the terms of the contracts are changed and the changes result in the revised expected cash flows being significantly different from the previously expected cash flows.

5.23 Furthermore, the IASB issued 'Amendments to International Accounting Standard 39 Financial instruments: Recognition and measurement – Embedded derivatives' in March 2009, which requires financial assets reclassified out of the fair value through profit or loss category (see chapter 6) to be assessed for embedded derivatives. The assessment is based on the circumstances that existed on the later date of (a) when the entity first became a party to the contract and (b) when a change in the terms of the contract significantly modifying the cash flows that otherwise would have been required under the contract. In the basis for

紧密相关标准的评估

5.21　很明确，在合同初始确认时，通常是合同开始时，就应对紧密相关的标准进行评估。然而，问题在于是否应在合同期内对初步评估进行重新评定。例如，主体可能基于合同开始时的市场条件，确定主合同中的嵌入式衍生工具是紧密相关的。之后市场条件发生了变化，主体认为该嵌入式衍生工具不再紧密相关。当然，也可能出现相反的情况。问题在于主体在何种情况下需要进行重新评估。

5.22　《国际财务报告解释公告第9号——重估嵌入式衍生工具》（“IFRIC 9”）处理了上述问题。IFRIC 9 再次确认了 IAS 39 中的处理方式，即当主体首次成为合同的一方时，应评估嵌入式衍生工具是否需要从主合同中分离，并作为衍生工具进行会计处理。初始评估不应修改，除非合同条款发生变化，并且相对之前预期的合同现金流，该变化对嵌入式衍生工具、主合同或两者兼有的现金流量有显著改变［IFRIC 9 第 7 段］。因此，如果市场条件发生变化，而且市场是确定主合同与嵌入式衍生工具是否紧密相关的主要因素，则不要求进行重新评估，除非合同条款变更并且变更导致修改后的预期现金流量与之前预期的现金流量相比发生了显著的变化。

5.23　此外，国际会计准则理事会（IASB）在 2009 年 3 月发布了“对国际会计准则第 39 号金融工具：确认和计量的修订——嵌入式衍生工具”，要求重分类“以公允价值计量且其变动计入损益”类别的金融资产时（参见第六章），需进行嵌入式衍生工具的评估。该评估应基于以下两个日期较晚之日所存在的情形进行：（a）主体首次成为合同一方之日；（b）合同条款发生变化，显著地改变合同所要求的现金流量之日。在修订稿结论基础中，理事会指出，在重分类时，任何确认的嵌入式衍生工具条款不应与假定在相关评估日就已确认的嵌入式衍生工具条款有所不同。

conclusions to the amendment the board noted that, upon reclassification, the terms of any embedded derivative recognised, should not be different to those that would have been recognised at the relevant date for assessment of embedded derivatives.

5.24 Similarly, a first time adopter of IFRS should assess whether an embedded derivative is required to be separated from the host contract and accounted for as a derivative on the basis of the conditions that existed at the later of the date it first became a party to the contract and the date a re-assessment is required by the above paragraph. [IFRIC 9 para 8]. It follows that as the conditions existing at the date the entity first adopts IFRS are of no relevance to the assessment of whether the embedded derivative is closely related or not, there is no difference in treatment between a continuing IFRS reporter and a first time adopter of IFRS. [IFRS 1 para IG 55].

5.25 Paragraph 16 of IFRS 3 requires a company that acquires another company (the 'acquirer') to re-assess all contracts of the acquired entity for embedded derivatives at the acquisition date. The rationale for this approach is that all such contracts (to which the acquirer becomes a party as a result of the acquisition) should be accounted for in the same way as if the acquirer had taken them out individually at the time of acquisition. Generally this will result in more embedded derivatives being separated from host contracts in the group's consolidated financial statements, as compared with the acquired entity's stand-alone financial statements. This is because the embedded derivative guidance links some of the criteria for separating embedded derivatives to market conditions existing at initial recognition of the host contract. These embedded derivatives will be accounted for at fair value through profit or loss separately from their host contracts in the consolidated financial statements, after the acquisition (unless they are designated in a valid hedge relationship in accordance with IAS 39).

Example – Re-assessment of embedded derivative

A UK entity entered into an 'own use' long-term electricity purchase contract in the late 1980s. At that time, there was no market for electricity. However, prices for gas and electricity were linked and, there was high correlation between the two prices. Hence, the price of the electricity contract was linked to gas prices. However, following deregulation of the energy market in the

5.24 同样，首次采用 IFRS 的主体应基于其成为合同一方之日与根据以上段落需要进行重新评估之日孰晚，评估嵌入式衍生工具是否必须从主合同中分离而作为衍生工具进行会计处理［IFRIC 9 第 8 段］。因而，主体首次采用 IFRS 之日存在的情况与评估嵌入式衍生工具是否紧密相关是不相关的，已经采用 IFRS 的报告主体与首次采用的主体在处理上没有任何区别。［IFRS 1 IG 第 5.5 段］。

5.25 IFRS 3 第 16 段规定，一家公司（“购买方”）在对另一家公司进行收购时，须在收购日重新评估被收购主体的所有合同，以确定其中嵌入式衍生工具的情况。采取此种做法的理由是，所有此类合同（收购以后购买方成为合同一方）应按照如同收购方在收购时单独取得这些合同的相同方式进行会计处理。一般来说，与被收购主体的个别财务报表相比，这将会使更多的嵌入式衍生工具在集团合并财务报表中，从主合同中分拆出来。这是因为嵌入式衍生工具的指引把分拆嵌入式衍生工具的某些标准与主合同订立之初时的市场条件联系起来。在收购以后，在合并财务报表中，这些嵌入式衍生工具将从主合同中分拆出来以公允价值进行会计处理且其变动计入损益（除非按照 IAS 39 被指定为有效的套期关系）。

示例——嵌入式衍生工具的重新评估

某英国主体在 20 世纪 80 年代末订立了一项长期的“自用”电力购买合同。在那时，还没有电力市场。但是，天然气和电力价格是相关联的，而且这两种价格间具有很大的相关性。因此，电力合同的价格与天然气的价格挂钩。然而，随着 20 世纪 90 年代中期英国能源市场放松管制，天然气和电力的价格已经不再相关。该主体在过渡到 IFRS 时，此合同的

UK in the mid 1990s, the prices of gas and electricity are no longer correlated. On transition to IFRS, the contract has a remaining maturity of two years.

When considered at the date of transition to IFRS the price adjustment feature would have been regarded as closely related, reflecting market conditions prevailing at the date the contract was entered into. Given that there were no amendments to the terms of the contract, in accordance with paragraph 5. 22 above, the initial assessment is not updated even though over time market conditions have changed and prices of gas and electricity are no longer correlated at the date of transition to IFRS.

On the other hand, if the entity entered into a similar contract after deregulation of the energy market, but before transition to IFRS, the price adjustment feature (electricity price in the contract is linked to gas prices and not market price of electricity) would not be regarded as closely related. Therefore, the embedded derivative would have to be separated and accounted for as a derivative at the date of transition to IFRS in accordance with paragraph 5. 24 above.

Application of closely related criterion to different types of hosts

5. 26 The application guidance to IAS 39 provides examples of situations where the embedded derivative is, or is not, closely related to the host contract. [IAS 39 paras AG30-AG33]. This guidance is not an exhaustive list of contract features or embedded derivatives but does contain many of the common features found in typical host contracts. Judgement will be required to analyse situations that are not included in the standard's examples. However, as determining what is closely related can prove challenging in practice, we have supplemented the standard's examples with the additional examples where relevant. The following paragraphs deal with the application of the closely related criterion to different types of hosts and embedded derivatives.

剩余期限还有两年。

当在过渡到 IFRS 之日进行考虑时，该价格调整特征会被视为紧密相关，以反映了合同订立时的市场条件。由于合同条款没有修订，根据上述第 5.22 段，即使随着时间推移，市场条件已经改变，天然气和电力价格在过渡到 IFRS 之日也不再相关，不应对初步评估进行更新。

另一方面，如果主体在能源市场放松管制以后，但在过渡到 IFRS 之前订立了类似的合同，该价格调整特征（合同电价与天然气价格挂钩，而不是市场电价）将不被视为紧密相关。因此，根据上文第 5.24 段，在过渡到 IFRS 之日，嵌入式衍生工具必须分拆出来，并作为衍生工具进行会计处理。

不同类型主合同的紧密相关标准的应用

5.26　IAS 39 的应用指南给出了嵌入式衍生工具是否与主合同紧密相关的示例［IAS 39 AG 第 30—33 段］。该指南并未穷尽所有合同特征或嵌入式衍生工具，但确实包含了典型主合同的许多普遍特征。对于准则的示例中没有包含的情况进行分析需要运用判断。然而，在确定什么是紧密相关的，在实务操作中非常具有挑战性，因此我们除了准则提供的示例之外，补充了额外的示例。以下各段将针对不同类型主合同及嵌入式衍生工具的紧密相关标准的应用进行讨论。

Embedded derivatives in debt host contracts

5.27 The most common host for an embedded derivative is a debt contract. However, it is first necessary to identify the host debt in the hybrid instrument. The implementation guidance states that the terms of the host debt instrument should reflect the stated or implied substantive terms of the hybrid instrument. [IAS 39 para IG C1]. For example, if the terms indicate that the host instrument has a stated or predetermined maturity and pays a fixed, floating or zero-coupon rate of interest, then its economic characteristics and risks are those of a debt instrument.

5.28 In the absence of implied or stated terms, the entity makes its own judgement of the terms. However, in exercising such judgement, the entity should not seek out a component that is not specified in the contract. Nor should it establish the terms of the host debt instrument in a manner that would separate an embedded derivative that is not clearly present in the hybrid instrument, that is to say, it cannot create a cash flow that does not exist. For example, if a five-year debt instrument has fixed interest payments of C40,000 annually and a principal payment at maturity of C1 million multiplied by the change in an equity price index, it would be inappropriate to identify a floating rate host contract and an embedded equity swap that has an offsetting floating rate leg in lieu of identifying a fixed rate host. The host contract is a fixed rate debt instrument that pays C40,000 annually, because there are no floating interest rate cash flows in the hybrid instrument. [IAS 39 para IG C1].

5.29 The value of a debt instrument is determined by the interest rate that is associated with the contract. The interest rate stipulated in the debt instrument is usually a function of the following factors:

- Risk free interest rate.
- Credit risk.
- Expected maturity.
- Liquidity risk.

债务主合同中的嵌入式衍生工具

5.27　附嵌入式衍生工具的最常见主合同是债务合同。然而，首先必须识别混合工具中的主债务合同。准则实施指南指出主债务工具的条款应当反映混合工具明示或暗含的实质性条款［IAS 39 IG 第 C1 段］。例如，如果条款表明，主工具包含明确或事先确定的到期日、支付固定、浮动或零息率利息，则其具有债务工具的经济特征和风险。

5.28　在没有明示或暗含条款的情况下，主体应自行判断其中的条款。但在进行这样的判断时，主体不应设法寻找合同中没有明确的成分，也不应设法拟定主债务工具的条款，造成分拆混合工具中并不明显存在的嵌入式衍生工具。也就是说，不能创造不存在的现金流量。例如，一项五年期的债务工具，每年需要支付 40,000 元的固定利息，到期支付本金，金额为 100 万元乘以权益价格指数的变动。如果将其识别为浮动利率主合同加上一个具有抵销效果的浮动利率端的嵌入权益互换，而不是识别为固定利率主合同，是不合适的。由于混合工具没有浮动利率现金流量，主合同是每年支付 40,000 元的固定利率债务工具。［IAS 39 IG 第 C1 段］。

5.29　债务工具的价值取决于与合同相联系的利率。债务工具中规定的利率通常是以下因素的函数：

- 无风险利率。
- 信用风险。
- 预计到期日。
- 流动性风险。

Thus, embedded derivatives that affect the yield on debt instruments because of any of the above factors would be considered to be closely related (unless they are leveraged or do not change in the same direction as interest rates and fail the test described in para 5.31. A detailed example is the inverse floater in example 3 of para 5.34 below). On the other hand, if the economic characteristics and risks of the embedded derivatives have features that are unrelated to interest rates (such as equity or commodity features), they would not be closely related to the debt host. Examples relating to the application of closely related criterion to a debt host and different embedded derivatives are considered in the following paragraphs.

Index linked interest payments

5.30 It is common for debt instruments to contain embedded interest rate indices that can change the amount of interest that would otherwise be paid or received. Typical interest rate indices are LIBOR and the prime rate index. More complex ones include leveraged interest rate indices, such as levered inverse floaters, range floaters, etc.

5.31 An embedded derivative in which the underlying is an interest rate or interest rate index that can change the amount of interest that would otherwise be paid or received on an interest-bearing host debt contract (or insurance contract) is closely related to the host contract unless:

- the combined instrument can be settled in such a way that the holder would not recover *substantially* all of its recognised investment; or
- the embedded derivative *could* at least double the holder's initial rate of return on the host contract *and could* result in a rate of return that is at least twice what the market return would be for a contract with the same terms as the host contract.

[IAS 39 para AG 33(a)].

Note that this assessment is made when the entity becomes party to the contract and on the basis of market conditions existing then (see para 5.22).

5.32 An example of an instrument meeting the first condition would be a bond callable by the issuer at an amount significantly lower than its issue price. Should

因此，由于上述任何因素而对债务工具的收益产生影响的嵌入式衍生工具将被认为是紧密相关的（除非其具有杠杆作用或与利率变化的方向不同，同时未能通过下文第5.31段所述的测试，比如下文第5.34段示例3中的逆向浮动等）。换言之，如果嵌入式衍生工具的经济特征和风险具有与利率无关的特征（如权益或商品特征等），其不会被认为与债务主合同紧密相关。紧密相关标准应用于债务主合同和不同类型嵌入式衍生工具的示例将在下面段落中讨论。

与指数挂钩的利息支付

5.30 债务工具中包含改变支付或收取的利息金额的嵌入利率指数是很常见的。典型的利率指数是伦敦银行同业拆放利率（LIBOR）及最优惠利率指数。复杂一点的指数还包括杠杆利率指数，诸如杠杆逆向浮动和区间浮动等。

5.31 以利率或利率指数为标的，且能改变带息债务主合同（或保险合同）需支付或收取的利息金额的嵌入式衍生工具，与主合同紧密相关，除非：

- 混合工具的结算可能造成持有人将无法收回*几乎所有*的已确认投资；或者
- 嵌入式衍生工具能够使持有人在主合同上的初始回报率至少翻倍，*并且能够使*回报率至少达到与主合同条款相同的合同的市场回报率的两倍。

［IAS 39 AG 第33（a）段］。

注意，应当在主体成为合同一方时，基于当时存在的市场条件进行此项评估（参见第5.22段）。

5.32 满足第一项条件的工具包括诸如发行人可以显著低于其发行价赎回的债券。如果发行人决定行使该看涨期权（即回购债券），则持有人必须将其出

the issuer decide to exercise the call option (that is, repurchase the bond) the holder would be required to sell it and, therefore, not recover substantially all of its recognised investment. The first condition that "*the holder would not recover substantially all of its recognised investment*" is not satisfied if the terms of the combined instrument permit, but do not require, the investor to settle the combined instrument in a manner that causes it not to recover substantially all of its recognised investment and the issuer has no such right (for example, a puttable debt instrument). An embedded interest rate derivative with such terms is regarded as closely related to the interest-bearing host contract. The condition that "*the holder would not recover substantially all of its recognised investment*" applies to situations in which the holder can be forced to accept settlement at an amount that causes the holder not to recover substantially all of its recognised investment. [IAS 39 para IG C10]. The term 'substantially all' is not defined in IAS 39 and, therefore, judgement should be exercised after considering all the relevant facts and circumstances that are specific to the situation.

5.33 The second condition has two parts and, therefore, both these parts should be met for the embedded derivative not to be considered closely related. So, for example, if the embedded derivative feature results in doubling the initial return under a possible future interest rate scenario no matter how remote, but, at the same time, that interest rate scenario would not result in a rate of return that is at least twice what the then-current market return would be for a contract that has the same terms as the host, then only one part of the condition would have been met and the embedded derivative would be regarded as closely related to the host.

5.34 The above provisions are intended to 'scope in' those embedded derivatives that cause the hybrid instrument to perform less like a debt instrument and more like a derivative (for example, hybrid instruments that are highly leveraged). The following examples illustrate the application of the above guidance to various interest rate index linked debt instruments.

Example 1 – Floating rate debt

Entity A takes out a floating rate loan with a bank. The contractually determined interest rate on the debt is six-month LIBOR plus two percentage points (assuming credit spread is two percentage points).

售，因此，将无法收回几乎所有的已确认投资。如果混合工具的条款允许，但并不要求投资者以使其无法收回几乎所有的已确认投资的方式进行结算，而且发行人也没有这样的权利（例如可回售债务工具），那么第一个条件“*持有人将无法收回几乎所有的已确认投资*”就不成立。带有此类条款的嵌入利率衍生工具被认为与带息主合同紧密相关。“*持有人将无法收回几乎所有的已确认投资*”的条件适用于持有人可能被迫接受以导致其无法收回几乎所有已确认投资的金额进行结算的情况。［IAS 39 IG 第 C10 段］。术语“几乎所有”并未在 IAS 39 中定义，因此，应在考虑了特定情况下的所有相关事实和情形后，再做出判断。

5.33　第二个条件分为两部分，因此，如果要认为嵌入式衍生工具并非紧密相关，两部分的条件均需要满足。所以，举例来说，如果嵌入式衍生工具特征在可能的未来利率情景下（不管可能性有多小）产生翻倍的回报率，但同时该利率情景不会造成回报率至少是届时与主合同条款相同的合同的市场回报率的两倍，则仅仅满足了一部分的条件，该嵌入式衍生工具仍将被视为与主合同紧密相关。

5.34　上述规定的目的在于将那些使得混合工具不像一个债务工具而更像一个衍生工具的嵌入式衍生工具“纳入范围”（例如，高度杠杆作用的混合工具）。下面的示例说明了上述指引在各种与利率指数挂钩的债务工具中的应用。

示例 1——浮动利率债务

主体 A 向银行借了一笔浮动利率贷款。合同确定的利率是 6 个月 LIBOR 再加两个百分点（假设信用利差为两个百分点）。

A plain vanilla floating rate instrument with a normal credit spread whose risk free interest rate component (for example, LIBOR) is periodically reset to market interest rate cannot contain an embedded derivative.

Example 2 – Floating rate debt with investor payment provision

Entity A issues a floating rate debt instrument with a face value of C50m. The contractually determined interest rate on the debt is six-month LIBOR. However, there is a provision that if six-month LIBOR increases by 200 basis points, the investor will pay C2m to the issuing company.

In this situation, the embedded derivative consists of a contingent payment provision that depends on LIBOR increasing by 200 basis points. The embedded derivative is not separated, because the investor will receive C50m and the C2m payment is not considered to reduce its initial investment substantially. Therefore, the first condition in paragraph 5.31 above is not met. Furthermore, there is no provision in the contract that causes the investor's yield to increase to at least twice the initial rate. Therefore, the second condition is not met. Accordingly, the embedded derivative is closely related to the debt host and no separation is necessary. The fact that LIBOR may increase by 200 basis points in a year is simply a condition that triggers the payment and is not relevant to determining whether the embedded derivative is closely related.

Example 3 – Leveraged inverse floater

Entity A takes out a loan with a bank. The contractually determined interest rate on the debt is calculated as 14.5% – 2.5 × three-month LIBOR (sometimes referred to as a leveraged inverse floater).
Three-month LIBOR at inception = 4% giving an initial yield of 4.5%.

The embedded derivative has an underlying that is highly leveraged such that there is the possibility of either a negative yield or a significantly higher than market yield. This is because, if under a future interest rate scenario three-month LIBOR increases to 8%, the yield would be negative, that is, –9.5% (14.5% – 24%) and the investor would not be able to recover substantially all of its recognised investment. Therefore, as the first condition in paragraph

具有正常信用利差的普通浮动利率工具，其无风险利率部分（例如 LIBOR）定期按照市场利率进行重新调整的，不会包含嵌入式衍生工具。

示例 2——含投资者支付条款的浮动利率债务

主体 A 发行了面值为 5,000 万元的浮动利率债务工具。该债务的合同确定利率为 6 个月 LIBOR。但合同规定，如果 6 个月 LIBOR 上升 200 个基点，投资者将支付 200 万元给发行主体。

在此情况下，嵌入式衍生工具由取决于 LIBOR 增加 200 个基点的或有支付条款所组成。该嵌入式衍生工具不应分离，因为投资者将收到 5,000 万元的款项，而支付的 200 万元不会被视为其初始投资的实质性减少。因此，上述第 5.31 段中的第一个条件没有得到满足。此外，并无合同条款会造成投资者的收益率增加到至少是初始投资回报率的两倍。因此，第二个条件也没有得到满足。因此，该嵌入式衍生工具与债务主合同紧密相关，没有必要进行分拆。LIBOR 可能会在一年内增加 200 个基点仅仅只是触发付款的条件，而与确定嵌入式衍生工具是否紧密相关没有关系。

示例 3——杠杆逆向浮动

主体 A 向银行借了一笔贷款。该债务合同确定的利率计算方式为：14.5% -2.5×3 个月 LIBOR（有时称为杠杆逆向浮动）。
合同开始时的 3 个月 LIBOR =4%，这样计算出来的初始收益率为 4.5%。

该嵌入式衍生工具的标的具有高度的杠杆作用，可能会产生负收益，也可能会产生显著高于市场收益率的收益。这是因为，如果在某个未来利率情景下，3 个月 LIBOR 上升到 8%，那么收益将是负数，即 -9.5%（14.5% -24%），投资者将无法收回其几乎所有的已确认投资。因此，由于满足了上述第 5.31 段的第一个条件，该嵌入式衍生工具不与主合同紧密相关，将单独进行会计处理。在实务中，有时不允许收益为负。为

5. 31 above is satisfied, the embedded derivative is not closely related to the host contract and will be accounted for separately. In practice sometimes the yield will not be allowed to go negative. To prevent this happening, a floor is often imposed on the coupon rate.

Note that in this example there is no need to evaluate the second condition in paragraph 5. 31 above. But if this condition were to be evaluated the result would be the same, that is, the embedded derivative would not be considered closely related to the host debt contract. This is because, for example, if under a future interest rate scenario, three-month LIBOR falls to 2%, the yield would be 9. 5% (14. 5% - 5%) which is more than twice the initial yield of 4. 5%. Furthermore, the yield of 9. 5% is also likely to be twice the then market yield for a contract with the same terms as the host.

Example 4 – Forward starting interest rate swap

Entity A issues a 8% fixed rate debt instrument that matures at the end of year 5. The entity has an option to convert the loan into a variable rate debt at LIBOR + 3% after two years. LIBOR at inception is 5%.

The embedded derivative included in the above debt host is an option on a forward starting interest rate swap that changes the fixed rate interest payments to floating rate after two years. In order to determine whether the option on the forward starting swap should be accounted for as a separate derivative, it is necessary to apply the second condition in paragraph 5. 31 above.

Accordingly, if, under a future interest rate scenario (however remote), LIBOR increases to 14%, the increase would have the effect of more than doubling the initial return on the investment from 8% to 17% (14% + 3%). However, that interest rate scenario of 14% does not result in a market rate of interest that is twice the current market rate for a contract with the same terms as the host contract, which is only 17% assuming no change in credit rating. Therefore, as only one part of the second condition in paragraph 5. 31 is satisfied, the embedded option on the forward starting interest rate swap is closely related to the debt host and no separation is permitted.

了防止这种情况的发生，通常会设置利率的下限。

注意，在这个示例中不需要评估上述第5.31段的第二个条件。但如果进行评估，结果将是相同的，那就是该嵌入式衍生工具不会被认为和主债务合同紧密相关。这是因为，举例来说，如果在某个未来利率情景下，3个月LIBOR下降至2%，收益将是9.5%（14.5% -5%），也就是4.5%的初始收益率的两倍。此外，9.5%的收益率也很可能是与主合同条款相同的合同的市场收益率的两倍。

示例4——远期生效的利率互换合同

主体A发行了5年期8%固定利率的债务工具，主体可以选择在两年后把该笔贷款转换为LIBOR +3%的浮动利率债务。合同开始时的LIBOR为5%。

上述债务主合同中包含的嵌入式衍生工具是一项远期生效的利率互换选择权，该选择权在两年后将固定利率付款转换为浮动利率付款。为确定该远期生效的利率互换选择权是否应当作为单独的衍生工具进行会计处理，有必要应用上述第5.31段的第二个条件。

因此，在某个未来利率情景下（不管可能性有多小），如果LIBOR增加至14%，那么将会出现从8%到17%（14% +3%）的增长，该增幅将超过翻倍后的初始投资回报率。但是，14%的利率情景下，主合同利率仅为17%（假设信用评级没有变化）不会造成市场利率是与主合同条款相同的合同的当前市场利率的两倍。因此，由于只是满足了第5.31段第二个条件的一部分，该嵌入的远期生效的利率互换选择权与主合同紧密相关，不允许分拆。

Inflation-linked interest and principal payments

5. 35 There is often a close relationship between interest rates and inflation in an economy. The nominal rate of interest is often thought of as the real interest rate (the amount earned on a sum loaned or deposited in a bank) plus the rate of inflation. The more precise version that allows for the compounding effect is given by the following relationship know as the Fisher equation:

$$1 + n = (1 + r)(1 + i)$$

where:

n = nominal interest rate
r = real rate of interest
i = expected inflation rate

5. 36 The above equation illustrates that the nominal interest rate reflects compensation to the lender for expected decreases, due to inflation, in the purchasing power of the principal and interest during the course of the loan. In other words, the nominal interest rate will vary directly with the expected rate of inflation, indicating that, in general, there is a strong correlation between the two.

5. 37 A strong correlation is particularly true for a country whose interest and inflation rates are managed together as part of the country's monetary policy decisions. For example, the Bank of England in the UK, like the Federal reserve system in the US, is responsible for setting interest rates that are aimed at accommodating economic growth in an environment of stable prices. Consider, however, countries in the Eurozone where the interest rate is set by the European Central Bank (ECB). Although the ECB sets short-term interest rates aimed at maintaining inflation rates in the Eurozone below, but close to, two per cent (measured by year-on-year increase in the Harmonised Index of Consumer Prices) over the medium term, the inflation rate in a particular country within the Eurozone may be different from overall Eurozone inflation due to, for example, differences in national rates of growth, local market regulation, etc.

5. 38 Therefore, where a company issues a debt instrument where the amount of interest or the principal to be repaid or both is linked to an inflation index, it would

与通货膨胀挂钩的利息和本金

5.35　经济领域中的利率和通货膨胀之间通常存在紧密关系。名义利率通常被认为是实际利率（银行在一笔贷款或存款上所赚取的金额）与通货膨胀率之和。可从以下名为 Fisher 的方程看出考虑复利影响后，两者间更为精确的关系：

$$1 + n = (1 + r)(1 + i)$$

此处：

n = 名义利率
r = 实际利率
i = 预期通胀率

5.36　上述公式表明，名义利率体现了给予出借人在贷款期内因通货膨胀造成的本金和利息预期购买力下降的一种补偿。换句话说，名义利率会直接因预期通货膨胀率而有所不同，这表明，在一般情况下，两者之间有很强的相关性。

5.37　对于把利率和通货膨胀率纳入国家货币政策而进行统一管理的国家来说，两者之间的相关性尤其紧密。例如，英国的英格兰银行，它和美国联邦储备体系一样，负责制定利率，旨在使经济增长有一个物价稳定的环境。然而，对于欧元区国家，利率由欧洲央行（ECB）制定。尽管欧洲央行制定短期利率旨在维持欧元区在中期内通货膨胀率低于但接近 2%（以消费价格协调指数的年同比增长进行计量），但鉴于诸如各国增长速度、本地市场管制等差异，某一特定国家的通胀率可能与欧元区整体的通胀率有所不同。

5.38　因此，当公司发行一项债务工具，其本金或利息或两者兼有的还款与通货膨胀指数挂钩时，就必须同时进行定性和定量分析，以确定标的通胀指

be necessary to perform both a qualitative and quantitative analysis to determine whether the underlying inflation index is closely related. This analysis should be performed on a case by case basis and would include at least the following considerations:

- Demonstration via a regression analysis to support the contention that there is a long run statistically significant relationship between the interest rate for the maturity specified in the debt instrument and the inflation measure to which that debt's coupon is linked.
- The inflation index is a recognised measure of inflation in the economic environment in which the loan originates. If the inflation index relates to a different economy or is not one that is commonly used for the purpose of lending and borrowing, the underlying inflation index will not be regarded as closely related to the debt host. In the UK, inflation indices that are most commonly used are the retail price index and the consumer price index. Therefore, no other inflation indices will be appropriate where the bond is linked to UK inflation rate indices.
- The inflation adjustment is related to the same period that the coupon payments relate.
- The resulting real rate of return delivered by the inflation linked debt is itself a rate that would not be considered an embedded derivative under IAS 39 and is not dissimilar to market estimates of real rates at the time when the debt is issued.
- The inflation index is not leveraged in any way (see para 5.14 – 15 for discussion of the term leverage and examples in paras 5.34 and 5.71).
- A judgemental qualitative analysis supports the view that any short term deviations from the defined relationship are not indicative that the two measures are no longer closely related. For example, it is likely that short-term deviations between the two measures may indicate a disparity in a country whose interest and inflation rates are not managed together as part of the country's monetary policy decisions aimed at maintaining price stability.

数是否紧密相关。这种分析应逐例进行，并应至少考虑以下因素：

- 通过回归分析来证明：债务工具中特定期限的利率与债务票息挂钩的通胀指标之间在统计上有着长期的重大关联。

- 该通胀指数是发放贷款的经济环境下用以计量通胀的公认指标。如果该通胀指数与不同的经济体相关，或者不是贷款和借款通常所采用的指数，则该通胀指数不会被视为与债务主合同紧密相关。在英国，最常用的通胀指数为商品零售价格指数和消费者价格指数。因此，当债券与英国通胀指数挂钩时，没有其他通货膨胀指数更为适合。

- 通胀调整与票息支付的有关期间相同。

- 通胀挂钩债务产生的实际回报率本身不属于按 IAS 39 需要认定为嵌入式衍生工具的利率，并且和发债时市场实际利率估计值并无不同。

- 通胀指数不以任何方式具有杠杆作用（见第 5. 14—15 段关于“杠杆作用”的讨论以及第 5. 34 段和第 5. 71 段中的示例）。
- 判断性的定性分析证实，对于这一确定关系的任何短期背离并不表明两种计量指数已不再紧密相关。例如，两种计量指数的短期背离可能表明某国的一个不同情况，即该国利率和通货膨胀率并未旨在维持物价稳定而纳入国家货币政策进行统一管理。

- Where a quantitative analysis is performed this should demonstrate that the inflation index would not result in the rate of return on the debt instrument that would at least double the holder's initial rate of return on the instrument or at any point would not exceed twice what the market rate would be a contract with the same terms as the host debt instrument.

5. 39 An entity issuing an inflation linked bond would need to perform the above analysis at inception to determine whether the inflation index is closely related to the host debt instrument. If the above conditions are not met, the embedded derivative would have to be separated from the host contract and accounted for as a derivative.

Example – Inflation-linked bond

A UK entity issues an inflation-linked sterling bond that pays a fixed interest of 5% per annum. The return of the principal amount is linked to UK Retail Price Index (RPI), which is a recognised headline measure of inflation in the economic environment in which the entity operates.

As the coupon on the bond is 5%, and the underlying principal of the bond is £100, the bond pays £5 interest per annum. If the inflation index increases to 10%, the principal of the bond would then increase to £110 and the interest payment increases to £5. 50 (5% × C110).

In this example, as the principal payment is not leveraged and it is indexed to the headline measure of inflation in the economic environment in which the entity operates and, assuming the other indicators in the above paragraph are met, the inflation index is regarded as closely related to the host debt instrument.

Equity and commodity linked interest and principal payments

5. 40 Equity-indexed interest or principal payments embedded in a host debt instrument or insurance contract – by which the amount of interest or principal is indexed to the value of equity instruments – are not closely related to the host instrument, because the risks inherent in the host and the embedded derivative are dissimilar. [IAS 39 para AG 30(d)].

■ 在进行定量分析时，应当证明通胀指数不会使债务工具的回报率出现至少为持有人初始回报率两倍的情况，或者在任何时点上都不会超过与主债务工具条款相同的合同的市场回报率的两倍。

5.39　主体发行与通胀挂钩的债券，需要在一开始就进行上述分析以确定通货膨胀指数是否与主债务工具紧密相关。如果上述条件不能满足，则该嵌入式衍生工具就必须从主合同中分拆，作为衍生工具进行会计处理。

示例——与通胀挂钩的债券

某英国主体发行一项与通胀挂钩的英镑债券，固定年利率5%。该债券的本金回报与英国零售价格指数（RPI）挂钩。该指数是主体经营所在经济环境下公认的首要通胀计量指数。

由于债券的利率为5%，标的本金为100英镑，所以债券每年支付的利息为5英镑。如果通胀指数上升到10%，债券的本金将增加至110英镑，需要支付的利息将增加到5.50英镑（5%×110元）。

在本示例中，由于本金支付没有杠杆作用，而且与该主体经营所在经济环境的首要通胀计量指数挂钩，假设上段所有其他条件都成立，该通胀指数会被视为与主债务工具紧密相关。

与权益和商品挂钩的利息和本金

5.40　嵌入主债务工具或保险合同中的与权益指数挂钩的利息或本金支付（利息或本金支付额与权益工具的价值挂钩）不与主工具紧密相关，因为内含在主合同和嵌入式衍生工具中的风险不同。[IAS 39 AG 第30（d）段]。

Similarly, commodity-indexed interest or principal payments embedded in a host debt instrument or insurance contract – by which the amount of interest or principal is indexed to the price of a commodity (such as gold) – are not closely related to the host instrument, because the risks inherent in the host and the embedded derivative are dissimilar. [IAS 39 para AG 30(e)]. Therefore, where interest and principal payments in a debt instrument are indexed to an equity-index that is not specific to the entity, a commodity index or any other non-financial index, the embedded derivative must be accounted for separately.

Example 1 – Cash settled put option in a convertible bond

Entity A issues convertible bonds to entity H. The term of the bonds is 3 years and the par value is C2m. Each bond pays fixed interest annually at 6% a year and is convertible at any time by entity H until maturity into a fixed number of entity A's ordinary shares. Entity H also has the option to put the convertible bond back to entity A for cash at par at any time.

Entity A has determined that the market rate for a loan with comparable credit status and providing substantially the same cash flows on the same terms, but without the conversion option, is 7%.

Entity A's management should separate the convertible bond's equity and liability elements. [IAS 32 para 28]. The conversion option is an equity instrument of entity A provided it can only be settled by physical delivery of a fixed number of shares for a fixed amount of cash or other financial assets. It is not accounted for as a derivative. [IAS 39 para 2(d)].

Paragraph 49 of IAS 39 states that the fair value of a liability with a demand feature is not less than the amount payable on demand, discounted from the first date that the amount can be required to be paid. Hence entity A would record the liability at its nominal value with any residual consideration received being attributed to the equity component.

The option to put the convertible bond back to entity A for cash at par is an embedded derivative. This option is closely related to the host debt instrument, as the exercise price is approximately equal to the bond's amortised cost before separating the equity element under IAS 32. [IAS 39

同样，嵌入主债务工具或保险合同中的与商品挂钩的利息或本金支付（利息或本金的支付与商品（如黄金）的价格挂钩）不与主工具紧密相关，因为内含在主合同和嵌入式衍生工具中的风险不同。[IAS 39 AG 第 30（e）段]。因此，债务工具中利息和本金支付额与并非该主体特定的权益指数挂钩，或与商品指数或其他任何非金融指数挂钩的嵌入式衍生工具必须单独进行会计处理。

示例 1——可转债中的现金结算看跌期权

主体 A 向主体 H 发行可转债，债券的期限为 3 年，面值为 200 万元。债券每年支付固定利率 6%，并且主体 H 可在债券到期前任何时候将债券转换为固定数量的主体 A 的普通股。主体 H 也可选择在任何时候将可转换债券按面值回售给主体 A 换取现金。

主体 A 已经确定，具有可比信用状况、在相同条款下几乎提供相同现金流量、但没有可转换期权的贷款市场利率为 7%。

主体 A 的管理层应该将可转换债券的权益和负债要素区分开来。[IAS 32 第 28 段]。如果可转换期权只能通过交付固定数量股票换取固定数额的现金或其他金融资产进行结算，其应为主体 A 的权益工具，不作为衍生工具进行会计处理。[IAS 39 第 2（d）段]。

IAS 39 第 49 段规定，带有即期偿付特征的负债的公允价值不应低于需即期偿付的金额自其能被要求支付第一天起折现后的金额。因此，主体 A 以名义价值记录该负债，而把收到对价剩余部分归为权益成分。

将可转债按面值回售给主体 A 换取现金的期权是嵌入式衍生工具。该期权与主合同紧密相关，因为其行权价格大致等于该债券在按照 IAS 32 分拆权益要素之前的摊余成本。

para AG30(g)].

Example 2 – Call option linked to an equity index

An entity issues a debt instrument at par with a term of five years. The debt is callable by the issuer 3 years after issue. If the debt is called, the holder will receive a sum that is the greater of the par value of the debt or the par value as adjusted by the percentage increase in the FTSE 100 index.

The embedded call option that is exercisable 3 years after the issue of the debt instrument is not closely related to the debt host as the payoff is indexed to an equity index. The equity linked feature provides an upside to the investor, which is linked to an index representing different risks from those of the ordinary debt instrument. Hence, the option should be separated from the host debt instrument and accounted for separately.

Example 3 – Payments linked to the price of a listed share

An entity issues a debt instrument at par with a term of five years. The debt is redeemable at par at any time. However, the loan agreement provides that during the term of the loan the entity will either receive or pay an amount based on the changes in the share price of an unrelated listed company A plc, the reference point being the market price of A plc at the date of issue of the debt instrument.

As the interest payments are based on the changes in the price of an equity instrument (equity risk), they are not closely related to the host debt instrument (characterised mainly by interest rate and credit risk). Therefore, the embedded equity linked amounts should be separated by both the issuer and the holder of the debt instrument and recorded on the balance sheet at fair value, with subsequent changes in fair value recognised in the income statement.

The answer would be the same if the interest or principal payments were linked to the movement in an equity index, such as S&P 500 and even if they were linked to the market price of the entity's own shares because the entity's own shares are an example of an underlying that is a financial variable (see

示例 2——与权益指数挂钩的看涨期权

主体按面值发行期限为 5 年的债务工具。发行人可在该债务发行 3 年后将其赎回。如果该债务被赎回，持有人将收到债务面值与按照FTSE 100指数增长率调整后的面值两者较高的金额。

该债务工具发行 3 年后可行权的嵌入看涨期权不与债务主合同紧密相关，因为其偿付金额与权益指数挂钩。权益挂钩特征使得投资者可以获得上调收益，其与一个代表了不同于普通债务工具风险的指数进行挂钩。因此，该期权应从主债务工具中分拆并单独进行会计处理。

示例 3——与上市股票价格挂钩的付款

主体按面值发行期限为 5 年的债务工具。该债务可在任何时候按面值赎回。但贷款协议规定，在贷款期限内主体将收到或支付基于一家非关联上市公司 A 的股价变化计算的金额，计算的参考点为债务工具发行时该非关联上市公司 A 的市场价格。

由于利息支付是基于权益工具价格变化的（权益风险），其不与主债务工具（主要具有利率和信用风险的特点）紧密相关。因此，无论发行人还是持有人均要将该嵌入的与权益挂钩金额分拆，并按公允价值计入资产负债表，其公允价值的后续变动在利润表中确认。

如果利息或本金的支付与股票指数，如与标准普尔 500 指数的变动挂钩，或者甚至与主体自身股票的市场价格挂钩（如上所述），答案也是一样。因为主体自身的股票也是一种金融风险的标的，且其内含的风险不同于利息风险（关于衍生工具的定义详见第四章）。

Chapter 4 for more details on the definition of a derivative) and the risks inherent in them are dissimilar to interest risk.

Example 4 – Equity linked bond with repayment floor

Entity A purchases a one-year debt instrument issued by bank B for its principal amount of C1, 000 on the issue date. Bank B will make no interest payments during the life of the instrument. At maturity the holder will receive the principal amount plus any increase in the S&P 500 index since the issue date. The fair value of an at-the-money European option maturing in one year is C48 at issuance date.

Entity A classifies the debt instrument as held-to-maturity.

Management should recognise the hybrid instrument as a combination of a call option and a zero-coupon debt instrument. Entity A should first determine the option contract's fair value and strike price. [IAS 39 para AG 28].

Since the holder only receives increases in the value of the index since the issue date, the embedded option is at the money at the date of issue and its fair value consists only of its time value and no intrinsic value. Consequently, its fair value at the issue date is C48 and the balance of the consideration given (C1000 – C48 = C952) is attributed to the carrying amount of the zero-coupon debt instrument.

The zero-coupon host contract should be recognised at amortised cost with interest accreted at the original effective interest rate of 6.3% to reach C1, 000 at maturity. The option should be recognised at its fair value, initially C48 against the benchmark of C1, 000, with subsequent gains or losses recognised in the income statement.

Example 5 – Commodity linked bond

A gold mining company issues a debt instrument with a face value of C10m and contingent interest payments in addition to a guaranteed minimum interest payment of 4% per annum. The contingent payments are linked to the price of gold such that an additional interest payment of 0.5% would be paid for every US $25 increase in gold price above US $260. The price of gold at

示例 4——带付款下限的权益挂钩债券

主体 A 在发行当日购买了由银行 B 发行的一年期债务工具，本金 1,000 元。银行 B 在该工具的存续期限内不支付利息。到期时，持有人将收到债券的本金加上自发行日起标准普尔 500 指数的增值。在发行当日，一年期平价欧式期权的公允价值为 48 元。

主体 A 把债务工具划分为持有至到期投资。

管理层应当将该混合工具确认为看涨期权和零息债务工具相结合的混合工具。主体 A 应首先确定期权合约的公允价值和行权价格。［IAS 39 AG 第 28 段］。

由于持有人只是收到自发行日起指数的增值，该嵌入期权在发行日为平价，其公允价值仅由时间价值构成，而无内在价值。因此，其发行日的公允价值为 48 元，其与支付对价的差额（1000 元 – 48 元 = 952 元）应归为零息债务工具的账面余额。

零息主合同应按摊余成本确认，其利息按 6.3% 的初始实际利率增加以在到期日达到 1,000 元的总额。该期权应按照初始 48 元的公允价值（相对于 1000 元的基准）确认，其后续利得或损失在利润表中确认。

示例 5——与商品挂钩的债券

某金矿开采公司发行了面值为 1,000 万元的债务工具，最低保证年利息为 4%，并附或有利息。或有利息与黄金价格挂钩，即黄金价格在 260 美元以上每增加 25 美元，将会额外支付 0.5% 的利息。债券发行日的黄金价格为每盎司 310 美元。没有该附加特征的固定利率贷款的市场利率为 5%。

issue date was US $ 310 per ounce. The market rate for a fixed interest loan without such additional features is 5%.

A commodity linked bond such as the one described above enables the issuer to reduce its financing cost by offering contingent payments to investors, whilst the investor is assured of a guaranteed minimum, but able to participate in any increase in the price of gold.

In this situation, the issuer would be viewed as having (a) issued a host debt instrument at a market rate of interest of 5%; and (b) purchased a swap contract to receive 1% fixed interest and pay a variable amount equal to the movement in the gold price above US $ 260. The swap contract is not closely related to the debt instrument as the factors that cause the swap to change in value (commodity price risk) are not the same as the factors that cause the debt host to change in value (interest rate risk).

Accordingly, the embedded swap contract should be separated from the host contract by both the issuer and the holder and recorded on the balance sheet at fair value, with subsequent changes in fair value recognised in the income statement.

5.41 Example 2 in the previous paragraph dealt with call options held by the issuer. A similar treatment arises in circumstances where the holder has the right to put the debt instrument back to the issuer in exchange for an amount of cash or other financial assets that varies on the basis of the change in an equity or commodity index that may increase or decrease. These instruments are commonly referred to as 'puttable instruments'. Unless the issuer on initial recognition designates the puttable instrument as a financial liability at fair value through profit or loss, it is required to separate an embedded derivative (that is, the indexed payment). [IAS 39 paras AG30(a), AG31].

Interest rate caps, floors and collars

5.42 Floating rate securities may have a maximum coupon that is paid at any reset date. The maximum coupon rate is called a cap. For example, suppose for a floating rate note with a coupon of three-month LIBOR + 50 basis points, there is a cap of eight per cent. If the three-month LIBOR at the coupon reset date is eight

如上所述的与商品挂钩的债券，使发行人通过为投资者提供或有利息减少其融资成本，而投资者可以确保得到一个最低金额，但同时能够从黄金价格上升中获利。

在这种情况下，发行人将被视为：（a）以5%的市场利率发行了主债务工具；（b）购买了一项互换合同，收取1%固定利息并按照260美元以上黄金价格的变动情况支付可变金额。该互换合同不与债务工具紧密相关，因为造成互换合同价值变动的因素（商品价格风险）与造成主债务合同价值变动的因素（利率风险）并不相同。

因此，发行人与持有人都应将嵌入的互换合同与主合同分拆，并按照公允价值计入资产负债表，并在利润表中确认后续公允价值变动。

5.41　前段中的示例2讨论了发行人持有看涨期权的情况。当持有人有权将债务工具回售给发行人，以换取基于可涨可跌的权益或商品指数变化而变化的现金或其他金融资产时，也会出现相同的处理情况。此类工具通常被称为“可回售工具”。除非发行人在初始确认时就将该可回售工具指定为以公允价值计量且其变动计入损益的金融负债，否则就必须把该嵌入式衍生工具（即挂钩支付）分拆。[IAS 39 AG 第30（a）、31段]。

利率上限、下限和上下限

5.42　浮动利率证券可能对在任何重设日支付的票息设定一个最大值。该最大票息率称为上限。例如，假设一个3个月LIBOR +50个基点的浮动利率票据，有个上限为8%。如果票息重设日的3个月LIBOR为8%，那么票息本应是8.5%。但是，该上限将把票息限定为8%。因此，上限可能对发行公司具

per cent, then the coupon rate would be eight and a half per cent. However, the cap would restrict the coupon rate to eight per cent. Therefore, a cap can be attractive to the issuing company as a protection against rises in interest rates. A cap can be thought of as an embedded option requiring no action by the issuer to be protected from a rise in interest rates. Effectively, the bondholder has granted to the issuer the right not to pay more interest than the cap. For the grant of this privilege, the issuer of the bond (the cap buyer) will have to pay a premium that will increase the overall cost of funds. If the relevant/market interest rate rises above the cap strike rate, then in effect payments are made by the cap seller to the cap buyer to compensate for the excess. This means that the cap is in-the-money whenever the strike rate is the lower than the relevant/market rate of interest. It is out-of-the-money whenever the strike rate is above the relevant/market rate of interest.

5.43 In contrast, there could be a minimum coupon rate specified for a floating rate security. The minimum coupon rate is called a floor. If the coupon formula provides a coupon rate that is below the floor, the floor rate is paid instead. A floor is the mirror image of a cap. While a cap benefits the issuer if interest rates rise, a floor benefits the bondholder if interest rate falls. As with other options, the buyer must pay a premium to the issuer of the bond (the floor seller) that will reduce the issuer's overall cost of funds. If the coupon rate falls below the floor strike rate then payments are made by the seller to the buyer to compensate for the shortfall. This means that the floor is in-the-money whenever the strike rate is the above the relevant/market rate of interest. It is out-of-the-money whenever the strike rate is lower than the relevant/market rate of interest.

5.44 A floating rate security can have a cap and a floor. This feature is referred to as a collar. The buyer of a collar limits the maximum rate that he will pay and sets a minimum rate that he will pay and, therefore, will be exposed to interest rate movements within a range. Hence, as long as interest rates are within this band the buyer of the collar pays floating interest, no compensating payment is made or received by the buyer under the terms of the collar and the collar is said to be out-of-the-money.

5.45 An embedded floor or cap on the interest rate on a debt contract is closely

有吸引力，因其被作为利率上升时的一种保护。上限可以被视为嵌入期权，在利率上升时发行人无需采取任何措施即可受到保护。实际上，债券持有人授予了发行人不支付超出票息上限利息的权利。因这项特殊权利的授予，债券发行人（上限买方）必须支付期权费，这会增加资金的总成本。如果相关/市场利率超出该上限的执行利率，那么实质上上限卖方会支付给上限买方以弥补超额部分。这就意味着，当执行利率低于相关/市场利率时，该上限是价内期权；当执行利率高于相关/市场利率时，该上限是价外期权。

5.43　与此相反，浮动利率证券也可能设定有最低票息利率。最低票息率被称为下限。如果票息公式计算出的票息低于下限，则只按下限进行支付。下限是上限的镜像。上限在利率上升的情况下有利于发行人；下限则在利率下降的情况下有利于债券持有人。与其他期权一样，买方必须向债券发行人（下限卖方）支付期权费，这会降低发行人资金的总成本。如果票息率跌至下限的执行利率以下，则卖方将对买方进行支付以弥补不足。这就意味着，当执行利率高于相关/市场利率时，该下限是价内期权；当执行利率低于相关/市场利率时，该下限是价外期权。

5.44　浮动利率证券可以既有上限也有下限，这一特征被称为上下限。上下限限制了买方将支付的最高利率和最低利率，并因而面临一定范围内利率波动的影响。因此，根据上下限的条款，只要利率在该范围内波动，则上下限的买方不会支付或收到补偿金额，这样的上下限被称为价外期权。

5.45　债务合同中嵌入的利率上限或下限与主合同紧密相关，只要在该工具

related to the host contract, provided when the instrument is issued:

- the floor is at or below the market rate of interest (out-of-the-money); or
- the cap is at or above the market rate of interest (out-of-the-money); and
- the cap or floor is not leveraged in relation to the host contract.

[IAS 39 para AG 33(b)].

5.46 The assessment of whether the cap or floor is closely related to the host is made when the entity becomes party to the contract and is not subsequently revised unless the terms of the debt instrument are changed significantly (see para 5.22 above). An entity would become party to the contract when the debt is issued at inception, bought in the secondary market or on the date of a business combination in which the debt was acquired. It follows from the above that only in-the-money caps and floors when the entity becomes party to the contract or leverage provision would fail the closely related test. Therefore, an interest rate floor embedded in a variable rate debt instrument that was out-of-the-money when the debt instrument was initially recognised would not be separated from the host debt, even if interest rates subsequently fall so that the floor becomes in-the-money. Similar considerations apply to caps.

Example – Debt subject to an interest rate collar

Entity A has borrowed cash from a bank. The debt is interest-bearing at a variable rate, but within a collar. The variable rate on the date of inception of the loan was 7%, the floor was 5% and the cap was 9%.

In this situation, the embedded derivative is a collar that modifies the cash flows of variable rate debt if the variable rate moves outside the range of the collar. IAS 39 does not specifically deal with collars in this context, although the guidance relating to caps and floors can be extended to collars. Since at the time when the variable rate debt instrument is issued, the interest rate is 7%, which is within the collar range, the collar is out-of-the-money. Hence, based on the guidance in paragraph 5.45 above, the embedded collar is regarded as closely related and separate accounting for the embedded derivative is prohibited.

发行时：

- 下限等于或低于市场利率（价外期权）；或
- 上限等于或高于市场利率（价外期权）；以及
- 上限或下限与主合同不存在杠杆关系。

［IAS 39 AG 第33（b）段］。

5.46　在主体成为合同一方时，就要对上限或下限是否与主合同紧密相关进行评估，其结果随后不得更改，除非债务工具的条款发生了重大变化（参见以上第5.22段）。主体在以下三种事项发生日，即成为合同的一方：债务最初发行日、主体进入二级市场购买该债务之日、或因业务合并而取得债务的业务合并发生之日。因而，只有当主体成为合同一方时是价内期权的上限和下限，或者具有杠杆作用的条款，才会导致紧密相关的测试失败。因此，嵌入到浮动利率债务工具中的利率下限在债务工具初始确认时是价外期权的，不会从主债务合同中分离，即使随后利率下降致使该下限成为价内期权。类似的考虑同样适用于上限。

示例——受利率上下限制约的债务

主体A从银行借入现金，该债务以浮动利率计息，但有上下限。贷款发放日的浮动利率为7%，利率下限为5%，利率上限为9%。

在此情况下，嵌入式衍生工具是在浮动利率超出上下限的范围以外时，将改变浮动利率债务现金流量的一个“利率上下限”。IAS 39并没有专门涉及上下限的讨论，尽管有关的上限及下限的指引可以延伸适用至上下限。由于浮动利息债务工具发行时的利率为7%，在上下限的范围之内，该上下限为价外期权。因此，基于上述第5.45段的指引，该嵌入上下限被视为紧密相关，禁止对该嵌入式衍生工具单独进行会计处理。

Calls, puts and pre-payment options

5.47 The terms of a debt instrument may include an issuer call option (a callable bond), that is, a right of the issuer (but not the investor) to redeem the instrument early and pay a fixed price (generally at a premium over the par value). There may also be other pre-payment features that cause the whole or part of the outstanding principal to be repaid early. Adding call options and/or other pre-payment options should make it less attractive to buyers, since it reduces the potential upside on the bond. As interest rates go down and the bond price increases, the bonds are likely to be called back. Alternatively, the investor may have a put option to force early redemption of the outstanding principal. Such call option, put option and pre-payment features that are embedded in the debt host are derivatives.

5.48 The application guidance explains that these embedded derivatives are not closely related to the host debt contract, unless the option's exercise price is approximately equal on each exercise date to the host debt instrument's amortised cost or the exercise price of a pre-payment option reimburses the lender for an amount up to the approximate present value of lost interest for the remaining term of the host contract. [IAS 39 para AG 30(g)].

Example 1 – Calls and puts in debt instruments

An entity issues the following debt instruments:

- 5 year zero coupon debt for proceeds of C7m with a face value of C10m; issue costs are insignificant. The debt is callable by the issuer at its amortised cost calculated on the basis of the effective interest rate method in the event of a change in tax legislation adversely affecting the tax deductions available to the issuer.

- 5 year zero coupon debt for proceeds of C7m with a face value of C10m; issue costs are insignificant. The debt is puttable at its face value in the event of a change of control of the issuer.

In both scenarios above, the zero coupon debt will be recorded initially at its fair value of C7m, which is the consideration received. The debt will accrete

看涨期权、看跌期权和提前还款权

5.47　债务工具的条款可能包括发行人的看涨期权（可赎回债券），即发行人（而不是投资人）有权提前赎回该工具并支付固定价格（通常按超出面值的溢价）。可能还有其他的提前还款特征会使得全部或部分的未偿本金被提前偿还。加入看涨期权和/或其他提前还款权应会减少工具对购买人的吸引力，因其会降低债券的潜在收益。因为随着利率的降低和债券价格的上涨，债券很有可能会被赎回。另外，投资人也可能会有一个看跌期权以强制提前偿付未偿还本金。此类嵌入到主债务合同中的看涨期权、看跌期权和提前还款权都是衍生工具。

5.48　准则应用指南阐明，这些嵌入式衍生工具不与主债务合同紧密相关，除非期权的行权价格在每个行权日均大致等于主债务工具的摊余成本，或者提前还款权的行权价格补偿贷款人的金额大致等于主合同剩余期限利息损失的现值。[IAS 39 AG 第30(g) 段]。

示例1——债务工具中的看涨和看跌期权

某主体发行了如下债务工具：

- 5年期零息债券，面值为1,000万元，收到资金700万元；发行成本不重大。发行人可以在税法变更并对发行人可获得的税务抵扣产生负面影响时，以基于实际利率法计算出的摊余成本，对该债务进行赎回。

- 5年期零息债券，面值为1,000万元，收到资金700万元；发行成本不重大。该债务可在在发行人的控制权发生变化时，按照面值回售。

在上述两种情景下，零息债券均按其700万元的公允价值进行初始确认，即收到的对价。该债务5年到期后将增加至终值1,000万元。因此，除

to its final value of C10m at maturity in year 5. Therefore, between inception and maturity the debt's amortised cost will not be the same as its face value, except in the period close to maturity.

In the first scenario, if the debt is called by the issuer at its amortised cost, the call option does not accelerate the repayment of principal as the option's exercise price is the same as the debt's amortised cost (the exercise price is not fixed but variable), even though the debt was initially issued at a substantial discount. Therefore, in accordance with paragraph AG 30(g) of IAS 39, the call option is closely related to the debt host and would not be accounted for separately.

In the second scenario, if the debt is put back by the holder at its face value before maturity, the put option's exercise price of C10m (fixed at the outset) would not be the same as the debt's amortised cost at exercise date. Therefore, in accordance with paragraph AG 30(g) of IAS 39, the put option is not closely related to the debt host. This means that the put option must be separately accounted for.

Both debt instruments contain terms that allow the debts to be called or put back on the occurrence of a contingent event (adverse change in tax legislation or change in control). These terms (relating to factors other than interest rate risk and credit risk of the issuer) are not closely related to the debt hosts. However, determining whether the call or the put option is closely related to the host contract is based solely on the difference between the option's exercise price and the debt's amortised cost.

Example 2 – Pre-payment option in debt instruments

Entity A takes out a fixed rate loan with a bank for C1m. The loan is repayable in quarterly instalments. The debt contains a pre-payment option that may be exercised by entity A on the first day of each quarter. The exercise price is the remaining capital amount outstanding on the debt plus a penalty of C100,000.

At inception, entity A would record the financial liability at its fair value of C1m. As entity A makes repayments of capital to the bank, the amortised cost

了临近到期日的期间，在开始日至到期日之间，该债务的摊余成本不会等于其面值。

第一种情景下，如果债务由发行人按其摊余成本赎回，由于期权的行权价格等同于债务的摊余成本（行权价格不固定而是浮动的），该看涨期权不会加速本金的偿还，即使该债务初始发行时的折扣很大。因此，根据IAS 39 AG 第30（g）段，该看涨期权与债务主合同紧密相关，不单独进行会计处理。

第二种情景下，如果在到期日前持有人按面值回售该债务，该看跌期权的行权价格1,000万元（一开始即已固定）将不同于该债务行权日的摊余成本。因此，根据IAS 39 AG 第30（g）段，该看跌期权不与债务主合同紧密相关。这就意味该看跌期权必须单独进行会计处理。

这两种债务工具都包含允许在或有事项发生时（税法的不利变化或控制权变动）赎回或回售债务的条款。这些条款（与发行人利率风险和信用风险以外的因素相关）不与债务主合同紧密相关。但是，确定看涨期权或看跌期权是否与主合同紧密相关，只是基于期权的行权价格与债务摊余成本之间的差额。

示例2——债务工具中的提前还款权

主体A向银行借了一笔100万元的固定利率贷款，该贷款按季偿还。该债务包含提前还款权，主体A可在每季度开始的第一天行权。行权价格为债务剩余金额加上10万元的罚金。

开始时，主体A以100万元的公允价值记录该金融负债。随着主体A向银行偿还资金，摊余成本将发生变化。

of the debt will change.

The exercise price of the pre-payment option at inception is C1m plus the penalty of C100, 000. Whether the entity will exercise its option to pre-pay the loan early may depend on a number of reasons, but the level of interest rates is a critical variable. If there is a significant decline in interest rates, any potential gain from early pre-payment may well be more than the cost of the pre-payment (the penalty payable).

Given the penalty payable is fixed, the option's exercise price (outstanding principal + penalty) will always exceed the debt's amortised cost at each option exercise date as the loan is paid off in instalments. Hence, the pre-payment option is not closely related to the debt host and should be separately accounted for. The fair value of the option would need to be calculated and this will be a positive value to the entity as the value of the pre-payable bond = value of straight bond – value of pre-payment feature. If interest rates decline, the option's value will increase making it more attractive to the entity to repay the debt early.

Sometimes the pre-payment option's exercise price is a 'market adjusted value'. A market adjusted value is calculated by discounting the contractual guaranteed amount payable at the end of the specified term to present value using the current market rate that would be offered on a new loan having a maturity period equal to the remaining maturity period of the current loan. As a result, the adjustment necessary to arrive at the market adjusted value may be positive or negative, depending upon market interest rates at each option exercise date. In that situation, the pre-payment option enables the holder simply to cash out of the instrument at fair value at the date of pre-payment. Since the holder receives only the market adjusted value, which is equal to the fair value of the loan at the date of pre-payment, the pre-payment option has a fair value of zero at all times. In fact, on a stand-alone basis, a pre-payment option with a strike price equal to market value would not meet the definition of a derivative, so it cannot be an embedded derivative per IAS 39 paragraph 11.

5.49 Paragraph AG30 (g) of IAS 39 contains another example of a pre-payment option which would be deemed to be closely related to the host contract. This states

开始时提前还款权的行权价是 100 万元加上 10 万元的罚金。主体是否会行使该选择权以提前偿还贷款，可能取决于多方面的原因，但利率水平是其中的关键变量。如果利率大幅下降，任何尽早提前还款的潜在利得都可能超过提前还款的成本（应付罚金）。

鉴于应付罚金是固定的，行权价格（未偿还本金 + 罚金）将永远超过每个行权日该债务的摊余成本，因为该笔贷款是分期偿还的。因此，提前还款权不与债务主合同紧密相关，应当单独进行会计处理。需要对该期权的公允价值进行计算，而这对于主体将是正值，因为该可提前还款的债券的价值 = 普通债券价值 - 提前还款特征的价值。如果利率下降，期权的价值将会增加，从而使主体更愿意提前偿还债务。

有时候，提前偿还权的行权价是一个“经市场调整的价值”。经市场调整的价值是将特定期限期末合同的应付金额折现为现值计算得出的，计算采用的折现率为发行一项新贷款的市场利率，且该新贷款期限与当前贷款的剩余期限相等。因此，为达到市场调整值而需要做的调整，可正可负，这取决于在每个行权日的市场利率。在这种情况下，提前还款权使得持有人仅仅按提前还款日的公允价值兑现了该工具。由于持有人收到的只是经市场调整的价值，该价值等于提前还款日贷款的公允价值，所以提前还款权的公允价值始终为零。事实上，单独来看，行权价等于市场价值的提前还款权不满足衍生工具的定义，所以根据 IAS 39 第 11 段，其不是嵌入式衍生工具。

5.49　IAS 39 AG 第 30（g）段给出了另一个提前还款权的示例，该提前还款权被视为与主合同紧密相关。如果提前还款权是向借款人补偿与主合同剩余

that if the pre-payment option reimburses the lender for an amount up to the approximate present value of lost interest for the host contract's remaining term it is closely related to the host contract. Lost interest is the product of the principal amount multiplied by the interest differential. The interest differential is the difference between the effective interest rate on the host contract less the effective interest rate that could be obtained by the lender if it invests the principal at the repayment date for the host contract's remaining term in a similar contract.

5.50 An embedded pre-payment option in an interest-only or principal-only strip (that is, an interest or principal cash flow stream that has been separated and payable at different dates) is closely related to the host contract provided the host contract:

- initially resulted from separating the right to receive contractual cash flows of a financial instrument that, in and of itself, did not contain an embedded derivative; and
- does not contain any terms not present in the original host debt contract.

[IAS 39 para AG 33(e)].

Term-extending options

5.51 Sometimes clauses are included in debt instruments that allow the issuer to extend the debt's term beyond its original maturity. An option or automatic provision to extend the remaining term to maturity of a debt instrument is not closely related to the host debt instrument, unless there is a concurrent adjustment to the approximate current market rate of interest at the time of the extension. [IAS 39 para AG 30(c)]. Thus, if there is no reset of interest rates at the time of the extension, the embedded derivative is not closely related to the debt host.

5.52 An alternative view is that the option to extend the term of the debt may be considered a loan commitment. Not all loan commitments fall within the scope of IAS 39, as set out in paragraphs 2(h) and 4 of IAS 39. In particular, only the following loan commitments are within the scope of IAS 39:

- Instruments that the entity designates as financial liabilities at fair value through profit or loss.

期限内所损失的利息现值大致相同的金额，则其与主合同紧密相关。损失的利息是本金乘以息差的积。息差是主合同的实际利率减去出借人如果在还款日对类似合同以主合同剩余期限投资本金所能够得到的实际利率。

5.50　嵌入到利息部分或本金部分（即已被分离且在不同的日期支付的利息现金流或本金现金流）的提前还款权与主合同密切相关，只要：

- 该主合同最初是通过分离收取金融工具合同现金流量的权利形成的，而该金融工具本身不包含嵌入式衍生工具；且

- 该主合同不包含任何原主债务合同中不存在的任何条款。

[IAS 39 AG 第33（e）段]。

展期权

5.51　有时债务工具会包含允许发行人延长债务期限超过原始到期日的条款。延长债务工具剩余期限的选择权或自动条款不与主合同紧密相关，除非展期的同时将利率调整至与当前市场利率大致相当的水平［IAS 39 AG 第30（c）段］。因此，如果在展期时没有重设利率，该嵌入式衍生工具不与债务主合同紧密相关。

5.52　另一种观点认为，延长债务期限的选择权可被视为贷款承诺。根据 IAS 39 第2（h）段和第4段，并非所有贷款承诺都在 IAS 39 范围内。从而，只有以下贷款承诺才在 IAS 39 的范围内：

- 主体指定为以公允价值计量且其变动计入损益的金融负债的工具。

- Loan commitments that can be settled net in cash or by delivering or issuing another financial instrument.

- Commitments to provide a loan at a below-market interest rate.

Loan commitments that are not in the scope of IAS 39 do not meet the definition of a derivative, as all derivatives must be financial instruments within the scope of IAS 39. [IAS 39 paras 9, 11]. Hence, an option to extend the term of a debt instrument that is considered to be a loan commitment, that is, out of the scope of IAS 39 could not be an embedded derivative that needs to be assessed for separation (see para 5.6). The approach adopted (that is, whether to treat an option to extend the term of a debt instrument as only within the embedded derivatives requirements or as also within the requirements for loan commitments) is an accounting policy choice that should be applied consistently.

In March 2012, the IFRS IC considered whether term-extending options in fixed rate debt instruments should be separated from the host contract but decided not to add this issue to its agenda at this stage. If the Boards do not address the issue as part of their redeliberations on IFRS 9 then the IFRS IC may revisit it.

Example 1 – Term-extending options not reset to market rates

An entity issues 6% fixed rate debt that has a fixed term of 3 years. The entity is able to extend the debt before its maturity for an additional 2 year period at the same 6% interest.

In this example, as the entity is able to extend the debt's term at the same interest rate and there is no reset to current market rates, the term extending option is not considered to be closely related to the debt host.

Such term-extending options could be valuable to an entity as it allows the issuer to refinance debt at the same interest rate when market rates are rising. Conversely, if market rates are falling, the entity would not exercise its option to extend. Therefore, the option is a derivative that would need to be accounted for separately at fair value through profit or loss, even though its value is closely related to interest rates that also affect the value of the underlying debt host.

■ 可以通过现金或提供或发行其他金融工具净额结算的贷款承诺。

■ 提供低于市场利率贷款的承诺。

不在 IAS 39 范围内的贷款承诺不符合衍生工具的定义，因为所有衍生工具必须是 IAS 39 范围内的金融工具。[IAS 39 第 9、11 段]。因此，延长债务工具期限的选择权，被认为是在 IAS 39 范围外的贷款承诺的，不能作为需要进行分拆评估的嵌入式衍生工具（参见第 5.6 段）。所采用的方法（即，是将延长债务工具期限的选择权按嵌入式衍生工具的要求进行处理，或是按贷款承诺的要求进行处理）是一个会计政策选择，需要一贯应用。

2012 年 3 月，IFRS IC 考虑了是否应当将固定利率债务证券的展期权与主合同分离，但决定不在目前阶段将此问题加入议程。如果理事会不将此作为 IFRS 9 重新审议的一部分，则 IFRS IC 可能会重新考虑。

示例 1——不重新调整至市场利率的展期权

某主体发行 3 年固定期限、6% 固定利率的债券。主体可以在债券到期之前按 6% 的相同利率把期限延长 2 年。

在这个示例中，由于主体可以以同一利率将债务展期，没有重新调整至当前市场利率，该展期权不被视为与债务主合同紧密相关。

由于展期权允许发行人在市场利率上升的情况下，以同样的利率再融资，因此可能对于主体来说具有价值。相反，如果市场利率下降，主体将不会行使其展期权。因此，该选择权是需要以公允价值单独进行会计处理且其变动计入损益的衍生工具，即使其价值与同样影响标的债务主合同价值的利率是紧密相关的。

The above treatment regarding term-extending options is justified, because otherwise such options could be used to circumvent the requirement to bifurcate a derivative in circumstances where the investor might not recover substantially all its initial recorded investment (see further para 5. 31 above). Term-extending options in host debts typically involve postponement of the repayment of the principal and, even though such postponement does not cause the failure to recover substantially all of its initial recorded investment, it can significantly reduce the fair value of the recovery of that investment.

Alternatively, if the term-extending option was considered to be a loan commitment out of IAS 39's scope, it would not be separated from the host debt instrument.

Example 2 – Term-extending option reset to market rates

An entity issues a 6% fixed rate debt that has a fixed term of 3 years. The company is able to extend the debt before its maturity for an additional 2 year period, but the rate for the period of extension is the market rate at the time of the extension.

In this example, as the option to extend the term causes the interest rate to reset to current market rates, the option is regarded as closely related to the host debt. Common sense would also suggest such an option has no real value to the entity other than providing liquidity. This is because if the market interest rate at the time of extension is 8%, the entity cannot extend the term without paying an additional 2% interest anyway. On the other hand, if the market interest rate drops to 4%, the extension is equivalent to taking out a new loan at 4%.

5. 53 If an entity issues a debt instrument and the holder of that debt instrument writes a call option on the debt instrument to a third party, the issuer regards the call option as extending the term to maturity of the debt instrument provided the issuer can be required to participate in or facilitate the remarketing of the debt instrument as a result of the call option being exercised. [IAS 39 para AG 30 (c)].

5. 54 It is interesting to note that a bond that has a put option is economically no

上述有关展期权的处理方式是有道理的，否则此类选择权可以在投资人无法收回几乎所有其初始投资的情况下，用来规避对衍生工具进行分拆的要求（详见以上第5.31段）。债务主合同中的展期权通常涉及延迟本金偿还，即使此类延迟不会造成投资人无法收回几乎所有其初始投资，但会显著降低投资所收回的公允价值。

或者，如果展期权被视为IAS 39范围外的贷款承诺，其不会从主债务工具中被分拆。

示例2——重新调整至市场利率的展期权

某主体发行3年固定期限、6%固定利率的债券。该公司可以在债券到期之前把期限延长2年，但是展期期间的利率为展期时的市场利率。

在这个示例中，由于延长期限的选择权把利率重新调整至当前的市场利率，该选择权被视为与主债务合同紧密相关。根据常识也可以看出，此类选择权除了可以提供流动性以外，对于主体并没有真正的价值。这是因为如果展期时的市场利率为8%，则主体不支付额外2%利息就不能延长期限。另一方面，如果市场利率下降至4%，展期与以4%的利息获得一笔新贷款是等效的。

5.53　如果主体发行一项债务工具，该债务工具的持有人向第三方签发一个针对该债务工具的看涨期权，如果因该看涨期权行权而能够要求发行人参与或促使该债务工具的转流通，则发行人应把该看涨期权视作将债务工具展期至到期日［IAS 39 AG 第30（c）段］。

5.54　有趣的是，包含一个看跌期权的债券从经济上看与包含一个展期权的

different to one that has a term-extending option, yet IAS 39 prescribes a different treatment for the derivatives embedded in them. Consider the following example:

Example – Comparison of put and extension option

An entity purchasers two bonds A and B with the following terms:

- Bond A has a stated maturity of 10 years, but the entity can put it back to the issuer at par after 3 years.
- Bond B has a stated maturity of 3 years, but after 3 years the entity can extend the maturity to 10 years (that is, 7 more years) at the same initial rate (that is, the interest rate is not reset to the interest rate at the date of extension).

Both bonds are issued by the same issuer at par and have a coupon rate of 6%.

Assume also that the following two scenarios exist at the end of year 3:

Scenario 1: For the issuer, the interest rate for 7 year debt is at 8%.

- The holder will put bond A back to the issuer and reinvest the par amount of the bond at 8%.
- The holder will not extend the maturity of bond B and, instead, will reinvest the principal at 8%.

Scenario 2: For the issuer, the interest rate for 7 year debt is at 4%.

- The holder will not put bond A back to the issuer and, instead, will continue to receive 6% for the next 7 years.
- The holder will extend the term of bond B and continue to receive 6% for the next 7 years.

As can be seen from the above, the entity is in the same position with respect to either Bond A or Bond B. However, IAS 39 prescribes a different treatment for the put and the term extension options embedded in Bond A and Bond B respectively.

As discussed in paragraph 5.48 above, the embedded put option derivative in

债券没有什么不同，然而 IAS 39 对于嵌入其中的衍生工具规定了的不同处理方式。考虑如下示例：

示例——看跌期权和展期权的比较

某主体购买 A 和 B 两只债券，其条款分别如下：

- 债券 A 的规定期限为 10 年，但主体可以在 3 年后按面值回售给发行人。
- 债券 B 的规定期限为 3 年，但是 3 年后主体可以将期限延长至 10 年（即另外增加 7 年），增加期限内的利率同初始利率（即利率不会重新调整至展期日的利率）。

两只债券都是由同一发行人按面值发行，利率都为 6%。

同时假设在第 3 年年末时，出现以下两种情景：

情景 1：对发行人而言，7 年期债券的利率为 8%。

- 持有人会把债券 A 回售给发行人，并将面值金额重新投资于 8% 的债券。
- 持有人不会延长债券 B 的期限，而将本金重新投资于利率为 8% 的债券。

情景 2：对发行人而言，7 年期债券的利率为 4%。

- 持有人不会把债券回售给发行人，而在未来 7 年继续收取 6% 的利率。
- 持有人将延长债券 B 的期限，并在未来 7 年继续收取 6% 的利率。

以上可以看到，主体对于债券 A 或债券 B 的状况是相同的。然而，IAS 39 对于嵌入到债券 A 和债券 B 的看跌期权和展期权分别规定了不同处理方法。

如上文第 5.48 段所讨论的，债券 A 中嵌入的看跌期权被视为与该债券紧

Bond A is regarded as closely related to the Bond as the bond's amortised cost based on the effective interest rate at the end of three years is the same as par, which is also the put option's exercise price. This is because the expected cash flows would take into account the possibility of the debt being pre-paid early for the purposes of calculating the effective interest rate. [IAS 39 para 9]. Therefore, the embedded put option would not be recognised separately and fair valued.

On the other hand, the embedded term extension option is not regarded as closely related to the host debt, because under Bond B's terms the interest rates are not reset when the option is exercised. Therefore, the option would be separated and fair valued. Alternatively, if the embedded term extension option was considered to be a loan commitment outside IAS 39's scope, the option would not be separated, as it would not meet the definition of a derivative.

The above example illustrates that two instruments that are economically similar, but different in form by virtue of the way in which the terms of the embedded options are expressed, can lead to different accounting treatments for the embedded options.

To be able to rationalise the apparent conflict in accounting treatment between these two economically identical situations, it is necessary to consider the issuer's expectation of the instrument's life for the purposes of the effective interest rate calculation. Thus the issuer will not necessarily follow the legal form of the terms, but the economics in determining whether the instrument has a put option or a term extending option and thus the appropriate accounting treatment.

Credit sensitive payments and credit derivatives

5.55 IAS 39 does not deal specifically with payments based on the creditworthiness of the issuer of an instrument. However, as the stated in paragraph 5.29 above, the creditworthiness of the issuer is a key factor in setting the level of interest rate on the debt instrument. Thus, for debt instruments that provide for the interest rate to be reset in the event of a change in the issuer's

密相关，因为3年年末该债券基于实际利率的摊余成本等于面值，同时也是看跌期权的行权价。这是因为用来计算实际利率的预期现金流量会考虑提前偿还债务的可能性。[IAS 39 第9段]。因此，嵌入的看跌期权将不会单独确认并以公允价值计量。

另一方面，嵌入的展期权不被视为与主债务合同紧密相关，因为债券B的条款规定，在行权时不会对利率进行重新调整。因此，该期权将被分拆出来，并以公允价值计量。或者，如果该嵌入展期权被认为是IAS 39范围外的贷款承诺，就不应对其进行分拆，因为不符合衍生工具的定义。

上面的示例说明，两种在经济上类似、但因嵌入期权条款表达方式而在形式上有所不同的工具，就会导致对于嵌入期权的不同会计处理。

为了合理处理经济上相同的两个情形在会计处理上的明显冲突，有必要在实际利率的计算上考虑发行人对工具寿命的预期。因此，发行人不一定依照条款的法律形式，而是应从经济上确定该工具是包含看跌期权还是展期权，从而采取适当的会计处理。

信用敏感型付款与信用衍生工具

5.55 IAS 39 并没有专门涉及基于工具发行人信用水平而进行的付款。然而，如上文第5.29段所述，发行人信用水平是设定债务工具利率水平的关键因素。因此，对于当发行人的公开信用评级发生变化（比如从A级降至BBB级）或者发行人的信用水平发生变化之时，需要重新调整利率的债务工具，嵌入式衍生工具与债务主合同紧密相关，所以将不会从主合同分拆。

published credit rating (say down from A to BBB) or a change in the issuer's creditworthiness, the embedded derivative would be closely related to the debt host, and so would not be separated from the host contract.

Example 1 – Credit sensitive payments

Entity A issues a bond with a coupon step-up feature that requires the issuer to pay an additional coupon to bondholders in the event of deterioration in the issuer's credit rating below a specified level. The coupon payable on the bond will return to the initial fixed rate in the event that the issuer's credit rating returns to the specified level.

The coupon step-up clause meets the definition of a derivative as the value fluctuates in response to an underlying (in this case the credit rating); it requires no initial net investment and it is settled at a future date.

The economic characteristics and risks of the embedded derivatives in both cases are closely related to the economic characteristics and risks of the host bond because:

- both the embedded derivative and the host contract are driven by changes in the indications of the issuer's credit risk; and
- such clauses do not transfer the credit risk to another party external to the original contractual relationships created by the debt instrument (see para 5.56 below).

The embedded derivative is not accounted for separately from the host debt contract.

5.56 IAS 39 does, however, deal with credit derivatives that are embedded in host debt instruments. A credit derivative is a financial instrument designed to transfer credit risk from the person exposed to that risk to a person willing to take on that risk. The derivative derives its economic value by reference to a specified debt obligation, often described as the 'reference asset'.

5.57 Credit derivatives that are embedded in a host debt instrument and allow one party (the 'beneficiary') to transfer the credit risk of a particular reference asset, which it may not own, to another party (the 'guarantor') are not closely related

示例1——信用敏感型付款

主体A发行带有票息递增特征的债券，该特征要求发行人在其信用评级恶化而低于某个特定水平时，向债券持有人支付额外的票息。发行人的信用评级重新回到特定水平时，债券的应付票息将返回到初始固定利率。

票息递增条款符合衍生工具的定义，因为其价值随着标的（这种情况下为信用评级）的波动而波动；不需要初始净投资且在未来的某一日期结算。

该嵌入式衍生工具的经济特征和风险在两种情况下都与主债券的经济特征和风险紧密相关，这是因为：

- 嵌入式衍生工具和主合同都受到发行人信用风险指标变化的影响；
- 这类条款不会将信用风险转移至形成债务工具的原合同关系之外的另外一方（参见下文第5.56段）。

该嵌入式衍生工具不能独立于主债务合同单独进行会计处理。

5.56 然而，IAS 39确实对于嵌入到主债务工具中的信用衍生工具进行了讨论。信用衍生工具是一种金融工具，旨在把信用风险从承担该风险敞口的人转移到愿意接受这种风险的人。该衍生工具通过参照某特定的债务（通常被描述为“参照资产”）衍生其经济价值。

5.57 嵌入到主债务工具并且允许一方(“受益人”）向另一方(“担保人”）转移某特定参照资产（受益人可能并不拥有该资产）信用风险的信用衍生工具，不与主债务工具紧密相关。此类信用衍生工具允许担保人承担与其并不直接

to the host debt instrument. Such credit derivatives allow the guarantor to assume the credit risk associated with the reference asset without directly owning it. [IAS 39 AG30(h)].

Example – Credit-linked note

An investment bank issues a credit-linked note to another party (the investor) in return for a consideration equal to the par value of the note. The coupon on the note is linked to the credit risk of a portfolio of third party bonds (the reference assets). In economic terms, the credit-linked note comprises a fixed income instrument with an embedded credit derivative.

The embedded credit derivative must be accounted for separately as it is linked to credit risks of debt instruments issued by third parties and not to the credit risk of the host debt instrument issued by the investment bank. The notion of an embedded derivative in a hybrid instrument refers to provisions incorporated into a single contract and not to provisions in separate contracts between different counterparties.

Equity conversion features

5.58 When an investor holds debt securities that are convertible into the issuer's equity shares at the investor's option, the equity conversion feature represents an embedded option written by the issuer on its equity shares. The embedded derivative is not closely related to the host debt instrument from the investor's perspective. [IAS 39 para IG C3]. From the issuer's perspective, the written equity conversion option is an equity instrument and excluded from IAS 39's scope provided it meets the conditions for that classification under IAS 32. [IAS 39 para AG 30 (f)]. If, on the other hand, the debt instrument is convertible (or exchangeable) into shares of another entity, both the issuer and the holder would have to separate the embedded derivative from the host contract.

5.59 As the holder of a convertible bond is required to separate the embedded derivative, they are generally precluded from accounting for the debt host contract as a held-to-maturity investment. This is because classification as a held-to-maturity investment would be inconsistent with paying for the conversion feature - the right to convert into equity shares before maturity. However, the investor could

拥有的参照资产相联系的信用风险。[IAS 39 AG 第 30（h）段]。

示例——信用挂钩票据

某投资银行向另一方（投资人）发行信用挂钩票据，以换取等值于票据面值的对价。票据的票息与第三方债券投资组合（参照资产）的信用风险挂钩。以经济术语来讲，该信用挂钩票据由带有嵌入式信用衍生工具的固定收益工具组成。

该信用衍生工具应单独进行会计处理，因为其与第三方发行的债务工具的信用风险挂钩，而不是与该投资银行发行的主债务工具的信用风险挂钩。混合工具中嵌入式衍生工具的概念是指单个合同中的条款，而不是各方之间各自独立合同中的条款。

权益转换特征

5.58　当某投资人持有可按其选择转换为发行人权益股份的债务证券时，该转股特征为发行人就其权益股份签发的嵌入期权。从投资人角度看，该嵌入式衍生工具不与主债务工具紧密相关。[IAS 39 IG 第 C3 段]。从发行人角度看，如果其签发的转股权符合 IAS 32 的分类条件，则成为权益工具，不在 IAS 39 的范围内。[IAS 39 AG 第30（f）段]。另一方面，如果该债务工具可转换（或兑换）为其他主体的股票，发行人和持有人都必须把该嵌入式衍生工具从主合同中分拆出来。

5.59　由于可转债的持有人需要对嵌入式衍生工具进行分离，则通常其不应将债务主合同作为持有至到期投资进行会计处理。这是因为分类为持有至到期投资与就该转换特征（到期日前转换为权益股份的权利）支付代价是矛盾的。不过，只要不是为交易目的而购买债券，投资人可将该债券分类为可供出售金融资产。如果该债券被分类为可供出售类（即在债券未出售或减值之

classify the bond as an available-for-sale financial asset provided it is not purchased for trading purposes. If the bond is classified as available-for-sale (that is, fair value changes are recognised directly in equity until the bond is sold or impaired), the equity conversion option (the embedded derivative) is separated. The accounting for the holder, which is significantly different from the issuer as as considered in chapter 7, is as follows:

- The embedded derivative's fair value (the equity conversion option from the issuer's perspective) is calculated first and comprises its time value and its intrinsic value, if any. The option has value on initial recognition even when it is out of the money.

  After initial recognition, the embedded derivative is constantly remeasured at fair value at each balance sheet date and changes in the fair value are recognised in profit or loss, unless the option is part of a cash flow hedging relationship.

- The carrying value of the host contract (the liability component from the issuer's perspective) is assigned the residual amount after deducting from the fair value of the instrument as a whole (the consideration paid to acquire the hybrid instrument) the amount separately determined for the embedded derivative.

If the convertible bond is measured at fair value with changes in fair value recognised in profit or loss, separating the embedded derivative from the host bond as illustrated above is not permitted. [IAS 39 para IG C3].

5.60 Another type of embedded derivative that is often found in practice relates to a type of funding provided by venture capital entities as illustrated in the example below.

Example – Equity kicker

A venture capital entity provides a subordinated loan that, in addition to interest and repayment of principal, contains terms that entitles the venture capital company to receive shares of the borrower free of charge or at a very low price (an 'equity kicker') in the event the borrower undergoes an IPO. As a result of this feature, the interest on the subordinated loan is lower than it would otherwise be.

前，公允价值变动直接在权益中确认），则该转股权（嵌入式衍生工具）应被分拆。对于持有人而言，其会计处理和发行人有显著区别，有关发行人的相关内容在第七章中进行阐述，持有人的会计处理如下所示：

- 首先应计算嵌入式衍生工具（从发行人的角度看，即转股权）的公允价值，公允价值由时间价值和内在价值（若有）组成。即使在初始确认时该期权为价外期权，其仍有价值。

  初始确认后，除非该期权属于现金流量套期关系的一部分，应在各资产负债表日持续对该嵌入式衍生工具以公允价值重新计量，其公允价值变动计入损益。

- 工具的整体公允价值（取得该混合工具支付的对价）扣除嵌入式衍生工具单独确定的金额后的余额，分配至主合同（从发行人角度看，即负债成分）的账面价值。

如果可转换债券以公允价值计量且其变动计入损益，则不允许根据上述说明将嵌入式衍生工具从主债券中分离出来。[IAS 39 IG 第 C3 段]。

5.60　实务中经常遇到的另一种嵌入式衍生工具与风险投资主体提供资金的一种方式有关，如下例所示。

示例——准权益条件

一家风险投资主体提供了一笔次级贷款，这笔贷款的条款除了利息和偿还本金以外，还包括当借款人进行首次公开发行股票（IPO）时，授权该风险投资公司免费或以极低价（“准权益条件”）获得借款人股票的权利。由于这个特征，该次级贷款的利息低于本应有的水平。

The 'equity kicker' meets the definition of a derivative even though the right to receive shares is contingent upon the future listing of the borrower. IAS 39 paragraph AG 9 states that a derivative could require a payment as a result of some future event that is unrelated to a notional amount. An 'equity kicker' feature is similar to such a derivative except that it does not give a right to a fixed payment, but an option right, if the future event occurs. Therefore, as the economic characteristics and risks of an equity return are not closely related to the economic characteristics and risks of a host debt instrument, the embedded derivative would be accounted for separately by the venture capital entity. [IAS 39 para IG C4].

Foreign currency features

5.61 An entity may issue debt in a currency other than its functional currency. Such a foreign currency loan is accounted for under IAS 21, 'The effects of changes in foreign exchange rates', which requires foreign currency gains and losses on monetary items to be recognised in profit or loss. As the foreign currency gains or losses are already recognised, a foreign currency derivative that may be embedded in such a host debt instrument is considered closely related and is not separated. This also applies to an embedded foreign currency derivative that provides a stream of principal or interest payments that are denominated in a foreign currency and embedded in a host debt instrument (for example, a dual currency bond). [IAS 39 para AG 33(c)].

Example – Dual currency bond

An entity with pound sterling as a functional currency issues a £10m debt instrument that provides for the annual payment of interest in euros and the repayment of principal in pound sterling.

This dual currency bond can be viewed as containing a foreign currency swap that converts the pound sterling interest payments to euro interest payments. As discussed above, this embedded swap is not accounted for separately as under IAS 21, any exchange gains and losses arising on the annual euro interest payments due to exchange rate changes are themselves reported in profit or loss. [IAS 21 para 28]. See also the example of the measurement of

该“准权益条件”符合衍生工具的定义，即使获得股票的权利取决于借款人日后是否上市。IAS 39 AG 第9段指出，衍生工具可要求因某些未来事项而导致支付与名义金额无关的款项。“准权益条件”的特征与这种衍生工具的特征类似，只是“准权益条件”并非给予得到固定款项的权利，而是一个如果未来事项发生才触发的期权。所以，由于权益回报的经济特征和风险不与主债务工具的经济特征和风险紧密相关，风险投资主体应分离该嵌入式衍生工具并单独进行会计处理。[IAS 39 IG 第 C4 段]。

外币特征

5.61　主体可能以不同于其功能货币的其他币种发行债务。这种外币贷款按照《国际会计准则第 21 号——汇率变动的影响》（“IAS 21”）的规定进行会计处理。IAS 21 规定货币性项目的汇兑损益应在损益中确认。由于汇兑损益已在损益中确认，所以可能嵌入到此类主债务工具中的外币衍生工具被认为紧密相关而不应分拆。这同样适用于嵌入到主债务工具中、提供以外币计价本金或利息流量的嵌入式外币衍生工具（比如双币种债券）。[IAS 39 AG 第 33（c）段]。

示例——双币种债券

一家以英镑作为功能货币的主体发行了 1,000 万英镑的债务工具，该工具以欧元支付年息，以英镑偿还本金。

这种双币种债券可以看作包含了一个把英镑利息付款转换为欧元利息付款的外币互换。如上所讨论的，该嵌入的互换不单独进行会计处理，因为根据 IAS 21 的规定，因外汇汇率变动所导致的年度欧元利息付款的任何汇兑损益，本身都已在损益中列报。[IAS 21 第 28 段]。同样参见第九章中关于双币种债券计量的示例。

a dual currency bond in chapter 9.

5. 62 Although many embedded foreign currency derivatives will not have to be separated from a foreign currency host debt instrument, some may. Consider the following examples:

Example 1 – Loan with foreign currency option

An entity issues a C10m loan at an above average market rate. The entity has the option to repay the loan at par for C10m or a fixed amount in a foreign currency, say €15m.

The debt instrument can be viewed as combining a loan at prevailing market interest rates and a foreign currency option. In effect, the issuer has purchased a foreign currency option that allows it to take advantage of changes in foreign currency exchange rates during the outstanding period of the loan. The premium for the option is paid as part of the higher interest cost. Similarly, the lender has written an option that exposes it to foreign currency risk. Because the borrower has the option of repaying the loan in its functional currency or in a foreign currency, the option is not closely related to the debt instrument (that is, it is not directly related to the currency of the loan or the interest rate that applies to that currency). The principle discussed in paragraph 5. 61 above does not apply since application of IAS 21 rules for revaluing of monetary items would not lead to revaluation of the foreign currency option. Accordingly, the embedded foreign currency option should be separated from the host contract and accounted for separately by both parties to the contract. In contrast, if both the principal and the interest payments were made in a foreign currency (that is, if no optionality was involved), there would be no embedded derivative.

Example 2 – Interest payments linked to foreign currency exchange rates

An entity issues a £10m debt security at par. Quarterly interest payments, which are payable in pound sterling, are computed based on a formula that is linked to the £/€ exchange rate.

In this example, the quarterly interest is not denominated in foreign currency

5.62 尽管许多嵌入式外币衍生工具不必从外币主债务工具中分离出来，但有些可能需要。考虑以下示例：

示例1——带外币期权的贷款

某主体发行了一笔1,000万元的高于平均市场利率的贷款。该主体可以选择以1,000万元的面值偿还贷款，或以固定金额的外币偿还，如1,500万欧元。

该债务工具可以看做是一个现行市场利率的贷款与外币期权的结合。实际上，发行人购买了一个在贷款未偿还期间可以利用外币汇率变动优势的外币期权。该期权的期权费是通过较高利息费用的一部分支付的。同理，出借人签发了一个使其面临外币风险的期权。因为借款人拥有以其功能货币或外币偿还贷款的选择权，所以该期权不与债务工具紧密相关（即与贷款币种或适用该币种的利率没有直接关系）。上文第5.61段讨论的原则不适用，因为应用IAS 21对货币性项目重估价的规则不会导致对外币期权的重估价。因此，合同双方均应将该嵌入的外币期权从主合同中分拆并单独进行会计处理。与此相反，如果本金和利息都以外币支付（即，如果不涉及选择），则不会有嵌入式衍生工具。

示例2——与外币汇率挂钩的利息支付

主体按面值发行了一笔1,000万英镑的债券。每季度以英镑支付利息，利息基于一个与英镑/欧元汇率挂钩的公式计算。

在该示例中，季度利息不以外币计价，因此，上文第5.61段所论述的原

and, therefore, the principle discussed in paragraph 5.61 above does not apply. Since the formula for computing the interest payable on a sterling bond is linked to the £/€ exchange rate and not based on an interest rate or an index based on interest rates, an inflation index or the creditworthiness of the debtor, it is an embedded derivative that is not closely related to the sterling bond. Hence, it should be accounted for separately. The embedded derivative is a forward foreign exchange contract.

Embedded derivatives in equity host contracts

5.63 For embedded derivatives in an equity host contract, an analysis should first be performed to determine whether the host contract is an equity host. In carrying out this analysis, it is necessary to determine whether the host contract has any stated or pre-determined maturity and, if not, whether the residual interest represents a residual interest in the entity's net assets (see chapter 7). Generally, when a host contract encompasses a residual interest that involves the rights of ownership, it is an equity host. The value of an equity instrument is a function of the underlying equity price or index. Therefore, an embedded derivative would need to possess equity characteristics related to the same entity to be regarded as closely related. [IAS 39 para AG 27].

Calls and puts

5.64 A call option embedded in an equity instrument that enables the issuer to re-acquire that equity instrument at a specified price is not closely related to the host equity instrument from the holder's perspective. From the issuer's perspective, on the other hand, the call option is an equity instrument provided it meets the conditions for that classification under IAS 32, in which case it is excluded from IAS 39's scope. [IAS 39 para AG 30(b)].

5.65 A put option that requires the issuer to re-acquire an equity instrument at a specified price is similarly not closely related to the host equity instrument from the holder's perspective. From the issuer's perspective, the put option is a written option that gives the counterparty the right to sell the issuer's own equity instrument

则不适用。由于计算应以英镑支付的利息的公式是与英镑/欧元汇率挂钩的，而不是以利率、基于利率的指数、通货膨胀指数或债务人信用水平为基础，所以这是一个不与英镑债券紧密相关的嵌入式衍生工具。因此，应单独进行会计处理。该嵌入式衍生工具是一项远期外汇合同。

权益主合同中的嵌入式衍生工具

5.63　对于权益主合同中的嵌入式衍生工具，首先应进行分析，以确定主合同是否为权益主合同。在进行此项分析时，需要确定主合同是否有任何约定的或事先确定的到期日，若没有，则再确定剩余权益是否代表了主体净资产的剩余权益（参见第七章）。通常，当主合同包含了涉及所有权权利的剩余权益时，即为权益主合同。权益工具的价值是标的权益价格或指数的函数。因此，嵌入式衍生工具若要被视为与主合同紧密相关，需要拥有与同一主体有关的权益特征。[IAS 39 AG 第 27 段]。

看涨期权和看跌期权

5.64　嵌入到权益工具中、使发行人能以特定价格回购该权益工具的看涨期权，从持有人角度看，不与主权益工具紧密相关。另一方面，从发行人角度看，如果该看涨期权符合国际会计准则第 32 号（“IAS 32”）的分类条件，则该看涨期权是权益工具。在这种情况下，其不在 IAS 39 的范围内。[IAS 39 AG 第 30（b）段]。

5.65　同样，从持有人角度看，要求发行人以特定价格回购权益工具的看跌期权也不与主权益工具紧密相关。从发行人角度看，该看跌期权是一项签出期权，其赋予交易对方将发行人自身权益工具以固定价格向其出售的权利。依据 IAS 32 第 23 段的规定，发行人应确认一项与赎回金额现值（即期权行权

to the entity for a fixed price. Under paragraph 23 of IAS 32, the issuer recognises a financial liability equal to the present value of the redemption amount (that is, the present value of the option's exercise price). See further chapter 7.

5.66 In the case of a puttable instrument that can be put back at any time for cash equal to a proportionate share of the entity's net asset value (such as units of an open-ended mutual fund or some unit-linked investment products), the effect of separating an embedded derivative and accounting for each component is to measure the combined instrument at the redemption amount that is payable at the balance sheet date if the holder exercised its right to put the instrument back to the issuer. [IAS 39 para AG 32]. This will apply to both the issuer and the investor in such an instrument, but for the issuer it is only relevant if the instrument is classified as a debt instrument in accordance with an amendment to IAS 32 and IAS 1, 'Puttable financial instruments and obligations arising on liquidation'.

5.67 The treatment of call and put options embedded in preference shares require careful consideration. This is because the terms of the preference share must be analysed first to determine whether the preference shares are more akin to an equity instrument or a debt instrument. Consider the following examples:

Example 1 – Puttable preference shares

An entity issues C50m mandatorily redeemable preference shares at par with a fixed dividend of 8% per annum. The preference shares are puttable to the company for cash at par if market interest rate exceeds 12%.

The mandatorily redeemable preference shares (including fixed dividend) are a financial liability of the issuer and akin to a debt instrument. Furthermore, the embedded put option's exercise price, which is par, is approximately equal to the preference's shares amortised cost. Hence, the put option is considered closely related to the debt host.

Example 2 – Convertible preference shares

An entity issues C50m of irredeemable preference shares that give the holders a preferential right to return of capital in a winding up, but which are also convertible into a fixed number of ordinary shares at the holder's option. Any

价的现值）相等的金融负债。参见第七章。

5.66　对于在任何时候能够以等价于主体净资产价值相应比例份额的现金回售的可回售工具而言（如开放式共同基金单位或部分投资连结型产品），分拆嵌入式衍生工具并对各组成部分进行会计处理的效果是假定持有人已行使其将工具回售给发行人的权利，从而以资产负债表日应付的赎回金额计量该组合工具。[IAS 39 AG 第 32 段]。这对该工具的发行人和投资人均适用。但是，对发行人而言，仅当该工具根据《对 IAS 32 和 IAS 1 的修订——可回售金融工具和清算产生的义务》被归类为债务工具时才适用。

5.67　在处理嵌入到优先股中的看涨和看跌期权时，需要仔细考虑。这是因为首先必须先分析优先股的条款，以确定该优先股更类似于权益工具还是债务工具。考虑以下示例：

示例 1——可回售优先股

某主体以面值发行 5,000 万元、每年 8% 固定股利的强制性可赎回优先股。如果市场利率超过 12%，则该优先股以等值于面值的现金回售给公司。

该强制性可赎回优先股（包括固定股利）是发行人的金融负债，属于债务工具。此外，嵌入看跌期权的行权价（即票面价值）大致等于该优先股的摊余成本。因此，该看跌期权被认为与债务主合同紧密相关。

示例 2——可转换优先股

某主体发行 5,000 万元的不可赎回优先股，持有人具有在清算时优先回收资本权利，但是持有人也可选择将上述优先股转换成固定数量的普通股。当年支付的所有股利均由发行人决定。

dividends paid in the year are at the discretion of the issuer.

As the preference shares are irredeemable and there is no obligation on the issuer to pay dividends, the shares are equity in nature. The conversion feature represents an embedded written call option on the company's ordinary shares, which on a free-standing basis would be an equity instrument of the entity. As both the embedded call option and the host are equity instruments, the entity does not account for the embedded option separately. Similarly, the investor would not have to account for the embedded option separately.

Embedded derivatives in lease host contracts

5.68 Embedded derivatives may be present in lease host contracts, whether the lease is an operating or a finance lease. The approach for determining whether an embedded derivative is closely related to a lease host is similar to the approach that is used for a debt host.

Inflation indexed rentals

5.69 An embedded derivative in a host lease contract is closely related to the host contract if the embedded derivative is an inflation-related index such as an index of lease payments to a consumer price index provided:

- the lease is not leveraged; and
- the index relates to inflation in the entity's own economic environment.

[IAS 39 para AG 33(f)].

5.70 The first bullet point makes it clear that an embedded inflation adjustment in the lease contract would not be closely related if it is considered to be leveraged. In determining whether inflation features embedded in lease contracts are leveraged, the guidance stated in paragraph 5.14 – 5.15 above should be followed. Generally, lease contracts often stipulate that payments will increase in line with inflation, in which case, the indexed linked lease payments would not be considered leveraged. Where this is not the case, an inflationary adjustment of greater than one would be considered sufficiently leveraged for the inflation feature

由于该优先股不可赎回且发行人无义务支付股利，因此该优先股本质上为权益。该转换特征代表针对公司普通股的嵌入签出看涨期权，若独立核算会作为主体的权益工具。由于该嵌入看涨期权和主合同均为权益工具，因此主体不应对该嵌入期权单独进行会计处理。同样，投资人也不会对该嵌入期权单独进行会计处理。

租赁主合同中的嵌入式衍生工具

5.68 嵌入式衍生工具可能出现在租赁主合同中，无论是经营租赁还是融资租赁。确定嵌入式衍生工具是否与租赁主合同紧密相关的方法和对于债务主合同所采用的方法类似。

与通胀挂钩的租金

5.69 如果租赁主合同中的嵌入式衍生工具是与通胀挂钩的指数，比如与消费价格指数挂钩的租赁付款额指数等，则该嵌入式衍生工具与主合同紧密相关，但前提是：

- 该租赁不具杠杆作用；且
- 该指数与主体自身经济环境中的通胀有关。

[IAS 39 AG 第 33（f）段]。

5.70 第一点表明，如果租赁合同中嵌入通胀调整被视为具有杠杆作用，则其并不紧密相关。在确定嵌入租赁合同的通胀特征是否具有杠杆作用时，应遵从上述第5.14 至5.15 段中的指引。一般来说，租赁合同往往会规定付款会随着通胀同步增加，在此情况下，该指数挂钩的租赁付款不会被视为具有杠杆作用。若非如此，大于 1 的通胀调整被认为是具有足够的杠杆作用而要单独进行会计处理。这是因为在实务中，当其他因素相同时，市场会预期商品和服务的价格是随通胀同步变化的。因此，租赁合同中的任何通胀调整，只要使指数化现金流量的增速大于正常的通胀率，则被视为具有杠杆作用。

to be accounted for separately. This is because, in practice, the market would expect the prices of goods and services to move in line with inflation, all other factors being equal. Therefore, any inflationary adjustments in a lease contract that increase the indexed cash flows by more than the normal rate of inflation are considered to be leveraged.

5.71 The second bullet point in paragraph 5.69 states that the index should relate to inflation in the entity's own economic environment. IAS 39 is silent as to whether this means the lessee's or the lessor's economic environment. It is reasonable to assume, however, that the economic environment that is most relevant to the lease contract is the one in which the leased asset is located, as the inflation index of that economic environment is the one that directly affects the lease rentals and, hence, the leased property's value. Consequently, the economic environment in which the lessee or the lessor operates is not relevant to the analysis.

Example 1 – Inflation linked rentals

A UK entity is the tenant in a 10 year lease of a property in the UK with rental payments in pound sterling that are contractually determined for the first year, but thereafter increase at a rate of one time the change in UK RPI (Retail Price Index).

The future cash flows (the rental payments) will change in response to changes in the inflation index of UK. The embedded inflation indexed payments are not leveraged and relate to the economic environment in which the leased asset is located. Therefore, the inflation adjustment is closely related to the lease contract and separation is not required.

Note: this is a lease payable in a currency that is the functional currency of the UK lessee. Foreign currency features in lease contracts are discussed further from paragraphs 5.78 below.

Example 2 – Inflation linked rentals (leveraged)

A UK entity is the tenant in a 10 year lease of a property in the UK with rental payments in pound sterling that are contractually determined for the first year,

5.71 第 5.69 段第二点指出，指数应与主体自身经济环境中的通胀有关。主体自身经济环境是否指承租人或出租人的经济环境，IAS 39 中无相关规定。但是可以合理地假设，与租赁合同最相关的经济环境是租赁资产所处的经济环境，因为该经济环境的通胀指数是直接影响租金进而影响租赁财产价值的。因此，承租人或出租人经营所处的经济环境与分析无关。

示例 1——与通胀挂钩的租金

某英国主体承租了位于英国的某房产，租期为 10 年。以英镑支付的租金第 1 年由合同确定，以后以英国零售价格指数变动率 1 倍的比率增加。

未来现金流量（租金）将随英国通胀指数的变化而变化。该嵌入的与通胀指数挂钩的支付不具有杠杆作用，且与租赁资产所处的经济环境有关。因此，该通胀调整被认为与租赁合同紧密相关，无需分拆。

注：该应付租金的币种是英国承租人的功能货币。在下文第 5.78 段中会进一步讨论租赁合同中的外币特征。

示例 2——与通胀挂钩的租金（具有杠杆作用）

某英国主体承租了位于英国的某房产，租期为 10 年。以英镑支付的租金第 1 年由合同确定，以后以英国零售价格指数变动率 1.5 倍的比率增加。

but thereafter increasing at a rate of one and a half times the change in UK RPI (Retail Price Index).

The future cash flows (the rental payments) will change in response to changes in the UK RPI. Since the cash flows change by an amount in excess of the change in RPI, such cash flows are considered to be leveraged as discussed in paragraph 5.70 above. Therefore, the embedded inflation indexed payments would be accounted for separately.

A question arises as to whether the embedded derivative should be measured by reference to half times UK RPI or one and a half times UK RPI.

Some would favour the former treatment on the grounds that as the leverage portion of the embedded derivative is the amount over and above the change in the UK inflation index, this portion (half times RPI) should be accounted for separately as a derivative. On this basis, the host contract would contain the non-leveraged portion (one times RPI) that is considered to be closely related.

However, we consider that splitting the change in the fair value of an indexed linked derivative between a leveraged amount and a non-leveraged amount is not appropriate for the following reasons:

- A derivative has a single value and splitting a portion out in the above manner is not permitted under IAS 39.
- The leveraged and non-leveraged portions relate to the same risk and, since the inflation is leveraged overall, the entire link to RPI is no longer considered closely related.
- The separation creates cash flow patterns that are not evident in the lease contract because, in practice, the actual cash flows would consist of the minimum rentals plus amounts relating to the entire change in the inflation adjustment.

Therefore, the leveraged portion of the embedded derivative should be based on the total change in the UK inflation index, that is, one and a half times RPI, whilst the host would consist of a non-inflation linked lease rental

未来现金流量（租金）将随英国零售物价指数的变化而变化。由于现金流量的变化超过了零售价格指数的变化，此等现金流量被认为具有上述第5.70段所述的杠杆作用。因此，该嵌入的与通胀指数挂钩的支付将单独进行会计处理。·

问题是该嵌入式衍生工具应参照英国零售价格指数的0.5倍还是1.5倍来计量。

有人会倾向于前者的处理方法，因为该嵌入式衍生工具中的杠杆部分为超过英国通胀指数变化部分的金额，因此该部分（零售价格指数的0.5倍）应作为衍生工具单独进行会计处理。在此基础上，主合同将包含被认为紧密相关的不具杠杆作用的部分（零售价格指数的1倍）。

但是，我们认为将与指数挂钩的衍生工具公允价值变动拆分为具有杠杆作用的金额和不具杠杆作用的金额是不适当的，原因如下：

- 衍生工具具有单一价值，用上述方法对其进行拆分在IAS 39下是不允许的。
- 具有杠杆作用的部分和不具杠杆作用的部分与同一风险有关，由于总体而言，通胀具有杠杆作用，因此与零售价格指数挂钩的整体不再被认为紧密相关。
- 分拆会创造租赁合同中并不存在的现金流量形式，因为在实务中，实际现金流量是由最低租金加上与通胀调整整体变动相关的金额所构成的。

因此，该嵌入式衍生工具中具有杠杆作用的部分应基于英国通胀指数的总体变动（也就是零售价格指数的1.5倍），而主合同由不与通胀挂钩的租赁合同构成。

contract.

Example 3 – Inflation linked rentals not related to the entity's economic environment

Facts are the same as in example 1 except that the inflation adjustment relates to a specified US annual inflation rate (for example, Retail Price Index, Consumer Price Index etc). The landlord is a US entity.

The future cash flows (the rental payments) will change in response to changes in the US inflation index. The embedded inflation indexed payments, although not leveraged, relate to a different economic environment to that in which the leased asset is located and the UK entity operates. Therefore, the inflation indexed payment is not closely related to the lease host contract and would be accounted for separately.

Example 4 – Upward only inflation-linked rentals

Entity A is a tenant in a 10 year UK property lease agreement. The rent for the first year is contractually determined at C100, 000. The rental payments will change in line with an index of UK prices so if, at the end of year 1, the index had increased by 3%, the rent for year 2 would be C103, 000. However, the lease provides that the rent may not be decreased. So if, during year 2, the index fell by 1%, the rent for year 3 would remain at C103, 000. The index shows that UK prices are generally increasing at the inception of the lease (that is, there is UK inflation).

The rental payments are linked to an index. They follow that index while it is increasing, but do not follow it if it decreases. This feature is often known as 'upward only'. However, this lease contains a floor in the rental payments because of the upward-only feature, so it is necessary to identify whether the floor is in or out-of-the-money at the inception of the lease. Because the upward-only feature of the rent reviews means that the rentals can never fall below the floor, the floor is always out-of-the-money (not influencing the cash flows) both at inception (even where the relevant index is negative at the date of signing) and subsequently. Therefore, its presence does not alter the expected cash flows and so the derivative is closely related.

示例3——与主体经济环境无关的、与通胀挂钩的租金

本例中，除了通胀调整与特定的美国年度通胀率（如零售价格指数、消费者价格指数等）相关之外，其他情况与示例1相同。出租方是一家美国主体。

未来现金流量（租金）将随美国通胀指数的变化而变化。该嵌入的与通胀挂钩的支付虽然不具有杠杆作用，但与租赁资产和英国主体经营所处的不同经济环境有关。因此，与通胀挂钩的支付不与租赁主合同紧密相关，将单独进行会计处理。

示例4——仅与通胀上升挂钩的"只涨"租金

主体A是某租期为10年的英国房产租赁协议的承租人。合同确定的第一年租金为100,000元。租金将随英国物价指数的变化而变化。这样，如果指数在第1年年末增加了3%，则第2年的租金将是103,000元。但是，租赁合同规定租金不能降低。因此，如果指数在第2年降低了1%，那么第3年的租金仍然是103,000元。指数显示，英国物价在租约开始时总的来说呈上涨趋势（即英国发生通胀）。

该租金与指数挂钩。指数增加时，租金跟着上涨，但指数下降时，租金不动。该特征通常称为"只涨"特征。但是，由于具有"只涨"特征，该租赁合同包含一个租金下限，因此需要辨别该下限在租约开始时是价内还是价外。由于租金的只涨特征意味着租金绝不可能下降至低于下限，因此无论是在租约开始时（即使签署协议之日的相关指数为负）还是以后期间，该下限总是价外的（不影响现金流量）。所以，其存在不会改变预期现金流量，故该衍生工具是紧密相关的。

Contingent rentals based on related sales

5.72 Lease contracts may include contingent rentals that are based on certain related sales of the lessee. Such a contingent rental-related embedded derivative is considered to be closely related to the lease host contract and would not be accounted for separately. [IAS 39 para AG 33(f)].

Example – Lease rentals related to sales

A UK entity leases a property located in the UK. The rentals consist of a base rental of C10,000 plus 5% of the lessee's sales each month.

The rental payments will vary, depending on an underlying, being the entity's sales.

However, as stated above, the portion of the contingent rentals based on related sales is considered to be closely related to the host lease contract. Therefore, the sales related payments should not be separated.

Contingent rentals based on a variable interest rate

5.73 Where lease contracts include contingent rentals that are based on variable interest rates, the contingent rental-related embedded derivative is considered to be closely related to the lease host contract and would not be accounted for separately. [IAS 39 para AG 33 (f)]. This is because a lease contract is akin to a debt instrument and, therefore, the obligation to make future payments for the use of the asset and the adjustment of those payments to reflect changes in a variable interest rate index such as the LIBOR are considered to be closely related.

Example – Lease rentals indexed to LIBOR

A UK entity leases a property located in the UK. The lease rentals are indexed to the UK LIBOR rate. The contract does not contain any leverage feature.

The embedded derivative does not need to be separated as the rentals are based on a variable interest rate index of the UK economy.

On the other hand, if the rentals were indexed to a variable interest rate of an

基于相关销售额的或有租金

5.72　租赁合同可能包含基于承租人相关销售额的或有租金。该或有租金相关的嵌入式衍生工具被认为与租赁主合同紧密相关，不再单独进行会计处理。[IAS 39 AG 第 33（f）段]。

示例——与销售额挂钩的租赁租金

某英国主体承租了位于英国的某房产。租金由基本租金 10,000 元和承租人每月销售额的 5% 组成。

租金将随着该主体的销售额这一标的变化而变化。

然而，如上文所述，基于相关销售额的或有租金部分被认为与主租赁合同紧密相关。因此，该与销售额有关的付款不应分拆。

基于浮动利率的或有租金

5.73　租赁合同包含了基于浮动利率的或有租金时，该或有租金相关的嵌入式衍生工具被认为与租赁主合同紧密相关，不再单独进行会计处理。[IAS 39 AG 第 33（f）段]。这是因为租赁合同类似于债务工具，因此，为使用资产而在未来支付租金的义务与旨在反映浮动利率指数（如 LIBOR）的变动所做的租金调整被认为是紧密相关的。

示例——与 LIBOR 挂钩的租金

某英国主体承租了位于英国的某房产。租金与英国的 LIBOR 挂钩。该合同不包含任何杠杆特征。

由于租金是基于英国经济下的浮动利率指数，因此无需分拆该嵌入式衍生工具。

然而，如果租金与租赁资产所处经济环境不同的经济环境下的浮动利率

economic environment that is different from the economic environment in which the leased asset is located, the related embedded derivative would not be regarded as closely related in the same way that a similarly indexed inflation payment would not be regarded as closely related (see para 5.63 above).

Purchase options in lease agreements

5.74 Often lease contracts include an option that allows the lessee to purchase the asset at the end of the lease term. Such a purchase option would not qualify as an embedded derivative for a number of reasons. First, the purchase option is based on a non-financial variable (the underlying price of the leased asset) that is specific to a party to the contract and, hence, currently fails the definition of a derivative. [IAS 39 para AG12A]. Secondly, in order to exercise the option, the lessee must pay the purchase price in cash and the lessor must physically deliver the leased asset (a non-financial asset). This constitutes gross settlement and, therefore, the option is not a financial instrument. However, if the terms in the contract allow either party to settle net in cash (considered unlikely) or the leased asset is readily convertible into cash (because an active trading market exists for the asset in question and, therefore, it is not specific to a party to the contract), the purchase option could qualify as a derivative (see chapter 3). [IAS 39 para 6].

Term extension or renewal options

5.75 A finance lease is viewed as being equivalent to debt for accounting and disclosure purposes. However, the right to extend the lease term is different from the right to extend the term of a debt instrument. The right to extend the lease is not a right to borrow funds for a further period as would be the case with a debt instrument; rather, the right to extend the lease is a right to use a non-financial asset for an additional period. Furthermore, under IAS 17 the extension term would either be included in the calculation of the minimum lease term if it is reasonably certain that, at the inception of the lease, the lessee will exercise the option; or the renewal would constitute a new lease because the leased asset and the corresponding liability (if either exists) would have been amortised to nil by the end of the original lease term. In either case, the renewal or the extension

挂钩，则相关嵌入式衍生工具不被视为紧密相关，这与和不同经济环境的通胀指数挂钩的支付的处理方式一样，嵌入衍生工具不会被视为紧密相关（参见上述第5.63段）。

租赁协议中的购买选择权

5.74　租赁合同经常会包含允许承租人在租赁期结束时购买该资产的选择权。由于很多原因，该购买选择权不属于嵌入式衍生工具。首先，购买选择权是基于合同一方特定的非金融变量（租赁资产的标的价格），因而通常不符合衍生工具的定义。[IAS 39 AG 第12A段]。其次，要行使该选择权，承租人必须以现金支付购买价格，且出租人必须实物交付租赁资产（非金融资产）。这构成总额结算，因此该选择权不是金融工具。但是，如果合同条款允许任何一方以现金净额结算（不太常见）或租赁资产容易转换成现金（由于相关资产有活跃的交易市场，因此这并非与合同一方特定相关），则该购买选择权可属于衍生工具（参见第三章）。[IAS 39 第6段]。

展期权或续约权

5.75　融资租赁在会计处理和披露上被视为相当于债务。但是，延长租赁期限的权利不同于延长债务工具期限的权利。延长租赁期限的权利不像债务工具那样是一种延长借款期限的权利。更确切地说，延长租赁期限的权利一种在额外期间内使用非金融资产的权利。此外，根据IAS 17的规定，如果在租约开始时可合理确定承租人将会行使该选择权，则该延长期限会纳入最短租赁期的计算；或者该续约会成为一项新的租赁，因为租赁资产和相应的负债在原租赁期结束时会摊销至零（只要有其一）。在上述的任一情况下，续约或展期权都不会符合衍生工具定义，因为其未包含净额结算条款。

option would not meet the definition of a derivative, as it does not contain a net settlement provision.

Residual value guarantee in lease agreements

5.76 Where a lease includes a residual value guarantee, the lessee undertakes to make a payment if the residual value of the asset at the end of the lease falls below a pre-determined amount. A residual value guarantee does not meet the definition of a derivative because it has an underlying (price of the leased asset) that is specific to a party to the contract. Furthermore, under IAS 17, the gross value amount of any residual value guarantee is treated as part of the minimum lease payments and is accounted for as such. Therefore, it does not need to be accounted for under IAS 39.

Termination clause in lease agreements

5.77 Lease agreements are generally irrevocable, that is, the lessee is obliged to lease the asset during the non-cancellable period of the lease. However, the lease may contain an early termination clause that allows the lessee to terminate the contract, but only on the payment of a penalty. This penalty payment (sometimes referred to as the 'stipulated loss value') ensures that the lessor will be able to recover its remaining investment in the lease. This situation is similar in substance to a pre-payment option in a debt instrument, which is considered closely related in circumstances where the option's exercise price is approximately equal to the amortised cost of the debt instrument. See example 2 in paragraph 5.48 above. In that example, where the penalty payment clause had a 'market adjusted value' exercise price it had a fair value of zero, until the option was actually exercised.

Lease payments in foreign currencies

5.78 Finance lease contracts that give rise to financial assets in lessors and financial liabilities in lessees are financial instruments. Therefore, as a finance lease denominated in a foreign currency is similar in nature to a foreign currency loan, no separation of the embedded foreign currency derivative is required,

租赁协议中的余值担保

5.76　租赁合同包含余值担保的，在租赁结束时，若资产的余值降至低于事先确定的金额，则承租人有义务支付一定款项。余值担保不符合衍生工具的定义，因为其有一个与合同一方特定相关的标的（租赁资产的价格）。此外，根据 IAS 17 的规定，余值担保的总额作为最低租赁付款额的一部分进行会计处理。因此，不需要根据 IAS 39 的规定进行会计处理。

租赁协议中的终止条款

5.77　租赁协议通常是不可撤销的，也就是说，承租人在不可撤销的租赁期间有义务承租相关资产。但是，租赁可能包含提前终止条款，允许承租人终止合同，但前提是必须支付违约金。该违约金款项（有时称之为“约定损失价值”）确保出租人能收回其在租赁中的剩余投资。该情形在本质上与债务工具中的提前还款权类似，在行权价大致等于债务工具的摊余成本时，被认为紧密相关。参见上述第 5.48 段的示例 2。该示例中，在违约金条款包含经市场价值调整的行权价的情况下，其公允价值直到实际行权时，均为零。

外币租赁款

5.78　形成出租人金融资产和承租人金融负债的融资租赁合同是金融工具。因此，由于以外币计价的融资租赁在本质上与外币贷款类似，无需将嵌入的外币衍生工具分离，因为外币应收租赁款和应付款都是按 IAS 21 进行会计处理的货币性项目。适用于外币贷款的指引同样适用于外币融资租赁（参见第

because the foreign currency lease receivable and payable are monetary items that are accounted for in accordance with IAS 21. The guidance that applies to foreign currency loans is also applicable to foreign currency finance leases (see para 5.61), that is, the embedded derivative is not separated.

5.79 On the other hand, an operating lease is not regarded as a financial instrument. Therefore, an operating lease agreement that provides for payments in foreign currency may contain foreign currency embedded derivatives that may require separation. Paragraph AG33(d) of IAS 39 contains provisions that deal with embedded foreign currency derivatives in a host contract that is not a financial instrument. These are considered in paragraph 5.91 below. That guidance has been applied to the examples given below.

Example 1 – Operating lease rentals denominated in foreign currency

A UK company enters into an operating lease for a property in francs with a European lessor that is denominated in euros. The functional currency of the lessee and the lessor are the pound sterling and the euro respectively.

Paragraph AG33(d) of IAS 39 provides that contracts, other than financial instruments, that specify payments denominated in the functional currency of any substantial party to the contract are closely related to the host contract.

In this example, the lease payments are denominated in the functional currency of the lessor – a substantial party to the contract. Therefore, the embedded derivative is closely related to the host contract and not separated. It is not appropriate to argue that because the payments are in a foreign currency and the UK lessee is exposed to currency risk there is an embedded foreign currency forward converting sterling payments to euros.

On the other hand, if the lease payments are denominated in a currency that is unrelated to either party's functional currency (for example, US dollars), the embedded foreign currency forward should be separated from the host contract and accounted for as a derivative. This applies to both parties to the contract.

Example 2 – Operating lease rentals denominated in foreign currency

On 1 June 20X2 entity A, a Russian oil refinery, entered into an arrangement

5.61 段），即不分拆该嵌入式衍生工具。

5.79 然而，经营租赁不被视为金融工具。因此，以外币支付的经营租赁协议可能包含可要求分拆的嵌入式外币衍生工具。IAS 39 AG 第 33（d）段包含了非金融工具主合同中嵌入的外币衍生工具的处理规定。相关内容在下文第 5.91 段进行讨论。该指引已应用于以下示例。

示例 1——以外币计价的经营租赁租金

某英国公司与某欧洲出租人签署了位于法国的相关房产的经营租赁协议，以欧元计价。承租人和出租人的功能货币分别为英镑和欧元。

IAS 39 AG 第 33（d）段规定，除金融工具之外的合同，如果规定付款以合同任一实质方的功能货币计价，则其与主合同紧密相关。

该示例中，租赁款以合同的某一实质方，即出租人的功能货币计价。因此，该嵌入式衍生工具与主合同紧密相关，不应分拆。如果认为因该款项是以外币计价的，英国承租人面临外币风险，所以存在将英镑转换为欧元的嵌入远期外汇工具，这是不妥的。

然而，如果租赁款是以与各方的功能货币均无关的货币计价的（如美元），则该嵌入远期外汇工具应从主合同中分离，并作为衍生工具进行会计处理。对合同双方均如此适用。

示例 2——以外币计价的经营租赁租金

20X2 年 6 月 1 日，主体 A——一家俄罗斯炼油厂，与主体 S 签署了承租

with entity S to lease a building in Moscow for a 10-year period. The lease is classified as an operating lease. Entity A's management has determined its functional currency to be the US dollar.

Entity S is a property management and development entity located in Russia. Its management has determined its functional currency to be the Russian Rouble.

Entity S set the monthly lease repayments in Swiss francs to avoid exposure to any devaluation in the Russian Rouble and to obtain a natural hedge for the repayment of its Swiss franc denominated bonds.

As the Swiss franc is neither the functional currency of one of the substantial parties to the lease contract, nor a currency commonly used in Russia, nor the currency in which leases are routinely denominated in the world, the lease contract contains an embedded derivative that is not closely related to the host contract.

From entity S's perspective, the lease contract contains a series of embedded forward contracts to buy Swiss francs against Russian roubles. These embedded derivatives are not closely related to the host contract (lease contract denominated in Russian Rouble) and, therefore, should be accounted for separately. Entity S may however be able to use the separated forward contracts in a formal hedge of the cashflows on its Swiss franc bonds – see chapter 10 on hedging for more details of when this could be permissible.

From entity A's perspective, the lease contract contains a series of embedded forward contracts to sell Swiss francs against US dollars. These embedded derivatives are not closely related to the host contract (lease contract denominated in USD) and, therefore, should be accounted for separately.

Example 3 – Subsidiary's foreign currency lease payments guaranteed by parent

A major French operating subsidiary of a US parent enters into a lease with a Swiss company that requires lease payments in US dollars. The lease payments are guaranteed by the US parent. The functional currencies of the

位于莫斯科的某建筑的租约，租期为 10 年。该租赁被归类为经营租赁。主体 A 的管理层已确定其功能货币为美元。

主体 S 是一家位于俄罗斯的物业管理和开发公司。其管理层确定其功能货币为俄罗斯卢布。

主体 S 规定每月的租金以瑞士法郎支付，以避免俄罗斯卢布的任何贬值风险并自然对冲其以瑞士法郎计价的债券还款。

由于瑞士法郎既不是租赁合同任何实质方的功能货币，也不是俄罗斯普遍使用的货币，也不是世界上通常使用的租赁计价货币，因此，该租赁合同包含一个不与主合同紧密相关的嵌入式衍生工具。

从主体 S 的角度看，该租赁合同包含了一系列以俄罗斯卢布买入瑞士法郎的嵌入远期合同。这些嵌入式衍生工具不与主合同（以俄罗斯卢布计价的租赁合同）紧密相关，因此应单独进行会计处理。不过，主体 S 能在条件允许的情况下，使用该单独的远期合同进行瑞士法郎债券现金流的正式套期——有关可以使用套期的详情参见第十章。

从主体 A 的角度看，租赁合同包含了一系列卖出瑞士法郎获得美元的嵌入远期合同。这些嵌入式衍生工具不与主合同（以美元计价的租赁合同）紧密相关，因此，应单独进行会计处理。

示例 3——母公司担保的子公司外币租赁款

某美国母公司的一家主要的法国运营子公司与一瑞士公司签署租赁协议，规定租赁款以美元支付。该租赁款由美国母公司担保。各主体的功能货币为各自的本国货币。

respective entities are their local currencies.

In this example, the substantial parties to the lease contract are the French lessee and the Swiss lessor. The guarantor is not a substantial party to the contract and, therefore, its functional currency is of no relevance to the analysis (see further para 5.92 below). Since the lease payments are made in US dollars, which is neither the functional currency of the lessee nor the lessor, the embedded foreign currency swap would need to be accounted for separately.

Embedded derivatives in executory contracts

5.80 Contracts to buy or sell a non-financial asset that qualify as executory contracts, including commitments (for example, take or pay contracts) that are entered into to meet the entity's expected purchase, sale or usage requirements and are expected to be settled by physical delivery, are not financial instruments. Accordingly, they are scoped out of IAS 39 under the own use purchase or sale exception. [IAS 39 para 5]. However, even though such contracts are not financial instruments, they may contain embedded derivatives. Embedded derivatives may also be present in some service contracts.

5.81 IAS 39 contains little specific guidance relating to derivatives embedded in such contracts, except for features involving foreign currency. Therefore, it is necessary to consider carefully the economic characteristics and risks of such contracts in assessing whether embedded derivatives are present and, if so, whether they should be separately accounted for. Both quantitative and qualitative factors should be considered. Sometimes it may be possible to draw on the guidance discussed above for other host contracts. Indeed, it would not be unreasonable to do so, particularly for features such as pricing adjustments, inflation adjustments and caps, floors and collars on prices and quantities.

Price adjustment features

5.82 Normal purchase and sale contracts may contain price clauses that modify the contract's cash flows. In assessing the closely related criterion for the embedded

该示例中，租赁合同的实质方为法国承租人和瑞士出租人。担保人并非合同的实质方，因此，其功能货币与相关分析无关（参见下文第 5.92 段）。由于租赁款以美元支付，而美元既不是承租人的功能货币也不是出租人的功能货币，因此，该嵌入的外币互换需要单独进行会计处理。

待执行合同中的嵌入式衍生工具

5.80　购买或出售非金融资产的合同，属于待执行合同的，包括诸如签署目的在于满足主体预期的购买、销售或使用要求，且预计以实物交付方式结算的承诺等，此等待执行合同不属于金融工具。相应地，根据“自用购买或销售例外规则”，此等待执行合同也不在 IAS 39 的范围内。[IAS 39 第 5 段]。但是，尽管此等合同不是金融工具，但其可能包含嵌入式衍生工具。嵌入式衍生工具也可能存在于一些服务合同中。

5.81　除了涉及外币的特征外，IAS 39 几乎没有关于嵌入到此等合同中的衍生工具的具体指引。因此，必须仔细考虑此等合同的经济特征和风险以评估是否存在嵌入式衍生工具，如有，则其是否需要单独进行会计处理。定量和定性的因素都应予以考虑。有时可从上述有关其他主合同的讨论中找到指引。事实上，这样做亦为合理，尤其是针对价格调整、通胀调整以及价格和数量的上限、下限和上下限等特征时。

价格调整特征

5.82　普通的购买和销售合同可能包含使合同现金流量改变的价格条款。在评估嵌入式衍生工具是否密切相关的标准时，必须确定纳入该合同的价格调

derivative, it would be necessary to establish whether the underlying in a price adjustment feature incorporated into such a contract is related or unrelated to the cost or fair value of the goods or services being sold or purchased.

Example 1 – Price adjustment linked to market prices of goods purchased

An entity (whose functional currency is pound sterling) contracts to purchase 200 tonnes of aluminium from a UK supplier in 12 months' time. The aluminium is intended for use in the course of business. The purchase price will be the market price at the contract date plus an amount determined by a specified index of aluminium prices. The contract does not contain any leverage feature.

The future cash outflows are linked to movements in the market price for aluminium. The purpose of the embedded derivative is to ensure that the price paid for the aluminium is the market price at the date of purchase/supply rather than the date the two parties entered into the supply contract. This ensures that the seller passes any price risk to the entity. As the underlying is related to the price of the aluminium purchased, the derivative is closely related to the aluminium supply contract (host) and would not be accounted for separately.

Example 2 – Coal purchase contract linked to changes in the price of electricity

An entity enters into a coal purchase contract that includes a clause that links the price of coal to a pricing formula based on the prevailing electricity price at the date of delivery. The entity purchases the coal for its own use and there are no provisions to settle the contract net.

The coal purchase contract is the host contract. The pricing formula that changes the price risk from coal price to electricity price is the embedded derivative. Although coal may be used for the production of electricity, the underlying based on electricity prices is not pertinent to both the changes in the cost and the changes in the fair value of coal. Therefore, the embedded derivative (the electricity price adjustment) is not closely related to the host contract and should be accounted for separately.

整特征的标的是否与出售或购买的商品或服务的成本或公允价值有关。

示例1——与购买商品的市场价格挂钩的价格调整

某主体（其功能货币为英镑）签订合同，在12个月的时间内从英国供应商购买200吨铝。这些铝计划用于该主体的业务过程。购买价格为合同签署日的市场价格加上一个由特定的铝价指数所确定的金额。该合同不包含任何杠杆特征。

未来现金流出与铝的市场价格的变动挂钩。该嵌入式衍生工具的目的是确保支付的铝价为购买/供应日的市场价，而非双方签署供应合同日的市场价。这确保了卖方将所有价格风险都转给了主体。由于标的与采购的铝的价格有关，该衍生工具与铝供应合同（主合同）紧密相关，不再单独进行会计处理。

示例2——与电价变化挂钩的购煤合同

某主体签订了一购煤合同，该合同包含条款将煤价与一个基于交付日现行电价的定价公式挂钩。主体购煤的目的是供自己使用，且没有合同净额结算的条款。

购煤合同是主合同。将煤价价格风险转换为电价价格风险的定价公式是嵌入式衍生工具。虽然煤可用于发电，但基于电价的标的与煤的成本变化和公允价值变化均不相关，因此该嵌入式衍生工具（电价调整）不与主合同紧密相关，应单独进行会计处理。

Example 3 – Supply contract subject to multiple pricing adjustments

An entity has entered into a contract with a customer to sell 10, 000 wooden chairs for a period of five years. The price per chair is contractually determined at C100 per chair for the first year and thereafter increases in line with changes in certain indices. 50% of the price of each chair is linked to an index of timber prices, 30% is linked to the UK wage inflation index. So if the timber index rises by 10% and the wage inflation index increases by 5%, the price for each chair will be C106. 50 (being C50 × 1. 1 + C30 × 1. 05 + C20). The sales contract in its entirety does not meet the definition of a derivative as it will be settled by physical delivery in the normal course of business.

There are two embedded derivatives contained in this contract, because the price of chairs over the contract term is linked to the two indices (timber and wage inflation). The purpose of these embedded derivatives is to protect the entity's profit margin over the contract term by ensuring that changes in the prices of inputs are passed on to the end customer.

Although both indices are considered to be relevant and pertinent to the cost or fair value of the chairs being sold, they would be considered to be closely related to the host contract if, and only if, the entity can reliably demonstrate that the standard mix of direct material and direct labour for each chair produced is maintained.

If, however, the entity is unable to demonstrate reliably the clear linkage, then the embedded derivatives *may* be leveraged (because the percentage of the price linked to each index may not accurately reflect the cost structure). In other words, the magnitude of the price adjustment may cause the price of the host contract to increase by more than an insignificant amount (see para 5. 15 above). In that situation, the indexed linked price adjustments would not be considered to be closely related.

5. 83 Where a contract to buy or sell non-financial assets does not qualify for the own use purchase or sale exception, the entire contract would fall to be treated as if it were a financial instrument (and in most cases a derivative). In that situation,

示例3——受多种价格调整影响的供应合同

某主体与客户签署了在五年的时间内销售10,000张木椅的合同。合同规定，第1年每张椅子的单价是100元，一年之后单价随相关指数的变化而增加。椅子单价的50%与木材价格指数挂钩，30%与英国工资通胀指数挂钩。这样，如果木材指数上升10%，工资通胀指数上升5%，则椅子的单价将是106.50元（等于50元×1.1＋30元×1.05＋20元）。该销售合同整体并不符合衍生工具的定义，因其在正常业务过程中通过实物交付进行结算。

此合同中包含两个嵌入式衍生工具，因为合同期内椅子的价格与两个指数（木材和工资通胀）挂钩。这两个衍生工具的目的是通过确保将投入价格的变化转移给最终客户，来保护合同期内主体的利润率。

虽然这两个指数都被认为与出售的椅子的成本或公允价值有关，只有当主体能可靠证明所生产的每张椅子的直接材料和直接人工的标准配比保持不变时，才能认为这两个指数与主合同紧密相关。

但是，如果主体无法可靠证明这种清晰的联系，则该嵌入式衍生工具可能具有杠杆作用（因为与各指数挂钩的价格百分比可能无法准确反映成本结构）。换言之，价格调整的幅度可能会导致主合同的价格上涨幅度超过一个不重大的金额（参见上述第5.15段）。在此情形下，与指数挂钩的价格调整不会被认为紧密相关。

5.83　购买或销售非金融资产的合同不符合“自用购买或销售例外规则”的，则整个合同将视作金融工具（在多数情况下为衍生工具）来处理。在此情形下，由于整个衍生工具合同将以公允价值计量且其变动计入损益，任何嵌入

as the entire derivative contract would be accounted for at fair value through profit or loss, any derivatives embedded in such contracts would no longer need to be accounted for separately.

Example – Contract not qualifying for 'normal' purchase or sale exception

An entity enters into a forward contract to purchase 10,000 tonnes of coal. The contract does not qualify for the 'normal' purchase or sale exception as there is a provision in the contract for net settlement and the entity's past practice indicates that it will settle the contract net. Settlement is based on changes in the fair value of coal during the contract's term plus a payment provision based on a formula linked to prevailing electricity prices.

Given that the own use exception does not apply, the entire forward contract to purchase coal will be accounted for as a derivative in accordance with IAS 39 with gains and losses on the entire contract reported in the profit and loss account. Therefore, there is no need to identify separately the leverage payment provision as an embedded derivative.

Volume adjustment features

5.84 Many contracts for the supply of goods usually give the buyer the right to take either a minimum quantity of goods or any amount based on the buyer's requirements. A minimum annual commitment does not create a derivative as long as the entity expects to purchase all the guaranteed volume for its 'own use'. However, if it becomes likely that the entity will not take physical delivery of the product and, instead pay a penalty under the contract based on the market value of the product or some other variable, a derivative or an embedded derivative may well arise. In this situation, since physical delivery is no longer probable, the derivative would be recorded at the amount of the penalty payable. Changes in market price will affect the penalty's carrying value until the penalty is paid. On the other hand, if the amount of the penalty payable is fixed or pre-determined, there is no derivative as the penalty's value remains fixed irrespective of changes in the market value of the product. In other words, the entity will need to provide for

到此类合同中的衍生工具都不再需要单独进行会计处理。

示例——不符合“普通”购买或销售例外规则的合同

某主体签署了购买 10,000 吨煤的远期合同。该合同不符合“普通”购买或销售例外规则，因为其包含了净额结算的条款，且该主体过去的惯例表明其会对合同进行净额结算。结算的支付条款基于合同期内煤公允价值的变动，加上一个基于与现行电价挂钩的公式。

鉴于自用例外规则不适用，则整个远期购煤合同将根据 IAS 39 作为一个衍生工具进行核算，整个合同的利得和损失将计入损益账户中。因此，无需将杠杆付款条款单独识别为一个嵌入式衍生工具。

数量调整特征

5.84　许多供货合同经常会给予买方提取最低数量的货物或根据买方的要求提取任何数量的货物的权利。一个年度最低量承诺不构成衍生工具，只要主体预期以“自用”为目的购买所有的保证量。但是，如果主体很有可能不会实物交付产品，而是依据合同基于产品的市场价格或其他变量支付违约金，则会产生衍生工具或嵌入式衍生工具。在此情形下，由于不可能再进行实物交付，衍生工具将以应付违约金的金额记录。市场价格的变化会影响违约金的账面价值，直至违约金支付。然而，如果应付违约金的金额是固定的或事先已确定，则不存在衍生工具，因为不管产品市场价格如何变化，违约金的价值均保持不变。换言之，一旦发现很可能不履约，主体将需要计提应付违约金。

the penalty payable once it becomes clear that non-performance is likely.

5.85 On the other hand, if the quantity specified in the contract is more than the entity's normal usage requirement and the entity intends to net settle part of the contract that it does not need in the normal course of the business, the contract will fail the 'own use' exemption. Chapter 3 sets out a number of ways in which the entity can settle the contract net. For example, the entity could take all the quantities specified in the contract and sell on the excess or it could enter into an offsetting contract for the excess quantity. In such situations, the entire contract falls within IAS 39's scope and should be marked-to-market.

5.86 From the supplier's perspective, however, the volume flexibility feature in the contract can be viewed in two ways. The first is to view the contract as a whole. The contract may include a written option for the element of volume flexibility. The whole contract should be viewed as one instrument and, if the item being supplied (electricity) is readily convertible to cash, entity A would be prevented from classifying the contract as 'own use' by paragraph 7 of IAS 39. This states that a written option on a non-financial item that is readily convertible to cash cannot be entered into for the purpose of the receipt or delivery of a non-financial item in accordance with the entity's expected purchase, sale or usage requirements. A second view is that the contract has two components, an 'own use' fixed volume host contract outside of IAS 39's scope for any contractually fixed volume element and an embedded written option potentially within IAS 39's scope for the volume flexibility element. The latter would be in IAS 39's scope if the item being supplied (electricity) is readily convertible to cash for the same reason as under the first view. In March 2010, the IFRS IC discussed the issue of volume flexibility and recognised that significant diversity exists in practice. However, the IFRS IC decided not to add the issue to its agenda because of the Board's project to develop a replacement for IAS 39.

5.87 As explained in chapter 3, such written options have to be accounted for in accordance with IAS 39 if they can be 'settled net in cash'. 'Settled net in cash' in this context means either that the contract allows net settlement or the item that is the subject of the contract is readily convertible into cash.

5.88 Therefore, it is necessary to consider whether the contract contains a written

5.85 另一方面，如果合同规定的数量大于主体正常使用的需求量，且主体打算对其正常业务过程中不需要的部分进行净额结算，则该合同将不符合“自用”例外规则。第三章规定了主体对合同进行净额结算的一系列方法。例如，主体可以提取合同规定的全部数量并出售超额部分，或者主体也可以签署有关超额部分的抵销合同。在此情形下，整个合同属于 IAS 39 的范畴，应按市值调整。

5.86 然而，从供应商的角度看，合同中的数量弹性特征可以两种方式看待。第一种观点是将合同视为一个整体。合同可能包含一个有关弹性数量要素的签出期权。整个合同应视为一个工具，并且如果供应的货物（例如电）容易转换成现金，则主体 A 将无法根据 IAS 39 第 7 段将合同归类为“自用”合同。该段指出，出于根据主体的预期购买、销售或使用要求而收取或交付非金融产品之目的，不可能签订一个针对容易转换成现金的非金融项目的签出期权。另一种观点是，合同由两部分构成，一个不在 IAS 39 范围内的、针对合同约定的固定数量要素的“自用”固定数量合同，及一个在 IAS 39 范围内的、针对数量弹性要素的嵌入签出期权。如果供应的货物（例如电）由于与第一种观点相同的原因容易转换成现金，那么后者将在 IAS 39 的范围内。2010 年 3 月，IFRS IC 讨论了数量弹性的问题，并确认在实务中存在的重大的多样化处理。但是，由于理事会的 IAS 39 替代项目，IFRS IC 决定不将该事项纳入议程。

5.87 正如第三章所述，如果此类签出期权能以“现金净额结算”，则其必须根据 IAS 39 进行会计处理。此处的“现金净额结算”指合同允许净额结算或合同标的容易转换成现金。

5.88 因此，必须考虑合同是否包含签出期权。如果买方没有为得到该期权

option. A contract will not contain a true written option if the buyer did not pay any premium to receive the option. Receipt of a premium to compensate the supplier for the risk that the buyer may not take the optional quantities specified in the contract is one of the distinguishing features of a written option. [IAS 39 IG F1.3(a)(b)]. Therefore, it would be necessary to consider whether a net premium is received either at inception or over the contract's life in order to determine the accounting treatment. Any penalty payable for non-performance by the buyer may well amount to the receipt of a premium. If no premium can be identified, other terms of the contract may need to be examined to determine whether it contains a written option, in particular, whether the buyer is able to secure economic value from the option's presence. Contracts need to be considered on a case-by-case basis in order to determine whether they contain written options.

Example 1

Entity A, a car manufacturer enters into a contract to sell cars to entity B that is engaged in renting cars. The contracts provide for entity A to supply 50 cars of a specific model at a specified future date at a fixed price. Entity B has the option to take between 90% and 110% of the contract quantity. Available market information indicates that a similar contract for 50 cars but without volume flexibility would also be priced at the same fixed price specified in the contract. Entity B cannot monetize the value of the contract by selling on any excess cars in the market.

The supply contract would not be considered a written option, as the pricing of the contract is the same as that for a similar contract with no volume flexibility. There is, therefore, no premium associated with the contract. Entity B cannot exercise any value from the option's presence; the contract is, therefore, not a written option and qualifies for the own-use exemption.

Example 2

Entity A, an electricity producer in the United Kingdom where there is an active electricity market, enters into a contract to sell electricity to entity B. The contracts provide for entity A to supply 100 units of electricity at a specified future date to entity B at a fixed price per unit. Entity B has the

而支付任何期权费，则合同不会包含真正的签出期权。因供应商面临的买方可能不会提取合同规定的可选数量的风险，而收取一定的期权费作为补偿，这是签出期权的显著特征之一。[IAS 39 IG 第 F1.3（a）（b）段]。因此，需要考虑是否在合同开始时或在合同期间收到了净期权费，以便确定会计处理方式。买方应支付的任何未履约违约金的金额可以等于收取的期权费。如不能识别期权费，则可能需要检查其他合同条款，以确定其是否包含签出期权，尤其是要确定买方是否能够从提供的期权中获得经济价值。需要对各项合同逐个进行分析，以确定其是否包含签出期权。

示例 1

汽车制造商主体 A 签署了向从事汽车租赁的主体 B 出售汽车的合同。合同规定主体 A 应在指定的未来某个日期以固定价格供应指定型号的汽车 50 辆。主体 B 有权提取合同数量的 90%—110%。现有市场信息表明，类似的不具备数量弹性的 50 辆汽车合同的供货价和本合同规定的固定价格相同。主体 B 不能通过在市场中出售任何超额汽车而将合同价值货币化。

该供应合同不会被认为是一个签出期权，因为合同的定价与类似的不具备数量弹性的合同的定价相同。因此，不存在与合同相联系的期权费。主体 B 不能从提供的选择权中的实现任何价值；因此，该合同不是签出期权，符合“自用”豁免的条件。

示例 2

英国有活跃的电力市场，位于英国的发电商主体 A 签署向主体 B 售电的合同。合同规定主体 A 应在指定的未来某个日期以固定的单位价格向主体 A 提供 100 单位的电。主体 B 有权提取合同数量的 90%—110%。提取的总量的定价为每单位 0.21 元。现有市场信息表明，类似的不具备数

option to take between 90% and 110% of the contract quantity. The total quantity taken will be priced at C0. 21 per unit. Available market information indicates that a similar contract for 100 units of electricity but without volume flexibility would be priced at C0. 20 per unit. Entity B is also a supplier of electricity and can, therefore, monetize the contract's value by selling on any excess power into the market, that is, it can readily convert the electricity contract to cash.

The pricing of the contract is not the same as that for a similar contract without volume flexibility. The price per cubic meter includes a premium for the additional risk accepted by entity A in offering volume flexibility. The contract is, therefore, a written option and entity A cannot claim the own-use exemption. In that situation, the contract will be marked-to-market in accordance with IAS 39. As noted above entity A can view the contract in two ways:

- as a written option in its entirety and hence entity A cannot claim the own-use exemption. In that situation, the contract will be marked-to-market in accordance with IAS 39; or
- as a fixed volume contract for 90 units of electricity for C0. 20 per unit for which the own use exemption could be claimed and a written option for 20 units at C0. 21 per unit, which is within IAS 39's scope.

Inflation related features

5. 89 It is not uncommon for purchase, sale or long-term service contracts to contain terms that are linked to an inflation index, particularly in periods of rising inflation. Inflation escalator clauses are included in such long-term contracts to protect the seller's margin in real terms. Although IAS 39 is silent on the treatment of inflationary adjustments in executory contracts, there is no reason, in principle, why the guidance on inflation adjustment features in lease host contracts would not be appropriate for such contracts. That guidance states that an embedded inflation-related index is closely related to the lease host contract if the index is not leveraged and it relates to inflation in the entity's own economic environment.

量弹性的 100 单位电合同定价是每单位 0.20 元。主体 B 也是一个供电商，因此，主体 B 可以通过向市场出售超额电量使合同价值货币化，也就是说，可以容易地将供电合同转换成现金。

该合同的定价与类似的不具备数量弹性的合同的定价不同。每立方米的价格包含了主体 A 因提供数量弹性而承担额外风险的期权费。因此，该合同是一个签出期权，主体 A 不能主张“自用”豁免。在此情形下，该合同将根据 IAS 39 按市价调整。如上所述，主体 A 可以两种方式看待该合同。

- 将合同整个视为签出期权，因而主体 A 不能主张“自用”豁免。在此情形下，该合同将根据 IAS 39 按市价调整；或
- 将合同视为一个可主张“自用”豁免的单价为 0.20 元的 90 单位固定数量供电合同，及一个单价为 0.21 元的 20 单位电的签出期权，该期权在 IAS 39 的范围内。

通胀有关的特征

5.89 购买、销售或长期服务合同中包含与通胀指数挂钩的条款，尤其是在通胀加剧的时期，是很常见的。在此类长期服务合同中纳入通胀调整条款是为了保护卖方的实际利润。虽然 IAS 39 未规定待执行合同中通胀调整的处理方法，但是在原则上，没有理由认为租赁主合同中对通胀调整特征的相关指引不适用于此类合同。该指引指出，如果嵌入的与通胀相关的指数不具有杠杆作用，且该指数与主体自身经济环境中的通胀有关，那么该指数与租赁主合同紧密相关。[IAS 39 AG 第 33（f）段]。本原则在租赁合同中的应用在上述第 5.69 段中讨论。我们认为，类似的考虑事项可以适用于购买、销售和服务合同。

[IAS 39 para AG 33(f)]. The application of this principle to lease contracts is considered from paragraphs 5.69 above. We believe similar considerations can be applied to purchase, sale and service contracts.

Example – Purchase contract linked to inflation

A UK entity contracts to purchase a fixed quantity of raw material from a UK supplier in 12 months' time. The raw materials are intended for use in the entity's business. The purchase price will be the market price at the contract date plus an adjustment for UK RPI from the beginning of the contract. The contract does not contain any leverage feature.

The future cash flows are linked to an inflation index that is not leveraged and the index is in the local economic environment. Therefore, the embedded derivative is closely related to the host purchase contract.

If, on the other hand, the entity is unable to demonstrate that these goods are to be used in the course of its business, that is, the own use exception does not apply, the entire contract would be treated as a forward purchase contract that would fall to be settled net. In that situation, the forward purchase contract meets the definition of a derivative and, is itself, accounted for at fair value through profit or loss. So there is no need to account separately for any derivatives that may be embedded in it.

Caps, floors and collars

5.90 Contracts to buy or sell a non-financial asset may contain provisions that provide for payments to be made at the market price at the time of payment, but set an upper or lower limit or both on the final price to be paid or received. Such caps, floors or collars included in contracts are embedded derivatives. IAS 39 states that provisions included in a contract to purchase or sell an asset (for example, a commodity) that establish a cap and a floor on the price to be paid or received for the asset are closely related to the host contract if both the cap and floor were out-of-the-money and are not leveraged. [IAS 39 para AG 33(b)]. This guidance can be extended to a collar that would be closely related if it was out-of-the-money at inception (see para 5.44 above).

示例——与通胀挂钩的购买合同

某英国主体签署了在 12 个月期间从某英国供应商购买固定数量的原材料的合同。原材料计划在该主体的业务中使用。购买价格为合同签署日的市场价格加上自合同签署日起英国零售价格指数的调整。合同不包含任何杠杆特征。

未来现金流量与不具有杠杆作用的通胀指数挂钩，且该指数为本国经济环境中的指数。因此，该嵌入式衍生工具与购买主合同紧密相关。

如果主体无法证明这些货物是在自身的业务过程中使用的，换言之，如果“自用例外规则”不适用，则整个合同将被作为一个将采用净额结算的远期购买合同处理。在此情形下，该远期购买合同符合衍生工具的定义，其本身将以公允价值计量且其变动计入损益。因此，任何可能嵌入到该合同中的衍生工具都无需单独进行会计处理。

上限、下限和上下限

5.90　购买或出售非金融资产的合同可能包含这样的条款，即规定以付款时的市场价格付款，但对将支付或收取的最终价格设定上限、下限或同时设定上下限。合同中包含的此等上限、下限和上下限均为嵌入式衍生工具。IAS 39 规定，包含在资产（如某种商品）购买或销售合同中的、对该资产支付或收取的价格确定上限和下限的条款，若该上限和下限均是价外的且不具有杠杆作用，则此等条款与主合同紧密相关。［IAS 39 AG 第 33（b）段］。该指引可延伸至上下限，若上下限在合同开始时是价外的，则其紧密相关（参见上文第 5.44 段）。

Example – Purchase contract with selling price subject to a cap and a floor

A manufacturer enters into a long-term contract to purchase a specified quantity of certain raw materials from a supplier. Under the contract, the supplier will provide the raw materials at the list price prevailing at the delivery date, but within a specified range. For example, the purchase price may not exceed C20 per kg or fall below C15 per kg. The current list price at inception of the contract is C18 per kg.

From the manufacturer's perspective, the embedded derivatives contained in the purchase contracts are two options; a purchased call option with a strike price of C20 per kg and a written put with a strike price of C15 per kg. These options would each meet the definition of a derivative if they were free standing, because they have a notional amount (the fixed quantity to be purchased), an underlying (the price per kg), require no initial net investment and will be settled in the future.

The economic characteristics and risks of the two options are closely related to the purchase contract, because the options are indexed to the asset's purchase price that is the subject of the contract and both the embedded cap (cap price of C20 is greater than current list price of C18) and the floor (floor price of C15 is lower than current list price of C18) are out-of-the-money at inception of the contract. Hence, the embedded derivatives are closely related and the host contract can be considered to be a purchase contract that requires delivery of the specified quantity of raw materials at a price equal to the current list price.

Foreign currency features

5.91 IAS 39 provides specific guidance for an embedded foreign currency derivative in a host contract that is not a financial instrument (such as a contract for the purchase or sale of a non-financial item where the price is denominated in a foreign currency). The embedded foreign currency derivative is closely related to the host contract provided it is not leveraged, does not contain an option feature and requires payments denominated in one of the following currencies:

示例——销售价格有上限和下限的购买合同

一制造商签署了从某供应商购买指定数量的原材料的长期合同。根据该合同，供应商将以交付当日的现行目录价格提供原料，但有指定价格范围。例如，购买价格不得超过每千克 20 元或不得低于每千克 16.3 元。合同开始日的现行目录价格为每千克 18 元。

从制造商角度看，购买合同中包含的嵌入式衍生工具为两个期权，即一个执行价为每千克 20 元的买入看涨期权和一个执行价为每千克 15 元的签出看跌期权。如果这两个期权是独立的，则其各自都符合衍生工具的定义，因为这两个期权有名义金额（将购买的固定数量），有标的（每千克的价格），不需要初始净投资，且会在未来结算。

这两个期权的经济特征和风险与购买合同紧密相关，因为这两个期权与合同标的资产的购买价格挂钩，且嵌入上限（上限价格 20 元高于现行目录价格 18 元）和下限（下限价格 15 元低于现行目录价格 18 元）在合同开始时都是价外的。因此，该嵌入式衍生工具紧密相关，该主合同可认为是一个要求以现行目录价格交付指定数量原材料的购买合同。

外币特征

5.91　IAS 39 提供了有关非金融工具主合同中的嵌入式外币衍生工具的具体指引（诸如购买或销售非金融产品的合同，其中价格以外币计价）。该嵌入的外币衍生工具与主合同紧密相关，前提是其不具有杠杆作用，不包含期权特征，且要求款项以下列币种之一计价：

- The functional currency of any substantial party to that contract.
- The currency in which the price of the related goods or service that is acquired or delivered is routinely denominated in commercial transactions around the world (such as the US dollar for crude oil transactions).
- A currency that is commonly used in contracts to purchase or sell non-financial items in the economic environment in which the transaction takes place (for example, a relatively stable and liquid currency that is commonly used in local business transactions or external trade).

[IAS 39 para AG 33(d)].

5.92 The term 'substantial party' to the contract referred to in the first bullet point above is not explained in IAS 39. Generally, it is taken to mean a party that is acting as principal to the contract, that is, the buyer/seller. A bank that provides a guarantee on behalf of a local importer to a foreign supplier that the buyer will meet its payment obligations in foreign currency under the contract's terms is not a substantial party to the contract. Furthermore, the guarantor's functional currency is of no relevance in determining whether the payments denominated in the foreign currency are closely related to the contract.

5.93 A question also arises in practice as to the efforts one party to a contract needs to employ to determine the functional currency of its counterparty. Generally, there would be a rebuttable presumption that the local currencies of the economic environment in which the counterparties operate would be their functional currencies. In addition, the local currency is always presumed to be commonly used. Therefore, if the contract requires payment in either one of the two local currencies of the counterparties, the condition in the first bullet point above would be met. The position is less clear if payments are denominated in a currency that is not the local currency of either party to the contract. In that situation, the contracting parties would need to determine whether that currency is the functional currency of their counterparty. In practice, this determination should be made on the basis of all available evidence and reasonable assumptions about the counterparty. Furthermore, the guidance for determining functional currency in IAS 21 would need to be considered in determining the functional currency. An

- 合同任何实质方的功能货币。
- 购买或交付的相关商品或服务的价格在全世界商业交易中通常使用的计价货币（如原油交易使用的美元）。
- 购买或销售非金融产品的合同在交易发生的经济环境中普遍使用的货币（如本国商业交易或对外贸易中普遍使用的相对稳定和流通的货币）。

[IAS 39 AG 第33（d）段]。

5.92　上述第一点中的合同的“实质方”这一术语在 IAS 39 中未有解释。通常，“实质方”被认为是指作为合同履行方，即买方或卖方。如果某银行代表某本国进口商向国外供应商提供担保，买方会根据合同条款以外币履行其付款义务，则该银行不属于合同的实质方。此外，担保人的功能货币与确定以外币计价的款项是否与合同紧密相关没有关系。

5.93　在实务中还会产生这样的问题，即合同一方需作出努力以确定对方的功能货币。通常，可以假定对方经营所处的经济环境中的本国货币是其功能货币。此外，一般假设本国货币为常用的货币。因此，如果合同要求款项以双方两种本国货币中的任何一种计价，则符合上述第一点的条件。如果付款的计价货币不是合同任一方的本国货币，则情况就比较复杂了。在此情形下，合同各方需要确定计价货币是否是对方的功能货币。在实务中，应该基于所有可取得证据和有关对方的合理假设来进行确定。此外，在确定功能货币时，需要考虑 IAS 21 有关确定功能货币的指引。主体不必一定依赖于诸如对方销售的计价货币等单个指标。相反，主体在确定对方的功能货币时，应当考虑所有可取得的相关信息。

entity should not necessarily rely on a single indicator such as the currency in which the counterparty's sales are denominated. Rather, the entity should consider all relevant available information in determining the counterparty's functional currency.

Example 1 – Payments denominated in the functional currency of a party to the contract

A UK entity (whose functional currency is pound sterling) contracts to sell goods to a French purchaser whose functional currency is the euro. The contract will be fulfilled by the physical delivery of goods and payments by the French buyer would be made in euros.

In this example, the payment in euros exposes the UK entity to currency risk as the cash flows under the contract will vary with the £/€ exchange rate. The contract can be viewed as a host contract that is denominated in sterling containing an embedded foreign currency swap that converts payments in pound sterling to euros or an embedded foreign currency forward contract to sell pound sterling and buy euros. However, the embedded swap or the forward contract is not separated as the payments are denominated in the functional currency of the French buyer who is a substantial party to the contract.

Example 2 – Payments denominated in a third currency

A UK entity (whose functional currency is pounds sterling) contracts to sell goods to a Swiss purchaser whose functional currency is the Swiss francs. The contract will be fulfilled by the physical delivery of goods and payments by the Swiss buyer would be made in euros. The goods are not commonly priced in euros.

In this example, the payment and the receipt in euros exposes both the substantial parties to the contract to exchange risk. Since the contract requires that payments be denominated in euros, which is not the functional currency of either party to the transaction, the embedded derivative is not closely related and should be accounted for separately at fair value by both the Swiss buyer and the UK seller. From the UK seller's point of view the embedded derivative would be to buy euros and sell sterling. In the books of the Swiss buyer the embedded derivative would be to sell euros and buy Swiss francs.

示例1——以合同一方的功能货币计价的付款

某英国主体（其功能货币为英镑）签署了向功能货币为欧元的法国买方出售货物的合同。执行合同需实物交付货物，法国买方将以欧元付款。

在该示例中，由于合同项下的现金流量将随英镑/欧元的汇率而变化，该欧元付款使得英国主体面临货币风险。该合同可看作是一个以英镑计价的主合同，包含了一个可将英镑计价的款项转换成欧元的嵌入外币互换，也可看作是一个卖出英镑买入欧元的嵌入外币远期合同。但是，该嵌入互换或远期合同不应分拆，因为付款以法国买方（合同的实质方）的功能货币计价。

示例2——以第三方货币计价的付款

某英国主体（其功能货币为英镑）签署了向功能货币为瑞士法郎的瑞士买方出售货物的合同。执行合同需实物交付货物，瑞士买方将以欧元付款。这种货物通常不是以欧元计价的。

该示例中，以欧元计价的付款和收款使得合同的两个实质方都面临外汇风险。由于合同要求以欧元付款，而欧元不是交易任何一方的功能货币，该嵌入式衍生工具不紧密相关，瑞士买方和英国卖方应以公允价值单独对该衍生工具进行会计处理。对英国卖方而言，嵌入式衍生工具是买入欧元卖出英镑。而在瑞士买方的账上，嵌入式衍生工具是卖出欧元买入瑞士法郎。该嵌入远期合约的名义金额等于供货合同条款规定的金额。

The nominal amount of the embedded forwards will be equal to the amount specified under the terms of the supply contract.

A particular issue arises in connection with the nature of the foreign currency embedded derivative in foreign currency purchase/sale contracts when the embedded derivative is required to be separated under paragraph AG 33(d). The issue is whether the embedded derivative is a forward contract that matures on the date on which goods are physically delivered, or on the date when cash settlement takes place.

Assume that the UK entity enters into the contract with the Swiss buyer to sell goods amounting to 100 on 1 March 20X6 for delivery on 30 June 20X6 and settlement on 31 July 20X6. The goods are not commonly priced in €. The UK entity's year end is 31 March 20X6. The following data is relevant.

Date	**Event**	**Spot €/£**	**Forward €/£ (maturity June 20X6)**	**Forward €/£ (maturity July 20X6)**
1 Mar 20X6	UK entity enters into a contract to sell goods for €100	0.70	0.725	0.72
31 Mar 20X6	UK entity's year end. Embedded derivative revalued	0.73	0.745	0.74
30 Jun 20X6	Goods delivered	0.75		0.77
31 Jul 20X6	Invoice amounting to €100 settled	0.78		

In this example, from the perspective of the UK seller, the firm commitment to sell goods is separated into two contracts – a host contact that is a firm commitment to sell goods in pound sterling and an embedded forward contract to buy euro and sell pound sterling with an inception date of 1 March 20X6. However, as stated above there is some debate regarding the deemed date of settlement/maturity of the embedded derivative.

如果要求依据 AG 第 33（d）段分拆外币购买/销售合同中的嵌入式外币衍生工具，那就会产生有关嵌入式外币衍生工具的性质这一问题。这个问题是，嵌入式衍生工具是在实物交付之日到期的远期合同，还是在现金结算之日到期的远期合同。

假设英国主体与瑞士买方于 20X6 年 3 月 1 日签署出售 100 欧元的货物的合同，货物将于 20X6 年 6 月 30 日交付，并于 20X6 年 7 月 31 日进行结算。这种货物通常并不是以欧元计价的。英国主体的年度结算日为 20X6 年 3 月 31 日。以下是相关数据。

日期	事件	即期汇率 欧元/英镑	远期汇率 欧元/英镑（20X6 年 6 月到期）	远期汇率 欧元/英镑（20X6 年 7 月到期）
20X6 年 3 月 1 日	英国主体签署出售 100 欧元货物的合同	0.70	0.725	0.72
20X6 年 3 月 31 日	英国主体的年度结算日。对嵌入式衍生工具重新估值	0.73	0.745	0.74
20X6 年 6 月 30 日	交付货物	0.75		0.77
20X6 年 7 月 31 日	结算金额为 100 欧元的发票	0.78		

该示例中，从英国卖方角度看，其出售货物的确定承诺分为两个合同，一个是以英镑出售货物的确定承诺的主合同，另一个是于 20X6 年 3 月 1 日开始的买入欧元卖出英镑的嵌入远期合同。但是，如上所述，关于认定嵌入式衍生工具的结算/到期日期存在一些争议。

Some take the view that the embedded derivative's settlement/maturity date is 30 June 20X6 when the goods are delivered. This is because the derivative that is embedded in the host firm commitment can no longer exist after that date as there is no host contract — the seller having fulfilled its commitment by delivering the goods to the customer. Following performance by the seller, the seller has an unconditional right to receive consideration from the customer. In other words, the embedded derivative is in the sales contract not in the receivable; the derivative being effectively settled by creation of a financial asset (receivable). Under this view, the accounting entries would be as follows:

Accounting for sale and embedded derivative

		Dr (Cr)				
		Sales	Debtors	Cash	Derivative	Profit and loss
Date	**Transaction**	£	£	£	£	£
1 Mar 20X6	Embedded derivative – nil fair value					
31 Mar 20X6	Change in fair value of embedded derivative – €100 @ (0.745 – 0.725) – ignoring discounting – there is a gain as, using the forward rate at the balance sheet date, to buy €100 would cost £74.5 compared to £72.5 using the contracted forward rate				2.0	(2.0)
30 Jun 20X6	Change in fair value of embedded derivative – €100 @ (0.75 – 0.745)				0.5	(0.5)
30 Jun 20X6	Recording sales at forward rate – 100 @ 0.725	(72.5)	72.5			
30 Jun 20X6	Embedded derivative settled against debtors		2.5		(2.5)	
31 Jul 20X6	Debtor carried at spot rate at 30 June 20X6 settled by receipt of €100 at spot rate – €100 @ 0.78		(75.0)	78		(3.0)
	Effect on profit or loss and balance sheet	(72.5)	–	78	–	(5.5)

有人认为该嵌入式衍生工具的结算/到期日为20X6年6月30日，即交付货物的日期。这是因为，卖方已通过向客户交付货物而履行了其承诺，由于没有了主合同，所以嵌入到主确定承诺中的衍生工具在该日期后不再存在。卖方履约后，卖方有无条件向客户收取对价的权利。换言之，该嵌入式衍生工具存在于销售合同中而非应收款中；通过产生金融资产（应收款）实际上结算了该衍生工具。根据这种观点，会计分录如下：

收入和嵌入式衍生工具的会计处理

		借方(贷方)				
		收入	应收款	现金	衍生工具	损益
日期	交易	英镑	英镑	英镑	英镑	英镑
20X6年3月1日	嵌入式衍生工具——无公允价值					
20X6年3月31日	嵌入式衍生工具公允价值变动——100欧元,汇率变动(0.745 - 0.725)——不考虑折现——采用资产负债表日的远期汇率购买100欧元将花费74.5英镑,相比采用合同规定的远期汇率将花费的72.5英镑,产生了利得				2.0	(2.0)
20X6年6月30日	嵌入式衍生工具公允价值变动——100欧元,汇率变动(0.75 - 0.745)				0.5	(0.5)
20X6年6月30日	以远期汇率记录收入——100,汇率0.725	(72.5)	72.5			
20X6年6月30日	以应收款结算嵌入式衍生工具		2.5		(2.5)	
20X6年7月31日	采用20X6年6月30日的即期汇率计量的应收款,通过以即期汇率收取100欧元进行结算——100欧元,汇率0.78		(75.0)	78		(3.0)
	对利润表和资产负债表的影响	(72.5)	–	78	–	(5.5)

Others take the view that the embedded derivative being a forward foreign exchange contract matures at the date of cash settlement on the grounds that the cash leg of the firm commitment is settled at that date. Under this view, the sale and the corresponding receivable are recognised in local currency using the forward rate when the goods are delivered, that is (C72). The embedded derivative and the debtor is settled when cash is received at 31 July 20X6 with any gain or loss arising on settlement recorded in profit or loss. Under this view, the accounting treatment would be as follows:

Accounting for sale and embedded derivative

		Dr (Cr)				
		Sales	**Debtors**	**Cash**	**Derivative**	**Profit and loss**
Date	**Transaction**	£	£	£	£	£
1 Mar 20X6	Embedded derivative – nil fair value					
31 Mar 20X6	Change in fair value of embedded derivative – €100 @ (0.74 – 0.72) – ignoring discounting – there is a gain as using the forward rate at the balance sheet date, to buy €100 would cost £74 compared to £72 using the contracted forward rate				2.0	(2.0)
30 Jun 20X6	Change in fair value of embedded derivative – €100 @ (0.77 – 0.74)				3.0	(3.0)
30 Jun 20X	Recording sales at forward rate – 100 @ 0.72	(72.0)	72.0			
31 Jul 20X6	Settlement date – receipt of €100 at spot rate – €100 @ 0.78		(72.0)	78	(5.0)	(1.0)
	Effect on profit and loss and balance sheet	(72.0)	–	78	–	(6.0)

而其他人认为，该嵌入式衍生工具是在现金结算日到期的远期外汇合同，因为确定承诺的现金端是在该日结算的。根据这种观点，收入和相应的应收款均使用交付货物时的远期汇率折算的本国货币确认，即（72 元）。该嵌入式衍生工具和应收款在 20X6 年 7 月 31 日收到现金时结算，因结算产生的利得或损失记录在损益中。根据这种观点，会计分录如下：

收入和嵌入式衍生工具的会计处理

		借方(贷方)				
		收入	应收款	现金	衍生工具	损益
日期	交易	英镑	英镑	英镑	英镑	英镑
20X6 年 3 月 1 日	嵌入式衍生工具——无公允价值					
20X6 年 3 月 31 日	嵌入式衍生工具公允价值变动——100 欧元，汇率变动(0.74 - 0.72)——不考虑折现——采用资产负债表日的远期汇率购买 100 欧元将花费 74 英镑，相比采用合同规定的远期汇率花费的 72 英镑，产生了利得				2.0	(2.0)
20X6 年 6 月 30 日	嵌入式衍生工具公允价值变动——100 欧元，汇率变动(0.77 - 0.74)				3.0	(3.0)
20X 年 6 月 30 日	以远期汇率记录收入——100，汇率 0.72	(72.0)	72.0			
20X6 年 7 月 31 日	结算日以即期汇率收款 100 欧元——100 欧元，汇率 0.78		(72.0)	78	(5.0)	(1.0)
	对利润表和资产负债表的影响	(72.0)	-	78	-	(6.0)

Although both views can be sustained, in practice, entities generally tend to adopt the first treatment as they view these types of contract as inherent in future sales.

Example 3 – Payments denominated in the functional currency of a party to the contract, but the functional currency changes subsequently

A UK entity (whose functional currency is pound sterling) contracts to sell goods to a Japanese purchaser whose functional currency is the yen. The contract will be fulfilled by the physical delivery of goods and payments by the Japanese buyer would be made in yen. Subsequently, because of changes in economic circumstances, the functional currency of the Japanese buyer changes to US dollars.

The UK entity is required to assess whether the embedded derivative should be separated from the host sales contract and accounted for as a derivative when it first becomes a party to the contract. At the time the UK entity entered into the contract, the functional currency of the Japanese buyer was the yen. Therefore, no separation of the embedded derivative is required as yen is the functional currency of a substantial party to the contract. The issue is whether this initial assessment should be revisited following the change in the functional currency of the Japanese buyer.

As explained in paragraph 5.22 above, IFRIC 9 prohibits reassessment unless there is a change in the contract's terms that meet certain criteria . In such an instance, reassessment is required. In this situation, the contract terms remain unchanged, that is, the UK entity will still take payments in yen irrespective of the fact that the functional currency of the Japanese supplier has subsequently changed to US dollars. Therefore, the contract continues to be accounted for in the same manner as before, irrespective of the fact that the factors that led to the initial assessment have changed. However, any yen denominated contracts entered into with the Japanese buyer after it has changed its functional currency to US dollar would fail the closely related criterion, as they would not be in the functional currency of either party to the contract.

The above treatment also applies to the Japanese buyer even though it will be

虽然两种观点都有道理，但是在实务中，主体通常倾向于采用第一种处理方法，因为其将此类合同视为内含在未来收入中。

示例 3——以合同一方的功能货币计价的付款，但期后功能货币发生变化

某英国主体（其功能货币为英镑）签署了向功能货币为日元的日本买方出售货物的合同。执行合同需实物交付，日本买方将以日元付款。期后，由于经济环境发生变化，日本买方的功能货币变为美元。

当该英国主体首次成为合同一方时，其应当评估是否应将嵌入式衍生工具从销售主合同中分拆，并作为衍生工具进行会计处理。在英国主体签署合同时，日本买方的功能货币是日元。因此，不要求分拆该嵌入式衍生工具，因为日元是合同一实质方的功能货币。问题是，在日本买方的功能货币发生变化后，是否应重新审定最初的评估。

如上文第 5.22 段所述，IFRIC 9 禁止重新评估，除非合同条款的变化符合某些标准，则在该情况下，要求重新进行评估。在本例的情形中，合同条款保持不变，即英国主体仍旧要收取日元付款，不考虑日本供应商的功能货币期后已经变为美元这一情况。因此，该合同继续以之前的方式进行会计处理，不考虑影响初始评估的因素已发生改变这一情况。但是，在日本买方的功能货币变为美元后，之后与日本买方签署的所有以日元计价的合同将不再符合紧密相关的标准，因为这些合同不再以合同任何一方的功能货币计价。

上述处理方法同样适用于日本买方，即使其在根据合同付款时将面临日元/

exposed to Yen/dollar currency risk when it makes payments under the contract. Such exchange gains and losses will fall to be accounted for in accordance with IAS 21. In other words, as long as the contract terms remain unchanged, the Japanese buyer cannot create an embedded currency exposure that did not exist at the date it became a party to the contract.

Example 4 – Option to make payments in alternative currencies

Facts are the same as in example 1 except that the contract contains an option to make payment in either euros or in Swiss francs.

In this example, the UK seller has written an option to receive payments in a currency that is not its functional currency and, therefore, exposes it to £/€ or £/€ Swiss Fr currency risk. Although euro is the functional currency of the other substantial party to the contract, there is no certainty at inception of the contract that settlement will be in euros. Hence, the foreign currency option is not closely related to the host.

Similarly, the French buyer has effectively purchased an option to make payments in its own functional currency (euros) or in a foreign currency (Swiss Fr) that exposes it to euros/Swiss Fr currency risk. Although the French buyer has the option to settle the contract in its own currency and eliminate any exchange risk, there is no certainty at inception of the contract that it would eventually exercise that option. Since the contract could also be settled in Swiss francs, the settlement can either be potentially favourable or unfavourable and is not closely related to the purchase contract.

Accordingly, the embedded option should be separated from the host contract and accounted for separately by both parties to the contract.

5.94 In relation to the second bullet point in paragraph 5.91 above, the currency in which the price of the related goods or services is routinely denominated in commercial transactions around the world is a currency that is used for similar transactions *all around the world*, not just in one local area. For example, if cross-border transactions in natural gas in North America are routinely denominated in US dollars and such transactions are routinely denominated in euros in Europe, neither the US dollar nor the euro is a currency in which natural gas is routinely

美元货币风险。此等汇兑损益将根据 IAS 21 进行会计处理。换言之，只要合同条款保持不变，则日本买方就不能创造出其在成为合同一方之日不存在的嵌入货币风险敞口。

示例 4——以替代货币付款的选择权

本示例其他情形与示例 1 相同，除了合同包含一个以欧元或瑞士法郎付款的选择权。

本示例中，英国卖方签出一个收取不是其功能货币付款的选择权，因此，其面临英镑/欧元或英镑/瑞士法郎的货币风险。尽管欧元是合同另一实质方的功能货币，但在合同开始时并不确定会以欧元进行结算。因此，该外币期权不与主合同紧密相关。

同样，法国买方实际上已经购买了用自身功能货币（欧元）或外币（瑞士法郎）付款的选择权，这使其面临欧元/瑞士法郎货币风险。尽管法国买方拥有以自身功能货币结算合同并消除所有外汇风险的选择权，但在合同开始时无法确定其会行使该选择权。由于合同还可以瑞士法郎结算，结算既可以是潜在有利的，也可以是潜在不利的，不与购买合同紧密相关。

因此，合同双方均应将该嵌入选择权从主合同中分拆并单独进行会计处理。

5.94　关于上文第 5.91 段中的第二点，相关商品或服务的价格在全世界商业交易中通常使用的计价货币是全世界范围内而非某局部区域内同类交易使用的货币。例如，如果北美的跨国天然气交易通常都是以美元计价，而在欧洲此类交易通常以欧元计价，则全世界天然气商业交易中通常的计价货币既不是美元也不是欧元。[IAS 39 IG 第 C9 段]。因此，除了原油和某些金属在国际贸易中通常是以美元计价外，极少商品（如有）能满足此要求。

denominated in commercial transactions around the world. [IAS 39 para IG C9]. Accordingly, apart from crude oil and some metals which are routinely denominated in US dollar in international commerce, very few items, if any, are likely to meet this requirement.

Example – Leveraged foreign currency provision

Entity A, whose functional currency is the euro, enters into a contract with entity B, whose functional currency is the Norwegian krone, to purchase oil in six months for US $ 10m. The host oil contract is not within IAS 39's scope, because it was entered into and continues to be for the purpose of delivery of a non-financial item in accordance with the entity's expected purchase, sale or usage requirements. The oil contract includes a leveraged foreign exchange provision that states that the parties, in addition to the provision of, and payment for, oil will exchange an amount equal to the fluctuation in the exchange rate of the US dollar and Norwegian krone applied to a notional amount of US $ 10m.

In the example above, the payment provision under the host oil contract of US $ 10m can be viewed as a foreign currency derivative because the US dollar is neither entity A's nor entity B's functional currency. This foreign currency derivative would not be separated, however, because it follows from the second bullet point of paragraph 5.91 above that a crude oil contract that requires payment in US dollars is not regarded as a host contract with a foreign currency derivative.

However, the leveraged foreign exchange provision that states that the parties will exchange an amount equal to the fluctuation in the exchange rate of the US dollar and Norwegian krone applied to a notional amount of US $ 10m is in addition to the required payment for the oil transaction. It is unrelated to the host oil contract and, therefore, should be separated from the host oil contract, and accounted for as an embedded derivative. [IAS 39 para IG C8].

5.95 The third bullet point in paragraph 5.91 refers to a currency that is commonly used in contracts to purchase or sell non-financial items in the economic

示例——具杠杆作用的外币条款

功能货币为欧元的主体 A 与功能货币为挪威克朗的主体 B 签署了在 6 个月后以 1,000 万美元购买石油的合同。主石油合同不在 IAS 39 的范围内，因为合同签署和存续的目的是根据主体预期的购买、销售或使用要求交付非金融产品。该石油合同包含一个具有杠杆作用的外币条款，其规定，除石油的供应和付款外，合同双方还要交换以 1,000 万美元名义金额计算的美元和挪威克朗的汇率波动金额。

在上述示例中，1,000 万美元的主石油合同中的付款条款可视作外币衍生工具，因为美元既不是主体 A 的功能货币，也不是主体 B 的功能货币。但该外币衍生工具不会被分拆，因为根据上文第 5.91 段第二点，以美元支付的原油合同不被视为含外币衍生工具的主合同。

但是，除了石油交易所要求的付款外，还存在具有杠杆作用的外币条款，规定合同双方交换以 1,000 万美元名义金额计算的美元和挪威克朗的汇率波动金额。这与购买石油主合同无关，因此，应该与购买石油主合同分拆，作为嵌入式衍生工具进行会计处理。[IAS 39 IG 第 C8 段]。

5.95　第 5.91 段第三点中提到购买或销售非金融产品的合同在交易发生的经济环境中普遍使用的货币（如本国商业交易或对外贸易中普遍使用的相对稳

environment in which the transaction takes place (for example, a relatively stable and liquid currency that is commonly used in local business transactions or external trade). This flexibility was added when IAS 39 was revised so that entities domiciled in small or developing economies may find it more convenient to denominate business contracts with entities from other small or developing economies in an internationally liquid currency (such as the US dollar or the euro) rather than the local currency of any parties to the contract.

5.96 Some have interpreted the 'commonly used' currency provision to be limited to those countries with small or developing economies and that do not have a currency that is freely convertible and able to be used in commercial transactions as set out in an example in the basis for conclusions in IAS 39. [IAS 39 para BC39]. However, others have noted that IAS 39 does not limit the application of this exception to only these territories, and so they have concluded that it also applies to contracts with entities in developed economies if the 'commonly used' criterion is met. For example, economic data supports that the US dollar is used in a wide variety of contracts by Canadian companies. It can, therefore, be argued that the US dollar is 'commonly used' in Canada even though it is not a small developing country. We see the merits of both points of view and, therefore, will accept either interpretation as an accounting policy election to be applied on a consistent basis.

5.97 The standard uses the term 'commonly used' to mean a currency that is relatively stable or liquid and that is commonly used in local business transactions or external trade. A currency is commonly used in local business transactions when monetary amounts are viewed by the general population not in terms of the local currency, but in terms of a relatively stable foreign currency and prices may be quoted in that foreign currency. [IAS 39 para BC40]. Indeed, undertaking business transactions in a stable or hard currency is fairly common for entities operating in a hyperinflationary economy as a protection against inflation. [IAS 29 para 3(b)]. It follows that the currency must be commonly used within the country, not just commonly used within a particular industry or particular market. This is an exemption to the general rule that foreign currency embedded derivatives need to be separated. The exemption's application should be supported by an appropriate analysis specific to the respective country.

定和流通的货币）。该灵活性是在修订 IAS 39 时加入的，如此一来，对处于小型和发展中经济体的主体来说，与来自其他小型和发展中经济体的主体签署的商业合同，以国际流通货币（如美元或欧元等）计价比采用合同任何一方的本国货币计价更方便。

5.96　有些人把“普遍使用”外币的规则解释为仅限于属于小型和发展中经济体的、没有可自由兑换并能够在商业交易中使用的货币的国家（如 IAS 39 结论基础中的示例所述）。[IAS 39 BC 第 39 段]。但也有人认为，IAS 39 并未将该例外的应用仅限于那些地区，因此，只要符合“普遍使用”标准，则处于发达经济体的主体所签订的合同同样适用。例如，经济数据证明，加拿大公司的各种合同广泛使用美元。因此，可以认为，美元在加拿大也是“普遍使用”的，即使加拿大并不是一个小型发展中国家。我们认可这两种观点各自的优点，因此，我们可以接受任何一种解释作为选定的会计政策并一贯应用。

5.97　准则中使用“普遍使用”一词来解释相对稳定和流通的货币，且是在本国商业交易或对外贸易中普遍使用的货币。只有当大众在国内的商业交易中不用本国货币而是用一个相对稳定的外币考虑金额并以此外币报价时，这一货币才是“普遍使用”的货币。[IAS 39 BC 第 40 段]。事实上，对于在恶性通胀经济体中经营的主体，为避免受通胀的影响，商业交易中使用稳定的或硬通货币是很普遍的。[IAS 29 第 3（b）段]。因而，该货币必须是本国普遍使用的货币，而不只是在特殊行业或特殊市场才普遍使用的货币。这是一个针对要求分拆嵌入式外币衍生工具通用规则的豁免。该豁免的应用应根据各个国家具体情况进行恰当的分析。

5.98 Many countries around the world use more than one stable or liquid currency in undertaking local business transactions or external trade. Therefore, where such countries undertake transactions in those stable or liquid currencies rather than in their local currencies, the foreign currency derivative would be viewed as closely related to the host contract and would not be accounted for separately. This assessment should be a made on a country by country basis and be supported by a detailed analysis.

Example – Contract denominated in a currency commonly used in local business transactions

An entity located in a country with a hyper-inflationary economy contracts to purchase raw materials for use in its manufacturing process. The contract is denominated in US $, a stable currency, and not in the local currency, as most local transactions and external trade are undertaken in US $.

The embedded foreign currency derivative (denominated in a currency other than the local currency) does not need to be separated as the contract is denominated in a currency that is commonly used in the local economic environment.

If, however, the contract was priced in another international stable currency say the euro rather than the US $, and euro is not a currency that is commonly used in local business transactions, the embedded derivative (euro versus the entity's functional currency) would have to be separated.

Flow chart for identifying embedded derivatives in executory contracts

5.99 As stated previously, IAS 39 provides little or no guidance on derivatives that may be embedded in purchase, sale or service contracts. As identification of such embedded derivatives can be complex, the flow charts given below are to aid in the identification process. It should be noted that the flow chart has been constructed from the discussions undertaken above and is based on a simple executory contract to buy or sell a good, that is, does not need to be assessed for an embedded lease under IFRIC 4. In practice, such contracts may contain other terms and conditions whose interaction with the host is not obvious. Options that

5.98 在进行本国商业交易或对外贸易时，世界上许多国家都使用不止一种稳定或流通货币。因此，当这些国家使用上述稳定或流通货币而非其本国货币进行交易时，外币衍生工具将被视为与主合同紧密相关，不会单独进行会计处理。这项评估应逐个国家分别进行，并有详细分析支持。

示例——以本国商业交易中普遍使用的货币计价的合同

处于某恶性通胀经济体中的某主体签署了购买其生产过程中使用的原材料合同。该合同以稳定的美元而非以本国货币计价，因为多数本国交易和对外贸易都采用美元。

该嵌入的外币衍生工具（以非本国货币计价）不需要分拆，因为该合同是以本国经济环境中普遍使用的货币计价的。

但是，如果合同是以另一种国际稳定货币计价，如欧元而非美元，而欧元并不是本国商业交易中普遍使用的货币，则该嵌入式衍生工具（欧元相对于主体功能货币）就必须分拆。

识别待执行合同中的嵌入式衍生工具的流程图

5.99 如上文所述，IAS 39 中几乎没有对可能嵌入到购买、销售或服务合同中的衍生工具作出相关规定或提供指引。由于识别此类嵌入式衍生工具可能很复杂，下面的流程图有助于如何进行识别。应注意的是，该流程图是依上述讨论构建，且基于简单的购买或销售商品的待执行合同，即无需根据 IFRIC 4 对嵌入租赁进行评估。在实务中，此类合同可能会包含其他与主合同相互影响不是很明显的条款和条件。这些条款或条件包括诸如允许通过支付违约金提前终止合同的选择权、改变交货数量的选择权以及延期交货的选择权等，这些情况可能存在疑问，需要仔细斟酌。

allow early termination of a contract by paying a penalty, options to change the quantities to be delivered and options to defer delivery are some examples of terms and condition that can be problematic and would require careful consideration.

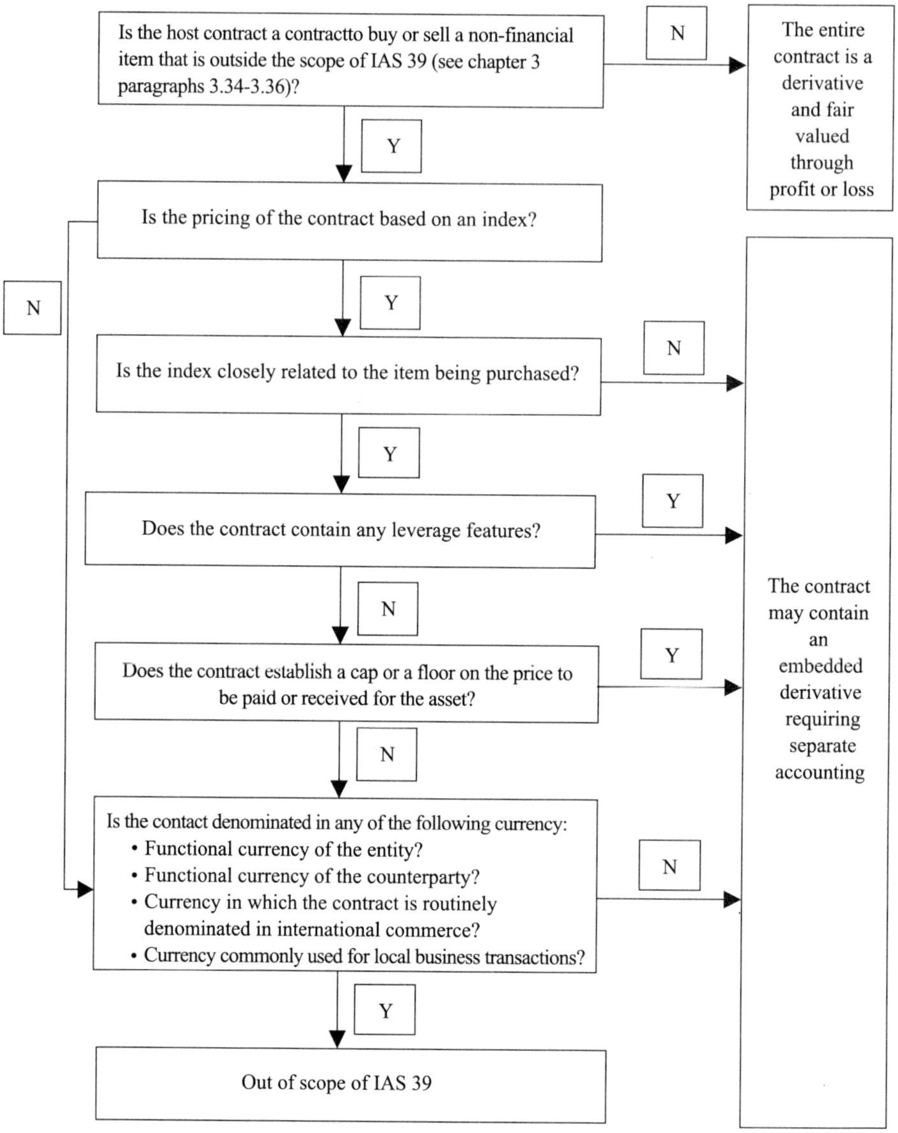

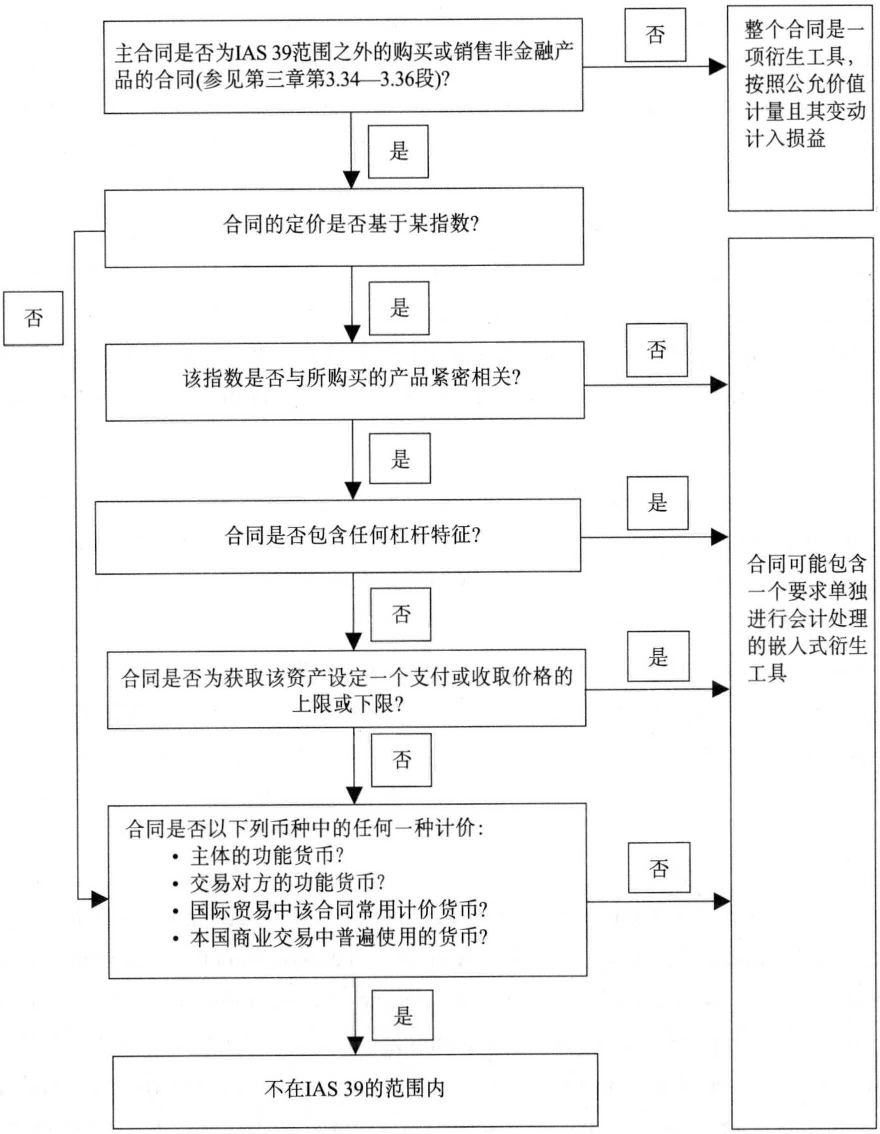
主合同是否为IAS 39范围之外的购买或销售非金融产品的合同(参见第三章第3.34—3.36段)?
否
整个合同是一项衍生工具，按照公允价值计量且其变动计入损益
是
合同的定价是否基于某指数?
否
是
该指数是否与所购买的产品紧密相关?
否
是
合同是否包含任何杠杆特征?
是
否
合同是否为获取该资产设定一个支付或收取价格的上限或下限?
是
否
合同是否以下列币种中的任何一种计价:
• 主体的功能货币?
• 交易对方的功能货币?
• 国际贸易中该合同常用计价货币?
• 本国商业交易中普遍使用的货币?
否
是
不在IAS 39的范围内
合同可能包含一个要求单独进行会计处理的嵌入式衍生工具

Embedded derivatives in insurance contracts

5.100 In recent years, a growing number of complex insurance products have been developed and many of them may contain embedded derivatives. As stated in chapter 3, derivatives embedded in insurance contracts or in contracts containing discretionary participation features are within IAS 39's scope. A derivative embedded in an insurance contract is closely related to the host insurance contract if the embedded derivative and host insurance contract are so interdependent that an entity cannot measure the embedded derivative separately (that is, without considering the host contract). [IAS 39 para AG 33(h)]. However, if a policy combines a derivative instrument with an insurance contract thereby creating a hybrid instrument, the embedded derivative may have to be separated from the insurance contract in accordance with IAS 39, unless the embedded derivative itself is an insurance contract. [IFRS 4 para 7].

5.101 Contracts such as equity indexed annuities, equity indexed life insurance and embedded guarantees of minimum returns may contain embedded derivatives that are not closely related to the host insurance contract and will have to be separated and accounted for under IAS 39. Much of the guidance discussed above also applies to embedded derivatives in insurance contracts as it does to any other contract. However, IFRS 4 paragraph 8 introduces a major exception to the principle of separation of embedded derivatives that are not closely related to the host contract. IFRS 4 permits an insurer to not separate a policyholder's embedded put option (also known as a cash surrender option) embedded in a host insurance contract when the option price is a fixed amount or a fixed amount and an interest rate. This exemption applies at all times even when the exercise price differs from the host insurance liability's carrying amount. The requirement to separate does, however, apply when the surrender value varies in response to a change in an equity or commodity price or index or a similar variable. [IFRS 4 para 8]. IFRS 4 paragraph 9 specifies that the same exemption applies to issuers of financial instruments with a discretionary participation feature. This area of accounting for embedded derivatives should always be considered in conjunction with IFRS 4. The implementation guidance to IFRS 4 contains many examples that illustrate the treatment of embedded derivatives contained in insurance contracts. [IFRS 4 paras

保险合同中的嵌入式衍生工具

5.100　近年来，越来越多的复杂保险产品被开发，其中很多产品都可能包含嵌入式衍生工具。如第三章所述，嵌入到保险合同或包含相机参与分红特征合同中的衍生工具都在 IAS 39 的范围内。如果嵌入保险合同的衍生工具与主保险合同相互依赖，致使主体无法单独计量该嵌入式衍生工具（即不考虑主合同），则该嵌入式衍生工具与保险主合同紧密相关。[IAS 39 AG 第 33（h）段]。但是，如果某保单将衍生工具与相关的保险合同相结合，而创造了一个混合工具，则可能必须根据 IAS 39 将嵌入式衍生工具与保险合同分拆，除非该嵌入式衍生工具自身就是一个保险合同。[IFRS 4 第 7 段]。

5.101　一些诸如与权益指数挂钩的年金、与权益指数挂钩的人寿保险以及嵌入最低回报担保等的合同可能包含不与主保险合同紧密相关的嵌入式衍生工具，这些嵌入式衍生工具必须根据 IAS 39 进行分拆并单独进行会计处理。上文讨论的适用于其他合同的指引多数也适用于保险合同中的衍生工具。但是，IFRS 4 第 8 段引入了针对分拆不与主合同紧密相关的嵌入式衍生工具原则的一个主要例外。IFRS 4 允许承保人不分拆投保人嵌入主保险合同的嵌入看跌期权（也称为现金退保期权），只要行权价为固定金额或固定金额加某一利率。该例外在任何时候均适用，即使行权价与主保险负债的账面价值不同。但是，如果退保金额随着权益或商品价格或指数或类似变量的变化而变化，则分拆要求还是适用。[IFRS 4 第 8 段]。IFRS 4 第 9 段明确，同样的豁免适用于相机参与分红特征的金融工具发行人。在该领域对嵌入式衍生工具进行会计处理时，应始终结合 IFRS 4 进行考虑。IFRS 4 的实施指南包含许多示例来说明保险合同所含的嵌入式衍生工具的处理方法。[IFRS 4 IG 第 3、4 段]。

IG 3, 4].

Accounting for embedded derivatives

5.102 On initial recognition, similar to all financial assets and liabilities, a financial instrument containing an embedded derivative is recognised at its fair value, that is, the fair value of the entire instrument. If the consideration paid / transaction price is not equal to the fair value of the instrument as a whole, then a day 1 gain or loss may arise. Whether such a gain or loss is recognised immediately within profit or loss depends on whether the conditions in paragraph AG76 of IAS 39 are met (as discussed in further detail in chapter 9). In summary, a day 1 gain or loss is recognised only when the fair value of the entire instrument is evidenced by either other observable current market transactions in the same instrument (without modification or packaging) or it is based on a valuation technique whose variables include only data from observable markets.

5.103 When an embedded derivative is required to be separated from a host contract, the derivative element must be measured at fair value on the balance sheet, with changes in fair value being accounted for through profit or loss, consistent with the accounting for a freestanding derivative. At initial recognition of the embedded derivative, the embedded derivative's fair value must be determined before that of the host contract. Paragraph AG28 of IAS 39 states that "*The initial carrying amount of the host instrument is the residual after separating the embedded derivative*". The host contract's carrying value at initial recognition is the difference between the fair value of the hybrid contract as a whole and the embedded derivative's fair value.

5.104 While a day 1 gain or loss may arise on the initial recognition of the entire instrument, if the criteria in paragraph AG76 of IAS 39 are met (see para 5.102), a day 1 gain or loss will not arise as a result of separating the embedded derivative from the host contract.

5.105 Published price quotations in an active market are normally the best evidence of fair value. Valuation techniques are used to determine the derivative's fair value if there is no active market for the embedded derivative. Valuing a

嵌入式衍生工具的会计处理

5.102 在初始确认时，类似于所有金融资产和负债，包含嵌入式衍生工具的金融工具以公允价值确认，即以整个工具的公允价值确认。如果支付的对价/交易价格不等于整个工具的公允价值，则可能会产生首日利得或损失。是否应立即将该利得或损失确认计入损益，取决于是否满足 IAS 39 AG 第 76 段的条件（如第九章中所详细讨论的）。总体而言，只有当整个工具的公允价值得到相同工具（无变更或打包的工具）的其他可观察到的当前市场交易证明或整个工具的公允价值是基于所用变量只包含可观察市场数据的估值技术时，才确认首日利得或损失。

5.103 当需要将嵌入式衍生工具与主合同分拆时，与独立存在的衍生工具的会计处理一致，该衍生工具要素必须在资产负债表上以公允价值计量且其公允价值变动计入损益。在初始确认嵌入式衍生工具时，应在主合同之前先确定嵌入式衍生工具的公允价值。IAS 39 AG 第 28 段规定：“*主工具的初始账面价值为分拆嵌入式衍生工具后的余值*”。主合同在初始确认时的账面价值为整个混合合同公允价值与嵌入式衍生工具公允价值的差额。

5.104 尽管在初始确认整个工具时可能会产生首日利得或损失，但如果符合 IAS 39 AG 第 76 的标准（参见第 5. 102 段），则不会因为从主合同中分拆嵌入式衍生工具而产生首日利得或损失。

5.105 活跃市场的公开报价通常是公允价值的最佳证据。如果没有有关嵌入式衍生工具的活跃市场，则采用估值技术确定衍生工具的公允价值。对衍生工具进行估值通常涉及管理层在进行某些估计时（如折现率、未来利率的外

derivative usually involves the exercise of judgement by management in making certain estimates such as the discount rate, extrapolation of future interest rates, foreign exchange rates and so on. The use of estimates for certain valuation parameters could be subjective, especially for long-term contracts that are common in the energy industry. Furthermore, certain embedded derivatives, in particular those arising from complex structured products, may contain several underlying variables making the valuation process complex.

5.106 If an entity is unable to determine reliably the fair value of an embedded derivative on the basis of its terms and conditions (for example, because the embedded derivative is based on an unquoted equity instrument), the embedded derivative's fair value is the difference between the fair value of the hybrid (combined) instrument and the host contract's fair value, if those can be determined reliably. [IAS 39 para 13]. If the entity is unable to determine the embedded derivative's fair value using this method either at initial recognition or at a subsequent financial reporting date, the entity should fair value the hybrid (combined) instrument and designate it as at fair value through profit or loss. [IAS 39 paras 12, 13]. Designation of financial instruments is discussed in chapter 6.

Example – Debt instrument that is exchangeable into shares of an unlisted entity

An entity issues a debt instrument that is exchangeable into shares of an unlisted entity whose fair value cannot be reliably measured. If the debt instrument is converted the unlisted equity investment would be recorded on the balance sheet at cost in accordance with paragraph 46(c) of IAS 39.

In this situation, the equity exchangeable feature is not closely related to the debt host and should be separated. However, although the equity instrument's fair value cannot be measured reliably, it would not be appropriate to measure the embedded derivative at cost. Instead, the entire combined contract is designated as a financial instrument at fair value through profit or loss. [IAS 39 para 12]. This presumes that the combined contract's fair value can be measured reliably.

推、汇率等）所做的判断。某些估值参数所采用的估计可能具有主观性，尤其对能源行业常见的长期合同而言。此外，部分嵌入式衍生工具，尤其是因复杂的结构性产品而产生的嵌入式衍生工具，可能包含若干标的变量，这些变量会使估值过程复杂化。

5.106 如果主体无法基于相关条款和条件可靠地确定嵌入式衍生工具的公允价值（例如，由于嵌入式衍生工具是基于一个无公开报价的权益工具），则该嵌入式衍生工具的公允价值为混合（组合）工具的公允价值与主合同公允价值的差额（若能可靠地确定这两个公允价值）。[IAS 39 第 13 段]。如果在初始确认时或在后续的财务报告日，若主体用此方法无法确定嵌入式衍生工具的公允价值，则主体应对混合（组合）工具进行公允价值估值，并指定为以公允价值计量且其变动计入损益。[IAS 39 第 12、13 段]。金融工具的指定在第六章中讨论。

示例——可兑换为未上市主体股票的债务工具

某主体发行了可兑换为未上市主体股票（无法可靠地计量其公允价值）的债务工具。如果该债务工具被转换，则该未上市权益投资将根据 IAS 39 第 46（c）段以成本记入资产负债表。

在此情形下，权益转换特征不与主债务合同紧密相关，应分拆出来。但是，尽管无法可靠地计量权益工具的公允价值，但以成本价计量嵌入式衍生工具也欠妥。相反，整个组合合同应被指定为以公允价值计量且其变动计入损益的金融工具。[IAS 39 第 12 段]。此时假设能可靠地计量组合合同的公允价值。

However, the entity might conclude that the combined instrument's equity component may be sufficiently significant to preclude it from obtaining a reliable estimate of the fair value of the entire instrument. In that case, the combined instrument is measured at cost less impairment. [IAS 39 para IG C.11].

It should be noted that as the fair value of the embedded derivative that is linked to, and must be settled by delivery of, the above unlisted equity instrument cannot be measured, the embedded derivative cannot be designated as a hedging instrument. [IAS 39 para AG 96].

5.107 The requirement to identify an embedded derivative in a hybrid instrument, assess whether it should be separated from the host contract and, for those that do need to be separated, measure the derivatives at fair value at initial recognition and subsequently, can be complex or may result in less reliable measures than measuring the entire instrument at fair value through profit or loss.

5.108 Therefore, if a contract contains one or more embedded derivatives, an entity may designate the entire hybrid (combined) contract as a financial asset or financial liability at fair value through profit or loss, unless:

- the embedded derivative(s) does not significantly modify the cash flows that otherwise would be required by the contract; or
- it is clear with little or no analysis when a similar hybrid (combined) instrument is first considered that separation of the embedded derivative(s) is prohibited, such as a pre-payment option embedded in a loan that permits the holder to pre-pay the loan for approximately its amortised cost.

[IAS 39 para 11A].

The option to designate the entire instrument at fair value through profit or loss may be particularly helpful to banks and other entities that issue structured products containing several embedded derivatives.

5.109 If an embedded derivative is separated, the host contract should be accounted for in accordance with IAS 39 if it is a financial instrument and in accordance with other appropriate standards if it is not a financial instrument. IAS

但是，主体可能会得出结论，认为组合工具的权益成分可能足够重大，以致会妨碍对整个工具的公允价值进行可靠估计。在此情形下，该组合工具应按成本减去减值准备计量。[IAS 39 IG 第 C. 11 段]。

应注意的是，由于该嵌入式衍生工具（与上述未上市主体工具挂钩且必须通过交付上述主体工具进行结算）的公允价值无法计量，其不能被指定为套期工具。[IAS 39 AG 第 96 段]。

5.107　识别混合工具中的嵌入式衍生工具、评估该嵌入式衍生工具是否需要与主合同分拆，对于确实需要分拆的衍生工具，要在初始确认及以后期间以公允价值计量，上述这些要求可能会比较复杂，或者会导致计量结果不如将整个工具计量为公允价值且变动计入损益那么可靠。

5.108　因此，如果某合同包含一个或多个嵌入衍生工具，主体可以将整个混合（组合）合同指定为以公允价值计量且其变动计入损益的金融资产或金融负债，除非：

- 嵌入衍生工具对合同所要求的现金流量没有改变；或

- 当首次考虑类似的混合（组合）工具时，仅进行少量分析或者不用分析就可以确定，不应分拆该嵌入式衍生工具，如一项贷款中嵌入的提前还款选择权，该选择权允许持有人以等于摊余成本的金额提前还款。

[IAS 39 第 11A 段]。

对于银行及其他发行包含多项嵌入式衍生工具的结构性产品的主体来说，将整个工具指定为以公允价值计量且其变动计入损益的选择权是非常有利的。

5.109　如果将嵌入式衍生工具分离，若主合同是金融工具，则该主合同应根据 IAS 39 进行会计处理；若主合同不是金融工具，则该主合同应根据其他适用的准则进行会计处理。IAS 39 并未规定嵌入式衍生工具是否应在资产负债

39 does not address whether an embedded derivative should be presented separately on the face of the balance sheet. [IAS 39 para 11].

Separating a non-option-based embedded derivative

5.110 When separating a non-option-based embedded derivative, such as an embedded forward or swap, the standard requires the embedded derivative to be separated from its host contract on the basis of its stated or implied substantive terms, so as to result in it having a fair value of zero at initial recognition. [IAS 39 para AG 28]. If it were permitted to separate embedded non-option derivatives on other terms, a single hybrid instrument could be decomposed into an infinite variety of combinations of host instruments and embedded derivatives. However, as already explained in paragraph 5.28 above, an embedded derivative that is not already clearly present should not be separated, that is a cash flow that does not exist cannot be created (with exception of, for example, assuming a functional currency cash flow in an embedded FX forward contract). If the terms of an embedded forward contract were determined so as to result in a fair value other than zero at the inception of the hybrid instrument, that amount would essentially represent a borrowing or lending. Therefore, it is inappropriate to separate an embedded non-option derivative on terms that result in a fair value other than zero at the inception of the hybrid instrument. [IAS 39 paras IG C1, C2]. This means that the forward price assumed in the embedded derivative should generally be at market rates observed when the embedded derivative is separated.

Example – Separation of a non-option-based derivative to produce zero fair value at inception

Entity X advances C900 to entity Y for one year at 6% interest rate and concurrently enters into an equity-based derivative in which it will receive any increase or pay any decrease in the current market price (C100) of entity Z's equity shares. The current forward price for one year for entity Z's equity shares is C200. These two transactions (the loan and the derivative) can be bundled into a structured note that could have almost an infinite variety of terms. Three possible contractual terms for the structured note that would be purchased by entity X for C900 are shown below.

表上单独列报。[IAS 39 第 11 段]。

分拆非基于期权的嵌入式衍生工具

5.110　分拆嵌入远期或互换等非基于期权的嵌入式衍生工具时，准则要求依据该嵌入式衍生工具明示或暗含的实质性条款将其从主合同分离，以使其在初始确认时的公允价值为零。[IAS 39 AG 第 28 段]。如果允许依据其他条款分拆嵌入式非期权衍生工具，则单个混合工具可被分解为无数各种各样主工具和嵌入式衍生工具的组合。但是，正如上文第 5.28 段所解释的，非明显存在的嵌入式衍生工具不应分拆，更确切地说，不能创造不存在的现金流量（但有例外情形，如嵌入外汇远期合同中假设存在的功能货币现金流量）。如果确定了嵌入远期合同的条款使得其公允价值在混合工具开始时的公允价值不为零，则该金额实际代表的是借入或借出款项。因此，在对嵌入式衍生工具进行分拆时，如果所依据的条款使得其在混合工具开始时的公允价值不为零，则依据该条款进行分拆是不适当的。[IAS 39 IG 第 C1、C2 段]。这意味着，嵌入式衍生工具中假设的远期价格通常应为该嵌入式衍生工具分拆时所观察到的市场利率。

示例——分拆非基于期权的衍生工具以使其初始公允价值为零

主体 X 向主体 Y 预付 900 元，为期 1 年，利率按 6% 计算，同时，主体 X 还签署了一个基于权益的衍生工具，根据该工具，主体 X 将收到或支付主体 Z 权益股票现行市价（100 元）的任何上升或下跌金额。主体 Z 权益股票一年期的现行远期价格是 200 元。这两个交易（贷款和衍生工具）可捆绑为一个几乎可有无数种条款组合的结构性票据。主体 X 以 900 元购买的结构性票据可能有三种合同条款，如下所示。

- Entity X to receive at the end of the year C954 plus any excess (minus any shortfall) in the current market price of entity Z's equity shares over (or under) C200.

- Entity X to receive at the end of the year C1,054 plus any excess (minus any shortfall) in the current market price of entity Z's equity shares over (or under) C300.

- Entity X to receive at the end of the year C755 plus any excess (minus any shortfall) in the current market price of entity Z's equity shares over (or under) C1.

All the above terms of the structured note will provide the same cash flows, given a specified market price of entity Z's shares. If the market price of entity Z's shares remains at C200 at the end of year 1, entity A will receive C954 under all the three options. Similarly, if the market price of entity Z's shares increases to C306, entity A will receive C1,060 under all the options.

As is apparent, the difference in terms under the above three options are totally arbitrary, because those differences have no impact on the ultimate cash flows under the structured note. Thus those differences are not substantive and should have no influence on how the terms of the embedded derivatives are identified. Therefore, the hybrid instrument's separation into an embedded derivative and a host debt instrument should be the same for all the three options described above for the structured note.

That separation would generally result in the structured note being accounted for as a debt host contract with an initial carrying amount of C900 and a fixed annual interest rate of 6% and an embedded forward contract with C200 forward price, which results in an initial fair value of zero.

Separating an option-based embedded derivative

5.111 An embedded option-based derivative (such as an embedded put, call, cap, floor or swaption) is separated from its host contract on the basis of the option feature's stated terms. The initial host instrument's carrying amount is the

■ 主体 X 将在年末收到 954 元，加上（减去）主体 Z 权益股票的现行市价高于（低于）200 元的所有超额部分（不足额）。

■ 主体 X 将在年末收到 1,054 元，加上（减去）主体 Z 权益股票的现行市价高于（低于）300 元的所有超额部分（不足额）。

■ 主体 X 将在年末收到 755 元，加上（减去）主体 Z 权益股票的现行市价高于（低于）1 元的所有超额部分（不足额）。

根据给定的主体 Z 股票的具体市价，所有上述结构性票据的条款都将提供相同的现金流量。如果主体 Z 股票的市价在第一年年末时仍然是 200 元，则主体 A 在这三个选项下均收到 954 元。同样，如果主体 Z 股票的市价增至 306 元，则主体 A 在这三个选项下均收到 1,060 元。

显然，上述三个选项的条款差异完全具有随意性，因为这些差异对结构性票据的最终现金流量并无影响。因而，上述差异是非实质性的，对如何识别嵌入式衍生工具的条款并不产生影响。因此，对结构性票据的上述三个选项来说，将混合工具分拆为嵌入式衍生工具和主债务工具应该是一样的。

通常，分拆将导致结构性票据作为一个主债务合同（初始账面价值为 900 元，固定年利率为 6%）和一个嵌入远期合同（远期价格为 200 元，其结果是初始公允价值为零）进行会计处理。

分拆基于期权的嵌入式衍生工具

5.111 基于期权的嵌入式衍生工具（如嵌入看跌期权、看涨期权、上限、下限或互换选择权）是基于期权特征所规定的条款从其主合同中分拆出来。主合同的初始账面价值为分拆嵌入式衍生工具后的剩余金额。[IAS 39 AG 第 28

residual amount after separating the embedded derivative. [IAS 39 para AG 28].

5.112 The implementation guidance explains that the economic behaviour of a hybrid instrument with an option-based embedded is fundamentally different from a non-option based derivative and depends critically on the strike price (or strike rate) specified for the option feature in the hybrid instrument.

5.113 If an entity were required to identify the terms of an embedded option-based derivative so as to achieve a fair value of the embedded derivative of zero, the strike price (or strike rate) generally would have to be determined so as to result in the option being infinitely out-of-the-money. This would imply a zero probability of the option feature being exercised. However, since the probability of the option feature in a hybrid instrument being exercised generally is not zero, it would be inconsistent with the likely economic behaviour of the hybrid instrument to assume an initial fair value of zero for the embedded derivative. Similarly, if an entity were required to identify the terms of an embedded option-based derivative so as to achieve an intrinsic value of zero for the embedded derivative, the strike price (or strike rate) would have to be assumed to equal the price (or rate) of the underlying variable at the initial recognition of the hybrid instrument. In this case, the option's fair value would consist only of time value. However, such an assumption would not be consistent with the likely economic behaviour of the hybrid instrument, including the probability of the option feature being exercised, unless the agreed strike price was indeed equal to the price (or rate) of the underlying variable at the initial recognition of the hybrid instrument. [IAS 39 para IG C.2].

5.114 Adjusting the strike price of an option-based embedded derivative, therefore, alters the nature of the hybrid instrument, whereas adjusting the strike price of a forward based embedded derivative does not necessarily alter the nature of the hybrid instrument. For example, if an option based embedded derivative is in-the-money, that intrinsic value does not represent a lending activity since the option may never be exercised (that is, it may expire out-of-the money due to a change in the underlying). Therefore, the separation of an option-based embedded derivative (including any embedded put, call, cap, floor, caption, floortion or swaption feature in a hybrid instrument) should be based on the stated terms of the

段]。

5.112　根据实施指南的解释，带有基于期权的嵌入式衍生工具的混合工具的经济行为与非基于期权的衍生工具存在根本上的不同，其关键取决于混合工具中规定的期权特征的行权价（或行权比率）。

5.113　如果要求主体识别基于期权的嵌入式衍生工具的条款来实现嵌入式衍生工具的公允价值为零，则通常必须确定一个使得该期权永久价外的行权价（或行权比率）。这意味着执行该期权特征的概率为零。但是，由于混合工具中的期权特征被执行的概率一般不为零，假定该嵌入式衍生工具的初始公允价值为零将与混合工具可能的经济行为不一致。同样，如果要求主体识别基于期权的嵌入式衍生工具条款来实现嵌入式衍生工具的内在价值为零，则必须假设行权价（或行权比率）等于混合工具初始确认时标的变量的价格（比率）。在这种情况下，期权的公允价值仅仅由时间价值构成。但是，如此假设将会与混合工具可能出现的经济行为（包括执行该期权特征的概率）不一致，除非议定的行权价确实等于混合工具初始确认时标的变量的价格（比率）。[IAS 39 IG 第 C.2 段]。

5.114　因此，调整基于期权的嵌入式衍生工具的行权价将改变混合工具的性质，而调整远期嵌入式衍生工具的行权价却并不一定会改变混合工具的性质。例如，当基于期权的嵌入式衍生工具在价内时，其内在价值并不代表一项借款活动，因为该期权可能不会被行权（即因标的变化导致期满时为价外）。因此，对基于期权的嵌入式衍生工具（包括混合工具中嵌入的任何看跌期权、看涨期权、上限、下限、上限选择权、下限选择权或互换选择权特征等）进行分拆应基于混合工具书面文件中规定的该期权特征的条款。其结果是，在混合工具初始确认时，嵌入式衍生工具的公允价值或内在价值不一定等于零。[IAS 39 IG 第 C.2 段]。

option feature documented in the hybrid instrument. As a result, the embedded derivative would not necessarily have a fair value or intrinsic value equal to zero at the initial recognition of the hybrid instrument. [IAS 39 para IG C. 2].

Multiple embedded derivatives

5. 115 A host contract may contain more than one embedded derivative. Each individual derivative must be identified and assessed to see whether they warrant separate accounting. Separate accounting is required in circumstances where the derivatives relate to different risk exposures and are readily separable and independent of each other. [IAS 39 para AG 29].

5. 116 Where, however, it is not possible to value each embedded derivative separately because of inter-dependencies, they should be treated as a single compound embedded derivative and valued in accordance with the guidance discussed from paragraph 5. 102 above. [IAS 39 para AG 29].

Example 1 – Callable convertible bond

An entity issues 20, 000 callable convertible bonds at a total par value of C2 million. Each bond pays fixed interest and is convertible, at the holder's option, at any time up to maturity into the entity's ordinary shares. Each bond also contains an embedded call option that gives the bond's issuer the right to call and redeem the bond at any time before maturity.

The bond has two embedded options that are held by different parties. The bond's holder has the option to convert the bond into a specified number of shares. The issuer has the option to call back the bond and pay an amount generally at a premium over par value.

From the issuer's perspective, the equity conversion option is an equity instrument of the issuer and, therefore, it is outside IAS 39's scope. Under IAS 32, the issuer must separate the equity and the liability elements of the compound instrument. As far as the issuer's call option (the right to call and redeem the bond) is concerned, this must be valued separately (using an option pricing model) as it is distinct in character and risk from the written

多种嵌入式衍生工具

5.115　主合同可包含一个以上的嵌入式衍生工具。必须识别和评估每个衍生工具，以判断其是否要独立进行会计处理。如果这些衍生工具与不同风险敞口相关联、容易分离且彼此独立，则要求单独进行会计处理。[IAS 39 AG 第 29 段]。

5.116　但是，因这些嵌入式衍生工具相互依存而无法对各衍生工具单独估值的，这些嵌入式衍生工具应该作为一个单一的复合嵌入式衍生工具按上文第 5.102 段起讨论的指引进行估值。[IAS 39 AG 第 29 段]。

示例 1——可赎回可转债

主体发行了 2 万张总面值为 200 万元的可赎回可转债。每张债券须支付固定利息，且持有人在到期前可以随时将其转换为主体的普通股。同时，每张债券还包括嵌入看涨期权，给予债券发行人在债券到期前随时赎回和偿付债券的权利。

该债券包含由不同方持有的两个嵌入期权。债券持有人拥有将该债券转换为特定数量股票的期权。发行人拥有通常以超出面值的溢价赎回该债券的期权。

从发行人的角度看，权益转换权是发行人的权益工具，不在 IAS 39 的范围内。根据 IAS 32 的规定，发行人必须分离复合工具中的权益和负债要素。就发行人的看涨期权（赎回并偿付债券的权利）而言，其必须单独进行估值（采用期权定价模型），因为其特征和风险与签出的权益转换权均不同。在按照 IAS 32 的规定将权益成分分离之前，其价值包含在负债部分中。该看涨期权需要单独进行会计处理，除非该期权的行权价在每

equity conversion option. This value is then included in the liability component before separating the equity component under IAS 32. The call option will need to be accounted for separately unless the option exercise price is approximately equal on each exercise date to the amortised cost of the host debt instrument or reimburses the lender for the present value of lost interest for the remainder of the host contract. [IAS 39 para AG 30(g); IAS 32 paras 31, IE 37].

From the holders' perspective, the purchased call option (to convert) and the written call (to redeem) are interlinked. This is because as the share price increases the issuer is likely to call the bond, thereby depriving the holder of the opportunity to make further returns on the bond. Although the optimal policy is to call the bond when its conversion price is equal to the call price, in practice, companies can establish a variety of call policies such as calling the instant the market value of the convertibles rises above the call price or waiting until the market value is well in excess of the call price. This interaction between the two options implies that they have to be valued together using an option pricing model. The single compound derivative is then accounted for separately from the host plain vanilla bond. Alternatively, the holder can designate the entire bond as at fair value through profit or loss as discussed in paragraph 5. 108 above.

Example 2 – Bond with embedded forward and option features

An entity issues a debt instrument at par with a term of 5 years. The debt is callable 3 years after the issue. If the debt is called, the holder will receive an amount that is adjusted by the percentage change in the FTSE 100 index and that amount doubles if the FTSE 100 index exceeds a certain level.

In the above instrument, there are two embedded derivatives – a forward contract that pays double if the FTSE 100 index exceeds a certain level and an option that is linked to changes in the FTSE 100 index. It is not appropriate to separate both a forward and an option on the equity index, because those derivative features relate to the same risk exposure. Instead the forward and option elements are treated as a single compound, embedded derivative.

个行权日都大致等于主债务工具的摊余成本。［IAS 39 AG 第30（g）段；IAS 32 第31 段，IE 第37 段］。

从持有人的角度看，其购买看涨期权（转换权）签出的看涨期权（赎回权）是相互关联的。这是因为当股价上涨时发行人很可能会赎回该债券，因而是持有人丧失了利用此债券获取更多回报的机会。尽管最佳的策略是当转换价格等于赎回价格时赎回债券，但在实务中公司可设立多种赎回策略，诸如当可转债的市场价超过赎回价格时立即赎回或等到市场价值大大超过赎回价格时才赎回。这两种期权的相互作用表明其需要采用期权定价模型一起进行估值。该单一复合衍生工具应与传统主债券分拆，单独进行会计处理。或者，持有人可以如上文第 5. 108 段所讨论的，将整个债券指定为以公允价值计量且其变动计入损益。

示例 2——带有嵌入远期和期权特征的债券

某主体按面值发行期限为五年的债务工具。发行人可在发行三年后赎回该债券。如果该债务被赎回，持有人将收到按照 FTSE100 指数变动比例调整的金额，且如果 FTSE100 指数到达一定水平，该金额将翻倍。

上述工具包含两个嵌入式衍生工具，一个是 FTSE100 指数超过某一水平时支付双倍金额的远期合同，另一个是与 FTSE100 指数变动挂钩的期权。由于这些衍生特征与同一风险敞口相关，将这两个都基于权益指数的远期合同和期权分离是不合适的。相反，该远期合同和期权要素应作为一个单一复合嵌入式衍生工具进行处理。

Embedded derivatives as hedging instruments

5.117 IAS 39 does not restrict the circumstances in which a derivative may be designated as a hedging instrument provided the hedge accounting criteria are met (subject to some limitations on written options). [IAS 39 para 72]. Therefore, embedded derivatives that are accounted for separately can be designated as hedging instruments, like any free standing derivatives, as long as the hedge accounting criteria are met. Hedge accounting is considered in chapter 10.

嵌入式衍生工具作为套期工具

5.117　只要满足套期会计运用条件（需考虑对签出期权的一些限制），IAS 39 对何种情形下能够将衍生工具指定为套期工具并没有限制。[IAS 39 第 72 段]。因此，单独进行会计处理的嵌入式衍生工具可以像任何独立存在的衍生工具一样被指定为套期工具，只要满足套期会计运用条件。套期会计在第十章中讨论。

Chapter 9 Measurement of financial assets and liabilities

Content

第九章　金融资产和金融负债的计量

目　录

Introduction

9.1 An entity recognises a financial asset or a financial liability when it first becomes a party to the contractual rights and obligations in the contract. It is, therefore, necessary to measure those contractual rights and obligations on initial recognition. Under IAS 39, all financial instruments are measured initially by reference to their fair value, which is *normally* the transaction price, that is, the fair value of the consideration given or received. However, this will not always be the case.

9.2 Subsequent to initial recognition, IAS 39's measurement approach is best described as a 'mixed attribute' model with certain assets and liabilities measured at cost and others at fair value. The model depends upon an instrument's classification into one of the four categories of financial assets or one of the two categories of financial liabilities discussed in chapter 6. For example, depending on the nature of the instrument and management's intentions, a fixed interest security intended to be held-to-maturity would be measured at amortised cost and not at fair value. Notwithstanding this, as explained in chapter 6, the standard gives entities the option to classify financial instruments that meet certain special criteria at fair value with all gains and losses taken to profit and loss. The ability for entities to use the fair value option simplifies the application of IAS 39 by mitigating some anomalies that result from the use of the mixed measurement model.

9.3 This chapter deals with IAS 39's basic measurement requirements and addresses the concepts of fair value and amortised cost, including the use of the effective interest method and the standard's impairment model. However, the special form of accounting that applies when a financial asset or liability is designated by management in a hedging relationship is covered in chapter 10.

9.4 In November 2009 the IASB issued the first part of IFRS 9 relating to classification and measurement of financial instruments. The new requirements apply a consistent approach to classifying financial assets based on the entity's business model for managing the financial assets and the contractual cash flow characteristics of the financial asset and replace the numerous categories of financial

引言

9.1　当主体首次成为合同中的合同权利和义务方时，应对金融资产或金融负债进行确认。因此，在初始确认时，需要对这些合同权利和义务进行计量。根据《国际会计准则第39号——金融工具：确认和计量》（“IAS 39”）的规定，初始计量时所有金融工具以其各自的公允价值为依据。公允价值通常为交易价格，即已支付或已接受对价的公允价值。但是也有例外的情况。

9.2　初始确认之后，IAS 39中的计量方法最宜被称为“混合计量”模型，即部分资产和负债按照成本计量，其他按照公允价值计量。金融工具依其分类，可划分为第六章中所述的四种金融资产或两种金融负债。例如：根据金融工具性质和管理层意图，对将要持有至到期的固定利率证券，以摊余成本而非公允价值进行计量。尽管如此，如第六章所述，该准则允许主体选择将满足某些特定标准的金融工具按公允价值计量，并将所有的利得和损失计入损益。主体对公允价值计量的选择权减少了由于使用混合计量模型而产生的某些异常情况，从而简化了IAS 39的应用。

9.3　本章说明了IAS 39的基本计量要求，阐述了公允价值和摊余成本的概念，包括实际利率法的使用以及该准则的减值模型。但是，对于管理层指定的套期关系中的金融资产或负债的特殊会计形式，将在第十章予以说明。

9.4　2009年11月，国际会计准则理事会（“IASB”）发布了《国际财务报告准则第9号——金融工具》（“IFRS 9”）第一部分，即金融工具分类和计量的相关内容。新规定以主体管理金融资产的业务模式及金融资产的合同现金流量特征为基础，运用一致的方法对金融资产进行分类，从而替换了IAS 39中金融资产的多种分类方法。金融资产将以摊余成本或公允价值计量，并保留

assets in IAS 39. Financial assets will be measured at amortised cost or fair value and the fair value option is retained but the presentation of gains and losses is changed. The IASB updated IFRS 9 in October 2010 to include guidance on classification and measurement of financial liabilities and on derecognition of financial instruments. The classification and measurement of financial liabilities under IFRS 9 remains the same as under IAS 39 except where an entity has chosen to measure a liability at fair value through profit or loss (see para 9.155). On 15 November 2011, the IASB tentatively decided to consider making limited modifications to IFRS 9 on an expedited basis to deal with specific application issues, interaction with the insurance project and convergence with the US-based FASB. A separate re-exposure draft 'Amortised cost and impairment of financial assets' is expected on the expected-loss impairment model and the IASB's tentative decisions to use a three bucket approach that determines the amount and timing of credit losses to be recognised. This model is expected to replace the numerous impairment methods in IAS 39 that arise from the different classification categories. It is the IASB's intention that IFRS 9 will ultimately replace IAS 39 in its entirety. IFRS 9 is dealt with in chapter 12.

9.5 In May 2011 the IASB issued IFRS 13. The standard provides a single source of fair value measurement guidance. It clarifies the definition of fair value, provides a framework for measuring fair value and requires disclosures for all assets and liabilities measured at fair value, on recurring (for example some financial instruments) or non-recurring (for example intangible assets acquired in a business combination) basis. The standard does not determine when fair value measurements are required. The measurement guidance in IFRS 13 will apply to all fair value measurements except for those within the scope of IFRS 2 or IAS 17, and certain other measurements that are required by other standards and are similar to, but are not, fair value. Disclosures are required for assets and liabilities measured at fair value with some exceptions. IFRS 13 amended IAS 39 and IFRS 9 to remove their guidance on fair value measurement. IFRS 13 is effective for annual periods beginning on or after 1 January 2013, with earlier application permitted, and it is applied prospectively as of the beginning of the annual period in which it is initially applied. IFRS 13 is dealt with in chapter 34 of the IFRS Manual of Accounting. In this chapter, certain guidance on fair value

了公允价值选择权，但利得和损失的列报有所改变。2010 年 10 月，IASB 更新了 IFRS 9，在其中纳入了金融负债分类和计量的指南和金融工具终止确认的指南。IFRS 9 中的金融负债分类和计量与 IAS 39 中的规定一致，但主体选择以公允价值计量且其变动计入损益的负债除外（参见第 9. 155 段）。2011 年 11 月 15 日，为了迅速应对特定应用问题、针对与保险项目的相互影响、与美国 FASB 趋同，IASB 暂时决定考虑对 IFRS 9 作有限的修改。将另有一份单独的再次征求意见稿“摊余成本和金融资产减值”提议预期损失减值模型，包括了 IASB 的暂时性决定，即使用三组别法来决定确认预期损失的金额和时间。这一模型将取代 IAS 39 中规定的针对不同分类的多种减值方法。IASB 意在以 IFRS 9 最终替代 IAS 39 的全部内容。第十二章将阐述 IFRS 9 的内容。

9. 5　2011 年 5 月，IASB 发布了《国际财务报告准则第 13 号——公允价值计量》（“IFRS 13”）。该准则作为公允价值计量的统一指南，澄清了公允价值的定义，提供了公允价值计量框架并针对经常性（例如某些金融工具）及非经常性（例如在业务合并中取得的无形资产）以公允价值进行计量的所有资产和负债提出了披露要求。该准则未规定何时需要运用公允价值计量。IFRS 13 中的计量指南适用于所有公允价值计量，但《国际财务报告准则第 2 号——股份支付》（“IFRS 2”）或《国际会计准则第 17 号——租赁》（“IAS 17”）以及一些特定的由其他准则规范的、虽然计量与公允价值相似但不属于公允价值计量的情形除外。准则要求对以公允价值计量的资产和负债进行披露，但也有一些例外情况。IFRS 13 对 IAS 39 和 IFRS 9 进行了修改，删除了其对公允价值计量的指南。IFRS 13 将于 2013 年 1 月 1 日或之后的期间生效，允许提前适用，且自首次实施年度之始在未来期间适用。《国际财务报告准则实务指引》第三十四章将探讨 IFRS 13 的内容。在本章节中，保留了 IAS 39 对公允价值计量的部分现行要求。采用 IFRS 13 的主体应参见《国际财务报告准则实务指引》第三十四章了解相关公允价值计量的规定。

measurements within the current context of IAS 39 are retained. Entities that have adopted IFRS 13 should refer to chapter 34 of the IFRS Manual of Accounting for the relevant fair value measurement guidance.

Initial measurement

Initial fair value

9. 6 When a financial asset or financial liability is recognised initially, IAS 39 requires the entity to measure it at its ' fair value ' plus, in certain situations, transaction costs (see para 9. 13 below). [IAS 39 para 43]. IFRS 13 currently defines fair value as the price that would be received to sell an asset or paid to transfer a liability in an ordinary transaction between market participants at the measurement date. [IFRS 13 para 9]. The consideration of fair value measurement are discussed in detail from paragraph 9. 94 below.

9. 7 Given that fair value is the price that arm's length market participants would pay or receive in a routine transaction under the market conditions at the date at which the asset or liability is to be measured for accounting purposes (the measurement date), it follows that a financial instrument's initial fair value will normally be the transaction price, that is, the fair value of the consideration given or received. [IAS 39 para AG 64].

9. 8 In some circumstances, the consideration given or received (say the face amount) may not necessarily be the financial instrument's fair value. For example, the fair value of a long-term note receivable that carries no interest is not equal to its face amount and, therefore, part of the consideration received is something other than its fair value. As the note receivable would have to be recorded initially at its fair value, its fair value has to be estimated. The instrument's fair value may be evidenced by comparison with other observable current market transactions in the same instrument (that is, without modification or repackaging) or based on a valuation technique whose variables include only data from observable markets. [IAS 39 para AG 76]. For a long-term loan or receivable with no stated interest,

初始计量

初始公允价值

9.6　对金融资产或金融负债进行初始确认时，IAS 39 要求主体按照其“公允价值”计量，在某些情况下，还要加上交易费用（参见下文第 9.13 段）。[IAS 39 第 43 段]。目前的 IFRS 13 将公允价值定义为：在计量日的有序交易中，市场参与者之间出售一项资产所能收到或转移一项负债将会支付的价格。[IFRS 13 第 9 段]。自下文第 9.94 段起探讨了公允价值计量时的考虑。

9.7　考虑到公允价值是出于计量当日（计量日）的会计目的，公平市场参与者在市场条件下的常规交易中愿意为所计量资产或负债支付或接受的价格。所以金融工具的初始公允价值通常为交易价格，即已支付或已接受对价的公允价值。[IAS 39 AG 第 64 段]。

9.8　在某些情况下，已支付或已接受对价（暂称票面金额）不一定是金融工具的公允价值。例如：不计利息的长期应收票据的公允价值并不等同于其票面金额，所以收到对价的一部分不属于其公允价值。因为应收票据需按其公允价值进行初始确认，所以需要对应收票据的公允价值进行估计。该工具的公允价值可通过与相同工具（即无变更或重新打包的工具）的其他可观察的当前市场交易做比较，或基于所用变量只包括可观察市场数据的估值技术来证实[IAS 39 AG 第 76 段]。对于无息的长期贷款或应收款项，通常用折现现金流的估值方法确定公允价值。按照此方法，参考同期发行的具有相似信用评级的类似金融工具（在币种、期限、利率类型及其他因素等方面类似）的现行市场利率，以全部未来现金收款折现后的现值来估算公允价值。任何

the fair value is normally arrived at by using a discounted cash flow valuation method. Under this method, the fair value can be estimated as the present value of all future cash receipts discounted using the prevailing market rate of interest for a similar instrument (similar as to currency, term, type of interest rate and other factors) with a similar credit rating issued at the same time. Any additional amount lent is an expense or a reduction of income, unless it qualifies for recognition as some other type of asset. [IAS 39 para AG 64].

9.9 A pragmatic measure, the standard permits short-term receivables and payables to be measured at the original invoice amount if the effect of discounting is immaterial. [IAS 39 para AG 79]. The IFRS IC also considered the accounting for extended payment terms, such as six-month's interest-free credit, and concluded that the accounting treatment under IAS 39 was clear. In such circumstances, the effect of the time value of money should be reflected when this is material. [IFRIC Update July 2004].

Example 1 – Interest free loan to a company

Entity A lends C1,000 to entity B for 5 years and classifies the asset under loans and receivables. The loan carries no interest. Instead, entity A expects other future economic benefits, such as an implicit right to receive goods or services at favourable prices.

On initial recognition, the market rate of interest for a similar 5 year loan with payment of interest at maturity is 10% per year. The loan's initial fair value is the present value of the future payment of C1,000 discounted using the market rate of interest for a similar loan of 10% for 5 years, that is, C621.

In this example, the consideration given of C1,000 is for two things – the fair value of the loan of C621 and entity A's right to obtain other future economic benefits that have a fair value of C379 (the difference between the total consideration given of C1,000 and the consideration given for the loan of C621).

Entity A recognises the loan at its initial fair value of C621 that will accrete to C1,000 over the term of the loan using the effective interest method (see further para 9.67 below).

额外出借的金额则均计入费用或抵减收入，除非该金额被确认为某些其他类型的资产。[IAS 39 AG 第 64 段]。

9.9 在实务中，若折现的影响不大，准则允许以原始的发票金额计量短期应收款和应付款。[IAS 39 AG 第 79 段]。国际财务报告解释委员会（"IFRIC"）还对延期支付条款的会计进行了考虑，例如六个月期的无息信贷，并作出 IAS 39 规定的会计处理是清晰明确的这一结论。在此类情况下，当影响重大时，则应反映货币的时间价值。[2004 年 7 月 IFRIC 的更新]。

示例 1——向公司提供无息贷款

主体 A 借给主体 B1,000 元，期限为 5 年，并将该资产分类为贷款和应收款项。虽然该贷款不计利息，但是主体 A 期望获得其他的未来经济利益，比如 A 有从 B 处以优惠价格获得商品或服务的隐性权利。

在初始确认时，类似的 5 年期到期付息的贷款市场年利率为 10%。通过类似 5 年期市场年利率 10% 的贷款，得出该贷款的初始公允价值为未来支付 1,000 元折现的现值，即 621 元。

在本示例中，给付的 1,000 元对价对应两项——贷款的公允价值 621 元和主体 A 获取其他未来经济利益的权利，其他未来经济利益的公允价值为 379 元（已支付的 1,000 元总对价与为贷款支付的 621 元对价间的差额）。

主体 A 确认贷款的初始公允价值为 621 元，使用实际利率法，该贷款在贷款期限结束时将增加到 1,000 元（参见下文第 9.67 段）。

The difference of C379 is not a financial asset, since it is paid to obtain expected future economic benefits other than the right to receive payment on the loan asset. Entity A recognises that amount as an expense unless it qualifies for recognition as an asset under, say, IAS 38, or as part of the cost of investment in subsidiary, if entity B is a subsidiary of entity A.

Example 2 – Interest free loan to an employee

An entity grants an interest free loan of C1, 000 to an employee for a period of two years. The market rate of interest to this individual for a two year loan with payment of interest at maturity is 10%.

The consideration given to the employee consists of two assets:

- The fair value of the loan, that is $C1,000/(1.10)^2 = C826$.
- The difference of C174 that is accounted for as employee compensation in accordance with IAS 19.

Example 3 – Interest free loan received from a government agency

An entity is located in an enterprise zone and receives an interest free loan of C500, 000 from a government agency. The loan carries no interest and is repayable at the end of year three.

Loans received from a government that have a below-market rate of interest should be recognised and measured in accordance with IAS 39. The benefit of the below-market rate of interest should be measured as the difference between the initial carrying value of the loan determined in accordance with IAS 39 and the proceeds received. [IAS 20 para 10A].

So if the fair value is estimated at C450, 000 under IAS 39, the loan would be recorded initially at its fair value of C450, 000. The difference between the consideration received and the fair value of the loan, that is, C50, 000, would fall to be accounted for as a government grant in accordance with IAS 20.

However, the IASB noted that applying IAS 39 to loans retrospectively may require entities to measure the fair value of loans at a past date. So the IASB decided that the amendment should be applied prospectively to government

379 元的差额不是金融资产，因为其支付目的是为预期未来经济利益，而非收取贷款资产的偿付。主体 A 将该笔金额确认为费用，除非该笔金额可被确认为例如 IAS 38 下的资产，或者如果主体 B 是主体 A 的子公司，该笔费用可被确认为对子公司投资成本的一部分。

示例 2——向职工提供无息贷款

一家企业向一位职工发放了为期 2 年的 1, 000 元无息贷款。该 2 年期到期付息的贷款市场利率为 10%。

向该员工支付的对价由两项资产组成：

- 贷款的公允价值，即 1, 000 元 $/(1.10)^2 = 826$ 元。
- 按照《国际会计准则第 19 号——员工福利》（“IAS 19”），174 元的差额被确认为职工薪酬。

示例 3——从政府机构得到的无息贷款

某主体位于经济开发区，从政府机构接受了 500, 000 元的无息贷款。该贷款不计利息，并应在第三年年底偿还。

从政府机构处得到的、低于市场利率的贷款按照 IAS 39 的规定进行确认和计量。低于市场利率的收益应以 IAS 39 所确定的贷款初始账面价值与收款之间的差额进行计量。[IAS 20 第 10 A 段]。

所以，如果按照 IAS 39 的规定，估计公允价值为 450, 000 元，该贷款应按其初始公允价值记为 450, 000 元。按照 IAS 20 的规定，收到的对价与贷款公允价值之间的差额，即 50, 000 元，在会计上作为政府补助处理。

但是，IASB 注意到，对该贷款追溯应用 IAS 39 可能要求主体按过去某个日期计量贷款的公允价值。所以 IASB 决定该修改应当未来适用于 2009 年 1 月 1 日起或之后期间所接受的政府贷款。

loans received in periods beginning on or after 1 January 2009.

9.10 In some circumstances, instead of originating an interest free loan, an entity may originate a loan that bears an off-market interest rate (for example, a loan that carries a higher or lower rate than the prevailing current market rate for a similar loan) and pays or receives an initial fee as compensation. In that situation, the entity still recognises the loan at its initial fair value, that is, net of the fee paid or received as illustrated below. The fee paid or received is amortised to profit or loss using the effective interest method. [IAS 39 para AG 65]. A similar requirement is included in IAS 18, where fees that are an integral part of a financial instrument's effective interest rate are generally treated as an adjustment to the effective interest rate. [IAS 18 para IE 14(a)].

Example – Off-market loan with origination fee

An entity originates a loan for C1,000 that is repayable in 5 year's time. The loan carries interest at 6%, which is less than the market rate of 8% for a similar loan. The entity receives C80 as compensation for originating a below market loan.

The entity should recognise the loan at its initial fair value of C920 (net present value of C60 of interest for 5 years and principal repayment of C1,000 discounted at 8%). This is equal to the net cash received (loan of C1,000 less origination fee of C80). The net amount of the loan of C920 accretes to C1,000 over the 5 year term using an effective interest of 8%.

In this example, the upfront fee received of C80 exactly compensates the entity for interest short fall of C20 for each of the next 5 years discounted at the market rate of 8%. Hence, no gain or loss arises on initial recognition.

9.11 A further exception to the general rule that the transaction price is not necessarily the financial instrument's initial fair value is of particular relevance to banking and insurance entities. Such entities often originate structured transactions and use models to estimate their fair values. Such models may show a 'day 1' gain (that is, the fair value exceeds the transaction price). However, IFRS permits departure from the transaction price only if fair value is evidenced by observable current market transactions in the same instrument or a valuation

9.10 在某些情况下，主体可能发放非市场利率的贷款（例如高于或低于类似贷款的当前市场利率），而非无息贷款，并支付或收取初始费用作为补偿。在这种情况下，该企业仍然按贷款的初始公允价值对其进行确认，即减去下文所示的已付费用或已收费用。已付费用或已收费用使用实际利率法摊销计入损益。[IAS 39 AG 第 65 段]。《国际会计准则第 18 号——收入》（"IAS 18"）纳入了类似要求，规定作为金融工具实际利率组成部分的费用，通常应被视为对实际利率的调整。[IAS 18 IE 第 14（a）段]。

示例——附初始费用的非市场利率贷款

主体发放了一笔 5 年期的 1,000 元贷款。该贷款的利率为 6%，低于类似贷款 8% 的市场利率。主体收取 80 元，作为发放低于市场利率贷款的补偿。

主体应以 920 元的初始公允价值确认贷款（5 年年息 60 元及 5 年到期归还本金 1,000 元的净现值，折现率为 8%）。该金额等于净现金收款（1,000 元贷款减去 80 元贷款初始费用）。使用 8% 的实际利率，在 5 年期内，920 元的贷款净额将增加到 1,000 元。

在本示例中，收取的 80 元初始费用正好补偿了主体在 5 年期中每年少收利息 20 元按照 8% 的市场利率折现的部分。所以，在初始确认时没有产生任何收益或损失。

9.11 交易价格不一定即为金融工具的初始公允价值，这一一般原则的例外特别常见于银行和保险公司。这些主体经常发起结构性交易，并采用模型估计其公允价值。这些模型可能呈现"首日"利得（即公允价值超出交易价格）。然而，只有在相同金融工具的公允价值可以通过可观察的当前市场交易确证，或估值方法的变量仅包括了来自于可观察市场的数据时，IFRS 才允许公允价值偏离交易价格。所以，很少在初始确认时确认"首日"利得。下文第 9.148 段还将对此问题进行进一步考虑。

technique whose variables include only data from observable markets. As a result, an immediate 'day 1' gain is rarely recognised on initial recognition. This issue is considered further in paragraph 9. 148 below.

Transaction costs

9. 12 Transaction costs are incremental costs that are directly attributable to the acquisition or issue or disposal of a financial asset or financial liability. An incremental cost is one that would not have been incurred if the entity had not acquired, issued or disposed of the financial instrument. [IAS 39 para 9].

9. 13 Transaction costs include fees and commissions paid to agents (including employees acting as selling agents), advisers, brokers and dealers, levies by regulatory agencies and securities exchanges and transfer taxes and duties. Transaction costs do not include debt premiums or discounts, financing costs or internal administrative or holding costs. [IAS 39 para AG 13].

9. 14 The standard defines transaction costs to include internal costs, provided they are incremental and directly attributable to the acquisition, issue or disposal of a financial asset or financial liability. [IAS 39 para BC222(d)]. However, in practice, other than payments made to employees acting as selling agents (common in insurance contracts that fall to be accounted for under IAS 39 as financial instruments), salary costs of employees that would be incurred irrespective of whether the loan was granted are not incremental, nor are allocated indirect administrative costs or overheads.

9. 15 The appendix to IAS 18, sets out a number of examples of financial services fees. IAS 18 distinguishes such fees between those that are an integral part of generating an involvement with the resulting financial instrument, those that are earned as services are provided and those that are earned on the execution of a significant act. Such fees may fall into two categories: fees associated with origination of a loan (loan origination fees) and fees associated with commitment to lend (commitment fees).

9. 16 Loan origination fees may consist of:

交易费用

9.12　交易费用是直接归属于金融资产或金融负债的购买、发行或处置的增量费用。增量费用是假如主体未购买、发行或处置金融工具，则不会产生的费用。[IAS 39 第9段]。

9.13　交易费用包括向代理人（包括作为销售代理的职工）、顾问、经纪人和经销商支付的费用及佣金，由监管机构和证券交易所征收的税费，及转让税和关税。交易费用不包括债务溢价或折价、融资费用及内部管理或持有成本。[IAS 39 AG 第13段]。

9.14　该准则规定，只有当内部费用为增量费用且直接归属于金融资产或金融负债的购买、发行或处置时，可将其包括在交易费用内。[IAS 39 BC 第222（d）段]。然而，在实务中，除了向作为销售代理的职工支付的款项（常见于作为金融工具纳入 IAS 39 适用范围的保险合同），其他职工工资成本无论发放贷款与否均将产生所以并非增量费用，同理，间接日常行政管理费用也非增量费用。

9.15　IAS 18 的附录列举了一系列融资服务费的示例。IAS 18 对形成金融工具的固有费用、提供服务收取的费用以及执行重要工作项目而收取的费用进行了区分。这些费用可划分为两类：与办理贷款相关的费用（贷款初始费用）和与贷款承诺相关的费用（承诺费）。

9.16　贷款初始费用可由以下几方面组成：

- Fees that are charged to the borrower as 'pre-paid' interest or to reduce the loan's nominal interest rate (explicit yield adjustments).
- Fees to compensate the lender for origination activities such as evaluating the borrower's financial condition, evaluating and recording guarantees, collateral and other security arrangements, negotiating the instrument's terms, preparing and processing documents and closing the transaction.
- Other fees that relate directly to the loan origination process (for example, fees that are paid to the lender as compensation for granting a complex loan or agreeing to lend quickly).

9.17 Commitment fees are fees that are charged by the lender for entering into an agreement to make or acquire a loan. Sometimes they are referred to as facility fees for making a loan facility available to a borrower. The accounting treatment depends on whether or not it is probable that the entity will enter into a specific lending arrangement and whether the loan commitment is within IAS 39's scope. If it is probable that the entity will enter into the lending agreement and the loan commitment is not within IAS 39's scope, the commitment fee received is regarded as compensation for an ongoing involvement with the acquisition of a financial instrument and, together with the transaction costs (as defined in IAS 39), is deferred and recognised as an adjustment to the effective interest rate. If the commitment expires without the entity making the loan, the fee is recognised as revenue on expiry. [IAS 18 App para 14(a)(ii)]. On the other hand, if it is unlikely that a specific lending arrangement will be entered into and the loan commitment is outside IAS 39's scope, the commitment fee is recognised as revenue on a time proportion basis over the commitment period. Loan commitments that are within IAS 39's scope are accounted for as derivatives and measured at fair value. [IAS 18 App para 14(b)(ii); IAS 39 para 9].

9.18 The borrower's accounting mirrors that of the lender as discussed above. Therefore, to the extent there is evidence that it is probable that some or all of the facility will be drawn down, the facility fee is accounted for as a transaction cost under IAS 39. Where this is the case, the facility fee is deferred and treated as a transaction cost when draw-down occurs; it is not amortised prior to the draw-down. For example, draw-down might be probable if there is a specific project for

- 向借款人收取的作为“预付”利息的费用，或减少贷款名义利率的费用（明确的收益调整）。

- 补偿贷款人贷款发放活动的费用，比如评价借款人的财务状况、评估和记录担保、抵押品和其他担保协议、协商金融工具的条款、准备和处理文件及完成交易。

- 与贷款发放过程直接相关的其他费用（例如，支付给贷款人作为发放复杂贷款或快速发放贷款的补偿费用）。

9.17　承诺费是订立提供或发放贷款的协议时由贷款人收取的费用。当向借款人提供贷款额度时，承诺费也被称为额度费。其会计处理取决于主体是否可能签订具体贷款协议且贷款承诺是否属于 IAS 39 的范围。如果主体可能签订贷款协议且贷款承诺不属于 IAS 39 的规定范围，则收取的承诺费被认为是与后续取得金融工具的补偿费，其与交易费用（依 IAS 39 定义）同样被递延且作为对实际利率的调整。如果承诺过期，但主体没有发放贷款，承诺费则在到期时被确认为收入。[IAS 18 附录第 14（a）（ii）段]。另一方面，如果不太可能签订具体贷款协议且贷款承诺不属于 IAS 39 的规定范围，承诺费则在承诺期内按时间比例被确认为收入。属于 IAS 39 范围的贷款承诺作为衍生工具核算，且以公允价值计量。[IAS 18 附录第 14（b）（ii）段；IAS 39 第 9 段]。

9.18　借款人会计与上述贷款人的会计对称，因此，如果确定存在支用部分或全部贷款的可能性，则将额度费作为 IAS 39 下的交易费用核算。在这种情况下，将额度费递延，且在支用时作为交易费用处理；而非在支用前摊销。例如，如果有某一特定项目并有商定的业务计划，则具有支用贷款的可能性。如果贷款额度为 2,000 万元，可能只支用其中 500 万元，额度费的 1/4 将代表这 500 万元贷款的交易费用，且递延至支用。如果无证据表明可能支用部分

which there is an agreed business plan. If a facility is for C20 million and it is probable that only C5 million of the facility will be drawn down, a quarter of the facility fee represents a transaction cost of the C5 million loan and is deferred until draw-down occurs. To the extent there is no evidence that it is probable that some or all of the facility will be drawn down, the facility fee represents a payment for liquidity services – that is, to secure the availability of finance on pre-arranged terms over the facility period. As such, to the extent draw down is not probable, the facility fee is capitalised as a prepayment for services and amortised over the period of the facility to which it relates. The availability of finance on pre-arranged terms provides benefit to an entity in a similar way to an insurance policy. If finance is needed in the future due to unforeseen events, the facility in place ensures that an entity can obtain this finance on known terms regardless of the economic environment in the future.

9.19 Direct loan origination costs relate to costs incurred by the entity for undertaking activities set out in the second bullet point of paragraph 9.16 above. Internal costs directly related to those activities should include only that portion of employee cost directly related to time spent performing those activities (see para 9.16 above).

9.20 It is apparent from the nature of the above fees that they are an integral part of generating an involvement with the resulting financial instrument and together with the related direct origination costs, are accounted for in a financial instrument's initial measurement as follows:

- When a financial asset or financial liability is recognised initially and not designated as at fair value through profit or loss, transaction costs (net of fees received) that are directly attributable to the acquisition or issue are added to the initial fair value. For financial assets, such costs are added to the amount originally recognised. For financial liabilities, such costs are deducted from the amount originally recognised. This applies to financial instruments carried at amortised cost and available-for-sale financial assets. [IAS 39 para 43].

- For financial instruments that are measured at fair value through profit or loss, transaction costs (net of any fees received or paid) are not added to or deducted from the initial fair value, but are immediately recognised in profit or loss on

或全部贷款，则额度费代表为流动性支持支付的款项，即在贷款额度期间，用来确保借款人可按照预定的条款获得融资。因此，如果不可能支用贷款，则将额度费作为服务的预付款进行资本化，并在相关的贷款额度期间进行摊销。主体按照预定条款取得融资的可能性，为主体带来类似保单利益。如果主体由于不可预见的事件而在未来有融资需求，则无论未来经济环境如何，安排好的额度确保了主体可按预定条款获得该笔融资。

9.19　贷款启动直接费用和主体因从事上述第9.16段第二点所示各项活动有关。与这些活动直接相关的内部费用只应包括相关职工成本中直接耗时于上述活动的部分（参见上文第9.16段）。

9.20　从上述费用的性质中可以明显看出这些费用是形成金融工具必不可少的一部分。这些费用与直接启动费用在金融工具初始计量时的会计处理如下：

■ 当对一项金融资产或金融负债进行初始确认，且未指定其为以公允价值计量且其变动计入损益时，直接归属于其购买或发行的交易费用（减去已收费用），被计入初始公允价值中。对于金融资产而言，将此类费用加入初始确认金额中。对于金融负债而言，将此类费用从初始确认金额中扣除。此方法用于以摊余成本计量的金融工具及可供出售金融资产。[IAS 39第43段]。

■ 对于以公允价值计量且其变动计入损益的金融工具而言，交易费用（减去已收费用或已付费用）不计入初始公允价值或从其中扣除，而是在初始确认时将其即时确认为损益。

initial recognition.

- Transaction costs expected to be incurred on a financial instrument's transfer or disposal are not included in the financial instrument's measurement.

[IAS 39 para IG E1. 1].

Example 1 – Initial measurement – transaction cost

An entity acquires an equity available-for-sale financial asset at its fair value of C100. Purchase commission of C2 is also payable. At the end of the entity's financial year, the asset's quoted market price is C105. If the asset were to be sold, a commission of C4 would be payable.

As the asset is not classified initially at fair value through profit or loss, the entity recognises the financial asset at its fair value that includes the purchase commission, that is, at C102. At the end of the entity's financial year, the asset is recorded at C105 without regard to the commission of C4 payable on sale. The change in fair value of C3 recognised in other comprehensive income includes the purchase commission of C2 payable at the acquisition date.

Example 2 – Allocation of transaction costs to a convertible instrument that contains a conversion option as an embedded derivative

An entity, with functional currency of C, issues a 5 year, euro-denominated convertible bond for C100. Transaction costs of C2 were incurred by the issuer. The host liability is to be accounted for at amortised cost. The fair value of the embedded derivative on initial recognition was C20.

Transaction costs relating to issuance of a convertible instrument for which the conversion feature is classified as an embedded derivative should be allocated to the host liability and the embedded conversion option in either of the following ways (that is, there is an accounting policy choice):

- Approach 1 – The convertible bond represents a liability in its entirety, as the conversion feature fails the fixed-for-fixed requirement for equity classification (see chapter 7). On initial recognition, the financial liability

■ 预期金融工具转让或处置时产生的交易费用，不计入金融工具计量中。

[IAS 39 IG 第 E1. 1 段]。

示例 1——初始计量——交易费用

主体以 100 元按公允价值购买了可供出售权益性金融资产，还支付了 2 元佣金。在该主体财年末，该资产的市场报价为 105 元，如果出售该资产，则应支付 4 元佣金。

因为该资产初始未分类为以公允价值计量且其变动计入损益，所以主体按照金融资产的公允价值确认该金融资产，并包括购买佣金，即 102 元。在该主体财年末，该资产计为 105 元，而不考虑 4 元出售佣金。在其他综合收益中确认的 3 元公允价值变动包括了在购买日支付的购买佣金 2 元。

示例 2——可转换工具的交易费用分摊，可转换工具含有作为嵌入式衍生工具的转股权

一个功能货币为“元”的主体，发行了五年期以欧元计价的 100 元可转换债券。发行人产生 2 元的交易费用。主债务以摊余成本进行会计处理。初始确认时嵌入式衍生工具的公允价值为 20 元。

与发行将转股特征分类为嵌入式衍生工具的可转换工具相关的交易费用，应按照以下任一方式分摊至主债务和嵌入式转股权（即可选择会计政策）：

■ 方法 1——当转股特征不能满足权益分类所需的固定换固定的要求时，可转换债券整体是一项负债（参见第七章）。在初始确认时，由于未对工具以公允价值计量且其变动计入损益，该金融负债（即整个金融工

(that is, the entire instrument) should be recognised at fair value less transactions costs that are directly attributable to its issuance since the instrument is not at fair value through profit or loss. As the embedded derivative's fair value at initial recognition is C20, the host liability is initially recognised at C78 (C100 – C20 – C2) and there is no impact on profit or loss.

- Approach 2 – Under this approach, transaction costs are allocated to each component in proportion to the allocation of proceeds. Therefore, costs allocated to the embedded derivative are charged to profit or loss on initial recognition, and those allocated to the host contract are deducted from its initial carrying amount. Accordingly, the embedded derivative is recognised initially at C20, with (20/100) of the transaction costs (that is, C0.4) being recognised in profit or loss. The host liability is recognised initially at C78.4 (C100 – C20 – (80/100) × C2).

9.21 Entities may also receive fees for the provision of a service, such as loan servicing fee, or for the execution of a significant act such as placement fees for arranging a loan between two third parties and loan syndication fees. These fees are not integral to lending or borrowing and, therefore, cannot form part of the financial instrument's measurement.

9.22 The treatment of transaction costs on the subsequent measurement of available-for-sale financial assets is considered in paragraph 9.33 below and those carried at amortised cost are considered in paragraph 9.75 below.

Settlement date accounting for regular way transactions

9.23 When an entity uses settlement date accounting for an asset that is subsequently measured at cost or amortised cost, the asset is recognised initially at settlement date, but measured at the fair value on trade date. [IAS 39 para 44]. This is an exception to the general rule in paragraph 9.6 above that a financial asset should be recognised at its fair value on initial recognition. The accounting for regular way trades is considered in chapter 8.

具）应以公允价值减去交易费用（直接归属于金融负债发行的费用）进行确认。由于在初始确认时嵌入式衍生工具的公允价值为 20 元，主债务初始确认时应为 78 元（100 元 - 20 元 - 2 元），不对损益造成影响。

- 方法 2——按照该方法，交易费用在发行收入的各组成部分之间按比例分摊。所以，在初始确认时分摊至嵌入式衍生工具的费用将计入损益，而分摊至主合同的费用将从其初始账面金额中扣除。因此，嵌入式衍生工具初始确认为 20 元，其中（20/100）的交易费用（即 0.4 元）计入损益。初始确认的主债务为 78.4 元（100 元 - 20 元 - （80/100）× 2 元）。

9.21 主体还可能因提供服务而收取费用，例如贷款服务费，或因执行一项重要工作项目而收取费用，例如安排两个第三方间贷款的费用和安排银团贷款的费用。这些费用不是贷款或借款的固有组成部分，所以不能构成金融工具计量的组成部分。

9.22 下文第 9.33 段将讨论可供出售金融资产后续计量中交易费用的处理，在下文第 9.75 段将讨论以摊余成本计量的金融工具的交易费用。

常规方式交易的结算日会计

9.23 当主体对一项后续以成本或摊余成本计量的资产使用结算日会计处理时，该资产将在结算日进行初始确认，但需以交易日的公允价值计量。[IAS 39 第 44 段]。这是上文第 9.6 段提到的金融资产应以公允价值进行初始确认这一一般原则的例外规定。第八章将讨论常规交易的会计处理。

Subsequent measurement of financial assets

General

9.24 As set out in chapter 6, financial assets are classified in one of four categories. Following their initial recognition, the classification determines how the financial asset is subsequently measured, including any profit or loss recognition. The following table summarises the requirements that are considered in detail in the remainder of this chapter.

Classification	Financial asset	Measurement basis	Changes in carrying amount	Impairment test (if objective evidence)
At fair value through profit or loss	Debt	Fair value	Profit or loss	No[5]
	Equity	Fair value	Profit or loss	No[5]
	Derivatives not designated as effective hedging instruments	Fair value	Profit or loss	–
Loans and receivables	Debt	Amortised cost	Profit or loss[3]	Yes
Held-to-maturity investments	Debt	Amortised cost	Profit or loss[3]	Yes
Available-for-sale financial assets	Debt	Fair value	OCI[2] Profit or loss[3]	Yes
	Equity	Fair value	OCI[2] Profit or loss[4]	Yes
	Equity[1]	Cost (fair value not reliably measurable)	Profit or loss[4]	Yes

1 Equity instruments that do not have any quoted market price in an active market and whose fair value cannot be reliably measured and derivative assets that are linked to and must be settled by delivery of such unquoted equity instruments.

2 Change in fair value including related foreign exchange differences other than those noted in note 3 or 4 below where relevant.

金融资产的后续计量

综述

9.24　正如第六章所述，金融资产共分四类。在初始确认后，分类决定了金融资产的后续计量方式，包括损益的确认。下表总结了相关的要求，我们将在本章余下的部分对其进行详细探讨。

类别	金融资产	计量基础	账面金额变动	减值测试（如果有客观证据）
以公允价值计量且其变动计入损益	债权	公允价值	损益	无[5]
	权益	公允价值	损益	无[5]
	未指定为有效套期工具的衍生工具	公允价值	损益	–
贷款和应收账款	债权	摊余成本	损益[3]	有
持有至到期投资	债权	摊余成本	损益[3]	有
可供出售金融资产	债权	公允价值	其他综合收益[2] 损益[3]	有
	权益	公允价值	其他综合收益[2] 损益[4]	有
	权益[1]	成本（其公允价值不能可靠计量）	损益[4]	有

1 指该权益工具在活跃市场中无任何市场报价，且其公允价值不能可靠计量，与其挂钩的衍生资产必须通过交付此类无报价的权益工具进行结算。

2 公允价值变动包括相应的汇兑差额，下文附注 3 或附注 4 相关说明除外。

3 Interest calculated using the effective interest method, foreign exchange differences resulting from changes in amortised cost, impairment and reversal of impairment, where relevant, are taken to profit or loss.
4 Dividends and impairment are taken to profit or loss. Foreign exchange difference on (non-monetary) equity AFS investments taken to equity and recycled to profit or loss on disposal or impairment.
5 Any impairment will be taken though profit or loss as part of the change in fair value and so separate impairment testing is not necessary.

9.25 Financial assets that are designated as hedged items are subject to measurement under the hedge accounting requirements. These requirements apply in addition to, and may modify, the general accounting requirements that are discussed below. Hedge accounting is covered in chapter 10.

Financial assets at fair value through profit or loss

9.26 After initial recognition, financial assets falling within this category (including assets held-for-trading and derivative assets not designated as effective hedging instruments and assets designated on initial recognition at fair value through profit or loss) are measured at fair value, without the deduction of transaction costs that the entity may incur on sale or other disposal. [IAS 39 para 46]. Such transaction costs are future costs that relate to the sale or the disposal and have no relevance to determining fair value. Therefore, they are properly included in the period in which the sale or the disposal takes place.

9.27 The standard's requirements for determining the fair value of instruments that fall to be measured on this basis are considered from paragraph 9.94 below. Investments in equity instruments that do not have a quoted market price in an active market and whose fair value cannot be reliably measured and derivatives that are linked to and must be settled by delivery of such unquoted equity instruments, are measured at cost (see further para 9.146 below). [IAS 39 para 46(c)].

9.28 All gains and losses arising from changes in fair value of financial assets falling within this category are recognised, not surprisingly, in profit or loss. [IAS 39 para 55(a)]. This means that assets falling within this category are not subject to review for impairment as losses due to fall in value (including impairment) would automatically be reflected in profit or loss.

3 使用实际利率法计算的利息，由摊余成本变化引起的汇兑差额，减值和减值转回计入损益。

4 股利和减值计入损益。（非货币性）可供出售权益投资的汇兑差额计入权益，并在处置或减值时转入损益。

5 因为任何减值均将作为公允价值变动的一部分计入损益，所以不需要进行单独减值测试。

9.25 对指定为被套期项目的金融资产应按照套期会计要求进行计量。套期会计的要求除了遵循下述的一般会计要求外，还可能有所修改。第十章中阐述了套期会计的内容。

以公允价值计量且其变动计入损益的金融资产

9.26 初始确认后，属于此类别的金融资产（包括交易性资产和未指定为有效套期工具的衍生工具资产，以及初始确认时指定为以公允价值计量且其变动计入损益的资产）以公允价值进行计量，不扣除主体销售或进行其他处置时可能产生的交易费用。[IAS 39 第 46 段]。这些交易费用是与销售或处置相关的未来成本，与公允价值的确定没有关系。所以，这些交易费用应被纳入销售或处置行为发生的相应期间。

9.27 准则对以公允价值计量的工具制定了相关的计量要求，将在自下文第 9.94 段起探讨。对于在活跃市场中无市场报价的权益工具投资，且其公允价值不能可靠计量及与其挂钩的衍生工具必须通过交付此类无报价的权益工具进行结算时，按照成本计量（详见下文第 9.146 段）。[IAS 39 第 46（c）段]。

9.28 本类别中金融资产公允价值变动产生的全部利得和损失均毫无例外地在损益中进行确认[IAS 39 第 55（a）段]。本类别中的资产不需进行减值复核，因为其价值下跌（包括减值）将自动反映在损益中。

Loans and receivables

9. 29 Loans and receivables, as defined in chapter 6, are measured at amortised cost using the effective interest method. [IAS 39 para 46(a)]. They are measured on this basis whether they are intended to be held-to-maturity or not. [IAS 39 para AG 68]. The amortised cost method of accounting is discussed from paragraph 9. 67 below.

9. 30 Gains and losses are recognised in profit or loss when loans and receivables are derecognised or impaired and throughout the amortisation process. Special rules apply for gain or loss recognition when loans and receivables are designated as hedged items. [IAS 39 para 56].

Held-to-maturity investments

9. 31 Held-to-maturity investments are also measured at amortised cost using the effective interest method. Gains and losses are accounted for in the same way as loans and receivables. [IAS 39 para 46(b)].

Available-for-sale assets

9. 32 Available-for-sale financial assets are measured at fair value. As with assets designated as at fair value through profit or loss, transaction costs that will be incurred on the sale or disposal of such assets are not deducted from the fair value. However, there is an exemption from measurement at fair value of an available-for-sale asset if its fair value cannot be measured reliably (see para 9. 27 above). This exemption only applies to unquoted equity instruments and derivative contracts based on those instruments. These instruments are measured at cost. [IAS 39 para 46(c)].

9. 33 As explained in paragraph 9. 20 above, transaction costs that are directly attributable to the acquisition of an available-for-sale financial asset are added to the initial fair value. For available-for-sale financial assets, transaction costs are recognised in other comprehensive income as part of a change in fair value at the

贷款和应收款项

9.29 在第六章中定义的贷款和应收款项，使用实际利率法以摊余成本计量。[IAS 39 第 46（b）段]。无论贷款和应收款项是否持有至到期，都以此作为计量基础。[IAS 39 AG 第 68 段]。从下文第 9.67 段起将对会计的摊余成本方法进行论述。

9.30 贷款和应收款项在终止确认、发生减值时或在整个摊销过程中确认损益。贷款和应收款项被指定为被套期项目时，对损益的确认应适用特殊规定。[IAS 39 第 56 段]。

持有至到期投资

9.31 持有至到期投资也使用实际利率法以摊余成本计量。收益和损失的会计处理与贷款和应收账款相同。[IAS 39 第 46（b）段]。

可供出售资产

9.32 可供出售金融资产以公允价值计量。与被指定为以公允价值计量且其变动计入损益的资产一样，销售或处置该资产时产生的交易费用不得从公允价值中扣除。然而，对于公允价值无法可靠计量的可供出售金融资产，则存在一项计量上的豁免（参见上文第 9.27 段)。该计量豁免只适用于无报价的权益工具和基于此工具的衍生工具合同。这些工具以成本计量。[IAS 39 第 46（c）段]。

9.33 根据上文第 9.20 段的解释，直接归属于取得可供出售金融资产的交易费用计入初始公允价值。对于可供出售金融资产，被确认在其他综合收益中的交易费用，作为在后续计量中公允价值变动的一部分。如果可供出售金融资产具有固定或可确定付款额，且无不确定的期限，则使用实际利率法将交

subsequent measurement. If an available-for-sale financial asset has fixed or determinable payments and does not have an indefinite life, the transaction costs are amortised to profit or loss using the effective interest method (see para 9.68 below). If an available-for-sale financial asset does not have fixed or determinable payments and has an indefinite life, the transaction costs are recognised in profit or loss when the asset is derecognised or becomes impaired and the cumulative gain or loss, including transaction costs, deferred in other comprehensive income is reclassified to profit or loss. [IAS 39 para AG 67].

9.34 All gains and losses arising from changes in fair value of available-for-sale financial assets are recognised directly in other comprehensive income except as follows:

- Interest calculated using the effective interest method is recognised in profit or loss (see further para 9.67 below). Dividends on an available-for-sale equity instruments are recognised in profit or loss when the entity's right to receive payment is established. [IAS 18 para 30(c)].
- Foreign exchange gains and losses on monetary financial assets are recognised in profit or loss (see further para 9.212 below).
- Impairment losses are recognised in profit or loss (see further para 9.201 below). Reversals of impairment of a debt instrument are also recognised in profit or loss, but reversals of impairment on equity instruments are not (see further para 9.204 below).

[IAS 39 para 55(b)].

9.35 When an available-for-sale financial asset is derecognised as a result of sale or is impaired, the cumulative gain or loss previously recognised in other comprehensive income is reclassified to profit or loss. [IAS 39 paras 55(b), 67]. For example, assume that an entity acquires an equity security for C500 that has a fair value at the end of the year of C600. A gain of C100 is recognised in other comprehensive income. In the following year, the entity sells the security for C550. In the year of sale, a profit of C50, being the difference between proceeds of C550 and original cost of C500 is recognised. This represents the difference between proceeds of C550 and previous carrying value of C600 (C50 loss) and the

易费用摊销计入损益（参见下文第9.68段）。如果可供出售金融资产不具备固定或可确定付款额，且期限无法确定，则在对资产终止确认或确认减值时，交易费用连同在其他综合损益中递延的累计利得或损失（包括交易费用）被转入损益。［IAS 39 AG第67段］。

9.34 可供出售金融资产公允价值变动产生的所有利得和损失，均在其他综合收益中直接确认，但以下情况除外：

- 使用实际利率法计算的利息，在损益中进行确认（参见下文第9.67段）。可供出售权益工具的股利在主体获得收款权利时，在损益中确认。［IAS 18第30（c）段］。
- 在损益中对货币性金融资产的外汇利得和损失进行确认（详见下文第9.212段）。
- 在损益中确认减值损失（详见下文第9.201段）。债务工具减值转回同样在损益中确认，但对权益工具减值转回不在损益中进行确认（详见下文第9.204段）。

［IAS 39第55（b）段］。

9.35 可供出售金融资产由于减值或销售导致确认终止后，之前在其他综合收益中确认的累计利得或损失被转入为损益。［IAS 39第55（b）段、第67段］。例如：假定主体购入了价值为500元的权益证券，截至年末其公允价值为600元。在其他综合收益中确认100元的利得。次年，该主体以550元的价格出售该证券。在销售当年，确认50元的利润，这50元利润是550元收入和500元原始成本之间的差额。其表示550元的收入和600元的账面价值（损失50元）之间的差额，及之前在其他综合收益中确认但转入损益的100元利得。

recycling to profit or loss of C100 gain previously recognised in other comprehensive income.

9.36 In the above example, a single security is used to illustrate the accounting for recycling. In practice, the entity may have acquired the same security in tranches at different dates and at different prices over a period of time. IAS 39 does not specify whether such fungible assets (or indeed any other fungible financial assets) should be considered individually or in aggregate, and, if in aggregate, which measurement basis (weighted average, first in first out (FIFO), specific identification) is appropriate for calculating the gain or loss on a partial disposal. This is in contrast to IAS 2, 'Inventories', which specifies the use of weighted average or FIFO in most circumstances. In practice, entities may opt, as an accounting policy choice, for any one of the methods. The method used should be applied consistently for both impairment and disposal and disclosed.

9.37 It is conceivable that within a group, portfolios have a different nature – for example, an available-for-sale portfolio held for liquidity purposes *versus* an available-for-sale portfolio held for long-term strategic investment purposes. In this instance, it may be possible to justify using different cost formulae within an entity for the same securities. However, whatever cost formula is used, it should be used for both impairment and measurement of gains and losses on disposal.

9.38 The subsequent measurement of available-for-sale financial assets with fixed and determinable payments is complicated by the fact that fair value changes are recognised in other comprehensive income, but interest income is recognised in each period in profit or loss using the effective interest method. In order to ensure that the change in fair value is correctly calculated at the measurement date, it would be necessary to compare the instrument's clean price (the fair value of the instrument less accrued interest) with its amortised cost, also excluding accrued interest, at that date. Therefore, although the instrument is measured at fair value, the amortised cost must still be calculated using the effective interest method in order to determine interest income.

9.36　上述示例是用一个单一证券阐释转入损益的会计处理。在实务中，主体可能在同一期间内的不同日期以不同的价格购入同种证券。IAS 39 没有规定是否应单独或合并考虑此等无差别的资产（或任何其他无差别的金融资产），而且如果合并考虑，IAS 39 也没有规定在部分处置时，以何种计量基础（加权平均、先进先出（FIFO）、个别认定）计算利得或损失。与《国际会计准则第 2 号——存货》（“IAS 2”）的规定对比，IAS 2 规定在大多数情况下，使用加权平均或先进先出法。在实务中，作为会计政策的选择，主体可选择任何一种方法。但该方法应一致地适用于减值和处置上，并进行披露。

9.37　人们认为，在同一组别中，不同组合具有不同的属性——例如，为流动性目的所持有的可供出售组合与为长期战略投资目的所持有的可供出售组合的属性不同。在这种情况下，则有理由对主体持有的同一证券使用不同的成本公式。然而，无论使用何种成本公式，都应同等地运用在减值和处置损益的计量上。

9.38　由于公允价值变动确认在其他综合收益中，但是使用实际利率法计算的各个期间的利息收入计入损益，这就造成了具有固定和可确定付款额的可供出售金融资产后续计量的复杂性。为确保在计量日准确计算公允价值的变动，必须在当日对比金融工具的净价（金融工具的公允价值减去应计利息）和其摊余成本，同样不包括应计利息。所以，虽然以公允价值计量金融工具，但为了确定利息收入，仍应使用实际利率法计算摊余成本。

Example – Debt security classified as available-for-sale investment

On 1 January 20X5, an entity purchases 10% C10 million 5 year bonds with interest payable on 1 July and 1 January each year. The bond's purchase price is C10, 811, 100. The premium of C811, 100 is due to market yield for similar bonds being 8%. Assuming there are no transaction costs, the effective interest rate is 8% (the effective interest method is discussed further in para 9. 68 below).

The entity classifies the bond as available-for-sale. The entity prepares its financial statements at 31 March. On 31 March 20X5, the yield on bonds with similar maturity and credit risk is 7. 75%. At that date, the fair value of this bond calculated by discounting 10 semi-annual cash flows of C500, 000 and principal payment of C10 million at maturity at the market rate of 7. 75% amounted to C11, 127, 710.

Since the bond is classified as available-for-sale, the bond will be measured at fair value with changes in fair value recognised in other comprehensive income.

At 1 January 20X5, the fair value of the bond is the consideration paid of C10, 811, 100 and the entry to record this is as follows:

	Dr	**Cr**
	C	**C**
At 1 January 20X5		
Available-for-sale investment	10, 811, 100	
Cash		10, 811, 100

On 31 March 20X5, the entity will record interest income for the 3 months at the effective interest rate of 8%, that is, C10, 811, 100 × 8% × 3/12 = C216, 222. Since the next coupon of C500, 000 is due on 1 July 20X5, the entity will record a three-month interest accrual of C250, 000. The difference of C33, 778 between the interest income accrued and that recognised in the profit or loss represents the amortisation of the premium. The entry to record

示例——分类为可供出售投资的债券

20X5 年 1 月 1 日，主体购买了 5 年期，利率为 10% 的 1,000 万元债券，每年的 7 月 1 日和 1 月 1 日支付利息。该债券的买价为 10,811,100 元。811,100 元的溢价归因于类似债券 8% 的市场收益率。假定无交易费用，则实际利率为 8%（下文第 9.68 段将对实际利率法进行详细阐述）。

主体将该债券分类为可供出售类。该主体在 3 月 31 日编制财务报表。20X5 年 3 月 31 日，类似到期日和信用风险的债券的收益率为 7.75%。通过对 10 个半年度利息 500,000 元和在到期日支付的 1,000 万元本金的现金流量按照 7.75% 的市场利率的进行折现，得出此债券的公允价值为 11,127,710 元。

因为该债券归类为可供出售类，所以将以公允价值计量，并在其他综合收益中确认其公允价值变动。

20X5 年 1 月 1 日，该债券的公允价值是已付对价 10,811,100 元，已付对价分录如下所示：

	借方	贷方
	元	元
20X5 年 1 月 1 日		
可供出售投资	10,811,100	
现金		10,811,100

20X5 年 3 月 31 日，该主体将按照 8% 的实际利率记录 3 个月的利息收入，即 10,811,100 元 × 8% × 3/12 = 216,222 元。因为接下来 500,000 元的利息到期日为 20X5 年 7 月 1 日，所以主体将记录 250,000 元三个月的应计利息。应计利息收入与损益中确认的应计利息收入之间 33,778 元的差额，表示溢价摊销。20X5 年 3 月 31 日的利息收入分录如下所示：

the interest income on 31 March 20X5 is as follows:

	Dr	Cr
	C	C
At 31 March 20X5		
Available-for-sale investment (accrued interest)	250,000	
Available-for-sale investment (premium)		33,778
Profit or loss – interest income		216,222

The bond's amortised cost at 31 March 20X5 is, therefore, C10, 777, 322 (10, 811, 100 – 33, 778)

The fair value of the bond at 31 March 20X5 is C11, 127, 710. This includes the accrued interest of C250, 000. To calculate the clean price of the bond, the accrued income is deducted from the fair value. Therefore, the clean price of the bond is C10, 877, 710.

A comparison of the clean price of the bond and its amortised cost at 31 March 20X5 results in a gain as follows:

	C
Fair value of bond at 31 March 20X5 – clean price	10,877,710
Amortised cost of bond at 31 March 20X5	10,777,322
Change in value – Unrealised gain	100,388

The entry to record the gain at 31 March 20X5 is as follows:

	Dr	Cr
	C	C
At 31 March 20X5		
Available-for-sale investments	100,388	
Other comprehensive income		100,388

	借方	贷方
	元	元
20X5 年 3 月 31 日		
可供出售投资（应计利息）	250,000	
可供出售投资（溢价）		33,778
损益——利息收入		216,222

所以，该债券在 20X5 年 3 月 31 日的摊余成本为 10,777,322 元（10,811,100 元 - 33,778 元）

20X5 年 3 月 31 日，该债券的公允价值为 11,127,710 元，其中包括 250,000 元的应计利息。为了计算债券的净价，从公允价值中扣除应计收入。所以，该债券的净价为 10,877,710 元。

20X5 年 3 月 31 日，该债券的净价与其摊余成本对比产生的利得如下所示：

	元
20X5 年 3 月 31 日该债券的公允价值——净价	10,877,710
20X5 年 3 月 31 日该债券的摊余成本	10,777,322
价值变动——未实现利得	100,388

20X5 年 3 月 31 日的收益分录如下所示：

	借方	贷方
	元	元
20X5 年 3 月 31 日		
可供出售投资	100,388	
其他综合收益		100,388

The movement in available-for-sale asset is shown below:

	C
At 1 Jan 20X5 – Fair value (inclusive of premium)	10,811,100
Accrued income (reflected in fair value)	250,000
Amortisation of premium	(33,778)
Fair value adjustment – gain	100,388
At 31 Mar 20X5 – Fair Value	11,127,710
	C
Recognised in profit or loss – income	216,222
Recognised in other comprehensive income – gain	100,388
Total change in fair value	316,610

9.39 As stated in paragraph 9.34 above, dividends on an available-for-sale equity instrument are recognised in profit or loss when the entity's right to receive payment is established. The right to receive payment is established when the equity instrument's issuer declares a dividend or in the case of quoted equity securities, at the ex-dividend date. When a share goes ex-dividend shortly before the dividend payment is actually due, the price will drop (other things being equal) by the amount of the dividend. Therefore, depending upon the ex-dividend date (when the dividend income is recognised) and the payment date (when the receivable is settled), the realisation of part of the fair value through dividend payment will affect both profit or loss and equity as illustrated below.

Example – Dividend on available-for-sale investments

An entity acquires 1,000 quoted equity shares in another entity for C20,000. The shares are classified as available-for-sale. Just prior to the entity's year end of 31 December 20X5, the security goes ex-dividend following declaration of a dividend of C1.50 per share. At 31 December 20X5, the quoted ex-dividend price of the shares amounts to C21 per share. The entity receives payment of the dividend on 6 January 20X6.

可供出售资产变动如下所示：

	元
20X5 年 1 月 1 日——公允价值(包括溢价)	10,811,100
计提收入(反映在公允价值中)	250,000
溢价摊销	(33,778)
公允价值调整——利得	100,388
20X5 年 3 月 31 日——公允价值	11,127,710
	元
在损益中确认——收益	216,222
在其他综合收益中确认——利得	100,388
公允价值总变动	316,610

9.39 按照上文第 9.34 段的说明，主体在其收款权利确立时，在损益中确认可供出售权益工具的股利。确立收款权利的时点是在权益工具发行方宣布股利时，或是有报价的权益类证券的除息日。如果在实际支付股利之前股票除息，则股价将按股息额下跌（其他条件不变）。因此，根据除息日（确认股利收入后）和付款日（应收款结算时），通过股利支付实现的部分公允价值将同时影响损益和权益，见下述说明：

示例——可供出售投资的股利

某主体以 20,000 元购入另一主体的 1,000 股有报价股票。这些股票被归类为可供出售类。在该主体截至 20X5 年 12 月 31 日的财年前，该股票宣布每股 1.50 元的股息并成为除息证券。在 20X5 年 12 月 31 日，该股的除息报价为 21 元。该主体于 20X6 年 1 月 6 日收到支付的股利。

At 31 December 20X5, the entity will recognise the dividend income in profit or loss and the change in the fair value of the shares in other comprehensive income as noted below:

	Dr	Cr
	C	C
Dividend receivable	1,500	
Profit or loss – dividend income – 1,000 @ 1.50		1,500
Available-for-sale financial asset	1,000	
Other comprehensive income – 1,000 @ (21 – 20)		1,000

The shares' quoted price prior to the dividend adjustment would have been C22.50 giving a total fair value change of C2,500. However, as part of this change (C1,500) is realised as a result of the dividend income recognised in profit or loss; there is an equal and offsetting change in other comprehensive income.

Designation as hedged items

9.40 Financial assets that are designated as hedged items are subject to measurement under IAS 39's hedging accounting requirements. [IAS 39 para 46]. These special accounting rules generally override the normal accounting rules for financial assets. Hedge accounting is covered in chapter 10.

Reclassifications between categories

9.41 The amendment to IAS 39 issued in October 2008 allows reclassification of certain financial assets after initial recognition out of a category measured at fair value (that is, held-for-trading or available-for-sale) and into another category under limited circumstances (see chapter 6 and IAS 39 para 50 A-E). The tainting rules applicable to the held-to-maturity category remain unchanged.

9.42 When a financial asset is reclassified, the fair value at the date of reclassification becomes its new cost or amortised cost. [IAS 39 para 50 C

20X5 年 12 月 31 日，该主体将在损益中确认股利收入，并在其他综合收益中确认股票的公允价值变动，如下所示：

	借方	贷方
	元	元
应收股利	1,500	
损益——股利收入——1,000 股×1.50 元		1,500
可供出售金融资产	1,000	
其他综合收益——1,000 股×(21 元－20 元)		1,000

股息调整前的报价应为 22.50 元，产生公允价值变动合计 2,500 元。但是，一部分变动金额（1,500 元）已在损益中确认为股利收入，因此在其他综合收益中有等额的抵销变动。

指定为被套期项目

9.40　对指定为被套期项目的金融资产应该按照 IAS 39 的套期会计要求进行计量。[IAS 39 第 46 段]。通常，针对金融资产，较之一般会计准则，应优先适用特定的会计准则。第十章中阐述了套期会计的内容。

不同类别之间重分类

9.41　2008 年 10 月发布的 IAS 39 的修订中，允许在有限情况下将一些金融资产在初始确认后从以公允价值计量的类别（即交易性或可供出售类），重分类至另一类别（参见第六章和 IAS 39 第 50 A-E 段）。适用于持有至到期资产类别的惩罚条款规定不变。

9.42　对一项金融资产进行重分类后，重分类当日的公允价值为其新的成本或新的摊余成本。[IAS 39 第 50C 段和 F 段]。已在损益中确认的任何利得或

and F]. Any gains or losses already recognised in profit or loss are not reversed. The new 'cost' is also used as the basis for assessing impairment in the future.

9.43 On reclassification, the effective interest rate is recalculated using the fair value at the date of reclassification. This new effective interest rate will be used to calculate interest income in future periods and considered as the original effective interest rate when measuring impairment.

9.44 For a financial asset denominated in a foreign currency that is reclassified to loans and receivables, the 'amortised cost' of the financial asset at the date of reclassification is calculated in the foreign currency and then translated at the spot rate to the functional currency at the date of reclassification. [IAS 39 para IG E3.4].

9.45 When an available-for-sale financial asset with fixed maturity is reclassified as held-to-maturity investment or loans and receivables, the fair value of the financial asset on that date becomes its new amortised cost. Any previous gain or loss on that asset that has been recognised directly in other comprehensive income is amortised to profit and loss over the investment's remaining life using the effective interest method. Any difference between the new amortised cost and the amount payable on maturity is also amortised in a similar manner, akin to the amortisation of a premium or a discount. If the financial asset is subsequently impaired, any gain or loss that has been recognised directly in other comprehensive income is recognised in profit or loss. [IAS 39 para 54(a)]. Essentially, interest income should not change as a result of reclassification and should continue to be based on the original amortisation schedule (that is, prior to reclassification). This is because the combination of the amortisation of the difference between the new amortised cost on the reclassified financial asset and the amount payable on maturity and the gain or loss to be amortised from other comprehensive income will result in the same net effective interest rate as originally determined prior to reclassification.

Example – Available-for-sale debt security reclassified to loans and receivables

On 1 January 20X9, an entity reclassifies a C9m bond from available-for-sale

损失不可转回。此外，新的“成本”将用作未来评估减值的基础。

9.43 在重分类时，使用重分类当日的公允价值对实际利率进行再计算。新的实际利率将用于计算未来期间的利息收入且在计量减值时，新的实际利率将被视为原始实际利率。

9.44 对于以外币计价的金融资产重分类为贷款和应收款项，以外币计算其在重分类日当日的“摊余成本”，然后按照即期汇率，换算至该日的功能货币。[IAS 39 IG 第 E3.4 段]。

9.45 具有固定到期日的可供出售金融资产被重分类为持有至到期的投资或贷款和应收款项后，该金融资产在重分类日的公允价值成为其新的摊余成本。在投资的剩余年限内，将该资产之前已直接在其他综合收益中确认的利得或损失以实际利率法摊销计入损益。并以同样的方式，把新的摊余成本和到期日应付金额之间的差额进行摊销，摊销的方式类似于溢价摊销或折价摊销。如果金融资产随后减值，已经直接在其他综合收益中确认的任何利得或损失应转至损益中。[IAS 39 第 54（a）段]。从本质上讲，利息收入不应由于重分类而改变，而应继续以原始的摊销进度表为基础（即重分类前的摊销进度表）摊销。原因在于重分类金融资产的新摊余成本与到期日应付金额之间的差额，与其他综合收益中待摊的利得或损失合并摊销产生的净实际利率，将与在重分类前确定的原实际利率相同。

示例——把可供出售债券重分类为贷款和应收款项

20X9 年 1 月 1 日，主体将 900 万元的债券从可供出售类重分类为贷款和

to loans and receivables. On the date of the reclassification, the bond's amortised cost is C9, 198, 571 and the original effective interest rate is 8.75%. The bond's fair value is C9, 488, 165, which becomes its new amortised cost. The excess of the new carrying amount over the amount receivable at maturity on 31 December 20Y0 (that is C488, 165) is amortised to profit or loss over the remaining term to give a new effective rate of 7% including interest coupons receivable, as shown below.

In addition, the cumulative gain of C289, 594 in other comprehensive income as at 31 December 20X8 (that is, the difference between the fair value of C9, 488, 165 and the amortised cost of C9, 198, 571) is also amortised to profit or loss during the remaining two years to maturity. The effect in profit or loss is the same as if the bond was classified as loans and receivables, as illustrated below:

	Cash received	Interest income@7%	New amortised cost
	C	C	C
1 Jan 20X9			9, 488, 165
31 Dec 20X9	900, 000	664, 172	9, 252, 337
31 Dec 20Y0	9, 900, 000	647, 663	
		1, 311, 835	
Amortisation of gain in other comprehensive income in 20X9 and 20Y0		289, 594	
Total amount recognised in profit or loss		1, 601, 429	

If the C9m bonds had not been reclassified as available-for-sale, the total amount recognised in profit or loss would have been as follows:

应收款项类。重分类时该债券的摊余成本为 9, 198, 571 元，原始实际利率为 8. 75%。该债券的公允价值 9, 488, 165 元即为其新的摊余成本。新的账面金额超过于 20Y0 年 12 月 31 日到期的应收金额的部分（即 488, 165 元）在余下的期间内摊销计入损益，并得出 7% 的新实际利率（包括应收利息），如下所示。

此外，在距到期日余下的两年内，截至 20X8 年 12 月 31 日其他综合收益中的累计利得 289, 594 元（即 9, 488, 165 元公允价值和 9, 198, 571 元摊余成本之间的差额）也摊销计入损益。结果是其对损益的影响与该债券一直被分类为贷款和应收款项类相同。如下所示：

	收到现金 元	利息收入 （利率 7%） 元	新摊余 成本 元
20X9 年 1 月 1 日			9, 488, 165
20X9 年 12 月 31 日	900, 000	664, 172	9, 252, 337
20Y0 年 12 月 31 日	9, 900, 000	647, 663	
		1, 311, 835	
20X9 年和 20Y0 年摊销在其他综合收益中的利得		289, 594	
损益中确认的合计金额		1, 601, 429	

如果 900 万元的债券未被分类为可供出售类，则在损益中确认的合计金额应为如下情况：

	Cash received	Interest income@8.75%	Amortised cost
	C	C	C
31 Dec 20X8			9, 198, 571
31 Dec 20X9	900, 000	804, 876	9, 103, 447
31 Dec 20Y0	9, 900, 000	796, 553	
Total income from date of reclassification to maturity		1, 601, 429	

9.46 When a held-to-maturity investment is reclassified as available-for-sale, it should be remeasured at fair value at the date of reclassification. The difference between its previous carrying amount and fair value should be recognised in other comprehensive income. [IAS 39 paras 51, 52].

Example – Held-to-maturity investment reclassified as available-for-sale financial asset

On 1 January 20X0, an entity purchases 10% C10m 10 year bonds with interest payable annually on 31 December each year. The bond's purchase price is C10, 811, 100. This results in a bond premium of C811, 100 and an effective interest rate of 8.75%. The bonds were classified by the entity as held-to-maturity.

On 31 December 20X5, when the bonds amortised cost and fair value amounted to C10, 407, 192 and C10, 749, 395 respectively, the entity sells C1m bonds and realises a gain as shown below:

	C
Fair value of C1m bond (10% of C10, 749, 395)	1, 074, 940
Carrying value of C1m bond (10% of C10, 407, 192)	1, 040, 719
Profit on disposal recognised in profit or loss	34, 221

Since the entity has sold more than an insignificant amount of its held-to-

	收到现金	利息收入（利率8.75%）	摊余成本
	元	元	元
20X8 年 12 月 31 日			9,198,571
20X9 年 12 月 31 日	900,000	804,876	9,103,447
20Y0 年 12 月 31 日	9,900,000	796,553	
从重分类日至到期日的总收益		1,601,429	

9.46　持有至到期的投资被重分类为可供出售类后，应以重分类日的公允价值重新计量。其之前的账面金额和公允价值之间的差额在其他综合收益中确认。[IAS 39 第 51 段、第 52 段]。

示例——将持有至到期的投资重分类为可供出售金融资产

20X0 年 1 月 1 日，主体购买了 1,000 万元利率为 10% 的 10 年期债券，每年 12 月 31 日为计息日。该债券的购买价格为 10,811,100 元，产生 811,100 元的债券溢价和 8.75% 的实际利率。该主体把该债券分类为持有至到期。

20X5 年 12 月 31 日，当该债券的摊余成本和公允价值分别为 10,407,192 元和 10,749,395 元时，该主体售出了 100 万元的债券，实现的利得如下所示：

	元
100 万元债券的公允价值（10,749,395 元的 10%）	1,074,940
100 万元债券的账面价值（10,407,192 元的 10%）	1,040,719
在损益中确认的处置利润	34,221

由于主体出售了“超过非重大金额”的持有至到期的投资，该投资组合

maturity investments, the portfolio is tainted. As a result, the entity has to reclassify the remaining C9m bonds as available-for-sale assets. The difference between the carrying value of C9m bonds and their fair value is recognised in other comprehensive income as shown below:

	C
Fair value of C9m bond (90% of C10,749,395)	9,674,455
Carrying value of C9m bonds (90% of C10,407,192)	9,366,473
Gain on reclassification recognised in other comprehensive income	307,982

Even though the remaining investment is classified as available-for-sale, the entity will continue to recognise the interest income and the amortisation of the premium using the effective interest method in profit or loss and fair value changes in other comprehensive income, as illustrated in the example in paragraph 9.45. After the tainting period is over, the entity may reinstate the bonds again to held-to-maturity. This will happen after 31 December 20X7 (two full financial years following the partial disposal).

Settlement date accounting for regular way transactions

9.47 As stated in paragraph 9.23 above, when an entity uses settlement date accounting for an asset that is subsequently measured at cost or amortised cost, the asset is recognised initially at its fair value at trade date. Any subsequent change in fair value between trade date and settlement date is not recognised (other than impairment losses). For assets that are subsequently measured at fair value, any change in fair value between trade date and settlement date is recognised:

- In profit or loss for assets classified as at FVTPL.
- In other comprehensive income for assets classified as available-for-sale.

9.48 When assets measured at fair value are sold on a regular way basis, the change in fair value between trade date (the date the entity enters into the sales contract) and settlement date (the date proceeds are received) is not recorded

受到“感染”。所以，该主体必须将剩余的900万债券重分类为可供出售资产。900万债券的账面价值与其公允价值之间的差额在其他综合收益中确认，如下所示：

	元
900万元债券的公允价值（10,749,395元的90%）	9,674,455
900万元债券的账面价值（10,407,192元的90%）	9,366,473
在其他综合收益中确认的重分类利得	307,982

即使把剩余的投资划分为可供出售类，该主体也将使用实际利率法，在损益中继续确认利息收入和溢价摊销，并在其他综合收益中确认公允价值变动，如第9.45段所示。“惩罚期”结束后，该主体可将该债券再次恢复至持有至到期类。这将在20X7年12月31日后进行（处置部分投资后满两个完整财年）。

常规方式交易的结算日会计

9.47　按照上文第9.23段的阐述，主体对于后续以成本或摊余成本计量的资产使用结算日会计核算时，该资产以交易日的公允价值进行初始确认。交易日与结算日之间公允价值的后续变化（减值损失除外）不予确认。对于后续以公允价值计量的资产，需按照下列方式确认交易日与结算日之间公允价值的变动。

- 对于以公允价值计量且其变动计入损益的资产，将该变动确认为损益。
- 对于可供出售类的资产，将该变动确认为其他综合收益。

9.48　以公允价值计量的资产按照常规方式售出后，不记录其在交易日（主体订立销售合同的日期）与结算日（取得收入的日期）之间公允价值的变动，因为卖方对公允价值变动享有的权利在交易日已终止（详见第八章）。

because the seller's right to changes in fair value ceases on the trade date (see further chapter 8).

Negative fair values

9.49 The standard clarifies that if a financial instrument that was previously recognised as a financial asset is measured at fair value and its fair value falls below zero, it becomes a financial liability that should be measured as considered below. [IAS 39 para AG 66].

Subsequent measurement of financial liabilities

9.50 After initial recognition, an entity should measure financial liabilities, other than those described in paragraphs 9.52 to 9.66 below, at amortised cost using the effective interest method as discussed from paragraph 9.67 below. [IAS 39 para 47].

9.51 Where a financial liability is carried at amortised cost, a gain or loss is recognised in profit or loss when the financial liability is derecognised or through the amortisation process. [IAS 39 para 56].

Financial liabilities at fair value through profit or loss

9.52 After initial recognition, financial liabilities falling within this category (including liabilities held-for-trading and derivative liabilities not designated as hedging instruments) are measured at fair value. However, a derivative liability that is linked to and must be settled by delivery of an unquoted equity instrument whose fair value cannot be reliably measured should be measured at cost. [IAS 39 para 47(a)].

9.53 A change in a financial liability's fair value in this category that is not part of a hedging relationship should be recognised in the profit or loss for the period. [IAS 39 para 55]. The standard's requirements for determining the fair value of instruments that fall to be measured on this basis are considered from paragraph 9.94 below.

负公允价值

9.49　准则澄清，如果一项以公允价值计量的金融工具之前被确认为金融资产，当其公允价值低于零时，则该工具成为金融负债，其计量考虑如下。[IAS 39 AG 第 66 段]。

金融负债的后续计量

9.50　初始确认后，除了下文第 9.52 段和第 9.66 段的情形之外，主体对于金融负债应使用下文第 9.67 段起所述的实际利率法，以摊余成本计量。[IAS 39 第 47 段]。

9.51　当金融负债以摊余成本计量时，在该金融负债终止确认时或在整个摊销的过程中确认损益。[IAS 39 第 56 段]。

以公允价值计量且其变动计入损益的金融负债

9.52　初始确认后，属于此类的金融负债（包括未被指定为套期工具的交易性负债和衍生工具负债）以公允价值计量。但是，与无报价的权益工具（其公允价值不能可靠计量）挂钩，并必须通过交付该权益工具结算的衍生工具负债应以成本计量。[IAS 39 第 47（a）段]。

9.53　此类金融负债的公允价值变动，且不属于套期关系部分，应在当期损益中确认。[IAS 39 第 55 段]。对于以此为计量基础的工具，有关其公允价值确定的准则规定参见自下文第 9.94 段起的说明。

Financial liabilities arising on transfers of financial assets

9.54 Certain financial liabilities may arise when a transfer of a financial asset does not qualify for derecognition, or is accounted for using the continuing involvement approach. For example, a sale of an asset that is accompanied by the seller giving a guarantee of the asset's future worth may, depending on the substance, give rise to the asset's derecognition and recognition of a liability in respect of the guarantee or it may result in the asset not being derecognised and the proceeds being shown as a liability. Special rules apply for the measurement of the transferred asset and the associated liability so that these are measured on a basis that reflects the rights and obligations that the entity has retained. [IAS 39 paras 29, 31, 47(b)]. See further chapter 8.

Financial guarantee contracts

9.55 Financial guarantee contracts are defined in chapter 3. Financial guarantee contracts that are accounted for as financial liabilities under IAS 39 by the issuer are initially recognised at fair value. If the financial guarantee contract was issued to an unrelated party in a stand-alone arm's length transaction, its fair value at inception would likely be to equal the premium received, unless there was evidence to the contrary. [IAS 39 para AG4(a)].

9.56 In some circumstances, an issuer expects to receive recurring future premiums from an issued financial guarantee contract (for example, it issues a five year guarantee with annual premiums due at the start of each year). In that situation, an issue arises as to whether the issuer should recognise a receivable for the discounted value of the expected future premiums or should it recognise only the initial cash received (if any). As stated above, IAS 39 requires the financial guarantee contract to be initially recorded at fair value; that is likely to equal the premium received. By analogy with derivative contracts the fair value will take into account any future cash flows on the instrument including those relating to premiums receivable.

9.57 IAS 39 does not explicitly prohibit the recognition of a separate receivable

转让金融资产产生的金融负债

9.54　金融资产转让不符合终止确认条件的，或使用继续涉入法进行会计处理时，可能会形成某项金融负债。例如，出售一项资产时，卖方对该资产的未来价值进行了担保，视具体情况而言，可能导致该资产终止确认，但对担保确认一项负债，或导致该资产不能被终止确认，而收款反映为负债。对于转让资产和相关负债的计量有专门规定，以便其计量基础能反映主体所保留的权利和义务。[IAS 39 第 29 段、第 31 段、第 47（b）段]。详见第八章。

财务担保合同

9.55　第三章中对财务担保合同进行了定义。按照 IAS 39 的规定，发行人将财务担保合同在会计处理中记为金融负债，并以公允价值进行初始确认。如果在独立的公平交易中与非关联方订立财务担保合同，除非有相反证据，该合同的初始公允价值很可能等于已收取的保费。[IAS 39 AG 第 4（a）段]。

9.56　在某些情况下，发行人希望从已签发的财务担保合同中获得未来分期保费（例如，发行人订立了一份五年期的财务担保合同，年保费于每年年初支付）。在这种情况下存在这样的问题，即发行人是否应将预期未来保费的折现价值确认为应收款，或只确认初始收款（如果有）。如上所述，IAS 39 规定财务担保合同应以公允价值进行初始计量，而公允价值很可能等于已收取的保费。与衍生工具合同同理，公允价值应将工具的所有未来现金流量，包括与应收保费相关的未来现金流量考虑在内。

9.57　IAS 39 没有明确禁止将未到期的未来保费确认为单项应收款。这点可

for future premiums not yet due. This is evidenced by the basis for conclusions, paragraph BC 23D, which states that the IAS 39 requirement for initial recognition at fair value is consistent with US GAAP as represented by FIN 45 (FIN 45 requires recognition of a liability for the guarantee and a separate receivable for future premiums). Accordingly, entities are permitted to recognise a separate receivable. The entity should select a presentation policy and apply it consistently to all issued financial guarantee contracts.

9.58 Subsequent to initial recognition, an issuer accounts for financial guarantee contracts at the higher of:

- the amount determined in accordance with IAS 37; and
- the amount initially recognised (fair value) less, when appropriate, cumulative amortisation of the initial amount recognised in accordance with IAS 18.

[IAS 39 para 47(c)].

9.59 However, the above requirements do not apply:

- if the financial guarantee contract was designated at fair value through profit or loss at inception. A contract designated at inception as at fair value through profit or loss is measured at fair value subsequently; or
- if the financial guarantee contract was entered into or retained on transferring financial assets or financial liabilities to another party and prevented derecognition of the financial asset or resulted in continuing involvement (see chapter 8).

[IAS 39 para 47(a)(b), AG 4].

9.60 From the perspective of the holder the contract is outside IAS 39's scope. The holder's accounting treatment depends on whether the guarantee is purchased in the context of the origination of a debt instrument or is purchased to guarantee pre-existing debt instruments. In the first case the purchaser of the financial guarantee contract, who could be either the borrower or the lender, should amortise the cost of the guarantee using the effective interest rate method, unless the debt instrument is measured at fair value through profit and loss. In the second case the cost is recognised as a pre-payment asset and amortised over the shorter of the life of the guarantee and the expected life of the guaranteed debt instruments. The asset is

以通过 BC 第23D 段的结论基础得以证明。BC 第23D 段阐述了 IAS 39 对于以公允价值进行初始确认的规定，与美国一般公认会计原则（US GAAP）的规定是一致的，后者体现在第 45 号解释（“FIN 45”，其要求将担保确认为负债，将未来保费确认为单项应收款）。所以，主体可以确认单项应收款。主体应选择一项列报政策，并将其一致地应用于所有已签发的财务担保合同。

9.58　初始确认后，发行人按照以下两者金额的较高者，对财务担保合同进行会计处理：

- 按照《国际会计准则第 37 号》（“IAS 37”）的规定确定的金额，及
- 初始确认的金额（公允价值）减去（在适当的情况下）根据 IAS 18 的规定所确认的初始金额的累计摊销。

[IAS 39 第 47（c）段]。

9.59　但是，以下情况不适用上述规定：

- 如果财务担保合同初始被指定为以公允价值计量且其变动计入损益。初始被指定为以公允价值计量且其变动计入损益的合同，后续以公允价值计量；或
- 向另一方转让金融资产或金融负债时订立或保留的财务担保合同，其阻碍了金融资产的终止确认或导致继续涉入（参见第八章）。

[IAS 39 第 47（a）（b）段、AG 第 4 段]。

9.60　从持有人的角度出发，财务担保合同不属于 IAS 39 的范围。持有人的会计处理取决于担保是在债务工具发行之初购买还是为现有的债务工具购买的。第一种情况中，除非债务工具是以公允价值且其变动计入损益计量，则财务担保合同的买方（既可以是借款人，也可以是贷款人）应使用实际利率法摊销担保成本。第二种情况中，该成本被认为是预付性质的资产，应在担保期限及被担保债务工具的预期期限二者孰短的期间内摊销。按照《国际会计准则第 36 号》（“IAS 36”）的规定，资产需进行减值测试。贷款人将摊销和减值作为利息收入的抵减，而借款人则将其视为一项额外财务费用。

tested for impairment under IAS 36. Lenders classify the amortisation and impairment charges as a reduction of interest income whilst borrowers treat it as an additional finance cost.

Intra-group financial guarantee contracts

9.61 As stated in chapter 3, intra-group financial guarantee contracts are not exempted from IAS 39's requirements and, on a stand-alone basis, will have to be measured in accordance with the standard. On a consolidation basis, the financial guarantee is not recognised as a separate contract, but is part of the group's liability to a third party (for example, a guarantee given by the parent to a subsidiary's bankers in the event the subsidiary fails to repay a loan to the bank when due). In the individual financial statements, the financial guarantee is recognised initially at fair value in accordance with IAS 39 (unless IFRS 4 applies).

9.62 Establishing such a fair value may be difficult if the financial guarantee contracts between related parties were not negotiated at arm's length and there are no comparable observable transactions with third parties. Given that intra-group guarantees are unlikely to be negotiated in a 'stand-alone arm's length transaction', fair value would have to be estimated.

9.63 As the fair value of an intra-group guarantee is unlikely to be equal to the fee charged, if any, the issuer would need to determine whether any difference should be treated as an expense or a capital contribution via an increase in investments in the subsidiary. This is an accounting policy choice. The method used should reflect the transaction's economic substance, be applied consistently to all similar transactions and be clearly disclosed in the financial statements. While each entity within a group can choose its own accounting policies, those policies must be aligned on consolidation.

9.64 Where a parent entity provides a guarantee to a bank that has advanced a loan to one of its subsidiaries, the subsidiary has obtained a benefit in that it would pay a lower rate of interest on the loan than it would have otherwise paid for an unguaranteed loan. The subsidiary could fair value the loan from the bank by reference to a normal market rate of interest it would pay on a similar but

集团内部财务担保合同

9.61 按照第三章的说明，集团内部财务担保合同并未从IAS 39规定中豁免，所以在单独报表上须按照该准则进行计量。在合并层面，财务担保不被确认为单独合同，而是集团对第三方负债的一部分（例如，在子公司未能在贷款到期时向银行还款的情况下，母公司向子公司银行机构提供的担保）。在单独财务报表中，按照IAS 39的规定，应以公允价值对财务担保进行初始确认（除非适用《国际财务报告准则第4号》（“IFRS 4”））。

9.62 如果关联方之间未按照公平的原则协商财务担保合同，且没有与第三方的交易可作为参考，则确定其公允价值可能有难度。考虑到集团内部担保不大可能在“独立的公平交易”条件下议定，往往需要估计公允价值。

9.63 因为集团内部担保的公允价值不大可能与所收取的费用相等，所以对于差额，发行人需要确定将其作为费用处理或视作对子公司投资增加而作为资本投入处理。这是一项会计政策选择。所采用的方法应反映交易的经济实质，并一致地应用于所有类似交易中，且在财务报告中清晰披露。虽然集团内的各主体可以选择各自的会计政策，但在合并报表中所选的会计政策必须一致。

9.64 当母公司为其子公司借款向银行提供担保时，该子公司因此获益，因为其将支付的有担保借款利率比无担保借款利率低。该子公司可以根据一般市场中获取无担保的类似借款的利率确定借款的公允价值，并将利差作为母公司资本投入计入权益。或者，该子公司可以将该计量单元视为担保借款，因此借款的公允价值即子公司收到款项的面值。IAS 39并没有规定财务担保

unguaranteed loan and take the benefit of the interest differential to equity as a capital contribution from the parent. Alternatively, the subsidiary could view the unit of account as being the guaranteed loan and therefore the fair value would be expected to be the face value of the proceeds the subsidiary receives. IAS 39 does not address the accounting for financial guarantees by the beneficiary and there is no requirement in IAS 24 to fair value non-arms length related party transactions. Therefore, there is an accounting policy choice as to whether a capital contribution is recognised in equity by the subsidiary for the benefit of the lower rate of interest on the loan than it would have otherwise paid for an unguaranteed loan. In practice, there is diversity on which accounting policy is applied, however, the majority of subsidiaries do not take the capital contribution to equity approach and instead recognise the fair value of the guaranteed loan.

Commitments to provide off-market loans

9.65 An entity may enter into a commitment to provide a loan at a below-market rate. After initial recognition at fair value, such a commitment is subsequently measured in the same way as a financial guarantee contract stated above. [IAS 39 para 47(d)].

Designation as hedged items

9.66 Financial liabilities that are designated as hedged items are subject to measurement under IAS 39's hedging accounting requirements. [IAS 39 para 47]. These special accounting rules generally override the normal accounting rules for financial liabilities. Hedge accounting is covered in chapter 10.

Amortised cost and the effective interest method

General

9.67 The amortised cost of a financial asset or financial liability is defined as the amount at which the financial asset or financial liability is measured at initial

收益方的会计核算方法，而 IAS 24 中也没有规定用公允价值计量关联方的非公平交易。因此，关于子公司是否应当将利率上相对无担保借款所获得的利益确认为资本投入，存在会计政策的选择。实务中有不同处理，然而，大部分子公司并不采用资本投入计入权益的方法，而是用公允价值确认有担保的借款。

提供低于市场利率贷款的承诺

9.65　某主体可能承诺以低于市场水平的利率提供贷款。以公允价值对其进行初始确认后，将按照上述财务担保合同同样的计量方式对此类承诺进行后续计量。[IAS 39 第 47（d）段]。

指定为被套期项目

9.66　对指定为被套期项目的金融负债应按照 IAS 39 的套期会计要求进行计量。[IAS 39 第 47 段]。通常，这些专门的会计规则优先于金融负债适用的一般会计准则。第十章中阐述了套期会计的内容。

摊余成本和实际利率法

综述

9.67　金融资产或金融负债初始确认时的金额，减去本金还款额，加上或减去使用“实际利率法”将初始金额和到期日应付金额之差摊销后的累计摊销

recognition minus principal repayments, plus or minus the cumulative amortisation using the 'effective interest method' of any difference between that initial amount and the amount payable at maturity and minus any reduction (directly or through the use of an allowance account) for impairment or uncollectibility. [IAS 39 para 9].

9.68 The effective interest method is a method of calculating the amortised cost of a financial asset or a financial liability (or group of financial assets or financial liabilities) and of allocating the interest income or interest expense over the relevant period. The method's principal features are as follows:

- The effective interest rate is the rate that exactly discounts estimated future cash payments or receipts through the financial instrument's *expected life* or, when appropriate, a shorter period, to the net carrying amount of the financial asset or financial liability (see para 9.76 below). The effective interest rate is sometimes termed the level yield to maturity or to the next repricing date and is the internal rate of return of the financial asset or liability for that period. The internal rate of return can be calculated using a financial calculator, or the IRR function in a spreadsheet.
- When calculating the effective interest rate, an entity should estimate cash flows considering all the financial instrument's contractual terms (for example, pre-payment, call and similar options), but should not consider future credit losses.
- The calculation should include all fees and points paid or received between parties to the contract that are an integral part of the effective interest rate, transaction costs, and all other premiums or discounts.

[IAS 39 para 9].

9.69 The effective interest rate method is grounded in historical transaction values, because its determination is based on the initial carrying amount of the financial asset or liability. Therefore, once determined it is not recalculated to reflect fair value changes in financial assets, for example, interest bearing available-for-sale assets due to changes in market interest rates. The effective interest method produces a periodic interest income or expense equal to a constant percentage of the carrying value of the financial asset or liability as illustrated in the example given in paragraph 9.78.

额，然后减去因减值或无法收回而产生的任何减少额（直接核销或通过备抵账户减少），所得出的金额即为金融资产或金融负债的摊余成本。[IAS 39 第9段]。

9.68　实际利率法是计算金融资产或金融负债（或金融资产组或金融负债组）摊余成本的方法，并且还是在相关期间内分配利息收入或利息支出的方法。该方法的主要特征如下：

- 实际利率是把预计未来现金付款或收款按照金融工具的预期期限或适用的更短期间，折现为金融资产或金融负债账面净值的利率（参见下文第9.76段）。实际利率有时被称为至到期日或下一个重新定价日的收益率，即此期间内金融资产或金融负债的内含收益率。可以使用金融计算器或电子数据表中内含收益率（IRR）函数计算内含收益率。

- 在计算实际利率时，主体应考虑金融工具的所有合同条款（例如提前偿付权、看涨期权和类似期权）来预计现金流量，但不得考虑未来信用损失。

- 计算应包括各方之间按合同支付或收取的所有作为实际利率构成的费用和贴息，交易费用和其他所有溢价或折价。

[IAS 39 第9段]。

9.69　实际利率法是以历史交易价值为基础的，因为其根据金融资产或金融负债的初始账面价值来确定。因此，一旦确定，就不再重新计算以反映金融资产的公允价值变动，例如，市场利率变动引起的带息可供出售资产的公允价值变动。实际利率法确定的期间利息收入或费用与金融资产或金融负债账面价值之间的比例是恒定的，说明见第9.78段的示例。

Estimation of cash flows

9.70 As noted in paragraph 9.68 above, the effective interest method uses a set of *estimated* future cash flows through the expected life of the financial instrument using all the financial instrument's contractual terms, rather than *contractual* cash flows. However, the financial instrument's expected life cannot exceed its contracted life. This applies not only to individual financial instruments, but to groups of financial instruments as well to achieve consistency of application. As the cash flows are often outlined in a contract or linked in some other way to the financial asset or financial liability in question, there is a presumption that the future cash flows can be reliably estimated for most financial assets and financial liabilities, in particular for a group of similar financial assets and similar financial liabilities. [IAS 39 para 9]. For example, for a portfolio of pre-payable mortgage loans, financial institutions often estimate pre-payment patterns based on historical data and build the cash flows arising on early settlement (including any pre-payment penalty) into the effective interest rate calculation.

9.71 However, in some rare cases it might not be possible to estimate reliably the cash flows of a financial instrument (or group of financial instruments). In those rare cases, the entity should use the contractual cash flows over the full contractual term of the financial instrument (or group of financial instruments). [IAS 39 para 9].

9.72 The standard requires that in estimating the future cash flows all the instrument's contractual terms, including pre-payment, call and similar options should be considered. [IAS 39 para 9]. Such pre-payment, call and put options, which are often embedded in the debt instruments, are derivatives. Therefore, as explained, in chapter 5, the entity must first determine whether such options need to be separately accounted for as embedded derivatives. Separate accounting for the embedded derivative will not be necessary if the option's exercise price is approximately equal to the instrument's amortised cost on each exercise date, or the exercise price reimburses the lender for an amount up to the approximate present value of the lost interest for the remaining term of the host contract, because in that situation the embedded derivative is regarded as closely related to the debt host. [IAS 39 para AG 30(g)].

9.73 Where a pre-payment, call or put option falls to be separately accounted

现金流量估计

9.70 如上文第9.68段所述，实际利率法采用的是根据金融工具合同的所有条款，在预期期限内的*预计*未来现金流量，而非*合同*现金流量。但是，金融工具的预期期限不能超过其合同年限。这项规定不仅适用于单项金融工具，也适用于金融工具组以保持一致。因为现金流量总是在合同中有所说明，或以其他方式与标的金融资产或金融负债相挂钩，所以可认为对于大部分金融资产和金融负债，特别是对类似的金融资产组和类似的金融负债组来说，可以对未来现金流量进行可靠估计。[IAS 39 第9段]。例如，对于可以提前还款的按揭贷款来说，金融机构通常以历史数据为基础，对提前偿付模式进行估计，并将提前结算产生的现金流量（包括任何提前偿付罚金）纳入实际利率计算。

9.71 但是，在极少数情况下，可能无法对一项金融工具（或金融工具组）的现金流量进行可靠估计。在这些极少数的情况中，主体应采用金融工具（或金融工具组）整个合同期间的合同现金流量。[IAS 39 第9段]。

9.72 该准则要求在估计未来现金流量时，应考虑工具的所有合同条款，包括提前偿付权、看涨期权和类似期权。[IAS 39 第9段]。这些常常嵌入在债务工具中的提前偿付选择权、看涨期权和看跌期权是衍生工具。所以，按照第五章的说明，主体必须首先确定是否需要将此等期权作为嵌入式衍生工具进行单独核算。如果期权的行权价格与工具在各行权日的摊余成本近似，或行权价格补偿给贷款人的金额与主合同剩余年限内其利息损失的现值近似，则无需对嵌入式衍生工具进行单独核算。因为在这种情况下，嵌入式衍生工具被认为与主债务紧密相关。[IAS 39 AG 第30（g）段]。

9.73 如果需要对提前偿付权、看涨期权或看跌期权进行单独核算，则确定

for, its impact on estimating the future cash flows for the purposes of determining the effective interest rate should be ignored. Although this is not explained in the standard, it is rather obvious as to do otherwise would result in double counting the effects of the embedded derivative in profit or loss - first through the option's fair value movement and, secondly, through its effect on the effective interest rate. In practice, this means that if the option is regarded as closely related and not separately accounted for, the entity, in determining the instrument's expected life, needs to assess whether the option is likely to be exercised in estimating the future cash flows at inception. Furthermore, this assessment should continue in subsequent periods until the debt instrument is settled, because the likelihood of the option being exercised will affect the timing and amount of the future cash flows and will have an immediate impact in profit or loss. On the other hand, if the option is accounted for as a separate derivative, such considerations are not necessary as the likelihood of the option being exercised will be reflected in its fair value. In that situation, the effective interest rate is based on the instrument's contractual term. See further paragraph 9. 84 below.

9. 74 The standard also makes it clear that expected or future credit losses (defaults) should not be included in estimates of cash flows, because this would be a departure from the incurred loss model for impairment recognition. However, in some cases, financial assets are acquired at a deep discount that reflects incurred losses (for example, purchase of impaired debt). As such losses are already reflected in the price, they should be included in the estimated cash flows when computing the effective interest rate. [IAS 39 para AG 5]. Accordingly, the effective interest rate of the acquired distressed loan would be the discount rate that equates the present value of the expected cash flows (this would be less than the contractual cash flows specified in the loan agreement because of incurred credit losses) with the purchase price of the loan. The alternative of not including such credit losses in the calculation of the effective interest rate means that the entity would recognise a higher interest income than that inherent in the price paid.

Transaction costs and fees

9. 75 Transaction costs and fees are discussed from paragraph 9. 12 above. To the

实际利率时不考虑其对预计现金流量的影响。虽然这点没有在该准则中明示，但如果不这样，显然将造成嵌入式衍生工具对损益影响的重复计算，即首先计入期权的公允价值变动，然后计入其对实际利率的影响。在实务上，意味着如果期权被认为紧密相关而未单独核算，则主体需要在初始预计未来现金流量时评估期权行使的可能性，以确定该工具的预计期限。而且，在后续期间也应继续进行该评估，直到该债务工具被结算。这是因为行权的可能性将影响未来现金流量的时点和金额，从而对损益造成即时影响。相反，如果把期权作为单独的衍生工具进行核算，因为行使期权的可能性将反映在其公允价值中，则无需进行上述评估。在这种情况下，实际利率将基于工具的合同期限。详见下文第 9. 84 段。

9. 74　该准则还明确规定了不得将预期信用损失或未来信用损失（违约）纳入现金流量预计中，因为这样会偏离用于减值确认的已发生损失模型。但是，在有些情况下，以大幅折价获得的金融资产反映了已发生损失（比如购买已减值债务）。因为此类损失已经反映在价格中，所以在计算实际利率时应将其纳入预计现金流量中。［IAS 39 AG 第 5 段］。因此，所获得的折价贷款的实际利率是使得预计现金流量的现值（因为已发生的信用损失，所以预计现金流量将少于贷款协议中规定的合同现金流量）等于该贷款买价的折现率。如果不把这些信用损失纳入到实际利率计算中，意味着主体将确认的利息收入高于支付价格中所含的利息收入。

交易成本和费用

9. 75　已在上文第 9. 12 段阐述了交易成本和费用。如果交易成本和费用是发

extent that they are integral to generating an involvement with a financial instrument, such costs and fees are included in the financial instrument's initial measurement. For financial instruments that are carried at amortised cost, such as held-to-maturity investments, loans and receivables, and financial liabilities that are not at fair value through profit or loss, transaction costs and fees are, therefore, included in calculating amortised cost using the effective interest method. This means that, in effect, they are amortised through profit or loss over the instrument's life (see para 9.68 above).

Amortisation period

9.76 Consistent with the estimated cash flow approach outlined from paragraph 9.70 above, the standard requires fees, points paid or received, transaction costs and other premiums or discount that are integral to the effective interest rate to be amortised over the instrument's expected life or, when applicable, a shorter period. A shorter period is used when the variable (for example, interest rates) to which the fee, transaction costs, discount or premium relates is repriced to market rates before the instrument's expected maturity. In such a case, the appropriate amortisation period is the period to the next such repricing date. [IAS 39 AG6]. The application of this requirement in the context of a floating rate instrument is considered in paragraph 9.84 below.

9.77 There is a presumption that the expected life of a financial instrument (or group of similar financial instruments) can be estimated reliably. However, in those rare cases when it is not possible to estimate reliably the expected life, the entity should use the full contractual term of the financial instrument (or group of financial instruments) as the amortisation period. [IAS 39 para 9]. The expected life cannot exceed the contractual term.

Illustrations of the effective interest rate method of amortisation

Fixed interest instruments

9.78 The examples that follow illustrate the application of the effective interest

行金融工具所固有的，则将这些成本和费用纳入金融工具的初始计量。因而对于以摊余成本计量的金融工具而言，例如持有至到期投资、贷款和应收款项以及并非以公允价值计量且其变动计入损益的金融负债，交易成本和费用纳入摊余成本计算中，并适用实际利率法。这意味着实际上其在工具的期限内摊销计入损益。(参见上文第 9. 68 段)。

摊销期间

9. 76　与上文第 9. 70 段所概述的现金流量预计方法一致，该准则规定属于实际利率组成部分的支付或收取的费用和贴息，交易费用和其他溢价或折价，在工具的预计年限或更短的期间（如适用）内进行摊销。当与收费、交易费用、折价或溢价相关的变量（例如利率），在工具的预计到期日之前，被重新定价为市场费率时，则采用更短的期间。在这种情况下，恰当的摊销期间为到下一个重新定价日的期间。[IAS 39 AG 第 6 段]。下文第 9. 84 段将说明如何对浮动利率工具运用该规定。

9. 77　一般来说，认为可以对某一金融工具（或类似金融工具组）的预计期限进行可靠估计，但在极少数情况下，如果不能对预计期限进行可靠预估，则主体应将金融工具（或金融工具组）的完整合同期限作为摊销期间。[IAS 39 第 9 段]。预计期限不能超过合同期限。

实际利率法摊销的说明

固定利率工具

9. 78　以下各示例是在固定利率贷款中使用实际利率法的演示。在示例 1 中，

rate method of amortisation to fixed interest loans. In example 1, the fixed rate loan asset is repayable only at maturity (a similar example is given in IAS 39 para IG B26). In example 2, the fixed rate loan asset is repayable in equal annual instalments. In example 3, the loan's pre-determined rate of interest increases over the instrument's term ('stepped interest').

Example 1 – Fixed interest loan asset repayable at maturity

On 1 January 20X5, entity A originates a 10 year 7% C1m loan. The loan carries an annual interest rate of 7% payable at the end of each year and is repayable at par at the end of year 10. Entity A charges a 1.25% (C12,500) non-refundable loan origination fee to the borrower and also incurs C25,000 in direct loan origination costs.

The contract specifies that the borrower has an option to pre-pay the instrument and that no penalty will be charged for pre-payment. At inception, the entity expects the borrower not to pre-pay.

The initial carrying amount of the loan asset is calculated as follows:

	C
Loan principal	1,000,000
Origination fees charged to borrower	(12,500)
Origination costs incurred by lender	25,000
Carrying amount of loan	1,012,500

As explained in paragraph 9.72 above, it is first necessary to determine whether the pre-payment option should be separately accounted for. In this example, as the loan's principal amount is likely to be approximately equal to the loan's amortised cost at each exercise date, the borrower's option to pre-pay is closely related and not separately accounted for.

As the entity expects the borrower not to pre-pay, the amortisation period is equal to the instrument's full term. In calculating the effective interest rate that will apply over the term of the loan at a constant rate on the carrying amount,

固定利率贷款资产仅在到期日偿还（IAS 39 IG 第 B26 段也给出了类似示例）。在示例 2 中，固定利率贷款资产为每年等额分期偿还。在示例 3 中，在合同存续期间，预定的贷款利率逐渐增加（“递增利率”）。

示例 1——在到期日偿还的固定利率贷款资产

20X5 年 1 月 1 日，主体 A 发放了一笔 10 年期、年利率为 7% 的 100 万元贷款，每年年末支付利息，并在第 10 年年末以面值清偿贷款。主体 A 向借款人收取 1.25%（12,500 元）的不可退还的贷款启动费，并产生了 25,000 元的贷款启动的直接费用。

该合同规定借款人可选择提前还款，且无需因提前还款支付任何罚金。在初始日，主体预计借款人不会提前还款。

贷款资产初始账面金额的计算结果如下所示：

	元
贷款本金	1,000,000
向借款人收取的贷款启动费	(12,500)
由放贷人产生的贷款启动费用	25,000
贷款的账面金额	1,012,500

按照上文第 9.72 段的说明，首先需要确定是否应对提前还款权进行单独核算。在该示例中，因为贷款的本金基本与贷款在各行权日的摊余成本大致相等，所以借款人的提前还款选择权是紧密相关的，因而不需要单独核算。

因为该主体预计借款人不会提前还款，所以摊销期间与合同的完整期限相等。计算的实际利率将在贷款期间以恒定利率应用于账面金额，以上计算出的折现率约为 6.823%，该折现率是通过将为期 10 年的每年付息

the discount rate necessary to equate 10 annual payments of C70,000 and a final payment at maturity of C1 million to the initial carrying amount of C1,012,500 is approximately 6.823%.

The carrying amount of the loan over the period to maturity will, therefore, be as follows:

	Cash in flows (coupon)	Interest income@ 6.823%	Amortisation of net fees	Carrying amount
	C	C	C	C
1 Jan 20X5				1,012,500
31 Dec 20X5	70,000	69,083	917	1,011,588
31 Dec 20X6	70,000	69,025	975	1,010,613
31 Dec 20X7	70,000	68,959	1,041	1,009,572
31 Dec 20X8	70,000	68,888	1,112	1,008,460
31 Dec 20X9	70,000	68,812	1,188	1,007,272
31 Dec 20Y0	70,000	68,731	1,269	1,006,003
31 Dec 20Y1	70,000	68,644	1,356	1,004,647
31 Dec 20Y2	70,000	68,552	1,448	1,003,199
31 Dec 20Y3	70,000	68,453	1,547	1,001,652
31 Dec 20Y4	70,000	68,348	1,652	1,000,000
	700,000	687,500	12,500	
31 Dec 20Y4	Repayment of principal			(1,000,000)
31 Dec 20Y4	Carrying value of loan			Nil

As can be seen from the above, the effective interest income for the period is calculated by applying the effective interest rate of 6.823% to the loan's amortised cost at the end of the previous reporting period. The annual interest income decreases each year to reflect the decrease in the asset's carrying value as the initial net fee is amortised. Thus the difference between the calculated effective income for a given reporting period and the loan's coupon is the

70,000 元，加上到期最终支付额 100 万元，折现为初始账面金额 1,012,500 元所得出的。

因此，该贷款在到期日前的各期账面金额如下所示：

	现金流入（票息）	利息收入（利率 6.823%）	净费用摊销	账面金额
	元	元	元	元
20X5 年 1 月 1 日				1,012,500
20X5 年 12 月 31 日	70,000	69,083	917	1,011,588
20X6 年 12 月 31 日	70,000	69,025	975	1,010,613
20X7 年 12 月 31 日	70,000	68,959	1,041	1,009,572
20X8 年 12 月 31 日	70,000	68,888	1,112	1,008,460
20X9 年 12 月 31 日	70,000	68,812	1,188	1,007,272
20Y0 年 12 月 31 日	70,000	68,731	1,269	1,006,003
20Y1 年 12 月 31 日	70,000	68,644	1,356	1,004,647
20Y2 年 12 月 31 日	70,000	68,552	1,448	1,003,199
20Y3 年 12 月 31 日	70,000	68,453	1,547	1,001,652
20Y4 年 12 月 31 日	70,000	68,348	1,652	1,000,000
	700,000	687,500	12,500	
20Y4 年 12 月 31 日	本金偿还			(1,000,000)
20Y4 年 12 月 31 日	贷款账面价值			0

由上表可以看出，通过把 6.823% 的实际利率运用到前一期报告期末的贷款摊余成本中，计算得出当期的实际利息收入。逐年减少的年利息收入反映了资产账面价值的减少，原因是初始费用净额被逐渐摊销。所以既定报告期所计算的实际利息与贷款票面利息的差额是当期净费用的摊销额。该贷款在上一期末的摊余成本加上本报告期的摊销额，得到该贷款在本期末的摊余成本。截至到期日，已收净费用全部摊销完毕，所以贷

amortisation of the net fees during that reporting period. The loan's amortised cost at the end of the previous period plus amortisation in the current reporting period gives the loan's amortised cost at the end of the current period. By maturity date, the net fees received are fully amortised and the loan's carrying amount is equal to the face amount, which is then repaid in full.

Example 2 – Fixed interest loan asset repayable in equal annual instalments

On 1 January 20X5, entity A originates a 10 year 7% C1 million loan. The loan is repaid in equal annual payments of C142, 378 through to maturity date at 31 December 20Y4. Entity A charges a 1. 25% (C12, 500) non-refundable loan origination fee to the borrower and also incurs C25, 000 in direct loan origination costs.

The contract specifies that the borrower has an option to pre-pay the instrument and that no penalty will be charged for pre-payment. At inception, the entity expects the borrower not to pre-pay.

The initial carrying amount of the loan is calculated as follows:

	C
Loan principal	1, 000, 000
Origination fees charged to borrower	(12, 500)
Origination costs incurred by lender	25, 000
Carrying amount of loan	1, 012, 500

As in the previous example, the pre-payment option will not be separately accounted for. In calculating the effective interest rate that will apply over the term of the loan at a constant rate on the carrying amount, the discount rate necessary to equate 10 annual payments of C142, 378 to the initial carrying amount of C1, 012, 500 is approximately 6. 7322%. The carrying amount of the loan over the period to maturity will, therefore, be as follows:

款的账面金额就等于票面金额，该金额于到期日偿还。

示例 2——本金每年等额偿还的固定利率贷款资产

20X5 年 1 月 1 日，主体 A 发放了一笔 10 年期、年利率为 7% 的 100 万元贷款。该贷款在 20Y4 年 12 月 31 日的到期日前，每年等额分期偿还 142, 378 元。主体 A 向借款人收取了 1. 25% （12, 500 元）的不可退还的贷款启动费，并产生了 25, 000 元的贷款启动的直接费用。

该合同规定借款人可选择提前还款，且无需因提前还款而收取任何罚金。在初始日，主体预计借款人不会提前还款。

贷款的初始账面金额计算如下所示：

	元
贷款本金	1, 000, 000
向借款人收取的贷款启动费	(12, 500)
由放贷人产生的贷款启动费用	25, 000
贷款账面金额	1, 012, 500

如前例，不单独核算提前还款选择权。计算的实际利率将在贷款期以恒定利率应用于账面金额，上述计算的折现率约为 6. 7322%，该折现率是通过将为期 10 年每年支付的 142, 378 元，折现为初始账面金额 1, 012, 500 元得到的。该贷款在到期日前各期的账面金额如下所示：

	Cash in flows	Interest Income@ 6.7322%	Carrying amount
	C	C	C
1 Jan 20X5			1,012,500
31 Dec 20X5	142,378	68,164	938,286
31 Dec 20X6	142,378	63,167	859,075
31 Dec 20X7	142,378	57,835	774,531
31 Dec 20X8	142,378	52,143	684,296
31 Dec 20X9	142,378	46,068	587,987
31 Dec 20Y0	142,378	39,584	485,193
31 Dec 20Y1	142,378	32,664	375,479
31 Dec 20Y2	142,378	25,278	258,379
31 Dec 20Y3	142,378	17,395	133,396
31 Dec 20Y4	142,378	8,982	–
	1,423,780	411,280	

Example 3 – Fixed interest loan asset with interest step-up

On 1 January 20X5, entity A originates a 5 year debt instrument for C1 million loan that is repayable at maturity. The contract provides for 5% interest in year 1 that increases by 2% in each of the following 4 years. Entity A also receives C25,000 in loan origination fees.

The loan's initial carrying amount is calculated as follows:

	C
Loan principal	1,000,000
Origination fees charged to borrower	(25,000)
Carrying amount of loan	975,000

	现金流入	利息收入(利率 6.7322%)	账面金额
	元	元	元
20X5 年 1 月 1 日			1,012,500
20X5 年 12 月 31 日	142,378	68,164	938,286
20X6 年 12 月 31 日	142,378	63,167	859,075
20X7 年 12 月 31 日	142,378	57,835	774,531
20X8 年 12 月 31 日	142,378	52,143	684,296
20X9 年 12 月 31 日	142,378	46,068	587,987
20Y0 年 12 月 31 日	142,378	39,584	485,193
20Y1 年 12 月 31 日	142,378	32,664	375,479
20Y2 年 12 月 31 日	142,378	25,278	258,379
20Y3 年 12 月 31 日	142,378	17,395	133,396
20Y4 年 12 月 31 日	142,378	8,982	-
	1,423,780	411,280	

示例 3——附有递增利率的固定利率贷款资产

20X5 年 1 月 1 日，主体 A 发放了一笔 5 年期的债务工具，贷款金额为 100 万元，到期偿还。合同规定第 1 年的利率为 5%，在后续四年中利率逐年增加 2%。主体 A 还收取了 25,000 元的贷款启动费用。

该贷款的初始账面金额计算如下：

	元
贷款本金	1,000,000
向借款人收取的贷款启动费	(25,000)
贷款的账面金额	975,000

In calculating the effective interest rate that will apply over the term of the loan at a constant rate on the carrying amount, the discount rate necessary to equate 5 annual step-up payments and a final payment at maturity of C1 million to the initial carrying amount of C975, 000 is approximately 9. 2934%.

	Interest income@ 9. 2934%	Cash in flows (coupon)	Carrying amount
	C	C	C
1 Jan 20X5			975, 000
31 Dec 20X5	90, 610	50, 000	1, 015, 610
31 Dec 20X6	94, 385	70, 000	1, 039, 995
31 Dec 20X7	96, 651	90, 000	1, 046, 646
31 Dec 20X8	97, 268	110, 000	1, 033, 914
31 Dec 20X9	96, 086	130, 000	1, 000, 000
	475, 000	450, 000	

If the borrower were to repay the entire loan of C1 million early, say in 20X9, when the loan asset's carrying value is C1, 033, 914, the excess amount of C33, 914 would have to be recognised in profit or loss. This effectively represents the excess income recognised in earlier periods that is now written back as shown below:

	C
Total income recognised to 31 Dec 20X8	378, 914
Amortisation of fees	(25, 000)
Cash received to 31 Dec 20X8	(320, 000)
Excess income recognised prior to pre-payment by borrower in 20X9	33, 914

计算的实际利率将在贷款期以恒定利率应用于账面金额，计算的折现率约为9.2934%，该折现率是通过将5年的递增利息支付额，加上到期最终支付额100万元，折现为初始账面金额975,000元得到的。

	利息收入（利率 9.2934%）元	现金流（票息）元	账面金额 元
20X5年1月1日			975,000
20X5年12月31日	90,610	50,000	1,015,610
20X6年12月31日	94,385	70,000	1,039,995
20X7年12月31日	96,651	90,000	1,046,646
20X8年12月31日	97,268	110,000	1,033,914
20X9年12月31日	96,086	130,000	1,000,000
	475,000	450,000	

如果借款人提前偿还所有的100万元贷款，比如在20X9年还款，贷款资产的账面价值达到1,033,914元，应将33,914元的超出金额确认在损益中。这实际表明了之前多确认的收入现在被转回，金额如下所示：

	元
在20X8年12月31日确认的总收入	378,914
费用摊销额	(25,000)
截至20X8年12月31日已收现金	(320,000)
在20X9年借款人提前还款之前已确认的超额收入	33,914

Changes in estimated cash flows

9.79 As explained above, the cash flows that are discounted to arrive at the effective interest rate are estimated cash flows that are expected to occur over the instrument's expected life. However, in practice, actual cash flows rarely occur in line with expectations. There is usually variation in the amount, timing or both. Differences from the original estimates present a problem for the effective interest rate. If the variation is ignored, either the asset or liability will amortise before all of the cash flows occur, or a balance may remain after the last cash flow.

9.80 The standard, therefore, requires an entity to adjust the carrying amount of the financial asset or financial liability (or group of financial instruments) to reflect actual and revised estimated cash flows whenever it revises its cash flow estimates. The entity recalculates the carrying amount by computing the present value of estimated future cash flows at the financial instrument's original effective interest rate, or, when applicable, the revised effective interest calculated in accordance with IAS 39 paragraph 92 (see chapter 10). The adjustment is recognised in profit or loss as income or expense. [IAS 39 para AG 8].

Example – Changes in estimates of cash flows

The facts arc thc samc as in example 1 in paragraph 9.78 above, except that on 1 January 20Y1, entity A revises its estimates of cash flows as it now expects that, because of a significant fall in interest rates during the previous period, the borrower is likely to exercise its option to pre-pay. Accordingly, entity A anticipates that 40% of the loan is likely to be repaid by the borrower in 20Y1, with the remaining 60% progressively at 20% in the following three years to maturity.

The revised cash flows are shown below. In accordance with paragraph 9.80 above, the opening balance at 1 January 20Y1 is adjusted. The adjusted amount is calculated by discounting the amounts the entity expects to receive in 20Y1 and subsequent years using the original effective rate of 6.823%. This results in the adjustment shown below. The adjustment is recognised in profit or loss in 20Y1.

现金流量估计的变动

9.79　如上所述，用于计算实际利率的现金流量是金融工具在其预期期限内的预计现金流量。但在实务中，实际现金流量很少按预期出现，通常会在金额或时点或是这两方面都有变化。因此。实际现金流量与原先预计现金流量之间的差异会给实际利率计算带来麻烦。如果忽略此等变动，会导致在全部现金流量发生之前资产或负债就已经摊销完毕，或者是在最后一次现金流量发生之后还有账面结余。

9.80　因此该准则要求，当一个主体修正预计现金流量时，需要调整金融资产或金融负债（或金融工具组）的账面金额，以反映实际修正后的预计现金流量。主体应按金融工具的原始实际利率，或者在适用时根据IAS 39第92段的规定计算的修正后实际利率（参见第十章），计算未来预计现金流的现值，从而重新计算出账面金额。相关调整应在损益中确认为收入或费用。[IAS 39 AG第8段]。

示例——现金流量的预计变动

本示例与上文第9.78段的示例1假设条件一样，但以下条件除外，即主体A预计因上期利率大幅下跌，借款人很可能选择提前还贷，故于20Y1年1月1日对预计现金流量进行了修正。因此，主体A预计借款人很可能于20Y1年偿还40%的贷款，余下的60%将于随后到期日前的三年期间逐年偿还20%。

修正后的现金流量如下所示。根据上文第9.80段所述，调整了20Y1年1月1日的期初余额。按原始实际利率6.823%对主体预计于20Y1年及随后年度的收款进行折现，便可计算出调整后的金额，调整结果如下所示。该项调整在20Y1年损益中确认。

				Carrying amount
1 Jan 20Y1	Opening amortised carrying amount before revision			1, 006, 003
	Adjustment for changes in estimate – profit or loss			2, 563
1 Jan 20Y1	Adjusted amortised carrying amount after revision			1, 003, 440
	Opening amortised carrying amount	**Interest income@ 6. 823%**	**Cash in flows (coupon + repayment of principal)**	**Closing amortised carrying amount**
	C	**C**	**C**	**C**
31 Dec 20Y1	1, 003, 440	68, 465	70, 000 + 400, 000	601, 905
31 Dec 20Y2	601, 905	41, 068	42, 000 + 200, 000	400, 973
31 Dec 20Y3	400, 973	27, 358	28, 000 + 200, 000	200, 331
31 Dec 20Y4	200, 331	13, 669	14, 000 + 200, 000	–

9. 81 For financial assets reclassified in accordance with IAS 39 paragraphs 50B, D and E (see para 9. 41), any increase in the estimates of expected future cash flows arising from recoveries is reflected by adjusting the effective interest rate prospectively, rather than as an adjustment to the carrying amount. Any increased recoverability of cash receipts is, therefore, spread over the debt instrument's remaining life. [IAS 39 para AG 8]. A decrease in the estimate of expected cash flows would be recorded as an impairment loss.

9. 82 An increase in estimates of future cash receipts can be determined on a discounted or undiscounted basis. It is an accounting policy choice and should be applied consistently to all reclassified financial assets. Entities may determine whether there is a change in recoverable cash receipts on an undiscounted basis. In such a case, an entity adjusts effective interest rate for any increase in the total amount of undiscounted cash receipts it expects to recover, but not for a change in recoverable amount (that is, discounted) due only to changes in the timing or pattern of cash receipts. Entities may alternatively determine whether there is a change in recoverable cash receipts on a discounted basis. In such circumstances, an entity adjusts the effective interest rate if there is a change in the present value of the estimated cash receipts, thus taking into account timing and pattern of receipt as well as quantum. In both cases, the reference to 'recoverability' indicates that

				账面金额
20Y1 年 1 月 1 日	修正前的期初摊余账面金额			1,006,003
	估计变动调整——损益			2,563
20Y1 年 1 月 1 日	修正后的经调整摊余账面金额			1,003,440
	期初摊余账面金额	利息收入（利率 6.823%）	现金流入（票息 + 本金偿还）	期末摊余账面金额
	元	元	元	元
20Y1 年 12 月 31 日	1,003,440	68,465	70,000 + 400,000	601,905
20Y2 年 12 月 31 日	601,905	41,068	42,000 + 200,000	400,973
20Y3 年 12 月 31 日	400,973	27,358	28,000 + 200,000	200,331
20Y4 年 12 月 31 日	200,331	13,669	14,000 + 200,000	-

9.81　对于按照 IAS 39 第 50B、50D、50E 段的规定进行重分类的金融资产（参见第 9.41 段），如果因可收回性改善导致预计未来现金流量增加，则通过调整预期实际利率而非账面金额予以反映。因此，任何基于可收回性改善的现金收款将摊销于债务工具的剩余期限内。[IAS 39 AG 第 8 段]。预计现金流量估计的减少将被确认为减值损失。

9.82　对预计未来现金收款的增加可按折现或未折现基础进行确定。这是可选择的会计政策，应一贯应用于所有重新分类的金融资产。主体可按未折现金额，确定可收回的现金收款是否有所变动。在这种情况下，主体就预计可收回金额的未折现额的增加调整实际利率，而不对仅仅由于现金收款时点或模式的变化所导致的可收回金额（即折现金额）变动而调整实际利率。同样，主体也可以按折现基础确定可收回金额是否有所变动。在这种情况下，主体根据预期收款金额的现值变化调整实际利率，因此其考虑了收款的时点、模式以及金额。在这两种情况下，“可收回性”均指信用损失转回所带来的收款。

such cash receipts arise from a reversal of credit losses.

Example 1 – Increase in expected future cash flows arising from recoveries

An entity has reclassified a floating-rate financial asset to loans and receivables on 1 July 20X8. The loan was originally purchased for C100. At the date of reclassification, the fair value of the instrument had decreased substantially as a result of a decline in the creditworthiness of the counterparty to C80, and the entity expects to get undiscounted cash receipts of C90. At 31 December, the credit rating of the counterparty has increased (for example, because of government backing) and the entity now expects to get undiscounted cash receipts of C100. The entity should recalculate its effective interest rate prospectively to reflect those new cash receipts. The increase in expected future cash receipts should be reflected in a new effective interest rate.

Example 2 – Decrease in expected future cash flows arising from recoveries

An entity reclassified a fixed rate asset to loans and receivables on 1 July 20X8. The loan was originally purchased for C100. At the date of reclassification, the fair value of the instrument had decreased substantially as a result of a decline in the creditworthiness of the counterparty to C60, and the entity expects to get undiscounted cash receipts of C75. At 31 December 20X8, the recoverability of cash receipts has decreased further to C50. The amendment to paragraph AG 8 requires the effective interest rate to be adjusted only where there are increases in the estimates of future cash receipts. Decreases in estimates of future cash receipts do not result in a downwards adjustment to the effective interest rate. The reduction in estimated cash receipts at 31 December 20X8 will be reflected as an impairment loss in profit or loss measured in accordance with paragraph 63 of IAS 39 (see further para 9. 173).

Example 3 – Increase in expected future cash flows arising from recoveries after impairment

An entity reclassified a fixed rate debt instrument to loans and receivables on 1 July 20X8. The loan was originally purchased for C100. At the date of reclassification, the instrument's fair value had decreased substantially as a result of a decline in the counterparty's creditworthiness to C60. At 31

示例1——预计未来收回现金流增加

某主体在20X8年7月1日将浮动利率金融资产重新归类为贷款和应收款项。此贷款的最初购买价为100元。在重分类日，因交易对方的信用水平下降导致工具的公允价值锐减至80元，主体预计将获得90元的未折现现金收款。在12月31日，交易对方的信用评级提高（例如，因获得政府支持），由此主体预计将获得100元的未折现现金收款。该主体应按预期重新计算其实际利率，以反映上述新增现金收款。未来预计现金收款的增加应在新实际利率中予以体现。

示例2——预计未来收回现金流减少

某主体在20X8年7月1日将固定利率资产重新归类为贷款和应收款项。此贷款的最初购买价为100元。在重分类日，因交易对方的信用水平下降导致工具的公允价值锐减至60元，主体预计将获得75元的未折现现金收款。在20X8年12月31日，可收回的现金收款进一步跌至50元。根据AG第8段修改的要求，仅当未来现金收款预计金额有所增加时，实际利率才应有所调整。而未来现金收款预计金额的减少不会导致实际利率的下调。在20X8年12月31日，预计现金收款的减少将根据IAS 39第63段的规定计量，作为减值损失在损益中反映（详见第9.173段）。

示例3——减值后预计未来收回现金流增加

某主体在20X8年7月1日将固定利率债务工具重新归类为贷款和应收款项。此贷款的最初购买价为100元。在重分类日，交易对手的信用水平下降导致工具的公允价值锐减至60元。在20X8年12月31日，可收回的现金收款下跌至50元，该主体将其确认为减值损失。在20X9年3月

December 20X8, the recoverability of cash receipts has decreased to C50, and the entity records an impairment loss. At 31 March 20X9, the recoverability of cash receipts has increased to C60. The entity should account for the increase in expected cash receipts as a reversal of the impairment recorded at 31 December 20X8 (see para 9.198).

9.83 When, subsequent to a reclassification, there is an increase in the cash flows expected to be recovered followed by a decrease in those expected cash flows, but the expected cash flows remain above the amount expected when the asset was reclassified (that is, there is not an impairment subsequent to reclassification), we consider that either of the following approaches would be acceptable:

- Only increases in cash flows are dealt with by amending the effective interest rate prospectively. Any decreases, even those after an increase and still above the cash flows expected at the reclassification date, are accounted for by means of a cumulative catch up in accordance with IAS 39 paragraph AG8 (using, as the discount rate, the effective interest rate on the reclassified instrument that was determined after the prospective change in the effective interest rate due to an increase in the cash flows).

- Increases and decreases above the level of cash flows expected on the reclassification date are dealt with prospectively by amending the effective interest rate. Any decreases below the cash flows expected on the reclassification date are accounted for by means of a cumulative catch-up in accordance with IAS 39 paragraph AG8, or as an impairment.

Issuer call option in debt instruments

9.84 The terms of a debt instrument may include an issuer call option, that is, a right of the issuer (but not the investor) to redeem the instrument early and pay a fixed price (generally at a premium over the par value). There may also be other pre-payment features that cause the whole or part of the outstanding principal to be repaid early. Adding call options and/or other pre-payment options should make the instrument less attractive to investors, since it reduces the potential upside on

31 日，可回收的现金收款上升至 60 元。该主体应将预期现金收款的增加作为对 20X8 年 12 月 31 日确认的减值的转回（参见第 9. 198 段）。

9. 83 如果重分类之后，预计收回的现金流量增加后又出现减少，但仍高于该资产被重新分类时的预计金额，即重分类之后未发生减值，我们认为下列任何一种方法都是可以接受的：

■ 只有现金流量增加时，才通过修改未来实际利率方法进行处理。对于现金流量减少的任何情况，包括增加后出现减少，即使减少后仍高于重新分类日预计的现金流量，都应根据 IAS 39 AG 第 8 段的规定，采用累计追调法进行会计处理（采用工具重分类时的实际利率作为折现率，其考虑了现金流量增加导致的未来实际利率变化）。

■ 对于增加情况和仍高于重分类日预计现金流量水平的减少情况，都按修改未来实际利率的方法处理。对于低于重分类日预计现金流量水平的任何减少情况，则根据 IAS 39 AG 第 8 段的规定，采用累计调整法进行会计处理，或作为减值处理。

债务工具中的发行人看涨期权

9. 84 债务工具的条件可能包括发行人看涨期权，即发行人（非投资方）支付一笔固定价格（通常按高于面值的溢价）提前赎回工具的权力。此外，可能还有其他会导致提前偿还全部或部分未偿本金的条款。添加看涨期权和/或其他可提前偿付选择权会降低工具对投资者的吸引力，因为这会缩小债券潜在的增值空间。当市场利率下降而债券价格上升（反映出其高于市场利率）时，债券很有可能被赎回。根据上文第 9. 72 段所述，此类嵌入主债务的看涨

the bond. As market interest rates go down and the bond price increases (reflecting its above market interest rate), the bonds are likely to be called back. As explained in paragraph 9.72 above, such a call option embedded in the debt host is a derivative and would fall to be separately accounted for if its exercise price is not approximately equal to the debt host's amortised cost at each exercise date. Consider the example given below.

Example – Issuer call option in debt instrument

Entity A issues a fixed rate loan for C1m and incurs issue costs of C30,000 resulting in an initial carrying value of C970,000. The loan carries an interest rate of 8% per annum and is repayable at par at the end of year 10. However, under the contract, entity A can call the loan at any time after year 4 by paying a fixed premium of C50,000.

As explained in paragraph 9.72 above, it is first necessary to determine whether the call option is closely related to the host debt instrument. As the fixed premium is required to be paid whenever the call option is exercised after year 4, it may or may not be equal to the present value of any interest lost during the remaining term after exercise of the option. Furthermore, as the call option's exercise price is C1,050,000 (inclusive of the premium), it is unlikely to be approximately equal to the debt instrument's amortised cost in year 4, or at any time subsequently. Therefore, the call option has to be separated from the host debt contract and accounted for separately. This assumes that the expected life of the instrument is the full 10 year term. However, if the expected life is assumed to be 4 years, the 10 year loan with a call option after 4 years is economically equivalent to a 4 year loan with a 6 year extension option. Since there is no concurrent adjustment to the interest rate after 4 years, the term extension option would not be closely related and would need to be accounted for separately (see chapter 5). Therefore, in this case whatever way the loan and option are viewed, the embedded derivative is separated.

Even though the option is out of the money at inception, because the option's exercise price is greater than the debt instrument's carrying value, it has a time value. Suppose the option's fair value is C20,000 at inception. Since the

期权是一种衍生工具，如果其行权价格未能与主债务在各行权日的摊余成本近似，则应对其进行单独核算。考虑以下示例。

示例——债务工具中的发行人看涨期权

主体 A 发行了 100 万元的固定利率贷款，因 30,000 元的发行成本而形成了 970,000 元的初始账面价值。此贷款的年利率为 8%，并于第 10 年年末按面值偿还。然而，根据合同，主体 A 若支付固定溢价 50,000 元，便可在 4 年后的任何时候提前赎回贷款。

根据上文第 9.72 段所述，首先需要确定看涨期权是否与主债务工具紧密相关。由于在 4 年后任何时候行使看涨期权都需要支付固定溢价，所以看涨期权的行权价不一定与可行权后剩余期内发生的利息损失现值持平。此外，由于看涨期权的行权价为 1,050,000 元（含溢价），所以它基本上无法与第 4 年或随后任何时候的债务工具摊余成本近似。因此，看涨期权应从债务主合同中分离出来并进行单独核算。以上假定这是一个预期为 10 年的工具。然而，如果假定其是预期为 4 年的工具，则附有看涨期权的 10 年期贷款从经济上来讲与附有 6 年展期选择权的 4 年期贷款相当。由于合同未约定在 4 年后对利率进行即时调整，所以此展期选择权与主合同非紧密相关，因此将需要进行单独核算（见第五章）。因此，在这种情况下，无论以何种方式看待贷款和期权，嵌入式衍生工具都需要分拆。

即使该期权在开始时为价外期权，即行权价高于债务工具的账面价值，其仍具有时间价值。假设期权在开始时的公允价值为 20,000 元。由于可赎回债券价值等于普通债券价值减去期权价值，在开始时的会

value of a callable bond is equal to the value of a straight bond less the value of the option feature, the accounting entries at inception would be as follows:

	Dr	Cr
	C	C
Embedded option (derivative asset)	20, 000	
Cash	970, 000	
Debt instrument (host)		990, 000

Since the call option will be fair valued and accounted for separately with fair value movements taken to profit or loss, it has no impact on the entity's estimate of future cash flows as explained in paragraph 9. 73 above and, accordingly, the amortisation period will be the debt host's period to original maturity. On this basis, the effective interest rate amounts to 8. 15%. The amortisation schedule is shown below.

	Opening amortised cost	**Interest expense@ 8. 15%**	**Cash payments**	**Closing amortised cost**
	C	C	C	C
Year 1	990, 000	80, 685	80, 000	990, 685
Year 2	990, 685	80, 741	80, 000	991, 427
Year 3	991, 427	80, 802	80, 000	992, 228
Year 4	992, 228	80, 867	80, 000	993, 095
Year 5	993, 095	80, 938	80, 000	994, 033
Year 6	994, 033	81, 014	80, 000	995, 047
Year 7	995, 047	81, 097	80, 000	996, 144
Year 8	996, 144	81, 186	80, 000	997, 330
Year 9	997, 330	81, 283	80, 000	998, 613
Year 10	998, 613	81, 387	1, 080, 000	–

The entity would recognise interest expense in profit or loss and the loan's amortised cost in the balance sheet each year in accordance with the above amortisation schedule.

In years 1 and 2, there is no change in interest rate since inception for an

计分录如下：

	借方	贷方
	元	元
嵌入期权（衍生资产）	20,000	
现金	970,000	
债务工具（主）		990,000

由于看涨期权将以公允价值计量并单独核算，且公允价值变动计入损益，所以如上文第9.73段所述，看涨期权对主体的预计未来现金流量不会产生影响，因此主债务的摊销期间为截至原始到期日的期限。在此基础上的实际利率为8.15%。下面为摊销进度表。

	期初摊余成本	利息费用（利率8.15%）	现金支付	期末摊余成本
	元	元	元	元
第1年	990,000	80,685	80,000	990,685
第2年	990,685	80,741	80,000	991,427
第3年	991,427	80,802	80,000	992,228
第4年	992,228	80,867	80,000	993,095
第5年	993,095	80,938	80,000	994,033
第6年	994,033	81,014	80,000	995,047
第7年	995,047	81,097	80,000	996,144
第8年	996,144	81,186	80,000	997,330
第9年	997,330	81,283	80,000	998,613
第10年	998,613	81,387	1,080,000	–

该主体每年将按照以上摊销进度表将利息费用计入损益，并将贷款摊余成本列示于资产负债表。

在第1年和第2年，具有类似到期日和信用评级的工具的利率自初始以

instrument of similar maturity and credit rating. The option's fair value (time value) at the end of year 2 is C10, 000. The decrease in fair value of C10, 000 since inception will be reported in profit and loss and the option will be recorded at C10, 000 at the end of year 2.

At the end of year 3, interest rates have fallen and the option's fair value increases to C18, 000. The increase in value of C8, 000 will be recorded in profit or loss and the option will be recorded at its fair value of C18, 000 at the end of year 3.

At the end of year 4, interest rates have fallen further. The option's fair value increases to C30, 000 and the company decides to repay the loan at the end of year 4.

The accounting entries to reflect the change in the option's fair value and the loan's early repayment at the end of year 4 are as follows:

	Dr	**Cr**
	C	**C**
Embedded Option	12, 000	
Profit or loss		12, 000
Early repayment of loan		
Debt instrument (host)	993, 095	
Embedded option (derivative asset)		30, 000
Cash		1, 050, 000
Loss on derecognition of liability	86, 905	

The loss of C86, 905 in profit or loss reflects the fact that the fair value of the host contract has gone up in value as interest rates have fallen compared to its carrying value at amortised cost. The fair value of the host contract is actually C1, 080, 000, which is the option's fair value plus the fair value of the consideration given. The market rate of interest that discounts the interest payments of C80, 000 for the next 6 years plus the principal repayment of C1, 000, 000 at maturity to the fair value of the host is 6.95%, indicating a

来未发生变动。第 2 年年末期权的公允价值（时间价值）为 10, 000 元。于是在第 2 年年末，自初始以来减少的 10, 000 元公允价值将计入损益，并以 10, 000 元记录期权价值。

在第 3 年年末，利率下降而期权的公允价值增至 18, 000 元。8, 000 元的增值将计入损益，该期权将以其公允价值 18, 000 元记账。

在第 4 年年末，利率进一步下降。期权的公允价值增至 30, 000 元，公司决定在第 4 年年底提前偿还贷款。

下表为反映在第 4 年年底期权的公允价值变动和贷款提前偿还情况的会计分录：

	借方	**贷方**
	元	**元**
嵌入期权	12, 000	
损益		12, 000
提前偿还贷款		
债务工具（主）	993, 095	
嵌入期权（衍生资产）		30, 000
现金		1, 050, 000
终止确认负债时的亏损	86, 905	

损益中确认的 86, 905 元亏损表明，主合同的公允价值（相较于按摊余成本计算的账面价值）随着利率下跌而增加。主合同的实际公允价值为 1, 080, 000 元，即期权的公允价值加上支付对价的公允价值。将未来六年每年支付的 80, 000 元利息加上到期日偿还的 1, 000, 000 元本金折现为主负债公允价值的市场利率为 6.95%，相较于工具的约定利率 8%，价值明显下跌。

significant fall in value compared to the instrument's stated interest rate of 8%.

Suppose that instead of an additional premium or penalty payable on early exercise, the option's exercise price is the fair value of the loan at each exercise date. In other words, the exercise price of the pre-payment option is a 'market adjusted value'. A market adjusted value is calculated by discounting the contractual guaranteed amount payable at the end of the specified term to present value using the current market rate that would be offered on a new loan with a similar credit rating and having a maturity period equal to the remaining maturity period of the current loan. As a result, the market adjusted value may be more or less than the loan principal, depending upon market interest rates at each option exercise date.

In that situation, the pre-payment option enables the issuer simply to pay off the loan at fair value at the pre-payment date. Since the holder receives only the market adjusted value, which is equal to the loan's fair value at the date of pre-payment, the pre-payment option (the embedded derivative) has a fair value of zero at all times. Since the pre-payment option, on a stand-alone basis, would not meet the definition of a derivative, it cannot be an embedded derivative, the loan is simply carried at its amortised cost as above, on the assumption that the loan is not going to be pre-paid. If, however, the entity expects to pre-pay the loan, the loan would be amortised over its expected life.

Floating rate instruments

9.85 As will be apparent from the above illustrations, the application of the effective interest rate method is relatively straight forward for fixed interest instruments with fixed terms. Indeed, it appears to be specifically designed for such instruments. However, the analysis is more complicated in the case of a financial instrument that provides for future cash flows that are determinable rather than fixed. Floating rate interest on a financial instrument that is linked to a reference rate such as LIBOR and a principal amount linked to a price index are examples of determinable cash flows. The apparent complication arises because, unlike fixed interest instruments where the effective interest rate generally stays constant over the instrument's term, for floating rate instruments, the periodic re-

假设期权的行权价为各行权日贷款的公允价值，而非提早行权的附加溢价或应付罚金。换句话说，可提前还款的期权行权价为经市场调整后价值。经市场调整后价值的计算是将特定期间期末的合同保证应付金额进行折现。计算时需采用当期市场利率，即适用于信用评级相似且期限等于当年贷款剩余期限的新贷款的市场利率。因此，经市场调整后价值可能高于或低于贷款本金，取决于各期权行权日的市场利率。

在这种情况下，提前偿付选择权使发行人只需按提前还款日的公允价值还清贷款即可。因为持有人收到的只是经市场调整后价值，其金额等于提前还款日的贷款公允价值，所以提前偿付选择权（即嵌入式衍生工具）的公允价值始终为零。由于独立存在的提前偿付选择权不符合衍生工具的定义，所以不能作为嵌入式衍生工具。该贷款将根据不会提前还贷的假设，简单地按上述摊余成本列报。但是，如果主体预计提前还贷，则该贷款将在预期期限内进行摊销。

浮动利率工具

9.85 根据上文所述，可以看出对具有固定期限的固定利率工具来说，应用实际利率法相对较为简单明了。其的确像是专门为此类工具而设的。然而，对于可确定而非固定的未来现金流的金融工具而言，其分析复杂得多。与参考利率（例如LIBOR）挂钩的金融工具的浮动利率以及与价格指数挂钩的本金就是现金流量可确定的例子。与固定利率工具（其实际利率在工具期限内一般保持恒定）不同，浮动利率工具明显复杂得多，因为需要定期重新估计待定的现金流量，以反映市场利率波动对工具实际收益的影响。

estimation of determinable cash flows to reflect movements in market rates of interest alters the instrument's effective yield.

9.86 However, although fluctuations in interest rates result in a change in the effective interest rate, there is usually no change in the instrument's fair value. Accordingly, where a floating rate instrument is acquired or issued and the amount at which it is recognised initially is equal to the principal receivable or payable at maturity, re-estimating the future interest payments normally has no significant effect on the carrying amount of the asset or liability. [IAS 39 para AG 7]. This means that the effective yield will always equal the rate under the interest rate formula (for example, LIBOR + 1%) in the instrument. The effect is that the carrying amount remains unchanged by the process, illustrated in paragraph 9.81 above, of re-estimating future cash flows and the effective interest rate. The result is that changes in LIBOR are reflected in the period in which the change occurs.

9.87 However, if a floating rate instrument is issued or acquired at a discount or premium, or the entity receives or incurs loan origination fees or costs, the question arises as to whether the premium or discount and other transaction fees or costs should be amortised over the period to the next repricing date, or over the instrument's expected life. The answer depends upon the nature of the premium or discount and its relationship with market rates.

- An amortisation period to the next repricing date should be used if the premium or discount on a floating rate instrument reflects interest that has accrued on the instrument since interest was last paid, or changes in market interest rate since the floating interest rate was reset to market rates. This is because the premium or discount relates to the period to the next interest reset date as, at that date, the variable to which the premium or discount relates (that is interest rates) is reset to market rates. In this case, the loan's fair value at the next repricing date will be its par value. This is illustrated in example 1 below.

- The instrument's expected life should be used as the amortisation period if the premium or discount results from changes in the credit spread over the floating rate specified in the instrument, or other variables that are not reset to market rates. In this situation, the date the interest rate is next reset is not a market-based repricing date of the entire instrument, since the variable rate is not

9.86　然而，尽管利率的波动导致了实际利率的变动，但工具的公允价值通常不会因此而改变。所以，如果购买或发行浮动利率工具，且初始确认的金额等于到期日应收或应付本金，那么对未来利息支付的重新估计通常不会对资产或负债的账面金额产生重大影响。[IAS 39 AG 第 7 段]。这也就意味着工具的实际收益率将始终等于采用利率公式（例如，LIBOR + 1%）计算出的利率。结果如上文第 9.81 段所述，账面金额在重新估计未来现金流量和实际利率的过程中保持不变。于是，LIBOR 的变化体现在了其变动发生的当期。

9.87　然而，如果浮动利率工具以折价或溢价发行或认购，或者主体收到或产生了贷款启动费用或成本，则产生的问题是，溢价或折价以及其他交易费用或成本是否应该在截至下一重新定价日的期间内摊销，还是在工具预期期限内摊销。此问题的答案取决于溢价或折价的性质及其与市场利率的关系。

- 如果浮动利率工具的溢价或折价反映自最后支付利息以来工具的应计利息，或自按照市场利率重新设定浮动利率以来的市场利率变动，则应采用至下一重新定价日的摊销期间。这是由于溢价或折价与截至下一重设日的这段期间相关，因为在该重设日，与溢价或折价相关的变量（即利率）按市场利率重新调整。在这种情况下，下一重新定价日贷款的公允价值即为其票面价值。相关内容在下文的示例 1 中进行阐述。

- 如果溢价或折价源于债务工具中明确规定的浮动利率之上的信用价差变动，或其他不按市场利率重设的变量，则应将工具的预计期限作为摊销期间。在这种情况下，下一重设日并非是整个工具基于市场的重新定价日，因为浮动利率并未因所发行的特定工具信用价差的变动而进行调整。相关内容在下文的示例 2 中进行阐述。

adjusted for changes in the credit spread for the specific issue. This is illustrated in example 2 below.

[IAS 39 para AG 6].

Example 1 – Amortisation of discount over the period to the next repricing date

On 15 May 20X6, an entity acquires a C100 nominal 5 year floating rate bond that pays quarterly interest at 3 month LIBOR + 50 basis points for C99.25. LIBOR at the last reset date on 30 March 20X6 was 4.50% which determines the interest that would be paid on the bond on 30 June 20X6. On the purchase date, LIBOR was 4.75%. The discount of 0.75 is amortised to the next repricing date, that is, 30 June 20X6.

Example 2 – Amortisation of discount over the expected life of the instrument

A 20 year bond is issued at C100, has a principal amount of C100, and requires quarterly interest payments equal to current 3 month LIBOR plus 1% over the instrument's life. The interest rate reflects the market-based rate of return associated with the bond issue at issuance. Subsequent to issuance, the loan's credit quality deteriorates resulting in a rating downgrade. Therefore, the bond trades at a discount. Entity A purchases the bond for 95 and classifies it as held-to-maturity.

In this case, the discount of C5 is amortised to net profit or loss over the period to the bond's maturity and not to the next date interest rate payments are reset, as there is no adjustment to the variable rate as a result of the credit downgrade.

9.88 There is no specific guidance in the standard as to how transaction costs incurred in originating or acquiring a floating rate instrument should be amortised. Since such costs are sunk cost and are not subject to repricing, they will be amortised over the instrument's expected life. Any methodology that provides a reasonable basis of amortisation may be used. For example, entities may find it appropriate to amortise the fees and costs by reference to the interest rate at inception ignoring any subsequent changes in rates or to simply adopt a straight-line

[IAS 39 AG 第6段]。

示例1——至下一重新定价日期间的折价摊销

20X6年5月15日，某主体以99.25元认购了面值为100元的5年期浮动利率债券，债券按季度支付利息（3个月期LIBOR+50个基点）。最近重设日（20X6年3月30日）的LIBOR为4.50%，并以此确定20X6年6月30日支付的债券利息。购买日的LIBOR为4.75%。0.75的折价将摊销至下一重新定价日，即20X6年6月30日。

示例2——在金融工具预期期限内的折价摊销

某20年期债券以100元发行，其本金金额为100元，且要求在工具的期限内按季支付利息，利率为现行3个月期LIBOR加上1%。该利率反映了与债券发行相关的基于市场的收益率。发行之后，贷款信用质量恶化导致等级下降。因此，债券折价交易。主体A用95元购买了该债券，并将其归类为持有至到期债券。

在这种情况下，5元折价将在截至债券到期日的期间内摊销到净损益中，而非在至下一利率支付重设日的期间内摊销，因为信用降低并未对浮动利率形成调整。

9.88　该准则未就发行或认购浮动利率工具过程中产生的交易费用的摊销办法提供具体指南。由于此类成本为沉没成本且无需重新定价，所以将在工具预期期限内摊销。只要摊销基础合理，任何方法都可采用。例如，主体可能认为适合通过参照期初利率而不考虑利率后续变化来摊销费用和成本，或者仅简单地采用直线摊销法。

amortisation method.

Inflation linked bond

9.89 Entities sometimes issue or invest in debt instruments whose payments (principal and interest) are linked to the change in an inflation index of the period. Such an inflation-linked bond needs to be assessed to determine if the inflation-linking mechanism is a closely related embedded derivative that does not need to be recognised and measured separately under IAS 39. There are two possible approaches to account for changes in estimated future cash flows for an inflation-linked bond where the inflation linking mechanism has been found to be closely related.

- Applying the guidance in IAS 39 paragraph AG7, under which the bond is treated as a floating-rate debt instrument with the inflation link being part of the floating-rate mechanism. The EIR at initial recognition is determined as the rate that sets the estimated future cash flows to be paid on the bond, based on the expected level of the inflation index over the expected term of the bond to equal the fair value of the bond (usually the issue proceeds). However, if in subsequent periods there is a change in inflation expectations, the entity reflects these changes by adjusting both the expected future cash flows on the debt and the EIR. It follows that such changes in the entity's expectations of future inflation result in no adjustment to the carrying amount of the debt and no gain or loss.

- Applying the guidance in IAS 39 paragraph AG8 under which the EIR is determined at inception in the same way as above. However, if in subsequent periods there is a change in the level of the inflation expectations for the bond's remaining term, the entity revises its estimates of the future cash flows to be paid on the bond accordingly. It recalculates the bond's carrying amount by discounting the revised estimated cash flows using the original EIR. The resulting adjustment to the bond's carrying amount is recognised immediately in the income statement as a gain or loss. The result is that a gain or loss is recognised in the current period for changes in the entity's expectations of the future level of the inflation index.

与通胀挂钩的债券

9.89　主体有时发行或投资本息与同一时期通胀指数变动挂钩的债务工具。与通胀挂钩的债券需要评估确定与通胀挂钩的机制是否为紧密相关的嵌入式衍生工具，即按照 IAS 39 的规定无需单独确认和计量的嵌入式衍生工具。当通胀挂钩机制确实紧密相关时，有两种方法对与通胀挂钩债券的预计未来现金流量的变动进行会计处理。

■ 应用 IAS 39 AG 第 7 段提供的指南：将该债券当作浮动利率债务工具处理，通胀挂钩关系作为浮动利率机制的组成部分。初始确认的实际利率（EIR）是根据使债券预计未来支付的现金流量（考虑了未来一定水平的通胀指数）与债券的公允价值（通常即发行所得）相等的利率而确定的。然而，如在随后期间内通胀预期出现变动，主体应通过同时调整债券预计未来现金流量及实际利率反映此等变动。所以，主体所预期的未来通胀变动不会引起对债券账面金额调整或影响损益。

■ 应用 IAS 39 AG 第 8 段提供的指南：实际利率按上述方法在初始时确定。然而，如果在随后期间通胀预期水平在债券剩余期限内出现变动，主体应对债券预计未来支付的现金流量估计进行相应修正。通过采用原始实际利率对修正后的预期现金流折现，即可重新计算出债券的账面金额。对债券账面金额所做的调整将在利润表中直接确认为利得或损失。所以，由于主体对未来通胀指数水平预期变动的影响将确认在当期损益中。

9.90 Given that the standard is not clear as to how the EIR method applies for instruments with variable cash flows, the IFRIC was asked to provide guidance on how to apply the effective interest rate method to a financial instrument whose cash flows are linked to changes in an inflation index. [IFRIC update July 2008]. The IFRIC noted that paragraphs AG6-AG8 of IAS 39 provide the relevant application guidance. Judgement is required to determine whether an instrument is a floating rate instrument within the scope of paragraph AG7 or an instrument within the scope of paragraph AG8. In view of the existing application guidance in IAS 39, the IFRIC decided not to add this issue to its agenda. However, since the application of the effective interest rate method has widespread application in practice, the IFRIC has decided to refer the matter to the IASB.

9.91 Until such time as the IASB provides clarification, we believe an entity should make an accounting policy choice as to which method is acceptable and apply this method to all similar instruments. The way in which the above guidance should be applied is illustrated in the example given below.

Example – Inflation-linked bond

On 1 January 20X5, an entity invests in an inflation-linked bond for C100,000. The term of the bond is 5 years. The bond pays a fixed coupon of 5% per annum (real) at the end of each year on principal that is adjusted annually by the applicable year's percentage change in the consumer price index. The principal repayable at the end of year 5 is similarly adjusted for inflation.

Terms of the bond	
Proceeds received on 1 Jan 20X5	100,000
Fixed coupon @ 5% per annum (real interest rate)	5,000
Term	5 years
Principal and real interest adjusted annually for changes in the consumer price index	

Following are data of actual inflation rates and annual expected inflation rates on various dates

9.90 鉴于准则未明确如何将实际利率法运用于可变现金流量的工具，国际财务报告解释委员会曾被要求就实际利率法如何运用于现金流量与通胀指数变动挂钩的金融工具提供指南。[IFRIC 2008 年 7 月的更新]。国际财务报告解释委员会指出，IAS 39 AG 第 6—8 段已提供了相关的应用指南。需运用判断，确定某工具是否属于 AG 第 7 段范畴内的浮动利率工具或者 AG 第 8 段范畴内的工具。根据 IAS 39 中现有的应用指南，国际财务报告解释委员会决定不将此问题纳入议程。但由于实际利率法在实务中的广泛应用，国际财务报告解释委员会决定将此事项提交 IASB。

9.91 在 IASB 作出澄清之前，我们认为主体应就可接受的会计政策作出选择，并将其适用于所有的类似工具。上述指南的应用方法在下文举例说明。

示例——与通胀挂钩的债券

某主体于 20X5 年 1 月 1 日投资认购了 100,000 元与通胀挂钩的债券，债券期限为 5 年。债券于每年年底按本金的 5% 支付年固定票息（实际利率），而本金的金额每年按适用年限的消费价格指数变动百分率进行调整。第 5 年年末应付的本金金额也进行相应的通胀调整。

债券条款	
20X5 年 1 月 1 日所得收入	100,000
年固定票息 5%（实际利率）	5,000
期限	5 年
本金和实际利息将每年因消费价格指数变动而进行调整	

下列数据为不同日期的实际通胀率以及年度预期通胀率

Annual expected percentage change in consumer price index						
	1 Jan 20X5	**1 Jan 20X6**	**1 Jan 20X7**	**1 Jan 20X8**	**1 Jan 20X9**	**Actual change**
20X5	0. 70%					1. 20%
20X6	2. 60%	1. 40%				2. 40%
20X7	2. 80%	1. 90%	1. 70%			0%
20X8	2. 80%	3. 50%	2. 10%	1. 20%		3. 40%
20X9	2. 80%	3. 50%	2. 60%	1. 60%	2. 50%	2. 50%

The expected inflation adjusted interest payments at the end of each year and the principal payment at the end of year 5 are shown below. The expected cash flows at the end of a year are calculated by multiplying the principal of C100, 000 by the expected change in the consumer price index in that year. So at the beginning of 20X5, the principal at the end of 20X5 is expected to be C100, 000 × 1. 007 = C100, 700. As the nominal coupon rate is 5%, the interest expected to be paid for 20X5 would be C5, 035 (C100, 700@5%). Similarly, at 1 Jan 20X6, the expected inflated adjusted principal at the end of year 20X6 would be C100, 000 × 1. 012 (the opening amount as adjusted by the actual increase in inflation during 20X5) × 1. 014 (expected increase during 20X6) = C102, 617 and the expected adjusted interest would be C5, 131 (C102, 617@5%).

Annual expected interest and principal cash flows						**Actual inflation adjusted cash flows**	
	1 Jan 20X5	**1 Jan 20X6**	**1 Jan 20X7**	**1 Jan 20X8**	**1 Jan 20X9**	**Interest**	**Principal**
20X5	5, 035					5, 060	
20X6	5, 166	5, 131				5, 181	
20X7	5, 311	5, 228	5, 270			5, 181	
20X8	5, 459	5, 411	5, 380	5, 244		5, 358	
20X9 – interest	5, 612	5, 601	5, 520	5, 328	5, 492	5, 492	
Principal	112, 242	112, 014	110, 401	106, 550	109, 831		109, 831
20X9	117, 854	117, 615	115, 921	111, 878	115, 323	26, 272	109, 831

年度预期消费价格指数的变动百分比						
	20X5 年 1 月 1 日	**20X6 年 1 月 1 日**	**20X7 年 1 月 1 日**	**20X8 年 1 月 1 日**	**20X9 年 1 月 1 日**	**实际变动**
20X5 年	0.70%					1.20%
20X6 年	2.60%	1.40%				2.40%
20X7 年	2.80%	1.90%	1.70%			0%
20X8 年	2.80%	3.50%	2.10%	1.20%		3.40%
20X9 年	2.80%	3.50%	2.60%	1.60%	2.50%	2.50%

下面是考虑了通货膨胀影响的每年年底的利息支付和第 5 年年末的本金支付。用本金 100,000 元乘以当年消费价格指数的预期变化，可算出每年年末的预期现金流量。因此在 20X5 年年初可算出本金在 20X5 年年末为 100,000 元 × 1.007 = 100,700 元。由于名义票息率为 5%，所以 20X5 年预期支付利息为 5,035 元（100,700 元 × 5%）。同样，在 20X6 年 1 月 1 日，20X6 年年底考虑了通货膨胀影响的预期本金为 100,000 元 × 1.012（按 20X5 年通货膨胀实际增长情况进行调整的期初金额）× 1.014（20X6 年的预期增长）= 102,617 元，调整后的预期利息为 5,131 元（102,617 元 × 5%）。

年度预期利息与本金现金流量						含实际通货膨胀调整的现金流量	
	20X5 年 1 月 1 日	**20X6 年 1 月 1 日**	**20X7 年 1 月 1 日**	**20X8 年 1 月 1 日**	**20X9 年 1 月 1 日**	**利息**	**本金**
20X5 年	5,035					5,060	
20X6 年	5,166	5,131				5,181	
20X7 年	5,311	5,228	5,270			5,181	
20X8 年	5,459	5,411	5,380	5,244		5,358	
20X9 年利息	5,612	5,601	5,520	5,328	5,492	5,492	
本金	112,242	112,014	110,401	106,550	109,831		109,831
20X9 年	117,854	117,615	115,921	111,878	115,323	26,272	109,831

Note that the principal expected to be paid at the end of 20X9 is adjusted for expected changes in the index since 1 Jan 20X5. For example, the expected principal payable in 20X9 estimated at 1 Jan 20X5 = 100, 000 × 1. 007 × 1. 026 × 1. 028 × 1. 028 × 1. 028 = 112, 242.

There are essentially two ways in which the bond could be amortised in accordance with the guidance provided in paragraph AG7 of IAS 39.

The first method views the EIR as a ‘floating inflation adjusted rate’—similar to LIBOR. In this method, the finance cost recognised in profit or loss is the actual inflation adjusted interest paid during the year plus the actual increase in principal as adjusted for inflation during the year. So the carrying amount is equal to the inflation adjusted amount at the end of the period. This method is simple and is often used in practice.

Amortisation of bond based on AG7 – Method 1

	Opening balance	Finance cost	Cash flow	Closing balance
31 Dec 20X5	100, 000	6, 260	5, 060	101, 200
31 Dec 20X6	101, 200	7, 610	5, 181	103, 629
31 Dec 20X7	103, 629	5, 181	5, 181	103, 629
31 Dec 20X8	103, 629	8, 881	5, 358	107, 152
31 Dec 20X9	107, 152	8, 171	115, 323	0
		36, 103	136, 103	

The second method complies strictly with the guidance in paragraph AG7. In this method, the finance cost in each period is based on an adjusted EIR, calculated by discounting the expected cash flows to equal to the carrying amount at the beginning of each period. No further gain or loss arises.

Amortisation of bond based on AG7 – Method 2

	Opening balance	Finance cost @ adjusted EIR (see below)	Cash flow	Closing balance
31 Dec 20X5	100, 000	7, 408	5, 060	102, 348
31 Dec 20X6	102, 348	7, 496	5, 181	104, 662
31 Dec 20X7	104, 662	7, 172	5, 181	106, 653
31 Dec 20X8	106, 653	5, 235	5, 358	106, 530
31 Dec 20X9	106, 530	8, 793	115, 323	0
		36, 103	136, 103	

值得注意的是，预计于20X9年年底支付的本金根据自20X5年1月1日以来指数的预期变动进行了调整。例如，20X5年1月1日估计的20X9年预期应付本金 = 100, 000 × 1. 007 × 1. 026 × 1. 028 × 1. 028 × 1. 028 = 112, 242。

按照IAS 39 AG第7段提供的指南，有两种基本方法可以用于该债券的摊销。

第一种方法是指将实际利率视为含通货膨胀调整的浮动利率，类似于LIBOR。在这种方法下，在利润表的财务成本中包括当年支付的根据实际通货膨胀调整的利息，加上因当年通货膨胀影响实际调增的本金。因此，账面金额等于经过通货膨胀调整后的金额。此方法简单且在实务中很常用。

遵照AG7的债券摊销——方法1

	期初余额	财务成本	现金流量	期末余额
20X5年12月31日	100, 000	6, 260	5, 060	101, 200
20X6年12月31日	101, 200	7, 610	5, 181	103, 629
20X7年12月31日	103, 629	5, 181	5, 181	103, 629
20X8年12月31日	103, 629	8, 881	5, 358	107, 152
20X9年12月31日	107, 152	8, 171	115, 323	0
		36, 103	136, 103	

第二种方法严格遵照AG第7段中的指南。采用此方法得出的各期财务成本基于调整后的实际利率，通过把预期现金流量折现至各期期初的账面金额得出。这种方法无其他损益影响。

遵照AG7的债券摊销——方法2

	期初余额	财务成本（调整后的实际利率，见下文）	现金流量	期末余额
20X5年12月31日	100, 000	7, 408	5, 060	102, 348
20X6年12月31日	102, 348	7, 496	5, 181	104, 662
20X7年12月31日	104, 662	7, 172	5, 181	106, 653
20X8年12月31日	106, 653	5, 235	5, 358	106, 530
20X9年12月31日	106, 530	8, 793	115, 323	0
		36, 103	136, 103	

Calculation of adjusted EIR based on expected cash flows							
	EIR %	**1 Jan 20X5**	**31 Dec 20X5**	**31 Dec 20X6**	**31 Dec 20X7**	**31 Dec 20X8**	**31 Dec 20X9**
20X5	7. 408	- 100, 000	5, 035	5, 166	5, 311	5, 459	117, 854
20X6	7. 324		- 102, 348	5, 131	5, 228	5, 411	117, 615
20X7	6. 853			- 104, 662	5, 270	5, 380	115, 921
20X8	4. 908				- 106, 653	5, 244	111, 878
20X9	8. 254					- 106, 530	115, 323

The original effective interest rate at inception is 7. 408%

The way in which the bond would be amortised in accordance with the guidance provided in paragraph AG8 of IAS 39 is shown below. As the finance cost in each period is based on the original EIR at inception, the carrying value at the end of each period is adjusted to the present value of the expected cash flows discounted at the original EIR. This gives rise to a further adjustment that is recognised as part of the finance cost in each period.

Amortisation of bond based on AG8							
	Opening balance	**Finance cost @ 7. 408%**	**Cash flow**	**Closing balance**	**AG8 adjustment**	**Adjusted closing balance (see below)**	**Total finance cost**
31 Dec 20X5	100, 000	7, 408	5, 060	102, 348	- 297	102, 050	7, 110
31 Dec 20X6	102, 050	7, 559	5, 181	104, 428	- 1, 305	103, 123	6, 255
31 Dec 20X7	103, 123	7, 639	5, 181	105, 581	- 3, 720	101, 860	3, 919
31 Dec 20X8	101, 860	7, 545	5, 358	104, 048	3, 321	107, 369	10, 866
31 Dec 20X9	107, 369	7, 953	115, 323	0	0	0	7, 953
			136, 103				36, 103

Present value of expected cash flows based on original discount rate					
	31 Dec 20X6	31 Dec 20X7	31 Dec 20X8	31 Dec 20X9	PV@ 7. 408%
31 Dec 20X5	5, 131	5, 228	5, 411	117, 615	102, 050
31 Dec 20X6		5, 270	5, 380	115, 921	103, 123
31 Dec 20X7			5, 244	111, 878	101, 860
31 Dec 20X8				115, 323	107, 369

基于预期现金流量计算的调整后实际利率							
		20X5 年	20X5 年	20X6 年	20X7 年	20X8 年	20X9 年
	实际利率（%）	1 月 1 日	12 月 31 日	12 月 31 日	12 月 31 日	12 月 31 日	12 月 31 日
20X5 年	7.408	-100,000	5,035	5,166	5,311	5,459	117,854
20X6 年	7.324		-102,348	5,131	5,228	5,411	117,615
20X7 年	6.853			-104,662	5,270	5,380	115,921
20X8 年	4.908				-106,653	5,244	111,878
20X9 年	8.254					-106,530	115,323

初始确认的原始实际利率为 7.408%。

下面为遵照 IAS 39 AG 第 8 段提供的指南对该债券的摊销方法。由于各期的财务成本以初始确认的原始实际利率为基础，所以各期期末的账面金额调整至按原始实际利率折现的预计现金流量现值，此调整将计入各期财务成本。

遵照 AG8 的债券摊销							
	期初余额	财务成本(利率 7.408%)	现金流量	期末余额	AG8 方式调整	调整后的期末余额（见下文）	财务成本合计
20X5 年 12 月 31 日	100,000	7,408	5,060	102,348	-297	102,050	7,110
20X6 年 12 月 31 日	102,050	7,559	5,181	104,428	-1,305	103,123	6,255
20X7 年 12 月 31 日	103,123	7,639	5,181	105,581	-3,720	101,860	3,919
20X8 年 12 月 31 日	101,860	7,545	5,358	104,048	3,321	107,369	10,866
20X9 年 12 月 31 日	107,369	7,953	115,323	0	0	0	7,953
			136,103				36,103

基于原始折现率的预期现金流量现值					
	20X6 年 12 月 31 日	20X7 年 12 月 31 日	20X8 年 12 月 31 日	20X9 年 12 月 31 日	现值(利率 7.408%)
20X5 年 12 月 31 日	5,131	5,228	5,411	117,615	102,050
20X6 年 12 月 31 日		5,270	5,380	115,921	103,123
20X7 年 12 月 31 日			5,244	111,878	101,860
20X8 年 12 月 31 日				115,323	107,369

Comparison between AG7 and AG8

	AG7 – Method 1		**AG7 – Method 2**		**AG8**	
	Finance cost	Loan balance	Finance cost	Loan balance	Finance cost	Loan balance
31 Dec 20X5	6, 260	101, 200	7, 408	102, 348	7, 110	102, 050
31 Dec 20X6	7, 610	103, 629	7, 496	104, 662	6, 255	103, 123
31 Dec 20X7	5, 181	103, 629	7, 172	106, 653	3, 919	101, 860
31 Dec 20X8	8, 881	107, 152	5, 235	106, 530	10, 866	107, 369
31 Dec 20X9	8, 171	0	8, 793	0	7, 953	0
	36, 103		36, 103		36, 103	

The comparisons between the two methods indicate that the finance cost calculated in accordance with AG7 is consistent with the trend in the actual inflation rate.

Perpetual debt instruments

9. 92 It is not uncommon for entities to issue debt instruments on terms with no redemption date, but on which interest payments are made, usually at a fixed rate or a variable market based rate (for example, a fixed margin over LIBOR) in perpetuity. At initial recognition, assuming there are no transaction costs, the debt instrument will be recorded at its fair value, which is the amount received. The difference between this initial amount and the maturity amount, which is zero if the interest rate at inception is the market rate for that instrument, will never be amortised, as there is no repayment of principal. This means that at each reporting date the debt instrument will be recorded at its principal amount, which is also its amortised cost. This is because the amortised cost, which is the present value of the stream of future cash payments discounted at the effective interest rate (fixed for fixed rate instruments or variable for floating rate instruments) equals the principal amount in each period. [IAS 39 para IG B24]. If, on the other hand, the entity incurs transaction costs, the debt instrument will be recorded in each reporting period at its initial amount, which is the amount received less transaction costs. The result is that the transaction costs are never amortised, but reflected in the carrying amount indefinitely.

AG7 与 AG8 之对比	AG7——方法 1		AG7——方法 2		AG8	
	财务成本	贷款余额	财务成本	贷款余额	财务成本	贷款余额
20X5 年 12 月 31 日	6, 260	101, 200	7, 408	102, 348	7, 110	102, 050
20X6 年 12 月 31 日	7, 610	103, 629	7, 496	104, 662	6, 255	103, 123
20X7 年 12 月 31 日	5, 181	103, 629	7, 172	106, 653	3, 919	101, 860
20X8 年 12 月 31 日	8, 881	107, 152	5, 235	106, 530	10, 866	107, 369
20X9 年 12 月 31 日	8, 171	0	8, 793	0	7, 953	0
	36, 103		36, 103		36, 103	

上述两种方法的对比表明，遵照 AG7 计算出的财务成本与实际通胀率的走势是一致的。

永续债务工具

9.92 主体发行无赎回日期但通常按固定利率或市场浮动利率（例如，LIBOR 加一个固定利差）无限期支付利息的债务工具的情况并不少见。假定在初始确认时无交易费用，则债务工具将按其公允价值（即已收到的金额）记录。如果期初的利率为该工具的市场利率，那么初始金额与到期金额之差为零，也就将不存在摊销，因为没有本金的偿还。这就意味着在每个报告日，债务工具都将以其本金金额（同样也是其摊余成本）记录。这是由于摊余成本与各期的本金金额相等，而摊余成本为按实际利率（对于固定利率工具，为固定利率；对于浮动利率工具，为浮动利率）折现的未来现金流量现值。[IAS 39 IG 第 B24 段]。另一方面，如果主体产生了交易费用，则在每个报告日，债务工具将以其期初金额（即收到的金额减去交易费用）记录。导致交易费用无需摊销，而是永远地反映在账面金额里。

9. 93 Sometimes perpetual debt instruments are repackaged in such a way that the principal amount is effectively repaid. One way of achieving this is to pay a high rate of interest for a number of years (the primary period) which then falls to a negligible amount. If the interest were simply charged to profit or loss, the company would bear an artificially high interest expense during the primary period and little or no interest expense thereafter to perpetuity. Such treatment might reflect the form of the loan agreement, but not its substance. From an economic perspective, some or all of the interest payments are repayment of principal as illustrated in the example below. A similar example is included in IAS 39 paragraph IG B25.

Example – Perpetual debt instrument with decreasing interest

An entity issues a perpetual bond for C100, 000 on which interest at 14% is paid annually for the first 10 years and thereafter at a nominal rate of 0. 125%.

It is clear that at the end of the ten year period, the bond has little or no value. The principal amount is repaid, in effect, over the initial 10 year primary period. Consequently, the interest payments during the primary period represent a payment for interest and repayment of capital. The effective interest rate calculated on the basis of C14, 000 for 10 years followed by C125 to perpetuity is 6. 84%.

	Opening amortised cost	Interest expense @ 6. 84%	Cash payments	Closing amortised cost
	C	C	C	C
Year 1	100, 000	6, 840	14, 000	92, 840
Year 2	92, 840	6, 350	14, 000	85, 190
Year 3	85, 190	5, 827	14, 000	77, 017
Year 4	77, 017	5, 268	14, 000	68, 285
Year 5	68, 285	4, 671	14, 000	58, 956
Year 6	58, 956	4, 033	14, 000	48, 989
Year 7	48, 989	3, 351	14, 000	38, 340
Year 8	38, 340	2, 622	14, 000	26, 962
Year 9	26, 962	1, 844	14, 000	14, 806
Year 10	14, 806	1, 013	14, 000	1, 819
		41, 819	140, 000	

9.93 有时，永续债务工具也会被打包成一种本金实际将会被偿付的方式。实现这一目标的方法之一是连续若干年（主要期间）支付高利率，然后降至可以忽略不计的数额。如果简单地将利息支付计入损益，则该公司将在债券主要期间承担被人为抬高的高额利息费用，而此后期间仅承担极少或没有利息费用。该处理方法可能反映贷款协议的形式，但非其本质。从经济角度来讲，部分或全部的付息属于本金偿还，如下面的示例所述。IAS 39 IG 第 B25 段中包含有类似的示例。

示例——利息递减的永续债务工具

主体发行了 100, 000 元的永续债券，前 10 年的利息按每年 14% 支付，此后以名义利率 0. 125% 支付。

显然，债券在头 10 年末已变得只有极小价值或无价值。实质上，本金在前 10 年期间已经被偿还。因此，主要期间的利息包含了对本息的支付。前 10 年按 14, 000 元计算，之后至无限期按 125 元计算，算得的实际利率为 6. 84%。

	期初 摊余成本	利息费用 （利率 6. 84%）	现金 支付	期末 摊余成本
	元	元	元	元
第 1 年	100, 000	6, 840	14, 000	92, 840
第 2 年	92, 840	6, 350	14, 000	85, 190
第 3 年	85, 190	5, 827	14, 000	77, 017
第 4 年	77, 017	5, 268	14, 000	68, 285
第 5 年	68, 285	4, 671	14, 000	58, 956
第 6 年	58, 956	4, 033	14, 000	48, 989
第 7 年	48, 989	3, 351	14, 000	38, 340
第 8 年	38, 340	2, 622	14, 000	26, 962
第 9 年	26, 962	1, 844	14, 000	14, 806
第 10 年	14, 806	1, 013	14, 000	1, 819
		41, 819	140, 000	

Although the carrying value at the end of year 10 is small, an amount of C100, 000 may fall to be repayable should the entity go into liquidation. In practice, however, there will usually be arrangements to enable the entity to repurchase the debt instrument for a nominal amount and, therefore, extinguish any liability on it.

Fair value measurement considerations

General

9. 94 The IASB believes that fair value is the most relevant measure for financial instruments and is the only relevant measure for derivative assets and liabilities. As a result, IAS 39 gives entities an option to measure all financial assets and liabilities that meet certain qualifying criteria at fair value. The importance of fair value in the measurement process arises because it is a market-based notion that is unaffected by the history of the asset or liability, the specific entity that holds the asset or the liability and the future use of the asset or the liability. Thus, it represents an unbiased measure that is consistent from year to year, within an entity and between entities. As a result, if an investor knows a financial instrument's fair value and has information about its essential terms and risks, it has all the information it needs to make decisions about that instrument. IFRS 13 amended IAS 39 and IFRS 9 to remove their guidance on fair value measurement. For entities still applying IAS 39, the guidance on 'day 1' gain or loss and unquoted equity investments and related derivatives continues to be applicable and is included below. The guidance on fair value measurements under IFRS 13 is included in chapter 34 of the IFRS Manual of Accounting.

[The next paragraph is 9. 145.]

Unquoted equity instruments and related derivatives

9. 145 Normally it is possible to estimate an equity instrument's fair value that does not have a quoted market price in an active market, as well as derivatives that are linked to and must be settled by delivery of such unquoted equity instruments

虽然第 10 年年末的账面金额较小，但如果此时该主体破产清算，可能仍需偿还 100,000 元。因而在实务中，往往有协议约定主体可以以名义金额回购债务工具，并解除相关负债。

公允价值计量的考虑

综述

9.94 IASB 认为，公允价值是金融工具最相关的计量属性，也是衍生资产和衍生负债唯一相关的计量属性。因此，IAS 39 允许主体选择以公允价值计量符合一定标准的所有金融资产和负债。由于公允价值是基于市场的概念，且不会受到资产或负债的历史、持有此类资产或负债的特定主体以及此类资产或负债未来使用的影响，所以其在计量过程中显得尤为重要。因此，公允价值作为一个公正的计量属性，在各年度、主体内部和主体之间都保持一致。如果投资者了解了金融工具的公允价值以及其基本条款和风险信息，就意味着其已掌握做出相关决策所需的所有信息。IFRS 13 修订了 IAS 39 和 IFRS 9，移除了这两项准则中对公允价值计量的规定。对于仍采用 IAS 39 的主体，有关“首日”损益与无报价的权益工具及其相关的衍生工具的指引仍然适用，并在下文中阐述。有关 IFRS 13 下的公允价值计量的指引包括在《国际财务报告准则实务指引》第三十四章中。

[下一段为第 9.145 段。]

无报价的权益工具及其相关衍生工具

9.145 通常而言，对于在活跃市场中没有市场报价的权益工具以及与该权益工具挂钩并须通过交付该权益工具结算的衍生工具，可使用基于合理假设的估值技术，充分可靠地估计其公允价值。此类工具的公允价值被视为能够可

with sufficient reliability by applying valuation techniques based on reasonable assumptions. The fair values of such instruments are deemed to be reliably measurable if:

- the variability in the range of reasonable fair value estimates is not significant for that instrument; or
- the probabilities of the various estimates within the range can be reasonably assessed and used in estimating fair value.

[IAS 39 para AG 80].

9.146 There are many situations in which the variability in the range of reasonable fair value estimates is likely not to be significant and, hence, the fair value is reasonably measurable. However, if the range of reasonable fair value estimates is significantly wide and the probabilities of the various estimates cannot be reasonably assessed, an entity is precluded from measuring the instrument at fair value. In that situation, such instruments are measured at cost, less impairment. [IAS 39 paras 46(c), AG81]. It is not permissible for the entity to measure the equity instrument at fair value, for instance, by judgementally picking a fair value estimate within a range.

9.147 A similar dispensation applies to derivative financial instruments that can only be settled by physical delivery of such unquoted equity instruments. It does not apply to derivative instruments in any other situations as illustrated in the following example.

Example – Reliability of fair value measurement

An entity acquires a complex stand alone derivative that is based on several underlying variables, including commodity prices, interest rates and credit indices. There is no active market or other price quotation for the derivative and no active markets for some of its underlying variables. The entity contends that the derivative's fair value cannot be reliably measured.

Notwithstanding the entity's contention, there is a presumption that the fair value of derivatives can be determined reliably by reference to appropriate market prices, or prices of similar instruments, or discounted cash flow or

靠计量的前提是：

■ 就该工具而言，公允价值合理估计的变动范围不大；或

■ 在该合理估计变动范围之内的各个估计的概率能被合理地评估，并用于估计公允价值。

[IAS 39 AG 第 80 段]。

9.146 在很多情况下，公允价值合理估计的变动范围可能不大，因此公允价值能够合理地计量。但是，若公允价值合理估计的范围很宽泛且不能合理评估各个估计的概率，则主体不能按公允价值计量该工具。在这种情况下，此类工具按成本减去减值计量。[IAS 39 第 46（c）段，AG 第 81 段]。不允许主体以公允价值计量该权益工具，例如，从某区间范围内武断地选取某个估计值作为公允价值。

9.147 对于只能通过交付此类无报价权益工具结算的衍生金融工具，也适用同样的处理方法。但不适用于其他情况下的衍生工具，如下所示。

示例——公允价值计量的可靠性

主体购买了一项复杂的、具有多种基础变量的、独立存在的衍生工具。基础变量包括商品价格、利率和信用指数。该衍生工具没有活跃市场或其他报价，且其中某些基础变量也没有活跃市场。主体认为，该衍生工具的公允价值不能可靠地计量。

尽管主体这样认为，但却存在这样一种假设，即衍生工具的公允价值可参考适当的市场价格、或类似工具的价格、或折现现金流量、或其他定价模型、或参考各组成部分的价格/利率，进行可靠地计量，但与无报价

other pricing models or by reference to prices/rates for components, with the exception only of derivatives that are linked to and must be settled by delivery of an unquoted equity instrument (see para 9.147 above). This is not the situation here and, therefore, the entity cannot measure the derivative at cost or amortised cost.

'Day 1' gain or loss

9.148 The best evidence of the instrument's fair value on initial recognition is the transaction price. However, it is possible that the instrument's fair value may not be the transaction price. The only exception to using the transaction price is if the fair value is evidenced by comparison with other observable current market transactions in the *same* instrument, or is based on a valuation technique whose variables include *only* data from observable markets. [IAS 39 para AG 76]. In such situations, the entity is required to use this value. Consequently, the difference between the estimated fair value using a valuation technique and the transaction price results in immediate 'day 1' recognition of a gain or loss. The IASB concluded that these conditions were necessary and sufficient to provide reasonable assurance that this fair value was genuine for the purposes of recognising up-front gains or losses. In all other cases, the transaction price gives the best evidence of fair value and 'day 1' gain recognition is precluded, an approach that achieves convergence with US GAAP. [IAS 39 para BC104].

Example – Day '1' gain or loss recognition

Entity A acquires a financial asset for C110, which is not quoted in an active market. The asset's fair value based on the entity's own valuation technique amounted to C115. However, that valuation technique does not solely use observable market data, but relies on some entity-specific factors that market participants would not normally consider in setting a price.

The entity cannot recognise a 'day 1' profit of C5 and record the asset at C115. The use of unobservable entity-specific inputs to calculate a fair value that is different from transaction price on 'day 1' is so subjective that its reliability is called into question. Hence, recognition of a 'day 1' gain or

权益工具挂钩并须通过交付该权益工具结算的衍生工具除外（参见以上第9.147段）。本示例不是例外情况，因此主体不能按成本或摊余成本计量该衍生工具。

“首日”损益

9.148 在初始确认时，工具公允价值的最佳证据是交易价格。但是，工具的公允价值也可能不是交易价格。对于采用交易价格的唯一例外是，如果公允价值源自同一工具的其他可观察当前市场交易，或公允价值估值方法中的变量仅取自可观察市场的数据。[IAS 39 AG 第76段]。在此情况下，主体应使用该价值。因此，使用估值技术得到的公允价值估计额与交易价格之间的差额会被立即确认为“首日”损益。IASB认为，这些条件是必要且充分的，足以合理保证首日损益是基于真实的公允价值。在所有其他情况下，交易价格是公允价值的最佳证明，不得确认“首日”利得，该处理同US GAAP是趋同的。[IAS 39 BC 第104段]。

示例——“首日”损益的确认

主体A以110元购买一项金融资产，但这项金融资产在活跃市场没有报价。基于该主体自行估值，该资产的公允价值为115元。但是，其估值方法并不是仅使用可观察的市场数据，还依赖于一些主体特定因素，但市场参与者在制定价格时通常不会考虑这些因素。

主体不能确认5元的“首日”利润，也不能将该资产记录为115元。使用不可观察的主体特定输入值，计算出不同于“首日”交易价格的公允价值是非常主观的，因而可靠性受到置疑。因此，确认“首日”损益是不适当的。所以，主体应将估值限于交易价格，将该资产记录为110元。

loss is not appropriate. Accordingly, the entity restricts its valuation to the transaction price and the asset is recorded at C110.

9.149 A question arises as to whether and how any gain or loss not recognised on 'day 1' should be recognised subsequently, or at all. An unrecognised 'day 1' gain or loss should be recognised after initial recognition only to the extent that it arises from a change in a factor (including time) that market participants would consider in setting a price. [IAS 39 para AG 76A]. It is not clear how the phrase "*a change in a factor (including time) that market participants would consider in setting a price*" should be interpreted. One interpretation is that a gain or loss should remain unrecognised until all market inputs become observable. Another interpretation is that it permits the recognition of 'day 1' gain or loss in profit or loss on a systematic basis over time, even in the absence of any observable transaction data to support such a treatment. Indeed, some constituents asked the Board to clarify whether straight-line amortisation was an appropriate method of recognising the difference. The Board decided not to do this. It concluded that although straight-line amortisation may be an appropriate method in some cases, it will not be appropriate in others. [IAS 39 para BC222(v)(ii)]. This would appear to suggest that an unrecognised 'day 1' gain or loss could be amortised either on a straight line basis or on another rational basis that reflects the nature of the financial instrument (for example, a non-linear amortisation for some option-based derivatives).

9.150 It should be noted that an unrecognised 'day 1' gain or loss is not separately identified in the balance sheet. However, IFRS 7 requires disclosure of the unrecognised amount, together with the change in the amount previously deferred, and the entity's accounting policy for determining when amounts deferred are recognised in profit or loss (see chapter 11).

Demand deposit liabilities

9.151 A demand deposit represents a promise by the deposit-taking institution to deliver cash either to the depositor or to third parties designated by the depositor. It imposes a contractual obligation that is a financial liability. A typical example is a current account in a bank. The current account holder can demand settlement at

9.149 问题是，对于"首日"未确认的损益，是否应随后确认或是不予确认。未确认的"首日"损益应在初始确认后确认，但仅限于因市场参与者在制定价格时会考虑的因素（包括时间）发生变化而产生的损益。[IAS 39 AG 第76A 段]。尚不清楚应如何解读"*市场参与者在制定价格时会考虑的因素（包括时间）发生变化*"这一措辞。一种解释认为，在所有市场输入值能被观察到之前，不确认损益。另一种解释认为，允许系统性地将"首日"损益逐期计入损益，即便缺少可观察的交易数据来支持这一处理方式。实际上，有人请求理事会澄清，直线摊销是否是确认此差额的合适方法。理事会决定不予澄清。理事会认为，尽管直线摊销法可能在某些情况下适合，但不一定适合其他情况。[IAS 39 BC 第222（v）（ii）段]。这似乎表明，未确认的"首日"损益既可根据直线法摊销，也可根据另一种反映金融工具性质的合理基础摊销（例如，适用于一些期权类衍生工具的非线性摊销）。

9.150 值得注意的是，在资产负债表中不单独列报未确认的"首日"损益。但是，IFRS 7 要求披露未确认金额和先前递延金额的变动，以及主体针对递延金额计入损益所采取的会计政策（参见第十一章）。

即期存款负债

9.151 即期存款代表存款机构向存款人或存款人指定的第三方支付现金的承诺。由于其背负了一项合同义务，因而属于金融负债。典型的例子是在银行开立的活期存款账户。活期存款账户持有人可在任何时候要求提款，银行通常有权在任何时候向存款人退款（即使银行很少行使这一权利）。常有争议认

any time and the bank generally has the right to return the depositor's money at any time (even though that right is seldom exercised). It is often argued that the fair value of the financial liabilities with a demand feature is less than the demand amount, because not all depositors withdraw their money at the earliest opportunity. Often there is a core of deposits (withdrawals replaced by new deposits) that is left outstanding for long periods of time.

9.152 However, the IASB was not prepared to concede that demand financial liabilities could have a fair value different from face value until further work had been done, particularly, in respect of insurance contract liabilities. Consequently, IAS 39 makes it clear that the fair value of a financial liability with a demand feature is not less than the amount payable on demand, discounted from the first date that the amount could be required to be paid. [IAS 39 para 49]. This follows from the fact that the maturity date of an item with no contractual repayment terms cannot be later than the earliest date on which payment can be demanded. The Basis for Conclusion section in IAS 39 notes that recognising a financial liability with a demand feature at less than the demand amount would give rise to an immediate gain on the origination of such a deposit, which is not considered appropriate. In substance, the gain represents the benefits of future interest free or low interest use of funds expected to occur as a result of the deposit relationship. Such benefits are not considered to be directly attributable to the rights and obligations that constitute the demand deposit liabilities existing at a measurement date and accordingly should not enter into the estimate of their fair value. The future benefit of the deposit relationship may be recognised as an intangible asset in circumstances where customer relationships are acquired, together with the related portfolio of demand deposits, if the recognition criteria in IAS 38 are met. However, the Basis for Conclusion section in IAS 39 notes that, absent such an acquisition, the market price observed for such financial liabilities is the price at which they are originated between the customer and the deposit-taker, that is, the demand amount. [IAS 39 para BC 94]. In the absence of an acquisition of a portfolio of demand deposits, this customer deposit intangible asset should not be recognised.

为，具有即期特征的金融负债的公允价值应低于可支取金额，因为不是所有的存款人在可支取时马上提款。通常，核心存款（新存款替代提款）会长期存在。

9.152 然而，在完成进一步研究之前，特别是有关保险合同负债的研究，IASB 并不准备允许即期金融负债的公允价值不同于其面额。因此，IAS 39 明确指出，具有即期特征的金融负债的公允价值不低于将要求支取时的应付金额从可支取的当天进行折现的现值。[IAS 39 第 49 段]。它遵循了一个这样的事实，合同未约定偿付条款的项目的到期日不应迟于可能被要求付款的最早日期。IAS 39 的结论基础备注说明，若具有即期特征的金融负债所确认的金额低于可支取金额，将导致存入该存款时立即产生一项利得，这样处理是不恰当的。实质上，利得代表未来使用无息或低息资金的收益，而预期能够获得这样的收益是因为存在存款关系。该收益不被认为直接归因于即期存款负债在计量日所具有的权利和义务，因此，不应纳入对公允价值的估计。如果满足《国际会计准则第 38 号》（“IAS 38”）中的确认标准，在同时获得客户关系及相关即期存款组合的情况下，存款关系的未来收益可被确认为无形资产。然而，IAS 39结论基础备注说明，若不存在上述取得情况，此类金融负债的可观察市场价格就是存款客户一开始存入存款接受人的金额，即可支取金额。[IAS 39 BC 第 94 段]。若没有获取即期存款组合，则不应当确认客户存款形成的无形资产。

Credit risk of liabilities

9.153 When financial liabilities are measured at fair value, changes in their credit risk should be reflected in their fair value measurement. Many question whether a liability's credit risk or changes in its credit risk should enter into the measurement of its liabilities. They argue that it is not useful to report lower liabilities when an entity is in financial difficulty precisely because its debt levels are too high and that it would be difficult to explain to users of financial statements the reasons why income would be recognised when a liability's creditworthiness deteriorates. The IASB, however, takes the view that because financial statements are prepared on a going concern basis, credit risk affects the value at which liabilities could be repurchased or settled. Accordingly, a financial liability's fair value reflects the credit risk relating to that liability. Therefore, the IASB decided to include credit risk relating to a financial liability in the fair value measurement of that liability for the following reasons:

- entities realise changes in fair value, including fair value attributable to the liability's credit risk, for example, by renegotiating or repurchasing liabilities or by using derivatives;
- changes in credit risk affect the observed market price of a financial liability and hence its fair value;
- it is difficult from a practical standpoint to exclude changes in credit risk from an observed market price; and
- a financial liability's fair value (that is, the price of that liability in an exchange between a knowledgeable, willing buyer and a knowledgeable, willing seller) on initial recognition reflects its credit risk. Therefore, it is inappropriate to include credit risk in the initial fair value measurement of financial liabilities, but not subsequently.

[IAS 39 para BC89].

9.154 It should be noted that the issue relates to the financial liability's credit risk, rather than the entity's creditworthiness. Although the two are closely related,

负债的信用风险

9.153 以公允价值计量金融负债时，金融负债信用风险的变化应在其公允价值计量中予以反映。许多人质疑，负债的信用风险或其信用风险的变化是否应纳入负债的计量之中。他们认为，在主体正因为其债务水平太高而陷入财务困境时，列报较低的负债不能提供有用的信息，且难以向财务报表使用者解释，为什么在债务信用状况发生恶化时反而确认了收益。但是，IASB 认为，因财务报表的编制基于持续经营假设，信用风险会影响负债被回购或清偿的价值。因此，金融负债的公允价值应反映与该负债相关的信用风险。所以，IASB 决定将金融负债的相关信用风险纳入该负债的公允价值计量，理由如下：

- 主体实现公允价值的变化，包括归因于负债信用风险的公允价值，例如：通过重新协商、或回购负债、或通过使用衍生工具；
- 信用风险的变化影响金融负债的可观察市场价格，从而影响其公允价值；
- 从实务角度，难以从可观察市场价格中剔除信用风险的变化；及
- 金融负债的公允价值（即熟悉情况的交易双方自愿交换该负债的价格）在初始确认时反映了其信用风险。因此，若将信用风险纳入金融负债的初始公允价值计量但不纳入后续计量，这样处理是不恰当的。

[IAS 39 BC 第 89 段]。

9.154 应当注意，这一问题与该金融负债的信用风险相关，而与该主体的信用状况无关。尽管这两者是密切相关的，但主体信用状况的恶化可能并不自

a deterioration of the entity creditworthiness may not, by itself, affect the credit risk of all the entity's liabilities in the same way. For example, the fair value of liabilities secured by valuable collateral, guaranteed by third parties or ranking ahead of virtually all other liabilities is generally unaffected by changes in the entity's creditworthiness. [IAS 39 para BC92]. If an entity designates a financial liability as at fair value through profit or loss, IFRS 7 requires it to disclose the amount of change in the fair value of the financial liability that is attributable to changes in the liability's credit risk (see further chapter 11).

9.155 In October 2010, the IASB updated IFRS 9. The new requirements retain the classification and measurement requirements of IAS 39 for financial liabilities, including bifurcation of embedded derivatives, except that the effects of changes in the credit risk of liabilities, designated under the fair value option would not affect profit or loss. Changes in fair value of a liability due to an entity's own credit risk will be recognised as a component of 'other comprehensive income'. The new requirements respond to the concern that recognising the effects of changes in the fair value of a liability attributable to the liability's credit risk in profit or loss is counter-intuitive and does not provide useful information, unless the liability is held for trading.

Impairment of financial assets

9.156 A financial asset measured at amortised cost is impaired when its carrying value exceeds the present value of the future cash flows discounted at the financial asset's original effective interest rate. A financial asset that is carried at fair value through profit or loss does not give rise to any impairment issues as diminution in value due to impairment is already reflected in the fair value and, hence, in profit or loss. It follows that impairment issues are only relevant to financial assets that are carried at amortised cost and available-for-sale financial assets whose fair value changes are recognised in other comprehensive income.

9.157 IAS 39 deals with impairment of financial assets through a two-step process. First, an entity must carry out an impairment review of its financial assets at each balance sheet date. The aim of this review is to determine whether there is

动地影响该主体所有负债的信用风险。例如，若该负债由有价值的担保物作抵押、由第三方作担保或其清偿顺序优于几乎所有其他负债，则其公允价值通常不受主体信用状况变化的影响。[IAS 39 BC 第 92 段]。若主体指定一项金融负债以公允价值计量且其变动计入损益，IFRS 7 要求披露该金融负债的公允价值因其信用风险变化而变化金额（另参见第十一章）。

9.155 2010 年 10 月，IASB 更新了 IFRS 9。新规定保留了 IAS 39 对金融负债的分类和计量要求，包括嵌入式衍生工具的拆分，但对于指定为公允价值计量的负债，其信用风险变化的影响将不再计入损益。主体自身信用风险导致的负债公允价值的变化将计入“其他综合收益”。新规定旨在回应人们的疑虑，即将因负债的信用风险而造成的公允价值变化计入损益是有违直觉的，且不能提供有用的信息，除非该负债是为交易目的而持有。

金融资产的减值

9.156 对于以摊余成本计量的金融资产，若其账面价值大于未来现金流量按该金融资产原实际利率折现的现值，则发生了减值。以公允价值计量且其变动计入损益的金融资产不存在减值问题，因为由减值造成的价值减损已经在公允价值中反映，因而已计入损益。因此，以摊余成本计量的金融资产和公允价值变动计入其他综合收益中的可供出售金融资产才会涉及减值问题。

9.157 IAS 39 通过两步法来处理金融资产的减值。首先，主体必须在各个资产负债表日对其金融资产进行减值评估。实施这一测试的目的在于确定是否存在客观证据表明金融资产发生了减值。[IAS 39 第 58 段]。自以下第 9.162

objective evidence that impairment exists for a financial asset. [IAS 39 para 58]. This is considered from paragraph 9.162 below.

9.158 Secondly, if there is objective evidence of impairment, the entity should measure and record the impairment loss in the reporting period. [IAS 39 para 58]. The measurement of impairment losses differs between financial assets carried at amortised cost (see para 9.173 below), financial assets carried at cost (see para 9.200 below) and available-for-sale financial assets (see para 9.201 below). There is also a difference on whether impairment losses can be reversed depending on whether the available-for-sale instrument is debt or equity (see para 9.204 below).

Incurred versus expected losses

9.159 Under IAS 39, a financial asset or a group of financial assets is impaired and impairment losses are incurred if, and only if, there is objective evidence of impairment as a result of one or more events that occurred after the asset's initial recognition (a 'loss event') and that loss event (or events) has an impact on the estimated future cash flows of the financial asset or group of financial assets that can be reliably estimated. It may not be possible to identify a single, discrete event that caused the impairment. Rather the combined effect of several events may have caused the impairment. In addition, the loss event must have a reliably measurable effect on the present value of estimated future cash flows and be supported by current observable data. [IAS 39 para 59].

9.160 Losses expected as a result of future events, no matter how likely, are not recognised. Possible or expected future trends that may lead to a loss in the future (for example, an expectation that unemployment will rise or a recession will occur) are also not taken into account. The standard states that to recognise impairment on the basis of expected future transactions and events would not be consistent with an amortised cost model.

9.161 As the impairment model in IAS 39 is based on the 'incurred loss' model and not on an 'expected loss' model, an impairment loss is not recognised at the time an asset is originated, that is, before a loss event can have occurred as

段起，将对该问题予以介绍。

9.158 其次，若存在减值的客观证据，主体应在报告期计量并记录减值损失。[IAS 39 第 58 段]。对于以摊余成本计量的金融资产（参见以下第 9.173 段）、以成本计量的金融资产（参见以下第 9.200 段）和可供出售金融资产（参见以下第 9.201 段）而言，减值损失的计量是不同的。此外，减值损失能否转回也存在差异，取决于是可供出售债务工具还是可供出售权益工具（参见以下第 9.204 段）。

已发生损失还是预期损失

9.159 根据 IAS 39，当且仅当资产在初始确认后，由于发生一个或多个事项（"损失事件"）而表明存在减值的客观证据，以及该损失事件影响了金融资产或金融资产组合能可靠估计的预计未来现金流量，则该金融资产或金融资产组已减值并且发生了减值损失。有时可能难以确认导致减值的单个、分散事件。更确切地说，多个事件的组合效应可能导致了减值。此外，损失事件对预计未来现金流量现值的影响必须是能够可靠计量的，且必须得到当前可观察数据的支持。[IAS 39 第 59 段]。

9.160 就未来事件而预估的损失，无论可能性有多大，都不予确认。可能导致在未来发生损失的可能或预计趋势（例如，预计失业率上升或发生经济衰退）同样不予考虑。准则认为，根据预期未来交易和事件确认减值不符合摊余成本计量模型。

9.161 因 IAS 39 的减值模型是基于"已发生损失"模型而不是基于"预期损失"模型，在资产原生时，即在损失事件发生前，不确认减值损失。参见以下示例：

illustrated in the following example:

Example – Recognition of an impairment loss on origination

Entity A lends C1,000 to a group of customers. Based on historical experience, entity A expects that 1% of the principal amount of loans given to the customers will not be collected.

Entity A is not permitted to reduce the carrying amount of a loan asset by C10 on initial recognition through the recognition of an immediate impairment loss.

Under the incurred loss model of IAS 39, an impairment loss is recognised only if there is objective evidence of impairment as a result of a past event that occurred after initial recognition. Furthermore, recognition of an immediate impairment loss based on future expectation would be inconsistent with the general rule that a financial asset should be initially measured at fair value. For a loan asset, the fair value is the amount of cash lent adjusted for any fees and costs (unless a portion of the amount lent is compensation for other stated or implied rights or privileges). [IAS 39 para IGE4.2]. In practice, however, the expectation of loss is built in to the credit spread for the customer.

Objective evidence of impairment

9.162 IAS 39 provides examples of factors that may, either individually or taken together, provide sufficient objective evidence that an impairment loss has been incurred in a financial asset or group of financial assets. They include observable data that comes to the attention of the holder of the asset about the following loss events:

- Significant financial difficulty of the issuer or obligor.
- A breach of contract, such as a default or delinquency in interest or principal payments.
- The lender, for economic or legal reasons relating to the borrower's financial

示例——发放时减值损失的确认

主体 A 借了 1,000 元给一组客户。根据历史经验，主体 A 预计发放给客户的贷款本金有 1% 不能被收回。

准则不允许主体 A 在初始确认时通过立即确认减值损失将贷款资产的账面价值减少 10 元。

根据 IAS 39 的已发生损失模型，只有在初始确认后发生的事件表明存在减值的客观证据时，才能确认减值损失。此外，根据未来预期而立即确认减值损失是不符合金融资产应按公允价值进行初始计量这一普遍规则的。对于贷款资产，其公允价值是所借资金并对收费和成本调整之后的金额（除非所借资金的一部分用于补偿其他约定的或隐含的权利或专用权）。[IAS 39 IG 第 E4.2 段]。在实务中，损失预期其实是被嵌入在客户的信用价差中。

减值的客观证据

9.162　IAS 39 列举了一些因素。这些因素可能单独或共同提供了充分的客观证据表明金融资产或金融资产组合发生了减值损失。其中包括使得资产持有人注意到下列损失事件的可观察数据：

- 发行人或债务人的严重财务困难。
- 合同违约，如利息或本金支付的拖欠或逾期。
- 借款人陷入财务困境，贷款人因经济或法律原因，才向借款人作出让步。

difficulty, granting to the borrower a concession that the lender would not otherwise consider.

- It becomes probable that the borrower will enter bankruptcy or other financial reorganisation.
- The disappearance of an active market for that financial asset because of financial difficulties.
- Observable data indicating that there is a measurable decrease in the estimated future cash flows from a group of financial assets since the initial recognition of those assets, although the decrease cannot yet be identified with the individual financial assets in the group, including:
  - adverse changes in the payment status of borrowers in the group (for example, an increased number of delayed payments or an increased number of credit card borrowers who have reached their credit limit and are paying the minimum monthly amount); or
  - national or local economic conditions that correlate with defaults on the assets in the group (for example, an increase in the unemployment rate in the geographical area of the borrowers, a decrease in property prices for mortgages in the relevant area, a decrease in oil prices for loan assets to oil producers, or adverse changes in industry conditions that affect the borrowers in the group).

[IAS 39 para 59].

9.163 A downgrade of an entity's credit rating is not, of itself, evidence of impairment, although it may be evidence of impairment when considered with other available information. Other factors that an entity considers in determining whether it has objective evidence that an impairment loss has been incurred include information about:

- The debtors' or issuers' liquidity.
- Solvency, business and financial risk exposures.
- Levels of and trends in delinquencies for similar financial assets.

- 借款人可能遭受破产或其他财务重组。

- 因财务困境，该金融资产的活跃市场消失。

- 虽然无法辨认金融资产组合中单项资产的现金流量是否减少，但根据可观察的数据分析发现，该金融资产组自初始确认以来的预计未来现金流量确已减少且可计量，包括：

  - 该组金融资产的借款人支付能力发生恶化（例如，延迟付款的数量增加，或已到信用额度且每月按最低还款额偿还的信用卡借款人的人数在增长）；或

  - 与该组合中资产的违约相关联的国家或地区的经济状况（例如，借款人所在地域的失业率上升，按揭房产价格下跌，对向石油生产商提供的贷款而言相关油价跌落，或影响该组合的借款人的行业状况发生不利变化）。

[IAS 39 第 59 段]。

9.163　尽管和其他可获得的信息一同考虑时，信用评级下降可能是减值的证据，但主体信用评级下降本身并不构成减值的证据。确认是否存在客观证据表明已经发生减值损失时，主体考虑的其他因素包括下列信息：

- 债务人或发行人的流动性。
- 偿付能力、经营和财务风险敞口。
- 类似金融资产发生拖欠的水平和趋势。

- National and local economic trends and conditions.
- The fair value of collateral and guarantees.

These and other factors may, either individually or taken together, provide sufficient objective evidence that an impairment loss has been incurred in a financial asset or group of financial assets. [IAS 39 para 60, IG para E4. 1].

9. 164 A decline in the fair value of a financial asset below its cost or amortised cost is not necessarily evidence of impairment (for example, a decline in the fair value of an investment in a debt instrument that results from an increase in the risk-free interest rate). Also, in contrast with the fifth bullet point mentioned in paragraph 9. 162 above, the disappearance of an active market because an entity's financial instruments are no longer publicly traded is not evidence of impairment. [IAS 39 para 60].

Evidence of impairment for equity instruments

9. 165 The standard provides additional guidance about impairment indicators that are specific to investments in equity instruments. They apply in addition to the impairment indicators described above, which focus on the assessment of impairment in debt instruments.

9. 166 The additional impairment indicators that may indicate that the equity investment's cost may not be recovered are:

- Significant adverse changes in the technological, market, economic or legal environment in which the issuer operates. For example, such changes include but are not limited to:
  - Structural changes in the industry or industries in which the issuer operates, such as changes in production technology or the number of competitors.
  - Changes in the level of demand for the goods or services sold by the issuer resulting from factors such as changing consumer tastes or product obsolescence.
  - Changes in the political or legal environment affecting the issuer's business,

■ 国家和地区经济形势和状况。

■ 抵押品和担保的公允价值。

这些以及其他因素可能单独或共同提供了充分的证据表明金融资产或金融资产组合发生了减值损失。[IAS 39 第 60 段，IG 第 E4.1 段]。

9.164　金融资产的公允价值跌至其成本或摊余成本之下，不一定是减值的证据（例如，无风险利率上调导致的债务工具投资的公允价值下跌）。此外，与以上第 9.162 段第五点不同，活跃市场的消失是由于主体的金融工具不再公开交易，这也并不形成减值的证据。[IAS 39 第 60 段]。

权益工具的减值证据

9.165　准则还对权益工具投资的减值迹象提供了额外指引。而上述主要适用于评估债务工具减值的减值迹象，亦同样适用。

9.166　可能表明权益投资成本无法收回的其他减值迹象包括：

■ 发行人所在的技术、市场、经济或法律环境发生重大不利变化。例如，这些变化包括但不限于：

　■ 发行人所在的行业发生结构性改变，如生产技术或竞争对手数量的变化。

　■ 消费者喜好改变或产品淘汰引起对发行人所出售的商品或提供的服务的需求发生变化。

　■ 政治或法律环境变化，影响发行人的业务，如新的环保、征税或贸易法

such as enactment of new environment protection, tax or trade laws.

- Changes in the issuer's financial condition evidenced by changes in factors such as its liquidity, credit rating, profitability, cash flows, debt/equity ratio and level of dividend payments.

- A 'significant' or 'prolonged' decline in the fair value of an investment in an equity instrument below its cost.

[IAS 39 para 61].

9.167 In the context of the last bullet point above, the IFRIC confirmed that a significant decline in fair value should be evaluated against the original cost at initial recognition and 'prolonged' should be evaluated against the period in which the fair value of the investment has been below that original cost. In May 2009 the IFRIC tentatively decided, that a significant or prolonged decline cannot be considered only an indicator of possible impairment in determining whether there is objective evidence. When such a decline exists, recognition of an impairment loss is required. Furthermore, any further declines in value after an impairment loss has been recognised in profit or loss should be recognised immediately in profit or loss. [IAS 39 para IG E4.9]. IAS 39 refers to original cost on initial recognition of an equity instrument and does not permit a prior impairment to establish a new deemed cost against which subsequent declines in fair value are evaluated. [IFRIC Update April 2005]. However, no guidance is provided on what is a 'significant' or 'prolonged' decline in the fair value of an equity instrument. Consequently, judgement is required.

9.168 Whether a decline in fair value below cost is considered as 'significant' must be assessed on an instrument-by-instrument basis. In our view, the assessment of significant should be based on both qualitative and quantitative factors. An entity should develop an accounting policy for assessing a 'significant' decline in fair value.

9.169 The expected level of volatility for an instrument may also be a factor that entities should take into consideration when assessing what is 'significant'. Volatility is a tendency of a stock's value to fluctuate. Stocks with higher volatility are considered riskier because their value changes more from day to day. Stocks

规的颁布。

- 发行人财务状况发生变化，特别是其流动性、信用评级、盈利能力、现金流量、负债/权益比和股息支付水平等。

- 权益工具投资的公允价值“严重”或“非暂时性”地低于其成本。

[IAS 39 第 61 段]。

9.167　在上述最后一点中，国际财务报告解释委员会确认，公允价值“严重”下跌的标准应基于初始确认时的初始成本评估；“非暂时性”下跌应基于投资的公允价值低于初始成本的期间评估。2009 年 5 月，国际财务报告解释委员会暂时决定，公允价值发生严重或非暂时性下跌不能仅仅认为是判断是否存在客观证据表明可能已发生减值的迹象。若出现这样的下跌，则应确认减值损失。此外，在减值损失计入损益后，公允价值的进一步下跌应立即计入损益。[IAS 39 IG 第 E4.9 段]。IAS 39 提及的是权益工具初始确认的初始成本，不允许考虑此前确认减值后创立出新的认定成本，并据以评估公允价值后续下跌是否减值。[2005 年 4 月 IFRIC 的更新]。但对于什么是权益工具公允价值“严重”或“非暂时性”下跌，没有提供指引。因此，需做判断。

9.168　公允价值跌至成本以下时是否被视为“严重”下跌，须逐个工具进行评估。我们认为，评估“严重”应基于定性与定量两方面因素。主体应制定一项会计政策，以评估公允价值是否“严重”下跌。

9.169　主体在评估什么是“严重”时，也可能考虑工具的期望波动率。波动率是指股票价值涨落的趋势。波动较大的股票风险较大，因为其价值天天发生较大变动。波动较小的股票更稳定，因此风险较小。例如，某公司持有一家知名超市连锁店和投机性矿业公司上市股票。在同一段时间内，这两家上

will a lower volatility are more stable and, therefore, viewed as less risky. For example, a company may hold listed shares in an established supermarket chain whose share price changes by 3% over a period of time and listed shares in a speculative mining enterprise whose share price fluctuates by 10% over the same period. In this case, a larger decline in the mining company's shares might be tolerated before an entity records an impairment loss, given its greater volatility compared with the supermarket chain. It is also important to note that where volatility is taken into account in a company's assessment of whether a decline is significant, the volatility is considered relative to the instrument's fair value at the date impairment is being considered, not its original cost. In addition, that volatility should be determined over a relatively long period. For example, a market downturn due to decline in the overall economy over a short period of time would not be considered adequate to establish an estimate of expected future volatility.

9.170 What is a 'prolonged' decline in fair value will also require judgement and a policy will need to be establishedIn general, a period of 12 months or greater below original cost is likely to be a 'prolonged' decline. However, the assessment of 'prolonged' should not be compared to the entire period that the investment has been or is expected to be held. For example, if a security's fair value has been below cost for 12 months, whether that security has been held or is intended to be held for two or 20 years is irrelevant. The assessment is whether the period of 12 months accords with the entity's chosen policy.

9.171 Following the amendment to IAS 39 described in paragraph 9.41, on reclassification of an equity instrument out of a category measured at fair value (that is, held-for-trading or available-for-sale) and into another category, the fair value at the date of reclassification becomes its new cost. [IAS 39 para 50C, F]. This new cost is the basis against which future 'significant' or 'prolonged' declines in fair value should be assessed.

9.172 In practice, an entity may have purchased securities in a company on multiple dates and at different prices. IAS 39 does not provide guidance on this point. By analogy to IAS 2, 'Inventories', in our view the basis for measuring the cost for calculating impairment could be a specific identification method, weighted

市公司的股价分别变化 3% 和 10% 。在这种情况下，鉴于矿业公司的股价比超市连锁店波动性大，因此，在决定是否确认减值损失之前，该公司可接受矿业公司股价较大的降幅。值得注意的是，在公司考虑波动率以评估价值下跌是否严重时，波动率是相对于工具确认减值当日的公允价值，而非初始成本。同时，还要考虑相对较长一段时间内的波动率。例如，短期内总体经济形势下滑引起的市场低迷，不足以构成估计未来波动率的因素。

9.170 什么是公允价值“非暂时性”下跌也需要进行判断，并需要制定相应的会计政策。通常来讲，跌至低于初始成本的时间达到 12 个月或更久很可能是“非暂时性”下跌。然而，评定是否“非暂时性”下跌不能与已经持有的时间或预期持有的时间相比较。例如，某证券的公允价值已低于其成本长达 12 个月，与原打算持有该证券的时间（20 年）或已持有该证券的时间（2 年）无关。应评估 12 个月的时间是否和主体选定的会计政策一致。

9.171 根据 9.41 段所述的对 IAS 39 的修改，在将以公允价值计量的权益工具（即交易类或可供出售类）从某一类别重分类至另一类别时，重分类当日权益工具的公允价值即为其新成本。[IAS 39 第 50C、50F 段]。该新成本成为未来评定公允价值发生“严重”或“非暂时性”下跌的基准。

9.172 在实务中，主体可能在不同日期以不同价格买入同一家公司的证券。IAS 39 未提供相关指引。我们认为，类比 IAS 2，用于计算减值的成本计量方法可以是个别认定法、加权平均成本法或先进先出法。用于计算减值的成本计量方法应与用于计算处置损益的成本计量方法保持一致，且各期保持不变。

average cost or FIFO method. The basis should be the same as the basis for calculating realised gains or losses upon disposal and should remain consistent across periods. This is an accounting policy choice and should be applied consistently.

Financial assets carried at amortised cost

General requirements

9.173 Financial assets carried at amortised cost are those that are classified as either loans and receivables or held-to-maturity. If there is objective evidence that an impairment loss on such an asset has been incurred, the amount of the loss should be measured as the difference between the asset's carrying amount and the present value of estimated future cash flows. The expected cash flows should exclude future credit losses that have not been incurred and should be discounted at the financial asset's original effective interest rate (that is, the effective interest rate computed at initial recognition). [IAS 39 para 63].

9.174 The standard allows the carrying amount of the asset to be reduced either directly by writing it down or through use of an allowance account such as a loan loss provision or provision for bad and doubtful debts. However, the amount of the loss should be recognised in profit or loss. [IAS 39 para 63]. The asset's carrying amount in the entity's balance sheet is stated net of any related allowance. [IAS 39 para AG 84].

9.175 In some circumstances, it may not be practicable to make a reasonably reliable direct estimate of the present value of future cash flows expected from an impaired financial asset measured at amortised cost. As a practical expedient, the carrying amount of the impaired asset may be determined in these circumstances on the basis of an instrument's fair value using an observable market price. [IAS 39 para AG 84].

9.176 A loan's observable market price is the loan's quoted price that can be obtained from reliable market sources. For example, loans with an active secondary market could be measured based on the observable market price. Similarly, an

这是一项会计政策选择，应当一贯运用。

以摊余成本计量的金融资产

一般要求

9.173 以摊余成本计量的金融资产分为贷款和应收款项或持有至到期投资。如有客观证据表明此类资产发生了减值损失，则损失金额应等于该资产的账面价值与预计未来现金流量现值之间的差额。预计现金流量不包括尚未发生的未来信用损失，且应按该金融资产的原实际利率（即初始确认时计算确定的实际利率）予以折现。[IAS 39 第 63 段]。

9.174 准则允许直接减少资产账面价值，或通过使用备抵账户减少资产账面价值，例如贷款损失准备金或呆坏账准备金。然而，损失金额应计入损益。[IAS 39 第 63 段]。在主体的资产负债表上，资产的账面价值以抵减了相关备抵账户的净额列示。[IAS 39 AG 第 84 段]。

9.175 在某些情况下，难以直接合理、可靠地估计以摊余成本计量的、已减值金融资产的未来现金流量的现值。作为一项实务便利，在此情况下，已减值资产的账面价值可基于该资产的可观察市场价格作为其公允价值予以确定。[IAS 39 AG 第 84 段]。

9.176 贷款的可观察市场价格即贷款的报价，可通过可靠的市场来源获得。例如，具有活跃二级市场的贷款可根据可观察市场价格计量。类似地，有批量处置贷款计划的主体可通过比较出售同类贷款所取得的净收款计量减值。

entity that has a viable plan to dispose of loans in a bulk sale could measure impairment by comparison to the net proceeds received on similar loan sales. However, it is likely that the use of the observable market price will be infrequent, because either there may not be a market for the loans or the market may be illiquid.

9.177 The expected future cash flows that are included in the calculation are the contractual cash of the instrument itself, reduced or delayed based on the current expectations of the amount and timing of these cash flows as a result of losses incurred at the balance sheet date. In circumstances where the amount outstanding is expected to be collected in full, but the collection period is delayed, an impairment loss must still be recognised, unless the creditor receives full compensation (for example, in the form of penalty interest) for the period of the delinquency, as illustrated in the example below.

Example – Impairment arising from changes in the amount and timing of cash flows

Entity A is concerned that, because of financial difficulties, customer B will not be able to make all principal and interest payments due on a loan in a timely manner. It negotiates a restructuring of the loan. Entity A expects that customer B will be able to meet its obligations under the restructured terms in any of the 5 scenarios indicated below.

- Customer B will pay the original loan's full principal amount 5 years after the original due date, but none of the interest due under the original terms.
- Customer B will pay the original loan's full principal amount on the original due date, but none of the interest due under the original terms.
- Customer B will pay the original loan's full principal amount on the original due date with interest only at a lower interest rate than the interest rate inherent in the original loan.
- Customer B will pay the original loan's full principal amount 5 years after the original due date and all interest accrued during the original loan term, but no interest for the extended term.

然而，用到可观察市场价格的几率可能很小，因为可能没有贷款市场或市场流动性不够。

9.177　由于资产负债表日已发生损失，基于对这些现金流量金额和时间的当前估计，用于计算减值的预计未来现金流量，即工具自身的合同现金流量，有所减少或延迟。如下例所示，若欠款预计能全部收回，但收款期被拖延，仍须确认减值损失，除非债权人就拖欠期间获得全额赔偿（例如，以罚息形式）。

示例——现金流量金额和时间发生变化而引起的减值

由于陷入财务困境，主体 A 担心客户 B 不能及时偿还贷款本金和利息，于是协商重组贷款。主体 A 希望客户 B 在以下所述的五种情况下，按重组条款履行其偿付义务。

- 客户 B 将在原贷款到期后五年内偿还原贷款的所有本金，而不支付原贷款条款下的应计利息。
- 客户 B 将在原贷款到期日偿还原贷款的所有本金，而不支付原贷款条款下的应计利息。
- 客户 B 将在原贷款到期日偿还原贷款的所有本金与利息，但利率比原贷款利率低。
- 客户 B 将在原贷款到期后五年内偿还原贷款的所有本金和原贷款期间所有应计利息，但不用支付展期利息。

- Customer B will pay the original loan's full principal amount 5 years after the original due date and all interest, including interest for both the loan's original term and the extended term.

[IAS 39 para IG E4. 3].

Given that customer B is in financial difficulties, an impairment loss has been incurred, as there is objective evidence of impairment. The amount of the impairment loss for a loan measured at amortised cost is the difference between the loan's carrying amount and the present value of future principal and interest payments discounted at the loan's original effective interest rate.

In the first four scenarios above, the present value of the future principal and interest payments discounted at the loan's original effective interest rate will be lower than the loan's carrying amount. Therefore, an impairment loss is recognised in those cases.

In the final scenario, even though the timing of payments has changed, the lender will receive interest on interest, and the present value of the future principal and interest payments discounted at the loan's original effective interest rate will equal the carrying amount of the loan. Therefore, there is no impairment loss. However, this fact pattern is unlikely given customer B's financial difficulties.

9. 178 Where an impaired financial asset is secured by collateral, the calculation of the present value of the estimated future cash flows of the collateralised financial asset should reflect the cash flows that may result from foreclosure less costs for obtaining and selling the collateral, whether or not foreclosure is probable. [IAS 39 para AG 84]. As the measurement of the impaired financial asset reflects the collateral asset's fair value, the collateral is not recognised as an asset separately from the impaired financial asset, unless it meets the recognition criteria for an asset in another standard. [IAS 39 IG para E4. 8].

9. 179 For financial assets reclassified to another category following the amendment to IAS 39 in October 2008, see paragraph 9. 45.

■ 客户 B 将在原贷款到期后五年内偿还原贷款的所有本金和利息，包括原贷款期和展期的应计利息。

[IAS 39 IG 第 E4.3 段]。

考虑到客户 B 陷入财务困境，有客观证据表明发生了减值损失。以摊余成本计量的贷款的减值损失，等于该贷款的账面价值与未来本金与利息按该贷款原实际利率折现的现值之差。

在上述前四种情况下，该贷款的未来本金与利息按其原实际利率折现的现值，小于其账面价值。因此，在这几种情况下要确认减值损失。

在最后一种情况下，尽管支付时点发生了改变，但贷款人按利滚利收取利息，于是该贷款未来本金与利息按其原实际利率折现的现值等于其账面价值。因此，没有减值损失。然而，如果客户 B 遭遇经济困难，这种情况不大可能发生。

9.178 如已减值金融资产有抵押品作担保，该被担保金融资产的预计未来现金流量现值的计算应反映可能来自于处置抵押品所得并扣除获得及出售抵押品的成本后的净现金流量，无论处置抵押品是否有可能。[IAS 39 AG 第 84 段]。由于已减值金融资产的计量已反映抵押资产的公允价值，因此该抵押物不再单独确认为一项资产，除非其满足其他准则中资产的确认条件。[IAS 39 IG 第 E4.8 段]。

9.179 对于依照 IAS 39 在 2008 年 10 月所做的修订而被重分类为其他类别的金融资产，参见第 9.45 段。

Appropriate discount rate

9. 180 As stated above, impairment of a financial asset carried at amortised cost is measured by discounting the expected future cash flows using the financial instrument's original effective interest rate. Since impairment reflects a fall in the asset's carrying amount, which is evidenced by a decrease in the estimate of expected cash flows to be received from the financial asset, discounting at a rate of interest that reflects a current market rate of interest would impose fair value measurement on the financial asset. This would not be appropriate for assets that are measured at amortised cost. [IAS 39 para AG 84]. The historical effective rate should be used as the discount rate even where it is lower or higher than the rate on current loans originated by the entity. In other words, loan impairments are based solely on the reduction in estimated cash flows rather than on changes in interest rates. This approach ensures that a financial asset carried at amortised cost that becomes impaired continues to be carried at an amount that considers the present value of all expected future cash flows, in a manner consistent with the asset's measurement before it became impaired.

Example – Impairment of fixed rate loan

The facts are the same as in example 2 in paragraph 9. 78 above, except that at 31 December 20X9 it became clear that as a result of structural changes in the industry in which the borrower operates, the borrower was in financial difficulties and its credit rating had been downgraded. At that date, the loan's amortised carrying value, calculated at the original effective rate of 6. 7322%, amounted to C583, 435.

Faced with this objective evidence, the entity believes that the borrower will be unable to make all the remaining 5 annual scheduled repayments of C142, 378. Accordingly, the entity restructures the loan under which the annual payment due on 31 December 20Y0 is waived followed by three annual payments of C175, 000 until 31 December 20Y3. The interest on the outstanding loan under the revised payment schedule is reduced to 6. 3071%.

The present value of the annual payments of C175, 000 due on 31 December

适当的折现率

9.180 如上所述，以摊余成本计量的金融资产的减值是基于该金融工具预计未来现金流量按其原实际利率折现来计量的。减值反映的是资产账面价值的下跌，即有证据表明预计未来从该金融资产所获的现金流量减少，若按当前市场利率折现，则使得该金融资产按公允价值计量。这不适合以摊余成本计量的资产。[IAS 39 AG 第 84 段]。无论是否低于或者高于主体当前发放贷款的利率，原实际利率应当被用作折现率。换言之，贷款减值只基于预计现金流量减少而不是利率变动。这种方法确保了当以摊余成本计量的金融资产发生减值时，仍以所有预计未来现金流量的现值计量，与该资产发生减值前的计量方式一致。

示例——固定利率贷款的减值

假设条件与以上第 9.78 段中的示例 2 一样，只是在 20X9 年 12 月 31 日，借款人所在的行业发生结构性改变，借款人遭遇财务危机，其信用评级下调。当日，按 6.7322% 的原利率计算，摊余后贷款的账面金额为 583,435 元。

鉴于客观证明，主体认为借款人无法偿付剩余账款（每年规定偿付 142,378 元）。因此，主体重组了贷款，取消了先前于到 20Y0 年 12 月 31 日到期的年还款，取而代之的是截至 20Y3 年 12 月 31 日分三次每年偿还 175,000 元。根据调整后的还款计划，未偿贷款的利息也下调至 6.3071%。

将分别于 20Y1 年、20Y2 年、20Y3 年的 12 月 31 日应付的年还款额

20Y1, Y2 and Y3, discounted at the original effective interest rate of 6.7322% amounts to C432,402. Accordingly, the entity recognises an impairment loss of C151,033 (C583,435 – C432,402) in profit or loss on 31 December 20X9. Therefore, the carrying amount is written down by the amount of the impairment loss.

9.181 Even if the terms of a loan, receivable or held-to-maturity investment are renegotiated or otherwise modified because of financial difficulties of the borrower, impairment is measured using the original effective interest rate before the terms were modified. [IAS 39 para AG 84]. However, in some situations, significant modification of the terms may result in derecognition of the existing asset and recognition of a new asset.

9.182 There are, however, three specific instances where the original discount rate is not used to measure impairment losses.

- For variable rate loans and variable rate held-to-maturity investments, the discount rate for measuring any impairment loss is the current variable rate determined under the contract. [IAS 39 para AG 84].

Example – Discount rate for loan impairment calculation

Entity A has provided a loan of GBP1m to entity B. In entity A's financial statements, the loan is classified as 'loans and receivables' in accordance with IAS 39. The loan was originally priced at three month GBP Libor + 300bp. However, entity B has run into financial difficulty and following renegotiations the loan has been re-priced at three month GBP Libor + 100bp.

Objective evidence that an impairment loss on the loan has been incurred is provided by the fact that the terms of the loan have been re-negotiated (that is, the price of the loan was reduced) in response to the counterparty being in financial difficulties.

The impairment loss should be measured as the difference between the carrying amount of the loan and the present value of estimated future cash flows. Estimated future cash flows should be based on the revised terms of the

175,000 元以 6.7322% 的原实际利率折现，得到现值为 432,402 元。因此，主体将 151,033 元（583,435 元减去 432,402 元）的减值损失计入 20X9 年 12 月 31 日的损益。减值损失既而减记了账面金额。

9.181　即使由于借款人陷入财务困境，贷款、应收款项或持有至到期投资的条款被重新协商或更改，仍按条款被修改前的原实际利率计算减值。[IAS 39 AG 第 84 段]。然而，在某些情况下，对条款的重大修改可能导致终止确认现有资产，并确认一项新的资产。

9.182　但在以下三种情况下，不使用原折现率计量减值损失。

- 对于浮动利率贷款和浮动利率持有至到期投资，用于计量减值损失的折现率是根据合同确定的当前浮动利率。[IAS 39 AG 第 84 段]。

示例——计算贷款减值的折现率

主体 A 向主体 B 提供了 100 万英镑贷款。在主体 A 的财务报表中，该贷款根据 IAS 39 被分类为“贷款和应收款项”。该贷款初始利率定为 3 个月 LIBOR + 300BP。然而，主体 B 发生了财务困难，经重新协商后，该贷款的利率改为 3 个月 LIBOR + 100BP。

贷款条款因借款人陷入财务困难而重新协商（借款费用已经减少），表明该贷款存在已发生减值损失的客观证据。

减值损失应为贷款账面价值与预计未来现金流量现值之间的差额。预计未来现金流量应当基于重新更改后的条款（利率为 3 个月 LIBOR + 100BP）。该预计未来现金流量应当按照贷款的实际利率进行折现，也就

loan – that is, GBP three month Libor + 100bp. These estimated future cash flows should then be discounted at the loan's effective interest rate, which in this case is the current GBP three month Libor + 300bp, according to the terms of the original loan. The amount of the loss should be recognised in profit and loss. It is the current GBP three month Libor plus the original spread of 300bp that should be used to measure any impairment loss.

In addition, following any impairment, management should consider whether the contractual rights to the financial asset have in substance expired – that is, whether the terms of the loan have been modified to such a large extent that it is in substance a new loan. If they have, the financial asset is derecognised under paragraph 17(a) of IAS 39, and a new asset is recognised for the new loan at its fair value. Derecognition is considered in chapter 8.

- For financial assets reclassified out of held-for-trading or available-for-sale, the effective interest rate will be recalculated using the fair value at the date of reclassification (see para 9.43). This new effective interest rate will be used to calculate interest income in future periods and considered as the original effective interest rate when measuring impairment. Subsequent to reclassification, an increase in the recoverability of cash flows would also result in an adjusted effective interest rate (see para 9.81).

- For a fixed rate loan that is designated as a hedged item in a fair value hedge of interest rate risk, the loan's carrying amount is adjusted for any changes in its fair value attributable to interest rate movements. The loan's original effective interest rate before the hedge, therefore, becomes irrelevant and the effective interest rate is recalculated using the loan's adjusted carrying amount. The adjusted effective rate is used as the rate for discounting the estimated future cash flows for measuring the impairment loss on the hedged loan. [IAS 39 para IG E4.4]. Hedge accounting is considered in chapter 10.

9.183 Consistent with the initial measurement requirements set out in paragraph 9.9 above, cash flows relating to short-term receivables are not discounted if the effect of discounting is immaterial. [IAS 39 para AG 84].

是最初条款中的当前3个月LIBOR+300BP。损失金额应计入损益。计算减值损失应采用当前3个月LIBOR加上最初的300BP。

此外，随着减值的发生，管理层应该考虑与金融资产相关的合同权利实质上是否已终止，也就是说对借款条款的修改是否重大，并实质上形成了新的借款。如果是这样，那么根据IAS 39第17（a）段，原金融资产被终止确认，而新贷款按公允价值确认成一项新资产。有关金融资产的终止确认，参见第八章。

■ 对于从交易类或可供出售类重分类出的金融资产，按重分类当日的公允价值，重新计算实际利率（参见第9.43段）。新的实际利率将用于计算未来期间的利息收入，并在计量减值时被视为原实际利率。重分类后，现金流量的可收回性增加也可导致调整实际利率（参见第9.81段）。

■ 对于在利率风险公允价值套期中被指定为被套期项目的固定利率贷款，其账面价值将按照因利率变化而导致的公允价值变动额进行调整。因此，套期前该贷款的原实际利率不再适用，而应根据该贷款调整后的账面价值重新计算实际利率。调整后的实际利率作为预计未来现金流量的折现率，用于计量被套期贷款的减值损失。［IAS 39 IG第E4.4段］。套期会计在第十章中讨论。

9.183　与第9.9段所述的初始计量要求一致，如折现影响不大，短期应收款项的现金流量不予折现。［IAS 39 AG第84段］。

Evaluation of impairment on a portfolio basis

9.184 IAS 39 contains specific guidance for assessing and measuring the impairment losses of a group of financial assets that is carried at amortised cost. The assessment process is as follows:

- First, financial assets that are considered to be individually significant are assessed for impairment individually based on whether objective evidence of impairment exists.
- Secondly, all other assets that are not individually significant are assessed for impairment. They may be assessed either individually or collectively on a group basis as indicated below.
- Thirdly, all assets that have been individually assessed for impairment, whether significant or not, but for which there is no objective evidence of impairment, are included within a group of assets with similar credit risk characteristics and collectively assessed for impairment.
- Fourthly, assets that are individually assessed for impairment and for which an impairment loss is (or continues to be) recognised are not included in a collective assessment for impairment.

[IAS 39 para 64].

9.185 It seems perhaps illogical and superfluous to subject individual loans that have been reviewed individually for impairment and found not to be impaired to be included again in a portfolio of similar loans for collective assessment. The Basis for Conclusions sets out in extensive detail the arguments for and against this requirement and concludes that impairment that cannot be identified with an individual loan may be identifiable on a portfolio basis. [IAS 39 paras BC111 to BC117].

9.186 There is no guidance in the standard as to what is meant by 'individually significant'. What is significant for one entity may not be significant to another, so each entity should assess what is significant based on its own facts and circumstances.

金融资产组合的减值评估

9.184　对于如何评估与计量以摊余成本计量的金融资产组减值损失，IAS 39 提供了具体指引。评估程序如下：

- 第一，基于是否存在减值的客观证据，对单项金额重大的金融资产单独进行减值评估。
- 第二，对单项金额不重大的所有其他资产进行减值评估。可以对其单独进行评估，或者如下所示，按组合进行整体评估。
- 第三，所有单独进行减值评估的资产，无论金额重大与否，如无表明已发生减值的客观证据，应归入具有类似信用风险特征的资产组合中，整体评估减值。
- 第四，单独进行减值评估的资产，若已被确认（或继续确认）减值损失，则不应纳入减值整体评估。

[IAS 39 第 64 段]。

9.185　将已单独进行减值评估且未发现已减值的单项贷款再次纳入具有类似贷款的组合中进行整体评估，似乎既不合理也无必要。结论基础详细列出了赞成与反对此要求的各类观点，并得出了结论，即在单项贷款层面无法识别减值时，或许可能在组合层面予以识别。[IAS 39 BC 第 111 至 117 段]。

9.186　对什么是“单项金额重大”，准则没有提供指引。对某主体而言金额重大的资产，对其他主体可能并不其然。因此，每个主体都应该根据自己的实际情况确定何为金额重大。

Example – Individual versus collection assessment

An entity has a portfolio of similar receivables amounting to C100m. The entity considers that within this portfolio are C30m of loans that are individually significant. It assesses these loans for impairment on an individual basis and determines that C20m of loans are impaired. Of the remaining C70m loans that are not significant, the entity selects C15m for individual assessment and finds them all to be individually impaired. The rest of the portfolio is subject to an impairment review on a collective basis.

The result of this assessment means that loans amounting to C35m that have been assessed for impairment on an individual basis, whether significant or not, and found to be impaired will not be included for collective assessment. The remaining C65m of loans (C10m of individually significant loans that are found not to be impaired and C55m that were not assessed for impairment on an individual basis) are included in the collective assessment.

However, loss probabilities and other loss statistics differ at a portfolio level between the C10m of individually evaluated loans that are found not to be impaired and the C55m of loans that were not individually evaluated for impairment. This means that a different amount of impairment may be required for these sub-portfolios. [IAS 39 AG 87].

9.187 For the purpose of a collective evaluation of impairment, financial assets should be grouped on the basis of similar credit risk characteristics that are indicative of the debtors' ability to pay all amounts due according to the contractual terms. This may be done on the basis of a credit risk evaluation or grading process that considers asset type, industry, geographical location, collateral type, past-due status and other relevant factors. If an entity does not have a group of assets with similar risk characteristics, it does not make the additional assessment. [IAS 39 para AG 87]. In that case, such assets are individually assessed for impairment.

9.188 It should be noted that as soon as information is available that specifically identifies losses on individually impaired assets in a group, those assets should be removed from the group. [IAS 39 para AG 88].

9.189 The Basis for Conclusions in IAS 39 provides detailed guidance on how to

示例——单项与组合评估

主体持有类似应收款项组合共计 1 亿元。主体认为该组合中有 3,000 万元的贷款是单项金额重大的，因而对这些贷款的减值情况进行了单独评估，结果发现有 2,000 万元的贷款已发生减值。对于余下的单项金额不重大的 7,000 万元贷款，主体从中挑选了 1,500 万元进行单独评估，结果发现都已减值。该组合的剩余部分将按整体进行减值测试。

这样评估的结果意味着，共计 3,500 万元的贷款，无论其单项金额重大与否，经单独进行减值测试，结果发现已发生减值，因而不再纳入整体评估。余下的 6,500 万元贷款（其中，1,000 万元单项金额重大的贷款，经评估未发现减值；5,500 万元未进行单独减值评估）将进行组合评估。

然而，经单独评估未发现减值的 1,000 万元贷款同未进行单独减值评估的 5,500 万元贷款，在组合层面的损失概率和其他损失统计是不同的。这意味着，这些子组合可能面临不同程度的减值。［IAS 39 AG 第 87 段］。

9.187 为进行组合减值评估，应基于类似信用风险特征（表明债务人按合同条款偿还所有到期金额的能力的特征）对金融资产进行分类。这可通过对信用风险进行评估或评级来完成。评估或评级应考虑资产类型、行业、地理位置、抵押品类型、逾期状态等其他相关因素。如果主体没有具类似风险特征的资产组合，则不再对其进行额外评估。［IAS 39 AG 第 87 段］。在这种情况下，这些资产将进行单独减值评估。

9.188 值得注意的是，一旦获得识别组合内单项资产减值损失的信息，这些资产应从该组合中移出。［IAS 39 AG 第 88 段］。

9.189 IAS 39 的结论基础就如何对金融资产组合进行减值评估提供了详细的

perform impairment assessments within groups of financial assets. Most of the detailed guidance will be highly relevant to banks and other financial institutions that have large portfolios of loans and receivables. The following elements are critical to an adequate process:

- Future cash flows in a group of financial assets should be estimated on the basis of historical loss experience for assets with credit risk characteristics similar to those in the group.
- Entities that have no entity-specific loss experience or insufficient experience should use peer group experience for comparable groups of financial assets.
- Historical loss experience should be adjusted on the basis of current observable data to reflect the effects of current conditions.
- Changes in estimates of future cash flows should be directionally consistent with changes in underlying observable data (such as changes in unemployment rates, property prices, payment status, or other factors indicative of changes in the probability of losses in the group and their magnitude).
- The methodology and assumptions used for estimating future cash flows should be reviewed regularly to reduce any differences between loss estimates and actual loss experience.

[IAS 39 para BC124].

9.190 Applying the above process ensures that the collective assessment of impairment for a group of financial assets is still an 'incurred' and not an 'expected' loss model that aims to reflect the loss events that have occurred with respect to individual assets in the group, but have not yet been identified on an individual asset basis. IAS 39 provides an example of an entity that determines, on the basis of historical experience, that one of the main causes of default on credit card loans is the death of the borrower. Although the death rate is unchanged from one year to the next, some of the borrowers in the group may have died in that year. This indicates that an impairment loss has occurred on those loans, even if, at the year-end, the entity is not yet aware which specific borrowers have died. It would be appropriate for an impairment loss to be recognised for these 'incurred

指引。这些指引大多与持有大量组合贷款和应收款项的银行和其他金融机构密切相关。以下要素对完善的评估流程至关重要：

- 金融资产组的未来现金流量应参考与该组合中具有类似信用风险特征的资产的历史损失经验进行估计。
- 主体无自有的损失经验数据或经验数据不足时，应借鉴同行在可比金融资产组的经验数据。
- 历史损失经验应基于当前可观察数据进行调整，以反映当前状况的影响。
- 未来现金流量估计的变化应与可观察的基础数据（如失业率、物业价格、付款状况或其他反映组合损失概率和幅度变动的因素）的变化方向保持一致。
- 应定期复核用于估计未来现金流量的方法和假设，以缩小损失的估计金额和实际金额之间的差异。

[IAS 39 BC 第 124 段]。

9.190　遵照上述步骤的目的是确保对金融资产组进行整体减值评估时，针对的是“已发生”损失模型，而非“预期”损失模型，旨在反映组合内各项资产已发生、但尚未单独识别的损失事件。IAS 39 提供了一个示例。该示例中，主体根据其以往的经验判定信用卡借款违约的一个主要原因是借款人死亡。尽管每年的死亡率保持不变，但组合中的某些借款人可能已在那一年过世。这意味着，即使主体在年底仍不清楚哪些借款人已经过世，那些贷款确已发生了减值损失。将“已发生未报告”（IBNR）损失确认为减值损失是适当的。但是，对于预计未来期间借款人发生死亡时的减值损失不应予以确认，因为必要的损失事件（借款人死亡）尚未发生。[IAS 39 AG 第 90 段]。

but not reported' (IBNR) losses. However, it would not be appropriate to recognise an impairment loss for deaths that are expected to occur in a future period, because the necessary loss event (the death of the borrower) has not yet occurred. [IAS 39 para AG 90].

9.191 The standard allows the use of formula-based approaches or statistical methods to determine impairment losses in a group of financial assets as long as they:

- Do not give rise to an impairment loss on a financial asset's initial recognition.
- Are consistent with the general requirements outlined above.
- Incorporate the effect of the time value of money.
- Consider the cash flows for all of the remaining life of an asset (not only the next year).
- Consider the age of the loans within the portfolio.

[IAS 39 para AG 92].

Measurement difficulties in the absence of observable data

9.192 Making a reasonably reliable estimate of the amount and timing of future cash flows from an impaired financial asset is a matter of judgement. The best estimate is based on reasonable and supportable assumptions and observable data concerning the ability of a debtor to make payments in relation to circumstances existing at the impairment measurement date.

9.193 However, sometimes observable data required to estimate the amount of an impairment loss on a financial asset may be limited or no longer fully relevant to current circumstances. For example, this may be the case when a borrower is in financial difficulties and there is little available historical data relating to similar borrowers. In such cases, an entity should use its judgement to estimate the amount of any impairment loss and to adjust observable data for a group of financial assets to reflect current circumstances. The use of reasonable estimates is an essential part of the financial statement's preparation and does not undermine their reliability. [IAS 39 para 62].

9.191　准则允许采用公式法或统计方法来确定金融资产组合的减值损失，只要满足以下条件：

■ 不会在金融资产初始确认时造成减值损失。

■ 与上述的基本要求一致。

■ 体现货币时间价值的影响。

■ 考虑资产所有剩余期限的现金流量（不只是下一年的）。

■ 考虑组合中贷款的年限。

［IAS 39 AG 第 92 段］。

缺少可观察数据时的计量困难

9.192　对已减值金融资产的未来现金流量金额和时间进行合理且可靠的估计，关键在于判断。最佳估计是基于合理且言之有据的假设和于减值计量日有关债务人还款能力的可观察数据。

9.193　金融资产减值损失金额的估计需要可观察数据，然而有时这些数据可能是有限的、或者可能与当前情况不再完全相关。例如，某借款人遭遇财务困境，而主体几乎没有类似借款人的历史数据。在此情况下，主体应当运用判断以估计减值损失的金额，并调整金融资产组的可观察数据以反映当前情况。合理运用估计是编制财务报表不可或缺的部分，并不损害财务报表的可靠性。［IAS 39 第 62 段］。

General provisions for bad and doubtful debts

9.194 It has not been uncommon for entities under previous GAAPs to determine bad debt provisions for non-performing loans based on a provision matrix or similar formula that specifies fixed provision rates for the number of days a loan or a debt is overdue. For example, the provisioning rates could be 0% if less than 90 days overdue, 20% if 90-180 days, 50% if 181-365 days and 100% if more than 365 days. Such a method of provisioning would not be acceptable under IAS 39, unless it produces a result that is sufficiently close to the one obtained by following a discounted cash flow methodology required by the standard, which is considered highly unlikely. [IAS 39 para IG E4.5].

9.195 Similarly, it was fairly common for entities under previous GAAPs to make a general provision for bad and doubtful debts on the grounds of prudence and set aside sums that are not specifically related to losses in a group of assets, but intended to cover unplanned and unexpected losses. Such provisioning methods are not allowed under IAS 39 as it results in impairment or bad debt losses that are in excess of those that can be attributed to incurred losses. Accordingly, amounts that an entity might want to set aside for additional possible impairment in financial assets, such as reserves that cannot be supported by objective evidence about impairment, are not recognised as impairment or bad debt losses under IAS 39. [IAS 39 para IG E4.6]. This does not prevent an entity designating part of its reserves in equity to cover such 'prudence' or related losses.

Recognition of interest on impaired assets

9.196 Once a financial asset or a group of similar financial assets has been written down as a result of an impairment loss, interest income is thereafter recognised using the rate of interest used to discount the future cash flows for the purpose of measuring the impairment loss. [IAS 39 para AG 93]. That is the discount in the carrying amount is unwound. This would be the original effective rate for fixed rate instruments carried at amortised cost and current interest rate for

呆坏账的一般准备金

9.194　主体通常根据先前 GAAP 的规定，对不良贷款按照拨备矩阵或类似公式来确定坏账准备金。这些公式按贷款或债务的逾期天数确定相应的拨备率。例如，当逾期少于 90 天时，准备金提取率为 0%；逾期 90—180 天时，准备金提取率为 20%；逾期 181—365 天时，准备金提取率为 50%；逾期大于 365 天时，准备金提取率为 100%。但 IAS 39 不认可这种准备金提取方法，除非其计算的结果与本准则要求的折现现金流方法所计算的结果非常接近，但这几乎不可能。[IAS 39 IG 第 E4.5 段]。

9.195　同样地，主体通常需根据先前 GAAP 的规定，基于审慎原则为呆坏账计提一般准备金，拨备的金额与资产组损失并无具体关联，而是旨在弥补计划之外的、非预期的损失。IAS 39 也不允许这种准备金提取方法，因为其提取的减值或坏账损失超过了已发生损失。因此，对于主体希望为金融资产可能的额外减值而拨备的金额，比如没有客观证据支持的减值准备金，按照 IAS 39 不能被确认为减值或坏账损失。[IAS 39 IG 第 E4.6 段]。但这不妨碍主体在权益中拨备准备金，以达到“审慎”目的或弥补相关损失。

确认减值资产的利息

9.196　一旦金融资产或类似金融资产的组合因发生减值损失被减记，其后，确认利息收入所用的利率即是计算减值损失时用于折现未来现金流量的利率。[IAS 39 AG 第 93 段]。这也就是摊销账面价值所用的利率。对于以摊余成本计量的固定利率工具，应是原实际利率；对于浮动利率工具，则是当前利率。

floating rate instruments.

9. 197 An entity should not stop accruing interest on loans that are non-performing. When non-performing loans are reviewed for impairment, the collection or non-collection of the future interest payments would be taken into account in the estimation of future cash flows for the purposes of the impairment calculation. Interest income would be recognised as the discount unwinds.

Example – Income recognition on impaired loans

The facts are the same as in the example in paragraph 9. 182 above. Following recognition of the impairment loss at 31 December 20X9, the amortised cost amounted to C432, 402.

On the assumption that cash inflows will occur as restructured, the amortisation schedule based on the revised cash flows and the original discount rate is shown below. In accordance with paragraph 9. 196 above, interest income is recognised at the rate of discount used to the measure the impairment.

	Cash in flows	Interest income @ 6. 7322%	Carrying amount
1 Jan 20Y0			432, 402
31 Dec 20Y0		29, 110	461, 512
31 Dec 20Y1	175, 000	31, 070	317, 582
31 Dec 20Y2	175, 000	21, 380	163, 962
31 Dec 20Y3	175, 000	11, 038	–
	525, 000	92, 598	

Reversal of impairment losses on assets held at amortised cost

9. 198 As stated in paragraph 9. 157 above, an impairment review should be carried out at each reporting date. If, in a subsequent period, the amount of the impairment loss decreases and the decrease can be related objectively to an event

9.197　主体不应当停止计提不良贷款的利息。对不良贷款进行减值测试时，减值计算中未来现金流量估计应考虑是否能收到未来利息。利息收入应随着折现转回而确认。

示例——减值贷款的利息收入确认

事实与以上第9.182段的示例相同。20X9年12月31日，确认减值损失后，摊余成本为432,402元。

基于贷款重组后现金流入假设，根据修改后的现金流量和原折现率编制的摊销进度表如下所示。如以上第9.196段所述，利息收入按计量减值用的折现率计算确认。

	现金流入	利息收入（利率6.7322%）	账面价值
20Y0年1月1日			432,402
20Y0年12月31日		29,110	461,512
20Y1年12月31日	175,000	31,070	317,582
20Y2年12月31日	175,000	21,380	163,962
20Y3年12月31日	175,000	11,038	-
	525,000	92,598	

以摊余成本计量的资产的减值损失转回

9.198　如以上第9.157段所述，应于每个报告日进行减值测试。在后续的会计期间，如果减值损失金额减少且该减少与减值确认后发生的事件（如债务人信用评级提高）存在客观联系，则之前确认的减值损失应直接转回或通过

occurring after the impairment was recognised (such as an improvement in the debtor's credit rating), the previously recognised impairment loss should be reversed either directly or by adjusting an allowance account. The reversal should not result in a carrying amount of the financial asset that exceeds what the amortised cost would have been had the impairment not been recognised at the date the impairment is reversed. The amount of the reversal should be recognised in profit or loss. [IAS 39 para 65]. This is in contrast with an equity instrument where an impairment loss is specifically not reversed (see para 9.204).

9.199 If a financial asset has been reclassified out of a category measured at fair value (that is, held-for-trading or available-for-sale) and into a category measured at amortised cost, an increase in cash flows would be a reversal of impairment only if the impairment loss was recognised after the date of reclassification. Any other increase in cash flows will be a change in expected cash flows and adjusted cumulatively in accordance with paragraph AG 8 of IAS 39 (see para 9.81).

Financial assets carried at cost

9.200 As set out in paragraph 9.145 above, an unquoted equity instrument that is not carried at fair value because its fair value cannot be reliably measured, or on a derivative asset that is linked to and must be settled by delivery of such an unquoted equity instrument, are measured at cost. For such instruments, if there is objective evidence that an impairment loss has been incurred, the amount of the impairment loss is measured as the difference between the carrying amount of the financial asset and the present value of estimated future cash flows discounted at the current market rate of return for a similar financial asset. Such impairment losses are not permitted to be reversed. [IAS 39 para 66].

Available-for-sale financial assets

9.201 When a decline in the fair value of an available-for-sale financial asset has been recognised directly in other comprehensive income and there is objective evidence that the asset is impaired, the cumulative loss that had been recognised directly in other comprehensive income should be reclassified from equity and

调整备抵账户转回。该转回不应使得该金融资产的账面价值超过假定未确认减值的情况下该金融资产在减值转回日的摊余成本。转回的金额应计入损益。[IAS 39 第65 段]。这与权益工具的减值损失不得通过损益转回不同（参见第9.204 段）。

9.199　如果将以公允价值计量的金融资产（即交易类或可供出售类）重分类至以摊余成本计量，只有对于在重分类日后确认了减值损失，现金流量的增加才能作为减值转回。其他现金流量的增加是预计现金流量变动，按照 IAS 39 AG 第 8 段累计调整（参见第 9.81 段）。

以成本计量的金融资产

9.200　如以上第 9.145 段所示，因公允价值不能可靠计量而不以公允价值计量的无报价权益工具，以及与该权益工具挂钩且须通过交付该权益工具结算的衍生资产，应按成本计量。若有客观证据表明已发生减值损失，则减值损失金额为该金融资产的账面价值与预计未来现金流量按类似金融资产当前市场回报率进行折现的现值之间的差额。该减值损失不得转回。[IAS 39 第 66 段]。

可供出售金融资产

9.201　当可供出售金融资产公允价值的下跌被直接计入其他综合收益，且有客观证据表明其已发生减值时，即使该金融资产还没有被终止确认，直接计入其他综合收益中的累计损失应从权益转至损益。[IAS 39 第 67 段]。不可以将低于成本的减少额的一部分作为减值，而将另一部分作为公允价值变动计

recognised in profit or loss even though the financial asset has not been derecognised. [IAS 39 para 67]. It is not appropriate to allocate part of the reduction below cost to impairment and part to a fair value movement through other comprehensive income.

9. 202 The amount of cumulative loss that is recycled to profit or loss is the difference between the acquisition cost (net of any principal repayment and amortisation) and current fair value, less any impairment loss on that financial asset previously recognised in profit or loss. [IAS 39 para 68]. Any portion of the cumulative net loss that is attributable to foreign currency changes on that asset that had been recognised in equity is also recognised in profit or loss (see para 9. 213 below). Subsequent losses, including any portion attributable to foreign currency changes, are also recognised in profit or loss until the asset is derecognised. [IAS 39 para IG E4. 9].

9. 203 For financial assets reclassified out of a category measured at fair value (that is, held-for-trading or available-for-sale) and into another category, see paragraph 9. 41.

Example – Impairment of available-for-sale debt security

On 1 January 20X3, an entity purchased C10 million 5 year bond with semi-annual interest of 5% payable on 30 June and 31 December each year. The bond's purchase price was C10, 811, 100, which resulted in a bond premium of C811, 100 and an effective interest rate of 8% (4% on a semi-annual basis). The entity classified the bond as available-for-sale.

The entity received all the interest due in 20X3 and 20X4 on a timely basis. At 31 December 20X4, the amortised cost of the bond amounted to C10, 524, 226. The cumulative amount recognised in equity to that date was a loss C266, 322.

The entity did not receive the half-yearly interest due on 30 June 20X5 and it soon became clear that the issuer was in financial difficulties. At 31 December 20X5, the entity reviews the issuer's financial condition and prospects for repayment of the bond and determines that the bond is impaired. On the basis of the information available at the time, the entity's best estimate of future

入其他综合收益。

9.202 转至损益的累计损失金额等于取得成本（扣除本金还款和摊销额）与当前公允价值之间的差额，减去该金融资产此前已计入损益的减值损失。[IAS 39 第 68 段]。累计净损失中任何因该资产汇率变动而产生的、计入权益的金额，也将转至损益（参见第 9.213 段）。后续损失，包括因汇率变动造成的损失，在该资产被终止确认前都应计入损益。[IAS 39 IG 第 E4.9 段]。

9.203 有关以公允价值计量的金融资产（即交易类或可供出售类）重分类至其他类别，参见第 9.41 段。

示例——可供出售债权类证券的减值

20X3 年 1 月 1 日，某主体购买了面值为 1,000 万元的 5 年期债券，其半年利率为 5%，利息于每年 6 月 30 日和 12 月 31 日支付。该债券的购买价格为 10,811,110 元，溢价 811,110 元，实际利率为 8%（半年利率为 4%）。主体将该债券分类为可供出售。

主体按时收到了 20X3 和 20X4 年到期的所有利息。于 20X4 年 12 月 31 日，债券的摊余成本为 10,524,226 元。截至该日，已在权益中确认的累计损失金额为 266,322 元。

主体没有收到于 20X5 年 6 月 30 日到期的半年期利息。不久后，主体发现该债券发行人出现了财务困难。于 20X5 年 12 月 31 日，主体审阅了该发行人的财务状况并探查了偿还债券的能力，确认该债券已减值。基于当时获得的信息，主体对未来现金流量（按年计）做出的最佳估计为：在预定还款日 20X6 年 12 月 31 日和 20X7 年 12 月 31 日的现金收款分别

cash flows (on a yearly basis) is cash receipts of C2m on 31 December 20X6 and C7m on 31 December 20X7, the scheduled repayment date.

Although the bond is non-performing, the entity recognises the interest income for the period to 31 December 20X5 at the original effective interest rate. On this basis, the bond's amortised cost at 31 December 20X5 amounts to C11, 383, 003.

As the bond is classified as available-for-sale, it is necessary to determine the bond's fair value at 31 December 20X5. As there is no observable market price for the bond, the bond's fair value, can only be obtained by discounting the expected cash flows at the current market rate. As a market rate for a comparable bond may not exist, it would be necessary to derive a current market rate for the bond. One way of estimating the current rate for a comparable bond with terms and credit risk profiles similar to the existing bond is by reference to a benchmark rate or the risk-free rate, which is part of the bond's effective rate of interest of 8%, and amending that rate by the original credit risk premium of the existing bond.

Assume that when the bond was purchased on 1 January 20X3, the risk-free rate was 6% for a debt instrument with the same terms as the one purchased by the entity. Thus, the credit risk premium of the bond is 200 basis points. At 31 December 20X5, the risk-free rate for a similar type of instrument is 8%. Therefore, using the bond's credit risk premium of 200 basis points, the current interest rate for discounting the expected cash flows is 10% (8% + 200 basis point). Using this rate of 10%, the present value of the expected cash flow of C2m and C7m arising on 31 December 20X6 and 31 December 20X7 amounts to C7, 603, 305.

Therefore, the impairment loss recognised in profit or loss is as follows:

为 200 万元和 700 万元。

尽管已是不良债券，但主体按原实际利率确认截至 20X5 年 12 月 31 日的当期利息收入。因此，于 20X5 年 12 月 31 日，该债券的摊余成本为 11, 383, 003 元。

因为该债券为可供出售类，所以有必要确认其在 20X5 年 12 月 31 日的公允价值。由于该债券没有可观察市场价格，其公允价值仅能通过将其预计现金流量按当前市场利率进行折现获得。因可能没有可比债券的市场利率，有必要为该债券推导出一个当前的市场利率。对于与现有债券有类似条款和信用风险状况的可比债券，估计其当前利率的一个方法是参照某个基准利率或无风险利率（为该债券 8% 实际利率中的一部分），并按照现有债券的原信用风险溢价加以调整。

该债券购于 20X3 年 1 月 1 日，假设与该债券具有相同条款的债务工具的无风险利率为 6%，则该债券的信用风险溢价为 200 个基点。于 20X5 年 12 月 31 日，同类债务工具的无风险利率为 8%。考虑到该债券 200 个基点的信用风险溢价，对预计现金流量进行折现的当前利率为 10%（8% + 200 个基点）。采用 10% 的当前利率，计算出将于 20X6 年 12 月 31 日和 20X7 年 12 月 31 日分别收取 200 万元和 700 万元的预计现金流量的现值是 7, 603, 305 元。

计入损益的减值损失如下：

Amortised cost at 31 December 20X4	10, 524, 226
Accrual of half-yearly interest to 30 June 20X5 @ 4%	420, 969
	10, 945, 195
Accrual of half-yearly interest to 31 December 20X5 @ 4%	437, 808
Amortised cost at 31 December 20X5 before impairment	11, 383, 003
Fair value of bond at 31 December 20X5	(7, 603, 305)
Impairment losses recognised in profit or loss during 20X5	3, 779, 698
Recycling of loss recognised in equity	266, 322
Bond stated in the balance sheet at 31 December 20X5	7, 603, 305

On 31 December 20X6, the holder received the expected cash flow of C2m. The amortised cost of the bond at 31 December 20X6 amounts to:

Amortised cost at 31 Dec 20X5	7, 603, 305
Accrual of interest to 31 Dec 20X6 @10%	760, 330
	8, 363, 635
Less cash received at 31 Dec 20X6	2, 000, 000
Amortised cost at 31 Dec 20X6	6, 363, 635

Note that once the bond has been written down as a result of an impairment loss, interest income is thereafter recognised using the rate of interest used to discount the future cash flows for the purpose of measuring the impairment loss. (See para 9. 196.) This rate is 10% as stated above.

During the year to 31 December 20X6, interest rates increased and as a result the bond's fair value at 31 December 20X6 fell to C6. 0m. There was no further change in the credit status/rating of the issuer and there is no evidence of any further credit-related impairment since the original assessment of impairment was made during 20X5. At 31 December 20X6, there is a difference between the bond's amortised cost and its fair value as shown below:

于20X4年12月31日的摊余成本	10,524,226
截至20X5年6月30日计提半年利息×4%	420,969
	10,945,195
截至20X5年12月31日计提半年利息×4%	437,808
减值前,于20X5年12月31日的摊余成本	11,383,003
于20X5年12月31日的债券公允价值	(7,603,305)
于20X5年计入损益的减值损失	3,779,698
权益中确认的损失转至损益金额	266,322
于20X5年12月31日资产负债表上所列债券	7,603,305

20X6年12月31日，持有人收到预计现金流量200万元。于20X6年12月31日该债券的摊余成本为：

于20X5年12月31日的摊余成本	7,603,305
截至20X6年12月31日计提利息×10%	760,330
	8,363,635
减去20X6年12月31日收到的现金	2,000,000
于20X6年12月31日的摊余成本	6,363,635

值得注意的是,一旦减值损失造成该债券减记,此后确认利息收入所用的利率是那个为了计算减值损失而用于折现未来现金流量的利率。(参见第9.196段)。如上所示,利率为10%。

在截至20X6年12月31日的年度内，由于利率上升，于20X6年12月31日该债券的公允价值降至600万元。发行人的信用状况/信用评级未再变化。自20X5年所做减值评估以来，没有证据表明发生与信用相关的进一步减值。截至20X6年12月31日，该债券的摊余成本和公允价值之间的差额如下：

Amortised cost at 31 Dec 20X6 as above	6, 363, 635
Fair value at 31 Dec 20X6	6, 000, 000
Further reduction	363, 635

The further reduction of C363, 635 is also the difference between the fair value of C7, 603, 305 at 31 December 20X5 after adjusting for interest income of 10% and the cash of £2m received and the fair value of C6, 000, 000 at 31 December 20X6.

The question arises as to whether the further decrease of C363, 635 should be taken to the AFS reserve in equity or recognised as a further impairment loss in profit or loss for the period to 31 December 20X6.

There are two acceptable views. An entity makes an accounting policy choice as to which view it accepts and applies this view to all similar transactions. If material, an entity discloses this policy in its financial statements.

View A – AFS reserve in equity

Without any further objective evidence of impairment, no further impairment charge is recognised in profit or loss. Hence, the change in fair value is recognised in equity.

This view is consistent with paragraph 58 of IAS 39, which requires an entity to assess at each balance sheet date whether there is any objective evidence that a financial asset is impaired. If such evidence exists, the entity should apply the requirement for available-for-sale financial asset considered in paragraphs 9. 201 and 9. 202 above. In this situation, at 31 December 20X6, as there is no new evidence of a further credit impairment, the requirements of those paragraphs do not apply and the further decrease of C363, 635 is recognised in equity. In addition, IAS 39 paragraph IG E4. 10 acknowledges that the AFS reserve in equity can be negative – for example, because of a decline in the fair value of an investment in a debt instrument that results from an increase in the basic risk free interest rate.

Similarly, had interest rates decreased resulting in an increase in fair value, it

如上表，于20X6年12月31日的摊余成本	6,363,635
于20X6年12月31日的公允价值	6,000,000
进一步减少额	363,635

该债券于20X5年12月31日的公允价值7,603,305元按10%利率计提利息收入并减去已收到的现金200万元，与该债券于20X6年12月31日的公允价值6,000,000元之间的差额，即为进一步减少额363,635元。

接下来的问题是，该减少额363,635元是计入权益中的可供出售公允价值变动，还是作为进一步的减值损失计入截至20X6年12月31日止的期间损益。

关于上述减少额的处理问题，有两种可接受的观点。主体可自行选择合适的会计政策，并对所有类似交易一贯运用。如果涉及金额重大，主体应在财务报表中披露所选会计政策。

观点A——权益中的可供出售公允价值变动

若没有客观证据表明发生了进一步的减值，则不计入损益。因此，公允价值的变化应计入权益。

此观点同IAS 39第58段的要求一致，即主体应在每个资产负债表日评估是否存在表明金融资产发生减值的客观证据。如果存在客观证据，主体应适用以上第9.152段和第9.153段中有关可供出售金融资产的规定。这种情况下，于20X6年12月31日，没有新的证据表明发生与信用相关的进一步减值。此时，不适用第9.201段和第9.202段的有关规定，进一步减少的金额363,635元应计入权益。此外，IAS 39 IG第E4.10段确认，计入权益的可供出售公允价值变动可以是负数——例如，由于基础无风险利率的上升导致债务工具投资的公允价值下跌。

同样，如果利率下降导致公允价值上升，可以将公允价值变动计入权益

would be appropriate to recognise that change in the AFS reserve in equity. This would not be considered a reversal of impairment as for a reversal to occur there should be an increase in fair value attributable to an improvement in the issuer's credit standing.

View B – impairment/reversal of impairment in profit or loss

This view is that, at the reporting date, there is still objective evidence of impairment since acquiring the asset and, therefore, a further decline in fair value is recognised in profit or loss as further impairment. Any changes in fair value (gains or losses) subsequent to impairment are reflected in profit or loss up to the asset's amortised cost and afterwards in equity.

This view interprets paragraph 58 of IAS 39 as referring to evidence of impairment since acquiring the asset. This view is also consistent with the treatment in a period in which objective evidence of impairment first arises on an asset where the entire change in fair value (IAS 39 para 68) is recognised in profit or loss, even if some of that change in fair value is market related (for example, due to an increase in interest rates). This is a broader reading of the term event in paragraph 70 of IAS 39 to mean any event rather than only a credit-related event.

This view is also consistent with paragraph IG E4. 9 of IAS 39. It states that for non-monetary AFS financial assets that became impaired in a previous period, any subsequent losses including the portion attributable to foreign exchange losses (that are also not additional impairments) are also recognised in profit or loss until the asset is derecognised.

Similarly, had interest rates decreased resulting in an increase in fair value and the increase can be objectively related to an event occurring after the impairment loss was recognised in profit or loss, it would be appropriate to recognise the change in profit or loss as a reversal of the previous impairment in accordance with IAS 39 paragraph 70.

中的可供出售公允价值变动。这不被视为减值转回，因为只有当公允价值系因发行人信用状况提升而增加时，才可以转回减值。

观点 B——减值/减值转回计入损益

观点 B 认为，在报告日，仍有自购买日后存在的客观减值证据，因此资产公允价值的进一步下跌应作为进一步减值计入损益。减值后，任何公允价值变化（利得或损失）均在损益中反映，但不超该过资产的摊余成本，超过后则计入权益。

观点 B 将 IAS 39 第 58 段解读为在取得资产后出现的减值证据。该观点与 IAS 39 第 68 段所要求的处理方式也是一致的，即某期间内首次出现资产减值的客观证据时，全部公允价值变动额计入损益，尽管公允价值的一些变化是与市场相关的（如利率上升）。这是对 IAS 39 第 70 段所用术语“事件”更宽泛的解释，不仅仅指信用相关事件，还包括所有其他事件。

IAS 39 IG 第 E4. 9 段规定，对于前期已确认减值的非货币性可供出售金融资产，任何后续损失（未必是新增的减值），包括因汇率变动造成的损失，都应计入损益，直至该资产被终止确认。观点 B 与此也是一致的。

同样，如果利率下降导致公允价值上升，且该上升与减值损失被计入损益之后发生的事项存在客观联系，则根据 IAS 39 第 70 段，可将公允价值变动作为转回此前的减值计入损益。

Reversal of impairment losses

9.204 It is possible that after an impairment loss has been recognised for an available-for-sale financial asset circumstances change in a subsequent period such that the fair value of the available-for-sale financial instrument increases. In those circumstances, the treatment required by the standard for reversals of impairment losses on available-for-sale debt instruments is different from those on available-for-sale equity instruments as noted below:

■ For available-for-sale debt instruments (monetary assets), past impairment losses should be reversed through the profit or loss when fair value increases and the increase can be objectively related to an event occurring after the impairment loss was recognised in profit or loss. [IAS 39 para 70].

■ For available-for-sale equity investments (non-monetary assets), past impairment losses recognised in profit or loss should not be reversed through profit or loss when fair value increases. [IAS 39 para 69]. This means that subsequent increases in fair value including those that have the effect of reversing earlier impairment losses are all recognised in equity. This is a significant change from the previous version of the standard.

9.205 The inability to reverse impairment losses recognised in profit or loss on available-for-sale equity instruments raises a particular issue for entities that have recognised such impairment losses in their interim reports. This is because, at the subsequent reporting or balance sheet date, conditions may have changed to such an extent that a loss would not have been recognised, or a smaller loss would have been recognised, if the impairment review were first carried out at that date.

9.206 The confusion arises because paragraph 28 of IAS 34, requires an entity to apply the same accounting policies in its interim financial statements as are applied in its annual financial statements. This suggests that an impairment loss recognised in the interim period should not be reversed at the subsequent balance sheet date. On the other hand, the same paragraph states that 'the frequency of an entity's reporting (annual, half-yearly, or quarterly) should not affect the measurement of

减值损失的转回

9.204　可供出售金融资产的减值损失被确认后，有可能在后续期间，由于情况发生变化导致该可供出售金融工具的公允价值上升。在这种情况下，有关减值损失的转回，准则对于可供出售债务工具与可供出售权益工具所要求的处理方式是不同的，具体如下：

- 对于可供出售债务工具（货币性资产），当公允价值上升且该上升与减值损失被计入损益之后发生的事项存在客观联系时，此前的减值损失应通过损益转回。[IAS 39 第 70 段]。

- 对于可供出售权益工具（非货币性资产），当公允价值上升时，此前计入损益的减值损失不得通过损益转回。[IAS 39 第 69 段]。这意味着，后续公允价值上升，包括在实际效果上转回早期的减值损失，都应计入权益。这与之前版本的准则有着很大的区别。

9.205　可供出售权益工具计入损益的减值损失不能转回，这为在中期报告中确认了此项减值损失的主体带来一个特别的问题。因为如果是在后续的报告日或资产负债表日首次进行减值测试，情况可能会有所不同，即不会确认减值损失或确认了较少的减值损失。

9.206　困惑的来源在于 IAS 34 第 28 段要求主体运用年度财务报表中的会计政策编制。一方面，该段暗含的意思是，中期确认的减值损失不得在其后的资产负债表日转回。另一方面，该段又规定主体报告的频率（年度、半年度或季度）不应影响对其全年业绩的计量。为此目的，编制中期财务报表时，计量应以“年初至今”为基础。这意味着，中期确认的减值损失可以在之后的资产负债表日转回。

its annual results. To achieve this objective, measurement for interim reporting purposes should be made on a 'year-to-date' basis. This suggests that an impairment loss recognised in one interim period can be reversed at the subsequent balance sheet date.

9.207 The IFRS IC considered the matter and issued IFRIC 10 in July 2006. The IFRS IC concluded that the prohibitions on reversals of recognised impairment losses on investments in equity instruments in IAS 39 should take precedence over the more general statement in IAS 34 regarding the frequency of an entity's reporting not affecting the measurement of its annual results. Therefore, any impairment losses that are recognised in a previous interim period in respect of an investment in an equity instrument may not be reversed in a later interim periods or when preparing the annual financial statements. [IFRIC 10 para 8].

Foreign currency financial instruments

General

9.208 Financial instruments are often denominated in foreign currencies. The way in which changes in foreign exchange rates in foreign currency financial assets and liabilities should be dealt with is covered in IAS 21. The measurement principles of IAS 39 generally do not override these rules, except in the area of hedge accounting which is considered in chapter 10.

9.209 Under IAS 21, all transactions in foreign currencies are initially recognised at the spot exchange rate at the date of the transaction. The spot exchange rate is the exchange rate for immediate delivery. It follows that on initial recognition, all foreign currency financial instruments are translated at the spot rate into the entity's functional currency, irrespective of whether the instrument is carried at cost, amortised cost or fair value.

9.210 Gains and losses associated with financial instruments, such as interest income and expense and impairment losses, are recognised at the spot exchange rate at the dates on which they arise. Dividends should be recognised in profit or

9.207 国际财务报告解释委员会仔细考虑了该事项后，于2006年7月发布了《国际财务报告解释公告第10号》（“IFRIC 10”）。国际财务报告解释委员会认为IAS 39禁止权益工具投资确认的减值损失转回，应优先于IAS 34关于主体报告频率不应影响对其全年业绩的计量的一般声明。因此，在之后的中期或在准备年度财务报表时，权益工具投资在之前中期确认的减值损失都不得转回。[IFRIC 10第8段]。

外币金融工具

综述

9.208 金融工具常常以外币计价。外币金融资产与负债的外汇汇率变化应遵照《国际会计准则第21号》（“IAS 21”）进行处理。IAS 39的计量原则一般不优先于这些规定，但第十章中讨论的套期会计除外。

9.209 IAS 21规定，所有外币交易应在交易当天按即期汇率进行初始确认。即期汇率为立即交割时使用的汇率。因此，所有外币金融工具进行初始确认时，不论这些金融工具是按成本、摊余成本还是公允价值计量，都应按即期汇率折算成主体的功能货币。

9.210 与金融工具相关的损益（如利息收入、利息费用和减值损失）都在其发生当日按即期汇率进行确认。股息应在股东有权收取时计入损益。[IAS 18第30（c）段]。当天（通常为股利宣告日）的汇率用于记录此项收入。如果

loss when the shareholder's right to receive payment is established. [IAS 18 para 30(c)]. The exchange rate ruling at that date, which is normally the dividend declaration date, is used to record the income. Entities are permitted to use an average rate where it represents an approximation to the spot rate in that period.

Subsequent measurement

9.211 The subsequent measurement of foreign currency financial assets and liabilities will depend on whether the assets and liabilities are monetary or non-monetary in nature. Monetary items are units of currency held and assets and liabilities to be received or paid in a fixed or determinable number of units of currency. [IAS 21 para 8]. It follows that financial assets and liabilities that are debt instruments are monetary items. Derivative financial instruments are also monetary items as they are settled at a future date, even though the underlying may be non-monetary. Non-monetary items are all items other than monetary items. In other words, the right to receive (or an obligation to deliver) a fixed or determinable number of units of currency is absent in a non-monetary item. This is the case for financial assets that are equity instruments.

Monetary financial assets

9.212 IAS 21 requires that an entity should translate its foreign currency monetary items outstanding at the balance sheet date using the closing spot rate at that date. [IAS 21 para 23(a)]. Exchange differences arising on translating monetary items or on the settlement of monetary items at rates different from those at which they were translated on initial recognition during the period or in previous financial statements, are recognised in profit or loss in the period in which they arise. [IAS 21 para 28]. However, exchange differences on monetary items that are designated as hedging instruments in cash flow hedges or net investments in foreign entities are recognised in equity. [IAS 39 para AG 83].

9.213 For the purpose of recognising foreign exchange gains and losses under IAS 21, a foreign currency monetary available-for-sale financial asset is treated as

某期平均汇率与即期汇率接近，允许主体使用平均汇率。

后续计量

9.211 外币金融资产与负债的后续计量取决于该资产与负债属于货币性还是非货币性。货币性项目为持有的货币和以固定或可确定数量的货币单位收取或支付的资产与负债。[IAS 21 第 8 段]。因此，债务工具的金融资产与负债为货币性项目。衍生金融工具也是货币性项目，因为其在未来日期结算，尽管其标的可能不是货币性项目。非货币性项目是指除货币性项目以外的所有其他项目。换句话说，非货币性项目中没有收取或支付固定或可确定数量的货币单位的权利或义务。金融资产为权益工具时即是此类情况。

货币性金融资产

9.212 IAS 21 要求主体在资产负债表日用当日收盘即期汇率折算外币货币性项目余额。[IAS 21 第 23（a）段]。由于货币性项目进行折算或结算采用的汇率，与当期或之前在财务报表中进行初始确认时采用的汇率不同，所产生的汇兑差额应计入发生当期的损益。[IAS 21 第 28 段]。但是，对于被指定为现金流量套期或境外经营净投资套期的套期工具的货币性项目所产生的汇兑差额，则应当计入权益。[IAS 39 AG 第 83 段]。

9.213 在计算 IAS 21 下的汇兑损益时，外币货币性可供出售金融资产被视为以摊余成本计量且同时以外币计价。因而，对于此类金融资产，由摊余成本

if it were carried at amortised cost in the foreign currency. Accordingly, for such a financial asset, exchange differences arising from changes in amortised cost, such as interest calculated using the effective interest method and impairment losses are recognised in profit or loss. All other gains and losses are recognised in equity. [IAS 39 para 55(b)]. An example illustrating the above treatment is included as example E3.2 in the Implementation Guidance to IAS 39. A similar example is given below.

Example – Available-for-sale debt security denominated in foreign currency

On 1 January 20X1, an entity whose functional currency is the local currency (LC) purchases a foreign currency (FC) denominated bond for its fair value of FC1,000. The bond has 5 years remaining to maturity and a principal amount of FC1,250. Interest is payable annually at 4.7% (that is, FC59) on 31 December each year. Assuming there are no transaction costs, the effective interest rate is 10%. The entity classifies the bond as available-for-sale.

The relevant foreign exchange rates are as follows:

	Average rate FC =	Closing rate FC =
1 January 20X1		LC 1.50
31 December 20X1	LC 1.75	LC 2.00
31 December 20X2	LC 2.25	LC 2.50
31 December 20X3	LC 2.35	LC 2.20
31 December 20X4	LC 2.05	LC 1.90
31 December 20X5	LC 2.10	LC 2.30

For the purpose of this illustrative example, it is assumed that the use of the average exchange rate provides a reliable approximation of the spot rates applicable to the accrual of interest income during the year.

The cumulative gain or loss that is recognised in equity is the difference

变化导致的汇兑差额——例如采用实际利率法计算的利息和减值损失——计入损益。所有其他的利得和损失应计入权益。［IAS 39 第 55（b）段］。IAS 39 实施指南中的示例 E3.2 为上述处理方法的举例说明。以下为类似的示例。

示例——以外币计价的可供出售债权类证券

20X1 年 1 月 1 日，功能货币为本国货币（本币）的某主体购买以外国货币（外币）计价的债券，其公允价值为 1,000 外币。该债券还有 5 年到期，本金金额为 1,250 外币。年息于每年 12 月 31 日支付，年利率为 4.7%，即 59 外币。假设没有交易费用，实际利率为 10%。主体将该债券分类为可供出售。

相关外汇汇率如下：

	平均汇率 外币 =	收盘汇率 外币 =
20X1 年 1 月 1 日		1.50 本币
20X1 年 12 月 31 日	1.75 本币	2.00 本币
20X2 年 12 月 31 日	2.25 本币	2.50 本币
20X3 年 12 月 31 日	2.35 本币	2.20 本币
20X4 年 12 月 31 日	2.05 本币	1.90 本币
20X5 年 12 月 31 日	2.10 本币	2.30 本币

为说明示例，假设使用平均汇率计算该年度计提的利息收入可合理地近似于应使用即期汇率计算的结果。

计入权益的累计利得或损失是该可供出售金融资产以主体功能货币计价

between the amortised cost (adjusted for impairment, if any) and the fair value of the available-for-sale financial asset in the entity's functional currency.

At 1 January 20X1, the fair value of the bond (FC1,000) translated in the entity's functional currency is LC1,500 and the entry to record this is as follows:

At 1 January 20X1	**Dr**	**Cr**
	LC	**LC**
Available-for-sale financial asset	1,500	
Cash		1,500

The amortisation schedule in foreign currency (FC) is as follows:

Date	**Interest income @10%**	**Cash inflow**	**Amortised cost**
1 Jan 20X1			1,000
31 Dec 20X1	100	59	1,041
31 Dec 20X2	104	59	1,086
31 Dec 20X3	109	59	1,136
31 Dec 20X4	113	59	1,190
31 Dec 20X5	119	59	1,250

As the entity classifies the bond as an available-for-sale investment, the asset is treated as an asset measured at amortised cost in foreign currency for the purposes of applying IAS 21. Therefore, the amortisation schedule in the entity's functional currency (LC) shown below is calculated from the above amounts at the appropriate exchange rates as follows:

的摊余成本（如有减值应调整）与公允价值之间的差额。

于20X1年1月1日，该债券的公允价值（1,000外币）折算成主体的功能货币金额为1,500本币，会计分录如下：

于20X1年1月1日	借 本币	贷 本币
可供出售金融资产	1,500	
现金		1,500

按外币金额计算的摊销进度表如下：

日期	利息收入 （利率10%）	现金流入	摊余成本
20X1年1月1日			1,000
20X1年12月31日	100	59	1,041
20X2年12月31日	104	59	1,086
20X3年12月31日	109	59	1,136
20X4年12月31日	113	59	1,190
20X5年12月31日	119	59	1,250

因为主体将该债券分类为可供出售投资，为适用IAS 21，该资产被视为以摊余成本计量且同时以外币计价。因此，以主体的功能货币（本币）计价的摊销进度表（参见下表），根据以上金额按适当的汇率折算，如下所示：

	Interest income @ 10% (average rate) LC	Cash inflow @4.7% (actual rate) LC	Amortised cost LC
1 Jan 20X1			1,500
31 Dec 20X1	175	118	1,557
31 Dec 20X2	234	148	1,643
31 Dec 20X3	256	130	1,769
31 Dec 20X4	232	112	1,889
31 Dec 20X5	250	136	2,003
	1,147	644	

	Amortised cost as above FC	Amortised cost translated at year end rate LC	Carrying amount as determined above LC	Cumulative exchange difference LC	Exchange difference recognised in profit or loss LC
31 Dec 20X1	1,041	2,082	1,557	525	525
31 Dec 20X2	1,086	2,715	1,643	1,072	547
31 Dec 20X3	1,136	2,498	1,769	729	(342)
31 Dec 20X4	1,190	2,261	1,889	372	(358)
31 Dec 20X5	1,250	2,875	2,003	872	500

As the debt instrument is classified as an available-for-sale investment, it is necessary to determine the bond's fair value at each balance sheet date. The bond's fair value at each balance sheet date is given below. The difference between the amortised cost and asset's fair value is the cumulative gain or loss that is recognised in equity. This difference will include exchange differences that would not be separated out from the overall movement recognised in equity. All other changes in foreign exchange rates are recognised in profit or loss as shown above.

	利息收入 10%（平均汇率）本币	现金流入 4.7%（实际汇率）本币	摊余成本 本币
20X1年1月1日			1,500
20X1年12月31日	175	118	1,557
20X2年12月31日	234	148	1,643
20X3年12月31日	256	130	1,769
20X4年12月31日	232	112	1,889
20X5年12月31日	250	136	2,003
	1,147	644	

	上述摊余成本 外币	按年末汇率折算的摊余成本 本币	上表中确定的账面价值 本币	累计汇兑差额 本币	计入损益的汇兑差额 本币
20X1年12月31日	1,041	2,082	1,557	525	525
20X2年12月31日	1,086	2,715	1,643	1,072	547
20X3年12月31日	1,136	2,498	1,769	729	(342)
20X4年12月31日	1,190	2,261	1,889	372	(358)
20X5年12月31日	1,250	2,875	2,003	872	500

因为债务工具被分类为可供出售投资，所以应于每个资产负债表日确定该债券的公允价值，具体情况参见下表。该资产的摊余成本与公允价值之差，即为计入权益的累计利得或损失。该差额包括未从计入权益的整体变动中分离出的汇兑差额。如上表所示，外汇汇率的所有其他变化计入损益。

	Fair value FC	Fair value at year end rate LC	Amortised cost at year end rate as above LC	Cumulative difference LC	Gain or loss recognised in equity LC
31 Dec 20X1	1,060	2,120	2,082	38	38
31 Dec 20X2	1,070	2,675	2,715	(40)	(78)
31 Dec 20X3	1,140	2,508	2,499	9	49
31 Dec 20X4	1,200	2,280	2,261	19	10
31 Dec 20X5	1,250	2,875	2,875	0	(19)

The movements in the fair value of the bond can be summarised as follows:

	Fair value at the beginning of the period LC	Interest income LC	Cash received LC	Exchange difference recognised in profit or loss LC	Gain or loss recognised in equity LC	Fair value at the end of the period LC
31 Dec 20X1	1,500	175	(118)	525	38	2,120
31 Dec 20X2	2,120	234	(148)	547	(78)	2,675
31 Dec 20X3	2,675	256	(130)	(342)	49	2,508
31 Dec 20X4	2,508	232	(112)	(358)	10	2,280
31 Dec 20X5	2,280	250	(136)	500	(19)	2,875

Dual currency bond

9.214 Dual currency bonds are bonds that are denominated in one currency, but pay interest in another currency at a fixed exchange rate. For example, an entity with pound sterling as a functional currency may issue a debt instrument that provides for the annual payment of interest in euros and the repayment of principal in pound sterling. Sometimes both the interest payments and the principal repayments may be denominated in currencies that are different from the entity's functional currency. For example, an entity with pound sterling functional currency may issue a euro denominated bond that pays interest in US dollars. Such a foreign currency bond can be viewed as a host debt instrument with principal and interest payments denominated in pound sterling and two embedded swaps that convert the

	公允价值外币	按年末汇率折算的公允价值本币	上表中按年末汇率折算的摊余成本本币	累计差额本币	计入权益的利得或损失本币
20X1 年 12 月 31 日	1,060	2,120	2,082	38	38
20X2 年 12 月 31 日	1,070	2,675	2,715	(40)	(78)
20X3 年 12 月 31 日	1,140	2,508	2,499	9	49
20X4 年 12 月 31 日	1,200	2,280	2,261	19	10
20X5 年 12 月 31 日	1,250	2,875	2,875	0	(19)

该债券公允价值的变动情况总结如下：

	期初公允价值本币	利息收入本币	收到的现金本币	计入损益的汇兑差额本币	计入权益的利得或损失本币	期末公允价值本币
20X1 年 12 月 31 日	1,500	175	(118)	525	38	2,120
20X2 年 12 月 31 日	2,120	234	(148)	547	(78)	2,675
20X3 年 12 月 31 日	2,675	256	(130)	(342)	49	2,508
20X4 年 12 月 31 日	2,508	232	(112)	(358)	10	2,280
20X5 年 12 月 31 日	2,280	250	(136)	500	(19)	2,875

双币种债券

9.214 双币种债券是指用某种货币计价，但用另一种货币按固定汇率支付利息的债券。例如，功能货币为英镑的某主体发行一种债务工具，其利息以欧元支付，偿还本金以英镑支付。有些情况下，利息支付和本金偿还均以不同于主体功能货币的货币计价。例如，功能货币为英镑的某主体发行一种以欧元计价的债券，却以美元支付利息。这种外币债券可视为本金和利息偿还均以英镑计价的主债务工具，加上两个嵌入互换。这两个互换分别是：将利息的支付由英镑换成美元；将本金的支付由英镑换成欧元。然而，如第 5.55 段所述，IAS 39 不允许将这些嵌入式外币衍生工具与主债务工具分离，因为 IAS 21 要求外汇汇兑收益和损失计入损益。[IAS 39 AG 第 33（c）段]。

pound sterling interest payments into US dollars and the pound sterling principal payments into euros. However, as explained in paragraph 5. 55, IAS 39 does not permit such embedded foreign currency derivatives to be separated from the host debt instrument, because IAS 21 requires foreign currency gains and losses to be recognised in profit or loss. [IAS 39 para AG33(c)].

9. 215 We believe the most appropriate accounting treatment would be to analyse the bond into its two components – the interest component that exposes the entity to US dollar exchange rate risk and the principal component that exposes the entity to euro exchange rate risk. Each component would be recognised at its fair value at initial recognition, being the present value of the future payments to be made on the respective components. This means that the entity would have an instalment bond with annual payments denominated in US dollars for the US dollar interest payments and a zero coupon bond denominated in euros for the euro principal payment. The carrying amount of each component would be translated to pound sterling at each period end using the closing exchange rate and the resulting exchange differences recognised in the income statement in accordance with paragraph 28 of IAS 21.

9. 216 Analysing the dual currency bond into its two components for measurement purposes reports the foreign currency risk on the principal on a discounted basis, recognising that the euro payment is not due until redemption and also captures the foreign exchange risk associated with the dollar interest cash flows inherent in the bond. The analysis is consistent with the rationale given in paragraph AG 33(c) of IAS 39 for not separating the foreign currency embedded derivative.

Example – Dual currency bond

On 1 January 20X5, an entity with pound sterling functional currency issued a €5m bond repayable in 3 year's time. The bond pays fixed interest at 6% per annum in US dollars, calculated on a notional dollar equivalent of the proceeds raised in euros. There is no issue cost.

The following exchange rates are relevant:

9.215　我们认为最合适的会计处理方式是将该债券分成两个组成部分：利息部分为使得主体面临美元汇率风险，本金部分使得主体面临欧元汇率风险。每个组成部分以公允价值，即该部分未来支付金额的现值，进行初始确认。这意味着，该主体有一个按美元计价的、于每年还款的分期付款债券（即美元利息部分），和一个按欧元计价的零息债券（即欧元本金部分）。每期期末用收盘汇率将每一个组成部分的账面价值折算成英镑，其产生的汇兑差额，按照 IAS 21 第 28 段计入损益。

9.216　为计量目的，将双币种债券解析成两个组成部分，使得本金的外汇风险以折现后的金额反映，体现了只在还本时支付欧元的约定，同时也涵括了该债券美元利息现金流带来的外汇风险。该解析同 IAS 39 AG 第 33（c）段所要求的不拆分外币嵌入式衍生工具的基本原理是一致的。

示例——双币种债券

20X5 年 1 月 1 日，功能货币为英镑的某主体发行了 500 万欧元的 3 年期债券。该债券每年按 6% 支付以美元计价的固定利息，计息基础为所募集的欧元资金按当时即期汇率计算的名义美元金额。无发行成本。

以下为相关汇率：

	01 Jan 20X5	31 Dec 20X5	13 Dec 20X6	31 Dec 20X7
£ 1 = Spot rate	€ 1. 4142	€ 1. 4530	€ 1. 4852	€ 1. 3571
Average rate		€ 1. 4627	€ 1. 4673	€ 1. 4621
£ 1 = Spot rate	$ 1. 9187	$ 1. 7208	$ 1. 9591	$ 1. 9973
Average rate		$ 1. 8207	$ 1. 8429	$ 2. 0018
€ 1 = Spot rate	$ 1. 3569			

In accordance with the treatment discussed above, the amounts that should be recognised in the income statement and the balance sheet at the end of each period are shown below:

	£	€	US $
Proceeds received		5, 000, 000	6, 784, 500
Interest payable @ 6% pa on USD amount			407, 070
Zero Coupon Bond = PV of € principal repayment at the end of year 3 discounted 6%	2, 968, 531	4, 198, 096	
Instalment Bond = PV of 3 yearly USD interest payments discounted at 6%	567, 104		1, 088, 103
Proceeds received for the single bond	3, 535, 635		

Note that the discounting is carried out at 6% assuming a flat yield curve. The actual proceeds of € 5, 000, 000 translated at the spot rate at 1 January 20X5 are actually £ 3, 535, 568. The small difference of £ 67 is due to the effect of discounting and cross exchange rate and is ignored.

Amortisation of instalment bond

	Balance brought forward US $	Finance cost @ 6% US $	Cash Payments US $	Balance carried forward US $
31/12/20X5	1, 088, 103	65, 286	407, 070	746, 319
31/12/20X6	746, 319	44, 779	407, 070	384, 028
31/12/20X7	384, 028	23, 042	407, 070	0

	20X5 年 1 月 1 日	20X5 年 12 月 31 日	20X6 年 12 月 31 日	20X7 年 12 月 31 日
1 英镑 = 即期汇率	1.4142 欧元	1.4530 欧元	1.4852 欧元	1.3571 欧元
平均汇率		1.4627 欧元	1.4673 欧元	1.4621 欧元
1 英镑 = 即期汇率	1.9187 美元	1.7208 美元	1.9591 美元	1.9973 美元
平均汇率		1.8207 美元	1.8429 美元	2.0018 美元
1 欧元 = 即期汇率	1.3569 美元			

根据以上讨论的处理方式，于每期期末在利润表和资产负债表中确认的金额如下：

	英镑	欧元	美元
收款		5,000,000	6,784,500
以美元计提的每年度应付利息 ×6%			407,070
零息债券 = 于第 3 年年末按 6% 对欧元本金还款额进行折现的现值	2,968,531	4,198,096	
分期还款债券 = 3 年内每年支付的美元利息按 6% 折现的现值	567,104		1,088,103
从单个债券取得的收款额	3,535,635		

值得注意的是，以上是按 6% 的水平收益率曲线进行折现的。实际收款 5,000,000 欧元按 20X5 年 1 月 1 日的即期汇率折算成 3,535,568 英镑。67 英镑的细小差异是由于折现和交叉汇率的影响造成的，可忽略不计。

分期付款债券的摊销

	承前余额 美元	财务费用 （利率 6%） 美元	现金支付 美元	结转下期余额 美元
31/12/20X5	1,088,103	65,286	407,070	746,319
31/12/20X6	746,319	44,779	407,070	384,028
31/12/20X7	384,028	23,042	407,070	0

	Balance brought forward	Finance cost at average rate	Payment at spot rate	Balance carried forward	Retranslated US $ @ year end rate	Exchange difference
	£	£	£	£	£	£
31 Dec 20X5	567, 104	35, 858	236, 559	366, 403	433, 705	67, 301
31 Dec 20X6	433, 705	24, 298	207, 784	250, 219	196, 023	- 54, 196
31 Dec 20X7	196, 023	11, 510	203, 810	3, 723	0	- 3, 723
		71, 666	648, 153			9, 382

Amortisation of zero coupon bond

	Balance brought forward	Finance cost@ 6%	Cash Payments	Balance carried forward
	€	€	€	€
31/12/20X5	4, 198, 096	251, 886	0	4, 449, 982
31/12/20X6	4, 449, 982	266, 999	0	4, 716, 981
31/12/20X7	4, 716, 981	283, 019	5, 000, 000	0

	Balance brought forward	Finance cost at average rate	Payment at spot rate	Balance carried forward	Translated US $ @ year end rate	Exchange difference
	£	£	£	£	£	£
31/12/20X5	2, 968, 531	172, 206		3, 140, 737	3, 062, 617	- 78, 120
31/12/20X6	3, 062, 617	181, 966		3, 244, 583	3, 175, 991	- 68, 592
31/12/20X7	3, 175, 991	193, 570	3, 684, 327	- 314, 766	0	314, 766
		547, 742	3, 684, 327			168, 054

Amortisation of single bond

	Opening balance sheet	Income statement	Cash payments	Finance cost	Exchange gain/ (loss)
	£	£	£	£	£
31/12/20X5	3, 535, 635	208, 064	- 10, 819	236, 559	3, 496, 322
31/12/20X6	3, 496, 322	206, 264	- 122, 788	207, 784	3, 372, 013
31/12/20X7	3, 372, 013	205, 081	311, 043	3, 888, 137	0
		619, 409	177, 436	4, 332, 480	

	承前余额 英镑	按平均汇率折算的财务费用 英镑	按即期汇率的支付 英镑	结转下期余额 英镑	重新折算美元(按年末汇率) 英镑	汇兑差额 英镑
20X5 年 12 月 31 日	567,104	35,858	236,559	366,403	433,705	67,301
20X6 年 12 月 31 日	433,705	24,298	207,784	250,219	196,023	-54,196
20X7 年 12 月 31 日	196,023	11,510	203,810	3,723	0	-3,723
		71,666	648,153			9,382

零息债券的摊销

	承前余额 欧元	财务费用(利率 6%) 欧元	现金支付 欧元	结转下期余额 欧元
31/12/20X5	4,198,096	251,886	0	4,449,982
31/12/20X6	4,449,982	266,999	0	4,716,981
31/12/20X7	4,716,981	283,019	5,000,000	0

	承前余额 英镑	按平均汇率折算的财务费用 英镑	按即期汇率的支付 英镑	结转下期余额 英镑	重新折算美元(按年末汇率) 英镑	汇兑差额 英镑
31/12/20X5	2,968,531	172,206		3,140,737	3,062,617	-78,120
31/12/20X6	3,062,617	181,966		3,244,583	3,175,991	-68,592
31/12/20X7	3,175,991	193,570	3,684,327	-314,766	0	314,766
		547,742	3,684,327			168,054

单个债券的摊销

	期初资产负债表 英镑	利润表 英镑	现金支付 英镑	财务费用 英镑	汇兑收益/(损失) 英镑
31/12/20X5	3,535,635	208,064	-10,819	236,559	3,496,322
31/12/20X6	3,496,322	206,264	-122,788	207,784	3,372,013
31/12/20X7	3,372,013	205,081	311,043	3,888,137	0
		619,409	177,436	4,332,480	

These amounts are calcultated by adding the bonds two components together.

Non-monetary financial assets

9. 217 Translation of non-monetary items depends on whether they are recognised at historical cost or at fair value. Items recognised at historical cost are not retranslated at subsequent balance sheet dates. This would apply to foreign currency denominated unquoted equity instruments that are measured at cost, because their fair values cannot be reliably determined. However, most non-monetary financial instruments, such as equity instruments, are measured at fair value. Non-monetary assets that are measured at fair value in a foreign currency are translated using the exchange rates at the date when the fair value was determined. [IAS 21 para 23(c)]. When a gain or loss on a non-monetary item is recognised directly in equity, any exchange component of that gain or loss should also be recognised directly in equity. Therefore, for available-for-sale equity instruments remeasured through equity the entire change in fair value is recognised in equity. [IAS 39 para AG 83].

Impairment of foreign currency financial asset

9. 218 Although not specifically dealt with in IAS 39, measuring impairment losses on financial assets that are denominated in foreign currency is, in principle, no different from those that are denominated in the entity's functional currency. Thus, for a foreign currency financial asset that is carried at amortised cost, the expected future cash flows denominated in the foreign currency are discounted at the financial asset's original effective interest rate. This amount is then translated into the entity's functional currency using the foreign exchange rate at the date when the impairment is recognised. The difference between the translated present value and the carrying amount in the entity's functional currency is the impairment loss that is recognised in profit or loss. Similarly, if in a subsequent period, circumstances change that result in a reversal of the impairment loss, in whole or in part, the reversal should be measured using the foreign exchange rate at the date when the reversal is recognised.

以上金额通过合并该债券的两个组成部分后计算得出。

非货币性金融资产

9.217　非货币性项目的折算取决于其是按历史成本还是公允价值进行确认。按历史成本确认的非货币性项目在后续的资产负债表日将不再进行折算。这适用于按成本计量并以外币计价的无报价权益工具，因为其公允价值不能可靠确定。然而，大多数非货币性金融工具（如权益工具）都按公允价值计量。以公允价值计量的非货币性外币资产，按公允价值确定当日的汇率进行折算。[IAS 21 第23（c）段]。当非货币性项目的利得或损失直接计入权益时，该利得或损失中的汇兑部分也应直接计入权益。因此，对于重估值计入权益的可供出售权益工具，全部公允价值变动均应计入权益。[IAS 39 AG 第83段]。

外币金融资产的减值

9.218　尽管IAS 39没有明确规定，但以外币计价的金融资产减值损失的计量，原则上与以主体功能货币计价的金融资产减值损失的计量方式是一致的。因此，对于以摊余成本计量的外币金融资产，其以外币计价的预计未来现金流量按该金融资产的原实际利率进行折现。该折现值再按减值确认当日的汇率折算成主体功能货币。经折算的现值与以主体功能货币计价的账面价值之间的差额，即为计入损益的减值损失。同样，如果在后续期间，由于情况的变化导致减值损失整体或部分转回，则转回金额应采用转回确认当日的外汇汇率进行折算。

9. 219 For foreign currency non-monetary assets that are held as available-for-sale with changes in fair value recognised in equity, the situation is different. In this case, the amount of the loss that is removed from equity and included in profit or loss is the difference between the asset's acquisition cost translated at the rate of exchange ruling at the acquisition's date and its current fair value translated at the rate of exchange ruling at the date of the impairment. [IAS 21 para 25]. This is because an impairment loss may be recognised in the foreign currency, but not in the entity's functional currency and vice versa as illustrated below.

Example – Foreign currency equity instrument designated as available-for-

On 1 January 20X3, an entity whose functional currency is the local currency (LC) purchases a foreign currency (FC) denominated equity instrument at its fair value of FC1, 000. The entity classifies the equity as available-for-sale. The exchange rate at acquisition was FC = LC1. 5. The asset's fair value at subsequent balance sheet dates in FC and the closing exchange rates are given below:

				Change in fair value recognised in OCI	
Date	**Exchange rate**	**Fair value of asset**		**Recognised in the period**	**Cumulative**
	FC	**FC**	**LC**	**LC**	**LC**
1 Jan 20X3	1. 5	1, 000	1, 500		
31 Dec 20X3	1. 7	900	1, 530	30	30
31 Dec 20X4	1. 6	800	1, 280	- 250	- 220
31 Dec 20X4 Loss reclassified from equity and recognised in profit or loss					220
31 Dec 20X5	1. 8	850	1, 530	250	250

As can be seen from the above, even though the asset's fair value measured in FC at 31 December 20X3 is less than the original cost in FC, no impairment loss is recognised in that year because any impairment of an equity AFS asset is determined in terms of an entity's functional currency (as confirmed by an agenda decision published in the IFRIC in July 2009). An impairment loss is recognised in the following year when the fair value measured in the entity's

9.219 如果非货币性外币资产为公允价值变动计入权益的可供出售类，那么情况则不同。在这种情况下，从权益转至损益的损失金额等于该资产按取得当日汇率折算的取得成本与按减值当日汇率折算的当前公允价值之间的差额。[IAS 21 第 25 段]。这是因为，按外币判断可能需要确认减值损失，但按主体的功能货币判断却不需要，反之亦然，如下例所示。

示例——指定为可供出售类的外币权益工具

20X3 年 1 月 1 日，功能货币为本国货币（本币）的某主体购买了公允价值为 1,000 外国货币（外币）的外币权益工具。主体将该权益工具分类为可供出售。购买日的汇率为 1 外币 =1.5 本币。该资产在后续资产负债表日以外币计价的公允价值以及期末汇率如下：

				计入其他综合收益的公允价值变化	
日期	汇率	资产的公允价值		当期确认金额	累计金额
	外币	外币	本币	本币	本币
20X3 年 1 月 1 日	1.5	1,000	1,500		
20X3 年 12 月 31 日	1.7	900	1,530	30	30
20X4 年 12 月 31 日	1.6	800	1,280	-250	-220
20X4 年 12 月 31 日从权益转至损益的损失					220
20X5 年 12 月 31 日	1.8	850	1,530	250	250

从以上示例可以看出，即使于 20X3 年 12 月 31 日，该资产按外币计价的公允价值小于其按外币计价的原始成本，20X3 年也没有确认减值损失，因为可供出售权益资产的减值基于主体的功能货币确定（2009 年 7 月 IFRIC 公布的议程决定对此进行了确认）。次年该资产的公允价值按主体的功能货币计价（1,280 本币）小于其购置价格（1,500 本币），此时确认减值损失。减值损失 220 本币从权益转至损益。即使此后情况发生变

functional currency (LC1, 280) is lower than the asset's acquisition price (LC1, 500). The impairment loss of LC220 is reclassified from equity and recognised in profit or loss. Even if circumstances change, as happens in 31 Dec 20X5, the loss recognised in profit or loss is never reversed. Instead, the change in fair value during the year of LC250 is recognised in equity (see further para 9. 204 above).

9. 220 For foreign currency monetary assets that are held as available-for-sale, past impairment losses recognised in profit or loss can be reversed through profit or loss as explained in paragraph 9. 204 above. Again the exchange rate at the date of the reversal should be used to measure the amount of the reversal. Since, for the purposes of recognising foreign exchange gains and losses under IAS 21, a monetary available-for-sale asset is treated as if it were carried at amortised cost in the foreign currency, all exchange differences arising on the reversal should be recognised in profit or loss.

Financial assets held in foreign operations

9. 221 An entity may have both financial assets that are classified as at fair value through profit or loss and available-for-sale investments. When such an entity is a foreign operation that is a subsidiary, its financial statements are consolidated with those of its parent. In that situation, IAS 39 applies to the accounting for financial instruments in the financial statements of the foreign operation and IAS 21 applies in translating the financial statements of a foreign operation for incorporation in the reporting entity's consolidated financial statements. Under IAS 21, all exchange differences resulting from translating the financial statements of a foreign operation are recognised in equity until disposal of the net investment. This would include exchange differences arising from financial instruments carried at fair value, which would include both financial assets classified as at fair value through profit or loss and financial assets that are available-for-sale as illustrated in the example below.

Example – Financial instruments held in a foreign entity – Interaction of IAS 39 and IAS 21

Entity A is domiciled in the UK and its functional currency and presentation

化，如发生上表中20X5年12月31日那样的情况，计入损益的损失再也不得转回。相反，公允价值在2005年的变动额250本币计入权益（参见以上第9.204段）。

9.220 如以上第9.204段所述，外币货币性可供出售资产此前计入损益的减值损失可通过损益转回。转回当日的汇率应当用于计量转回金额。为了计算IAS 21下的汇兑损益，货币性可供出售资产被视为是以摊余成本计量且同时以外币计价，转回时产生的所有汇兑差额应计入损益。

境外主体持有的金融资产

9.221 主体可能同时持有以公允价值计量且其变动计入损益的金融资产和可供出售金融资产。当这样的主体为境外经营的子公司时，其财务报表与其母公司的财务报表进行合并。在此情况下，IAS 39适用于境外经营财务报表中金融工具的会计处理，IAS 21则适用于将境外经营财务报表进行折算，以并入报告主体的合并财务报表。IAS 21规定，所有因折算境外经营财务报表而产生的汇兑差额应计入权益，直至处置该净投资。如下例所示，外币报表折算差额包括以公允价值计量的金融工具（包含以公允价值计量且其变动计入损益的金融资产和可供出售金融资产）所产生的汇兑差额。

示例——境外主体持有的金融工具——IAS 39和IAS 21的相互作用

主体A位于英国，其功能货币和列报货币均为英镑。主体B为主体A的

currency is pound sterling. Entity A has a foreign subsidiary, entity B, in France whose functional currency is the euro. Entity B is the owner of a debt instrument, which is held-for-trading and, therefore, carried at fair value under IAS 39. [IAS 39 para IE 3. 3].

In entity B's financial statements for year 20X5, the fair value and carrying amount of the debt instrument is €400. In entity A's consolidated financial statements, the asset is translated into pound sterling at the spot exchange rate applicable at the balance sheet date, say €1 = £0. 50. Thus, the carrying amount in the consolidated financial statements is £200.

At the end of year 20X5, the fair value of the debt instrument has increased to €440. Entity B recognises the trading asset at €440 in its balance sheet and recognises a fair value gain of €40 in its income statement. During the year, the spot exchange rate has increased from €1 = £0. 50 to €1 = £0. 75, resulting in an increase in the instrument's fair value from £200 to £330 (€440 @ 0. 75). Therefore, entity A recognises the trading asset at £330 in its consolidated financial statements.

Since entity B is a foreign entity, entity A translates the income statement of entity B in accordance with IAS 21 "*at the exchange rates at the dates of the transactions*". Since the fair value gain has accrued through the year, entity A uses the average rate of €1 = £0. 625 as a practical approximation. Therefore, while the fair value of the trading asset has increased by £130 (£330 – £200), entity A recognises only £25 (€40 @ 0. 625) of this increase in consolidated profit or loss. The resulting exchange difference, that is, the remaining increase in the debt instrument's fair value £105 (£130 – £25) is classified as equity until the disposal of the net investment in the foreign operation.

法国子公司，功能货币为欧元。主体 B 持有一项交易性债务工具。该债务工具按照 IAS 39 以公允价值计量。[IAS 39IE 第 3.3 段]。

20X5 年，在主体 B 财务报表中，该债务工具的公允价值和账面价值均为 400 欧元。在主体 A 的合并财务报表中，该资产采用资产负债表日的即期汇率（即 1 欧元 = 0.50 英镑）折算成英镑。因此，在合并财务报表中的账面价值为 200 英镑。

20X5 年年底，该债务工具的公允价值升至 440 欧元。主体 B 在资产负债表中确认交易性资产 440 欧元，在利润表中确认公允价值收益 40 欧元。20X5 年，即期汇率从 1 欧元 = 0.50 英镑升至 1 欧元 = 0.75 英镑，导致该债务工具的公允价值从 200 英镑升至 330 英镑（440 欧元 × 0.75）。因此，主体 A 在合并财务报表中确认交易性资产 330 英镑。

由于主体 B 为境外主体，所以主体 A 按照 IAS 21 "*按交易当天的汇率折算*" 折算主体 B 的利润表。由于该公允价值收益是于整个年度赚取的，主体 A 将平均汇率（即 1 欧元 = 0.625 英镑）作为实际近似值。因此，虽然交易性资产的公允价值增加了 130 英镑（从 200 英镑增至 330 英镑）时，但主体 A 于合并损益中只确认了其中的 25 英镑（40 欧元 × 0.625）。所产生的汇兑差额，即该债务工具公允价值的其余增长额 105 英镑（130 英镑 - 25 英镑）计入权益，直至处置该境外经营净投资。

PwC Assurance Service Contacts
联系普华永道审计业务部

北京 Beijing
梁伟坚 Thomas Leung
电话 Tel：+86（10）6533 2838
电子邮件 Email：thomas. w. leung@ cn. pwc. com

重庆 Chongqing
李松波 Bobby Lee
电话 Tel：+86（23）6393 7388
电子邮件 Email：bobby. lee@ cn. pwc. com

大连 Dalian
关兆文 Dorman Kwan
电话 Tel：+86（411）8379 1666
电子邮件 Email：dorman. kwan@ cn. pwc. com

广州 Guangzhou
何国辉 Timothy Ho
电话 Tel：+86（20）3819 2888
电子邮件 Email：timothy. kf. ho@ hk. pwc. com

青岛 Qingdao
张国俊 Kevin Zhang
电话 Tel：+86（532）8089 1818
电子邮件 Email：kevin. zhang@ cn. pwc. com

上海 Shanghai
李丹 Daniel Li
电话 Tel：+86（21）2323 3388
电子邮件 Email：daniel. li@ cn. pwc. com

深圳 Shenzhen
张展豪 Albert Cheung
电话 Tel：+86（755）8261 8833
电子邮件 Email：albert. cheung@ cn. pwc. com

苏州 Suzhou
汪超 Arthur Wang
电话 Tel：+86（512）6273 1998
电子邮件 Email：arthur. wang@ cn. pwc. com

天津 Tianjin
郑广安 Kwong On Cheng
电话 Tel：+86（22）2318 3003
电子邮件 Email：kwong. on. cheng@ cn. pwc. com

西安 Xi'an
叶骏 Joe Ye
电话 Tel：+86（29）8720 3998
电子邮件 Email：joe. ye@ cn. pwc. com

PwC Accounting Consulting Services Contacts
联系普华永道会计专业咨询服务

金以文 Yvonne Kam
电话 Tel：+86（21）2323 3267
电子邮件 Email：yvonne. kam@ cn. pwc. com

方毅贤 Ian Farrar
电话 Tel：+852 2289 2313
电子邮件 Email：ian. p. farrar@ hk. pwc. com

吴慧莹 Monica Ng
电话 Tel：+852 2289 1218
电子邮件 Email：monica. wy. ng@ hk. pwc. com

陈保郎 Baolang Chen
电话 Tel：+86（21）2323 2555
电子邮件 Email：baolang. chen@ cn. pwc. com

陈燕华 Tracy Chen
电话 Tel：+86（21）2323 3070
电子邮件 Email：tracy. yh. chen@ cn. pwc. com

戴奈尔 Nigel Dealy
电话 Tel：+852 2289 1221
电子邮件 Email：nigel. dd. dealy@ hk. pwc. com

苏虹 Shelley So
电话 Tel：+852 2289 2955
电子邮件 Email：shelley. so@ hk. pwc. com

沈洁 Jie Shen
电话 Tel：+86（21）2323 3659
电子邮件 Email：jie. shen@ cn. pwc. com

孙宇辉 Yuhui Sun
电话 Tel：+86（10）6533 7331
电子邮件 Email：yuhui. sun@ cn. pwc. com

梁少宝 Dorothy Leung
电话 Tel：+852 2289 2151
电子邮件 Email：dorothy. sp. leung@ hk. pwc. com

陈嘉怡 Clarry Chan
电话 Tel：+852 2289 2169
电子邮件 Email：clarry. chan@ hk. pwc. com

阮慧瑶 Elza Yuen
电话 Tel：+852 2289 2314
电子邮件 Email：elza. yuen@ hk. pwc. com

许心莹 Samying Huie
电话 Tel：+86（10）6533 2965
电子邮件 Email：samying. s. huie@ cn. pwc. com

白鸿安 Hendry Pai
电话 Tel：+86（10）6533 7760
电子邮件 Email：hendry. pai@ cn. pwc. com

For further help，please contact：
如需更多帮助，请联系：

北京 Beijing
中国北京市
朝阳区东三环中路 7 号
北京财富中心写字楼 A 座 26 楼
邮政编码 100020
26/F Office Tower A
Beijing Fortune Plaza
7 Dongsanhuan Zhong Road
Chaoyang District
Beijing 100020，PRC
电话 Tel：+86（10）6533 8888
传真 Fax：+86（10）6533 8800

重庆 Chongqing
中国重庆市渝中区邹容路 68 号
大都会商厦 19 楼 1905 室
邮政编码 400010
Room 1905
19/F Metropolitan Tower
68 Zou Rong Road
Chongqing 400010，PRC
电话 Tel：+86（23）6393 7888
传真 Fax：+86（23）6393 7200

大连 Dalian
中国大连市西岗区中山路 147 号
森茂大厦 8 楼
邮政编码 116011
8/F Senmao Building
147 Zhongshan Road
Xigang District
Dalian 116011，PRC
电话 Tel：+86（411）8379 1888
传真 Fax：+86（411）8379 1800

广州 Guangzhou
中国广州市天河区珠江新城
珠江西路 10 号
普华永道中心 18 楼
邮政编码 510623
18/F PwC Center
10 Zhujiang Xi Road
Pearl River New City
Tianhe District
Guangzhou 510623，PRC
电话 Tel：+86（20）3819 2000
传真 Fax：+86（20）3819 2100

杭州 Hangzhou
中国杭州市下城区环城北路208号
坤和中心3205室
邮政编码 310006
Room 3205, Canhigh Center
208 Huancheng Road North
Xiacheng District
Hangzhou 310006, PRC
电话：+86 (571) 2807 6388
传真：+86 (571) 2807 6300

宁波 Ningbo
中国宁波市江东区民安东路268号
宁波国际金融服务中心E座1203室
邮政编码 315040
Room 1203, Tower E
Ningbo International Financial Center
268 Min An Road East
Jiangdong District
Ningbo 315040, PRC
电话 Tel：+86 (574) 8187 1788
传真 Fax：+86 (574) 8187 1700

香港 Hong Kong
中国香港中环太子大厦22楼
22/F Prince's Building
Central
Hong Kong, PRC
电话 Tel：+852 2289 8888
传真 Fax：+852 2810 9888

青岛 Qingdao
中国青岛市市南区延安三路234号
海航万邦中心1号楼37楼
邮政编码 266071
37/F Tower One, HNA IMC Center
234 Yanan Third Road, Shinan District
Qingdao 266071, PRC
电话 Tel：+86 (532) 8089 1888
传真 Fax：+86 (532) 8089 1800

澳门 Macau
中国澳门苏亚利斯博士大马路323号
中国银行大厦29楼
29/F Bank of China Building
323 Avenida Doutor Mario Soares
Macau, PRC
电话 Tel：+853 8799 5111
传真 Fax：+853 8799 5222

上海 Shanghai
中国上海市黄浦区湖滨路202号
企业天地2号楼
普华永道中心11楼
邮政编码 200021
11/F PwC Center
2 Corporate Avenue
202 Hu Bin Road
Huangpu District
Shanghai 200021, PRC
电话 Tel：+86 (21) 2323 8888
传真 Fax：+86 (21) 2323 8800

南京 Nanjing
中国南京市鼓楼区中央路201号
南京国际广场南塔12A层01室
邮政编码 210009
Room 12A01, South Tower
Nanjing International Center
201 Zhongyang Road
Gulou District
Nanjing 210009, PRC
电话 Tel：+86 (25) 6608 6288
传真 Fax：+86 (25) 6608 6210

深圳 Shenzhen
中国深圳市罗湖区深南东路5016号
京基100－A座34楼
邮政编码 518001
34/F Tower A, Kingkey 100
5016 Shennan East Road
Luohu District
Shenzhen 518001, PRC
电话 Tel：+86 (755) 8261 8888
传真 Fax：+86 (755) 8261 8800

新加坡 Singapore
新加坡 048424 邮区
PWC 大厦
克罗士街 8 号 17 楼
8 Cross Street # 17 – 00
PWC Building
Singapore 048424
电话 Tel：+65 6236 3388
传真 Fax：+65 6236 3300

天津 Tianjin
中国天津市和平区
南京路 189 号
津汇广场 2 座 36 楼
邮政编码 300051
36/F The Exchange Tower Two
189 Nanjing Road
Heping District
Tianjin 300051, PRC
电话 Tel：+86（22）2318 3333
传真 Fax：+86（22）2318 3300

苏州 Suzhou
中国苏州市苏州工业园区
旺墩路 188 号建屋大厦 1501 室
邮政编码 215028
Room 1501, Genway Tower
188 Wang Dun Road
Suzhou Industrial Park
Suzhou 215028, PRC
电话 Tel：+86（512）6273 1888
传真 Fax：+86（512）6273 1800

厦门 Xiamen
中国厦门市思明区鹭江道 8 号
国际银行大厦 11 楼 B 室
邮政编码 361001
Unit B, 11/F
International Plaza
8 Lujiang Road
Siming District
Xiamen 361001, PRC
电话 Tel：+86（592）210 7888
传真 Fax：+86（592）210 8800

台湾 Taiwan
中国台北市信义区 110
基隆路一段 333 号 27 楼
International Trade Building
27F, 333 Keelung Road, Section 1
Taipei 110, Taiwan
电话 Tel：+886 2 2729 6666
传真 Fax：+886 2 2757 6371

西安 Xi'an
中国西安市南关正街 88 号
长安国际中心 D 座 7 楼
邮政编码 710068
7/F, D Block, Chang'an Metropolis Center
88 Nanguan Street
Xi'an 710068, PRC
电话 Tel：+86（29）8469 2688
传真 Fax：+86（29）8469 2600

如欲了解更多资讯，敬请登陆公司网站：
For more information, please visit our websites at：
pwccn. com
pwchk. com

图书在版编目（CIP）数据

国际财务报告准则实务指引．第5章，主合同中的嵌入式衍生工具、第9章，金融资产和金融负债的计量：汉英对照／陈燕华等编译．—北京：中国财政经济出版社，2014.3
（普华永道国际财务报告准则实务指引．金融工具系列）
ISBN 978-7-5095-5043-4

Ⅰ.①国… Ⅱ.①陈… Ⅲ.①会计准则-世界-汉、英 Ⅳ.①F233.1

中国版本图书馆CIP数据核字（2013）第318598号

责任编辑：吴　敏　　　　责任校对：张　凡

中国财政经济出版社出版
URL：http：//www.cfeph.cn
E-mail：cfeph@cfeph.cn

社址：北京市海淀区阜成路甲28号　邮政编码：100142
营销中心电话：88190406　财经书店电话：64033436
北京富生印刷厂印刷　新华书店经销
787×1092毫米　16开　25印张　425 000字
2014年4月第1版　2014年4月北京第1次印刷
定价：63.00元
ISBN 978-7-5095-5043-4/F·4090
（图书出现印装问题，本社负责调换）
本社质量投诉电话：010-88190744
反盗版举报热线：88190492、88190446